Knowledge and Coordination

Knowledge and Coordination

A Liberal Interpretation

Daniel B. Klein

OXFORD
UNIVERSITY PRESS

OXFORD
UNIVERSITY PRESS

Oxford University Press is a department of the University of Oxford.
It furthers the University's objective of excellence in research, scholarship,
and education by publishing worldwide.

Oxford   New York
Auckland   Cape Town   Dar es Salaam   Hong Kong   Karachi
Kuala Lumpur   Madrid   Melbourne   Mexico City   Nairobi
New Delhi   Shanghai   Taipei   Toronto

With offices in
Argentina   Austria   Brazil   Chile   Czech Republic   France   Greece
Guatemala   Hungary   Italy   Japan   Poland   Portugal   Singapore
South Korea   Switzerland   Thailand   Turkey   Ukraine   Vietnam

Oxford is a registered trade mark of Oxford University Press
in the UK and certain other countries.

Published in the United States of America by
Oxford University Press
198 Madison Avenue, New York, NY 10016

© Oxford University Press 2012

First issued as an Oxford University Press paperback, 2013.

Library of Congress Cataloging-in-Publication Data
Klein, Daniel B.
Knowledge and coordination: a liberal interpretation / Daniel B. Klein.
p. cm.
Includes bibliographical references and index.
ISBN 978-0-19-979412-6 (cloth : alk. paper); 978-0-19-935532-7 (paperback)
1. Liberalism.   2. Economics.   I. Title.
HB95.K53 2011
330.1–dc22
2011003596

To Beckski

Somewhere in Holland there lived a learned man, he was an orientalist and was married. One day he did not come to the midday meal, although he was called. His wife waits longingly, looking at the food, and the longer this lasts the less she can explain his failure to appear. Finally she resolves to go over to his room and exhort him to come. There he sits alone in his work-room, there is nobody with him. He is absorbed in his oriental studies. I can picture it to myself. She has bent over him, laid her arm about his shoulders, peered down at the book, thereupon looked at him and said, "Dear friend, why do you not come over to eat?" The learned man perhaps has hardly had time to take account of what was said, but looking at his wife he presumably replied, "Well, my girl, there can be no question of dinner, here is a vocalization I have never seen before. I have often seen the passage quoted, but never like this, and yet my edition is an excellent Dutch edition. Look at this dot here! It is enough to drive one mad." I can imagine that his wife looked at him, half-smiling, half-deprecating that such a little dot should disturb the domestic order, and the report recounts that she replied, "Is that anything to take so much to heart? It is not worth wasting one's breath on it." No sooner said than done. She blows, and behold the vocalization disappears, for this remarkable dot was a grain of snuff. Joyfully the scholar hastens to the dinner table, joyful at the fact that the vocalization had disappeared, still more joyful in his wife.

Søren Kierkegaard (1978: 126)

CONTENTS

PREFACE

In 1917 or so, the pre-eminent English economist Alfred Marshall wrote the following words intended for publication:

> But the more I studied economic science, the smaller appeared the knowledge which I had of it, in proportion to the knowledge that I needed; and now, at the end of nearly half a century of almost exclusive study of it, I am conscious of more ignorance of it than I was at the beginning of the study.
>
> (qtd. in Keynes 1951: 138)

Marshall tossed the sheet with those words into the wastepaper basket, where it was retrieved by Mrs. Marshall. It remained unpublished. Perhaps Marshall had the impulse to confess his ignorance of "economic science" as a way of highlighting something central to economic wisdom, but he lost his nerve.

This book dwells in the richness of knowledge. It dwells in the significance of that richness for actors within economic processes. It also dwells in the significance of that richness for the aspirations of the *analyst* to know economic processes.

As students and scholars, we read what others write about the economy. We listen to what others say. But is this like reading descriptions of how to ride a bicycle? Do we know the economy itself?

The "economy" is a metaphor of organizational management, and yet no one supervises the organization. Still, we somehow speak from a perspective of some imagined beholder of it all. What pleases that beholder? What is the beholder's "objective function"?

Friedrich Hayek spoke of the division of knowledge, or dispersed knowledge. But even these expressions may not go far enough. Knowledge is not merely divided, like a sandwich cut down the middle, or dispersed, like a crowd formerly amassed, but *disjointed*, living and moving in separate interpretive frames, taunting the will to know.

Theorists often make a particular move in their descriptions of things so as to ensure that interpretation is final and symmetric, a move that also makes it common to the agents existing within the description. The move is to assume that the working interpretation is *common knowledge* (Lewis 1969: 52f; Chwe 2001).

When teaching a course in game theory, in a classroom of students seated in an inward-looking circle, I demonstrated the idea by holding up a large blue marker and announcing: "I am holding up a blue marker." It was common knowledge that I had held up a blue marker.

What made it common knowledge was not that everyone knew I had held up a marker, but also that everyone knew that everyone knew, and everyone knew that everyone knew that everyone knew, and so on.

The higher-order conditions matter: I know and you know that we both would prefer to meet at the Japanese restaurant, but if I think you think I prefer the Thai place, then maybe I head there.

When we play poker, it is common knowledge that we look at our own hand and not at one another's. That which is common knowledge might be a condition of asymmetric information.

To make things "rigorous," game theorists and economic equilibrium model builders assume that conditions of the model are common knowledge to the agents within the model.[1] That is mainly how theorizing goes in professional economics. The common-knowledge precept flattens knowledge down to information. It is flattering to the theorist and seductive to others.

But maybe the common knowledge assumption is misplaced. Society is not a set of agents gathered in an inward-looking circle. If the economy is a cosmos of disjointed knowledge, involving asymmetric interpretations, maybe an idiom rooted in common-knowledge precepts and instincts will neglect important facets of the problem. When Adam Smith (TMS: 234) remarked on the planner's hubris, he pointed out that the actual human being on the ground has not only information and circumstances of its

---

1. Here are quotations from some game theory textbooks: "Game theorists usually assume that the rules of the game and the preferences of the players are common knowledge" (Binmore 1992: 150); "For clarity, models are set up so that information partitions are common knowledge. . . . Making the information partitions common knowledge is important for clear modeling" (Rasmusen 1989: 51); "in this book, complete information games are restricted to games in which complete information is common knowledge" (J.W. Friedman 1986: 11).

own, but "a principle of motion of its own, altogether different from that which the legislature might chuse to impress upon it."

Not that people are purely individual, or that the individual is sacred. Smith (134) said that the strange applications of some clerics have alienated many people altogether from the contemplation of higher aspirations and more sacred virtues. Likewise, strange applications have alienated many people from contemplation of the primacy of the social good. Political individualists sometimes fall into making their ethics individualistic. It was not by downgrading the social good that Adam Smith authorized liberal policy and the pursuit of honest profit.

The way that economists talk has often forsaken the virtues of classical-liberal principles. Maybe, as Alfred Marshall suspected, what is most important in economic wisdom are discursive verities about how things work *by and large*, not axiomatically or categorically, and the awareness *that we generally cannot know the economic system well enough to intervene into it beneficially.* This was Adam Smith's central message for public policy, and it authorized a presumption of liberty. Exceptions to liberty should be treated as exceptional and bear the burden of proof.

But partisans of liberty have sometimes led us into cul-de-sacs. I suggest that classical liberals be more competently Smithian. By confessing the looseness of its judgments and the by-and-large status of its claims, laissez-faire liberalism makes its economic verities more robust and its presumption of liberty more viable.

And I ask—nay, I *demand*—that those of the center and the left recognize faithfully that political individualists, those who take seriously what Smith called "natural liberty," are not necessarily ethical individualists, nor theorists who flatten down the human experience, nor seers who deduce categorical truths from first principles. The mainline of liberal individualism still travels with the Scottish enlightenment.

A NOTE ABOUT CITATION PRACTICE

I use author-date citations except for Adam Smith works, which are cited according to the system employed in the Glasgow Edition of the Works and Correspondence of Adam Smith, published by Oxford University Press (and reprinted by Liberty Fund): TMS = *The Theory of Moral Sentiments*; WN = *An Inquiry into the Nature and Causes of the Wealth of Nations*; LRBL = *Lectures on Rhetoric and Belles Lettres*; EPS = *Essays on Philosophical Subjects*; Corr. = *Correspondence of Adam Smith*; LJ = *Lectures on Jurisprudence*.

ACKNOWLEDGMENTS

Many of the ideas offered here were tested in articles produced over many years. I like to think, however, that in revising substantially and writing three wholly new chapters this work makes an integrated whole. I thank for guidance, kindness, indulgence, and assistance especially important to me, since my beginnings, Gerald Klein; since my teens, Tyler Cowen and Walter Grinder; and, since 1996, Charlotta Stern. Also, Niclas Berggren, for his steady interest and feedback. I am grateful to the many friends and associates who contributed feedback to the emergent pieces of this book, but I refrain from repeating here the acknowledgments that appeared in rudimentary articles. Four of those articles were written by a coauthor and me: I thank Aaron Orsborn, Henry Demmert, Fred Foldvary, and Jason Briggeman for their collaboration and permission to use our joint work. I thank Terry Vaughn and Joe Jackson of Oxford University Press for their generous interest and support for this project and Molly Morrison for superbly and cheerfully seeing it through production. I thank for copyediting Pat Morris, for excellent proofreading Linda Wootton, for index help Paul Mueller, and, especially, for editing and proofing Jason Briggeman. For the image used in the cover design, I thank the creator Luke Kelly at Popartmachine.com. For the cartoon used in chapter 15, I thank the creator P.S. Mueller.

I take this opportunity to express thanks for support I have received since 1980. I thank the individuals Warren Lammert, Robert and Susan Finocchio, T.J. Rodgers, David and Annette Jorgensen, Christopher Roofer, Walter Williams, and Lou Carabini; and the institutions the Institute for Humane Studies, the Earhart Foundation, the Austrian Economics Program at New York University, the Charles G. Koch Foundation, the Atlas Economic Research Foundation, the American Institute for Economic Research, Santa Clara University, the George Mason University Department of Economics, the Pierre and Enid Goodrich Foundation, the Bowling Green Social Philosophy & Policy

Center, the Mercatus Center at George Mason University, and the Ratio Institute.

* * *

Many of the chapters draw on previously published material, as follows:

Chapter 1: This chapter is adapted from the article by the same name published at Econlib (May 1, 2006), published by Liberty Fund, and reprinted in *Economic Affairs* 26(4) (2006): 64–67.

Chapter 2: This chapter is adapted from a chapter in *Uncertainty and Economic Evolution: Essays in Honor of Armen A. Alchian*, edited by John R. Lott (Routledge, 1997).

Chapter 4: The chapter draws heavily on an article by the same title coauthored with Aaron Orsborn published in *Journal of Economic Behavior and Organization* 72 (2009): 176–187.

Chapter 5: Parts of this chapter are taken from "Social Order, Convention, and the Two Coordinations," *Constitutional Political Economy*, 8, (1997): 319–335, and from the article coauthored with Aaron Orsborn, "Concatenate Coordination and Mutual Coordination," *Journal of Economic Behavior and Organization* 72 (2009): 176–87.

Chapter 6: Parts of this chapter are adapted from "Social Order, Convention, and the Two Coordinations," *Constitutional Political Economy* 8 (1997): 319–335, copyright Kluwer Academic Publishers, Boston, and from the article coauthored with Aaron Orsborn, "Concatenate Coordination and Mutual Coordination," *Journal of Economic Behavior and Organization* 72 (2009): 176–87.

Chapter 7: This chapter is adapted from an article of the same title in *Review of Austrian Economics* 11 (1999): 47–76.

Chapter 8: This chapter is based on "Experiment on Entrepreneurial Discovery: An Attempt to Demonstrate the Conjecture of Hayek and Kirzner," by Henry G. Demmert and Daniel B. Klein, *Journal of Economic Behavior and Organization* 50 (2003): 295–310.

Chapter 10: Some of the material of this chapter is used also in the article by the same title in *The Independent Review* 15(1) (Summer, 2010): 109–121.

Chapter 11: This chapter draws on "Planning and the Two Coordinations, with Illustration in Urban Transit," *Planning and Markets* 1(1) (1998).

Chapter 12: This chapter is adapted from a chapter in *Market Failure or Success: The New Debate*, eds. T. Cowen and E. Crampton (Edward Elgar, 2002): 172–192.

Chapter 13: This chapter is adapted from the introduction to *The Half-Life of Policy Rationales: How New Technology Affects Old Policy Issues,* edited by Fred E. Foldvary and Daniel B. Klein (New York University Press, 2003).

Chapter 14: This chapter is adapted from an article in *The Adam Smith Review* (forthcoming).

Chapter 16: This chapter is adapted from an article of the same title by D.B. Klein and Jason Briggeman, *Journal of Private Enterprise* 25(2) (Spring 2010): 1–53. Professor Kirzner replied in the same issue of the journal, and I rejoined in the Fall 2011 issue.

Chapter 17: This chapter uses some material that appeared in *Journal des Économistes et des Études Humaines* 12(1) (March 2002), an issue edited by Mario J. Rizzo on the occasion of Professor Kirzner's retirement.

Chapter 18: This chapter is adapted from an article of the same title in *Society* 47 (2010): 83–84

Knowledge and Coordination

Some Smith-Hayek Homiletics

Wikipedia's entry on *homiletics* begins, "[I]n theology the application of the general principles of rhetoric to the specific department of public preaching."

One definition of *homily* is "an admonitory or moralizing discourse."

The two chapters that follow offer moralizing discourse. The first focuses on coordination, the second on discovery or new knowledge.

CHAPTER 1

ᦔᚋᦕ

Rinkonomics

A Window on Spontaneous Order

At a roller rink, you can see something that holds insights into great questions of politics and society.

At a roller rink you see 100 people skating—but wait!—

Rather than imagine what you know happens at a roller rink, imagine that you have never seen or heard of a roller rink. Nor an ice skating rink. Long ago, people didn't know anything of skating. Imagine yourself one of them. Imagine that a friend walks up to you and tells you with great enthusiasm about his new idea for a business:

> "I'll build a huge arena with a smooth, hard, wooden floor and around the perimeter a naked iron handrail. I'll invite people to come down to the arena and strap wheels onto their feet and skate round and round the arena floor. They won't be equipped with helmets, shoulder pads, or knee pads. I won't test their skating competence nor separate skaters into lanes. Speedsters will intermingle with toddlers and grandparents, all together, they will just skate as they please. They'll have great fun. And they'll pay me richly for it!"

Knowing nothing of skating, you would probably expect catastrophe. You exclaim:

> "How are 100 people supposed to skate around the arena without guidance or direction? Each skater traces out a pattern, and the patterns must mesh so skaters avoid injury. That's a complex problem. It would require smart

leadership. But it won't get solved! The arena will be a scene of collision, injury, and stagnation. Who will pay for that?!"

If you knew nothing of skating, you would expect catastrophe. Before they knew of skating, people knew about dance performance, such as ballet, and that to achieve a complex coordination requires a choreographer. Everyone knows that.

Intuition leads us to think that complex problems require complex, deliberate solutions. In a roller rink, the social good depends on getting the patterns to mesh. But no one is minding that good. As your friend describes the business idea, not even the owner intends to look after it. How can the social good be achieved if no one is looking after it?

Yet, we have all witnessed roller skating, and we know that somehow it does work out. There are occasional accidents, but mostly people stay whole and have fun, and pay good money to join in. The spectacle is counterintuitive. How does it happen?

Suppose you and I step into roller skates and join the other skaters on the floor of the rink. In skating, I do not aim to solve the big problem of coordinating all the skaters. I do not try to get all 100 patterns to mesh. I show common courtesy, but, basically, I am out for myself. I want to have fun and, so, certainly don't want to get hurt. Looking out for myself, I promote my interest in avoiding collision with you.

An important quality of collision is *mutuality*. If I collide with you, then you collide with me. If I don't collide with you, you don't collide with me. In promoting my interest in avoiding collision with you, *I also promote your interest in avoiding collision with me*.

The key to social order at the roller rink is this *coincidence of interest*. I do not intend to promote your interest. I am not necessarily even aware of it. Still, by looking out for myself, I am to that extent also looking out for you. My actions promote your interest.

Skating on the floor of the roller rink is an example of what Friedrich Hayek called *spontaneous order*. The process is beneficial and orderly, but it is also spontaneous. No one plans or directs the overall order. Decision making is left to the individual skater. It is decentralized.

The contrast is centralized decision making. Again, intuition tells us that the only way the complex social good can be achieved is by central planning. Yet, Hayek tells us that sometimes another way it can work is "decentral" planning. He tells us, in fact, that, often, decentral planning is the *only* way it can work.

Suppose the social good on the floor of the roller rink were entrusted to central planning. The rink owner appoints a really smart, really nice guy to look out for the social good. He hires a man with the reputation of a saint, and with two PhDs from Yale, one in civil engineering and one in ethics. This smart saint stands in the organ booth, holds a bullhorn up to his mouth, and calls out directions: "You in the blue jacket, speed up and veer to the left." "You in the black overalls, I want you to slow down and move toward the inside." And so on.

The results would be terrible. The smart saint could not come close to achieving the brisk, dynamic order that spontaneous skating achieves. The main reason he could not is that he lacks knowledge of individual conditions. Using his Yale learning, he looks closely and does his best, but he has 100 skaters to watch, and the conditions of each are changing moment by moment. The planner's college knowledge is useless in informing him of the particular conditions of your situation. The planner tries to apply engineering principles, but each skater has principles of motion all his own: Do I feel like going faster? Am I losing my balance? Can I handle this turn? Do I have to go to the bathroom? Am I content to follow the planner's directions?

Your local conditions—your opportunities, constraints, and aspirations— are best known by you. No one else comes close. College knowledge is no substitute for what Hayek called *local knowledge*.

Moreover, even if somehow the smart saint from Yale has all the local knowledge of the individual skaters, what would he do with it? How would he interpret it? How would he integrate it? If he came up with orders for how to direct our skating, how would he communicate those orders to 100 people simultaneously?

Being smart and saintly, the planner would recognize his limitations and just slow things down. To prevent collisions, he would have to impose regimentation. Skating would be slow and simple. Skaters would be bored. Moreover, they would not find the joy and dignity that come from making one's own course.

On the floor of the roller rink, the social good can *only* be achieved by spontaneous order. As Hayek explained, the case for leaving action spontaneous is stronger *the more complex social affairs are*, because greater complexity only exacerbates the planner's knowledge problems. When the situation is simple, central planning can succeed. If there were just four skaters on the floor of the rink, central planning might not be so bad. With 100 skaters, it is preposterous.

If, besides being smart and saintly, the planner were also *wise*, he would beseech the rink owner to abandon central planning. Or, he might take it upon himself to implement that peculiar sort of plan that commands the people: *Fay çe que vouldras*—Do as thou wouldst—as did a reluctant friar in the Abbey of Thélème (Rabelais 1533/1946: 200).

The principles find direct application in economics. Just as we want to discourage collisions, we want to encourage voluntary exchange. In both cases, the key is mutuality. Gains from trade are mutual, giving rise to coincidence of interest: In promoting my interest in gaining in a voluntary exchange with you, *I also promote your interest in gaining in a voluntary exchange with me*. You would not enter into the exchange if you did not stand to gain.

Once again, actors buzz about spontaneously to advance their own interests, but in the process they are advancing the social good. As merchants, we garner the honest dollar by serving our customers—that is, by serving society. As consumers, we obtain stuff by rewarding suppliers for services rendered.

Again, individuals act on their knowledge of local conditions, which change moment by moment. A chief component of your local conditions is the array of prices you face. If you produce comic books, you pay attention to the prices of the ink, the paper, and the labor that go into your comic books, and you pay attention to the prices you can command for your product. The array of prices, for inputs and outputs, is how the business owner adjusts his activities to the activities of the vast number of players. Myriad players work to satisfy the comic reader, who, after all, provides the funding for all the activities flowing into comic book production. If you don't adjust properly, the reader will buy from another comic book provider who offers better quality or lower prices.

Prices are not only a means by which actors calculate things known, but an evocation of things unknown. This point is best illuminated by Israel Kirzner (1979): "What the market process does is to systematically translate unnoticed opportunities for mutually profitable exchange...into forms that tend to excite the interest and alertness of those most likely to notice what can be spontaneously learned. In this way the opportunities for social improvement...tend to be most rapidly discovered and exploited" (150). Understanding the role of free-market prices in both allocation and evocation, we again see why, if someone were to presume to plan the economy, the result would be disaster. The patterns being fabulously complex, it is ever more necessary that planning be decentral.

In political economy, the substance of "spontaneous" is liberty. Liberty means others not messing with your stuff, including yourself, your person.

Here, we use the skating rink as an analogy for human society. In the following quotation from *Theory of Moral Sentiments*, Adam Smith used the metaphor of a chessboard:

> The man of system...is apt to be very wise in his own conceit; and is often so enamoured with the supposed beauty of his own ideal plan of government, that he cannot suffer the smallest deviation from any part of it. He goes on to establish it completely and in all its parts, without any regard either to the great interests, or to the strong prejudices which may oppose it. He seems to imagine that he can arrange the different members of a great society with as much ease as the hand arranges the different pieces upon a chess-board. He does not consider that the pieces upon the chess-board have no other principle of motion besides that which the hand impresses upon them; but that, in the great chess-board of human society, every single piece has a principle of motion of its own, altogether different from that which the legislature might chuse to impress upon it. If those two principles coincide and act in the same direction, the game of human society will go on easily and harmoniously, and is very likely to be happy and successful. If they are opposite or different, the game will go on miserably, and the society must be at all times in the highest degree of disorder. (233–234)

When the government tells you that you can't enter certain contracts, can't use your property in certain ways, and can't keep 35% of your earnings, it treads on your liberty. It is making affairs less spontaneous and more centrally directed or controlled.

Liberty sounds self-centered—"others not messing with your stuff." But the principle would go for everyone, so it also requires you not to mess with others' stuff. Liberty implies not only security and freedom in ownership, but also duties to respect ownership by others.

More important, we live in a world of mutualities. I want others not to mess with my stuff so that I can use my stuff to best participate in mutual relationships. The point is not self-centeredness; it is to center control over stuff in the owner, so that action draws on local conditions and advances mutual betterment.

For Adam Smith, it was a social ecology of sympathy. The bonds of mutual relationships form the vast network of society, and when its members are individually empowered and motivated to advance those bonds, we have a society that is well cared for. Thus, one might embrace an understanding of "one's stuff" and of "messing with" stuff that is individualistic or atomistic without seeing the social good as individualistic or atomistic. Ethical sensibilities that are not atomistic may recommend a basic social grammar that is.

Spontaneous-order principles argue against full-fledged central planning, but do they condemn all incursions on liberty? The key is coincidence of interest. In some activities, such as polluting the air, maybe there isn't coincidence of interest. Maybe there is conflict of interest. In cases like that, there is less of a case for spontaneous arrangements.

Likewise, in the roller rink, there are occasions for simple rules, such as signaling to skaters when the direction for skating is to be reversed or when the floor is open only to ladies or only to couples. These rules are largely self-enforcing.

In the great roller rink of human society, however, many government restrictions are more like the central planner imposing foolish restrictions on ordinary skating. Spontaneous-order principles ought to have more purchase than they do.

Consider restrictions on the freedom to sell your services in certain occupations. Occupational licensing restrictions are justified by the idea of protecting consumers from quacks and charlatans. It is supposed that conflicts of interest, not coincidences of interest, prevail.

What the regulators neglect is that the very hazard or problem posited would generate awareness and opportunity for new practices and institutions, which reassert the primacy of coincidence of interest. Just as skaters will spontaneously adjust to an aberration on the floor of the rink, such as an obstruction, people in the market creatively adjust to aberrations from coincidence of interest. The aberrations create new opportunities for mutual gains, opportunities that summon our entrepreneurial propensities to resolve or avoid the initial aberration. We witness myriad private institutions and practices to certify practitioners and assure the quality of their services. Economists who study occupational licensing agree that, rather than protect consumers, the requirements hurt consumers by restricting the range and competition of spontaneous developments.

The principle of spontaneity, of liberty, is not an all-or-nothing proposition, but the principles of local knowledge, coincidence of interest, and resilient adaptation have much more power than is generally recognized. People have a hard time understanding how spontaneous order works or even that it exists. At a roller rink, spontaneous order happens before our very eyes. In the great rink of society, though, each of us is immersed deep within the spontaneous order, focused on our own particular situation. Each has no window on the whole, not even a glimpse. Economic insight can, however, help us see the principles at work. Economics cannot make the whole actually visible to us, but it can clue us in to how the whole would be seen, how it would be interpreted, by some divine being who was able to behold it.

Jonathan Swift said that vision is the art of seeing things invisible. In that sense, economics gives us vision.

CHAPTER 2

ᴄᴡᴏ

Discovery Factors of Economic Freedom

When an economist stands at the blackboard and draws a supply-and-demand diagram, he tells a story, and he assumes that the storyteller knows all that is relevant to the agents in the story. The storyteller knows all the opportunities. The story is sealed in a container, and the storyteller holds the container in his mind.

When stories are given exact formulation, especially in math or diagrams, they are called *models*. A resolution is called *equilibrium*. Economists and game theorists typically ensure closure by assuming that agents interpret things in a definite and final way, and that such interpretations are symmetric among the agents and among time periods for a single agent—the "common knowledge" assumption.

Models teach us much about competition, investment, and many other important topics in economics. But overexposure to models and the common knowledge assumption can impair our ability to see other important facets of economic processes. We forget that there is so much that is *not* known, even unknowable. We forget that the knowledge we articulate rests on knowledge that is personal and tacit.

Focusing on blackboard models limits our appreciation of economic freedom. Equilibrium stories of price controls and entry barriers lead us to think of markets as neat procedures and of freedom as little more than the freedom to choose within these neatly characterized settings. It may be the freedom of tenants to choose high-rent apartments, of laborers to choose low-wage employment, or of consumers to choose the services of unlicensed electricians. Because equilibrium stories posit the industry, the preferences, the constraints, and the opportunities, all that freedom accomplishes is individual optimization within given conditions. Knowledge is flattened down to mere information. Agents act like machines; they "optimize."

Economists often talk of asymmetric information, but they rarely talk of asymmetric *interpretation*. They rarely talk of discovery, imagination, or serendipity, and, consequently, they tend to neglect these as vital factors of economic progress. They often carry their mental habits over to public policy. In consequence, they are insensible to the fact that government restrictions on freedom tend to choke off or divert the vital discovery factors. Hayek noted the affinity between how one judges free enterprise and how one thinks about economics:

> To use as a standard by which we measure the actual achievement of competition the hypothetical arrangements made by an omniscient dictator comes naturally to the economist whose analysis must proceed on the fictitious assumption that *he* knows all the facts which determine the order of the market.
>
> (Hayek 1979: 67)

We might think, for example, that in making policy for urban transit, government experts can, after much careful study, adequately determine the transit system that would suit the city's needs and then implement it. But freedom to choose among a set of given alternatives is only one facet of freedom. I will discuss other facets of freedom. Each facet points to a kind of discovery.

SEARCH AND RESPONDENCE

As consumers, we do not know fully what products the stores are offering or what prices they are charging. To gain information we engage in *search*. It takes time and trouble, but we learn more about what alternatives are available and about the details of an alternative.

In other cases, information simply comes to us without our looking for it. Perhaps by chance, we encounter advertisements that alert us to valuable opportunities. Perhaps we get into a conversation and learn valuable information we hadn't been actively searching for. Then we revise our plans and respond appropriately to the new information. Merchants, too, sometimes confront a continual gale of new information and come to resemble a busy switchboard operator. I call *respondence* our rather automatic responding to new bits of information that simply rain down on us. Respondence is like search, except that you weren't actually searching for the information acquired. Search is active and costly, while respondence is passive.

Whether the individual searches for information or simply receives it in the course of pursuing other goals, let's assume that the newly acquired information fits into his original plans or intentions. He now pursues his plans somewhat differently in light of the new information, but he does not change his basic interpretation of what he is doing.

Economists can incorporate search and respondence into their formal models. Doing so, however, will certainly complicate the model, and, typically, such complications are not worth the trouble. In practice, economists usually leave such features out of their storytelling, unless those features are the very focus of the investigation.

Some economists explore the importance of respondence and freedom. They explore how uncertainty gives rise to economic practices that economists might otherwise have difficulty explaining—practices like queuing, order backlogging, second sourcing, and vertical integration. In "The Problem of Social Cost," Coase (1960/1988: 19) pressed the point that to understand an institutional or regulatory issue we would need "detailed investigation of the actual results of handling the problem in different ways" (see also Coase 1972). Coase's 1938 writing on "Business Organization and the Accountant" emphasizes that "courses of action may have advantages and disadvantages" that depend on the particulars of any point in time (1938/1981: 103, see also 106, 128). These points often show an appreciation for individuation and uncertainty in local conditions, and they suggest that infringements on freedom prevent proper respondence.

Unrestricted respondence carries not only a flexibility in making one's choices in isolation but also the freedom to form elaborate contracts that grant one flexibility in relations with others. Though hoping to follow plan A, one might contract in advance for the *option* of pursuing plan B, or plan C, or whatever plan would best respond to the contingency. For example, Arthur DeVany and Ross Eckert tell how, in the golden age, motion picture companies worked on a contract system with film stars and other talents, and vertically integrated into the movie house business, because of severe and pervasive uncertainties on both the supply side and the demand side of the industry. They argue that the Supreme Court's *Paramount* decision in 1948, which broke up the production-house system, was based on an oversimplified notion of "restraint of trade" and resulted in losses for filmmakers and audiences alike (DeVany and Eckert 1991).

In our example of free-enterprise urban transit, severe uncertainty and individuation might be fundamental, and adaptation crucial. Carriers might not expect current conditions to persist. New competitors might invade their routes, or current competitors drop out. The carrier companies may wish to abandon certain routes or add others. For such reasons, they may wish to lease their buses and vans and to form contracts that permit them to alter on short notice how they use their vehicles. They may form flexible contracts with their drivers, allowing the company to alter hours and remuneration. In unregulated private enterprise, such flexible respondence is an important source of both cost reduction and effective service. It is seldom captured in equilibrium storytelling.

EPIPHANY

It is one thing for the entrepreneur to greet fortune when it comes knocking. It is something else to apprehend fortune in its hidden forms and seize it. Here, we have the distinction between responding to the realization of events within a framework of recognized variables and relationships and the discovery of a fresh opportunity to embrace a new and better framework or interpretation. This element of epiphany, of finding fortune by interpreting the world differently, is the subtle and vital element in human decision making. Yet, it is absent from equilibrium model building. In equilibrium stories, agents never have a "light bulb" moment.

An illustration is found in the short story by W. Somerset Maugham called "The Verger" (1952). A new vicar came to St. Peter's, Neville Square, and called in the church verger to discuss a troubling matter. "I discovered to my astonishment that you could neither read nor write," he told Albert Edward Foreman, the verger of sixteen years. When directed to learn to read and write, Albert Edward replied, "I'm too old a dog," and bid the vicar a friendly farewell. He hung up his verger's gown and went into the street. He was a nonsmoker, but with a certain latitude, and it occurred to him that a cigarette would comfort him. He looked up and down the long street without finding a shop that sold cigarettes.

> "I can't be the only man as walks along this street and wants a fag," he said. "I shouldn't wonder but what a fellow might do very well with a little shop here. Tobacco and sweets, you know."

He gave a sudden start.

"That's an idea," he said. "Strange 'ow things come to you when you least expect it."

He turned, walked home, and had his tea.

"You're very silent this afternoon, Albert," his wife remarked.

"I'm thinking," he said.

The former verger set up in business as a tobacconist and news agent. Soon, he set up more shops, and in time he accumulated a small fortune. Now a man of means, he went to the bank to put his wealth into securities and startled the bank manager by announcing that he could not read or write. "Good God, man, what would you be now if you had been able to?" "I can tell you that, sir," replied Mr. Foreman. "I'd be verger of St. Peter's, Neville Square."

Maugham's story tells of a man who not only discovers something he isn't looking for but discovers something he quite possibly might not have discovered at all. In Israel Kirzner's terms, the verger was alert to a profit opportunity. The verger's apprehension of the street as a bad place to find a cigarette was a realization in his working interpretation. Apprehending it as a good place to set up a tobacco shop was not. The opportunity could have been missed entirely or noticed only fleetingly.

Economists give some attention to innovation in the sense of significant and identifiable technological advance, but they give very little attention to alertness or epiphany in all manifestations—buzzing, blooming, and too particularistic to chronicle. The verger's story is material for neither a news headline nor an elegant model. Nor is it well captured by any variable called "education," "search," or "R&D." It is nonetheless the kind of breakthrough everyone makes now and then, which, in aggregate, accounts for significant economic improvement. It is creativity and imagination, the "light bulb" moment, achieved countless times over, in the individuated worlds of individuals. Whereas search/respondence explores the individual's adaptation within his individuated world, Kirzner's alertness is the individual's re-interpretation of that world.[1] This human experience of re-interpreting one's world, this element of epiphany, is, at best, only poorly captured within an equilibrium model.[2]

---

1. Kirzner (1985: 7): "The crucial element in behavior expressing entrepreneurial alertness is that it expresses the decision maker's ability spontaneously to transcend an existing framework of perceived opportunities."

2. See Kirzner (1979: 155), in which he says that the distinctive aspect of entrepreneurial activity is "its inability to be compressed within the equilibrium conception of the market."

Too often, economists neglect the effects of public policy on the discovery process. Kirzner however queries: What economic and political institutions can be expected most successfully to evoke entrepreneurial alertness?

In the Maugham story, the verger noticed something that was now in his interest to notice. At the heart of Kirzner's argument for economic freedom is his recognition that two people walking down the same street will see different things. That difference, he writes, "can be ascribed, in part, to the *interests* of the two individuals. Each tends to notice that which is of interest *to him*" (Kirzner 1985: 28). The claim is natural enough and beyond doubt. It implies that profit opportunities will be best discovered and seized in a legal framework that gives individuals an interest in discovering them.

In some formal models, economic freedom (and a host of other assumptions) leads to perfectly efficient outcomes. Kirzner's argument for freedom is totally missed by such logic and arises only because the ancillary assumptions of the model do not hold. In real life, many opportunities lie hidden from view. Not only are preferences, constraints, and opportunities minutely individuated, but each actor's interpretation of them is individuated and apt to change moment by moment.

The market process generates a system of human activities, each of which is performed in partial ignorance. There are always discrepancies between available opportunities and market recognition of them. We therefore value, Kirzner argues, a legal system "which offers entrepreneurs the required incentives for the discrepancies to be noticed and corrected" (30). The legal system that best does so is economic freedom, which keeps individuals alert to profit opportunities because it grants them an interest in seizing them. To Kirzner, the most impressive aspect of the free enterprise system is not its ability to generate efficient allocations within a framework of fully recognized ends and means. Rather, "[T]he most impressive aspect of the market system is the tendency for [previously unrecognized ends and means] to be discovered" (30). Yet this most impressive aspect, which cannot be captured in the language of mainstream economics, is poorly recognized in academic economic research and poorly imparted in economic education.

In the matter of urban transit, it is very common that the local government fixes the price of taxi services and requires official meters in taxicabs. An economist might argue that this policy remedies problems of bad consumer information, infrequent dealings, and cabby opportunism. With a model of supply and demand in his head, he might reason that so long as regulators don't set the price too far from "the equilibrium price," the downside of price fixing may not be so bad.

Kirzner would argue that his reasoning is glaringly inadequate. Price competition is crucial to the vibrancy of the market and should not be seen in isolation from other activities in the market process.

Perhaps an upstart company seeks to enter a sleepy local taxi market. It plans to utilize a new maintenance system to keep the cabs in repair or a new dispatching system to provide prompter service to customers. It might offer new, stylish cabs and bring this new service to the consumer's attention by clever advertising. Finally, it plans on cracking the traditional market by offering—at least temporarily—a well-publicized low price, the lowest in town.

Kirzner's point is that when the government fixes taxi rates, besides running the risk of getting a shortage or a surplus, we run the risk of regimenting the industry and choking off the vital process of discovery. If the upstart company cannot offer a new low price, then it is likely to forgo the campaign altogether. Society loses not merely some "quantity supplied" but an entire foray into a local economic terrain, a vital entrepreneurial investigation into new services and new ways of producing them. In carrying out the would-be campaign, the upstart company would have encountered a series of fresh problems and undergone a series of fresh decisions, each of which would have prompted the interpretive powers and fresh discoveries. The overtrained economic perspective fails to appreciate this larger social loss from government incursions on freedom (cf. Kirzner 1992a: 53–54).

SERENDIPITY

In discussing search and respondence, we saw how freedom allows individuals to adapt by responding to changes and by forming contingent contracts and agreements. In discussing entrepreneurial discovery, we saw how freedom sparks individuals to adapt their interpretations of local conditions, to incorporate available but undiscovered profit opportunities into their interpretive framework. There is yet another kind of discovery that helps match opportunity and appropriate behavior.

In a famous article entitled "Uncertainty, Evolution, and Economic Theory," Armen Alchian pointed out that, in markets, not only does behavior tend to adapt appropriately to opportunity, but opportunity tends to adopt appropriate behavior. The survivors in a market, he explains, "may appear to be those having *adapted* themselves to the environment, whereas the truth may well be that the environment has *adopted* them" (1950: 22).

Alchian gives an unreal but useful example:

> Assume that thousands of travelers set out from Chicago, selecting their roads completely at random and without foresight...[O]n but one road are there any gasoline stations...[T]raveler will *continue* to travel only on that road; those on other roads will soon run out of gas...If gasoline supplies were now moved to a new road, some formerly luckless travelers again would be able to move; and a new pattern of travel would be observed, although none of the travelers had changed his particular path...All that is needed is a set of varied, risk-taking (adoptable) travelers. The correct direction of travel will be established. (22)

Alchian asks for an economic understanding that does not limit behavior to the tidy forms of optimization that make equilibrium models cohere. He asks for a more evolutionary understanding that allows "imitative, venturesome, innovative, trial-and-error adaptive behavior" (32). Such behavior may find serendipity. Serendipity is a major discovery that one was not looking for, that alters one's own interpretation of what one is doing, and that is obvious to the discoverer. Unlike the epiphany, serendipity does not depend on alertness or insight. It hits you in the face.

Alchian's idea of opportunity adopting appropriate behavior points us toward another discovery factor of economic freedom, one again eclipsed by equilibrium model building. Alchian's point tells us to value freedom even for human behavior that is foolhardy, romantic, or arbitrary. Economic freedom carries the freedom to act regardless of permits, licenses, certification, or other forms of government permission to use one's own property or to enter consensually into dealings with others.

In conjunction with the freedom to experiment comes the responsibility of failure: Only if the individual or firm carries the responsibility of failure will the selection mechanism of the competitive market operate to adopt appropriate behavior.

Once a way of supplying a restaurant, of distributing auto parts, of manufacturing textiles hits upon success, that behavior is imitated and the social benefits increase. Behavior that does not hit upon success perishes. Alchian introduces a ballistics metaphor to make the point: "[s]uccess is discovered...not by the individual through a converging search...[but] by the economic system through a blanketing shotgun process" (31). I think of Jed Clampett, the television character on the TV show *The*

Beverly Hillbillies, who inadvertently discovered crude oil while out shooting for some food.[3] That epitomizes *serendipity*. Freedom produces the widest and fullest blanket of buckshot, and the honest dollar rewards the pellets that hit the mark.

Sometimes, serendipity comes about not by random shotgunning but by mistake. Many of us have had the experience of making a mistake in using our word-processing program, and, in figuring out how to fix the mistake, discovering some wonderful feature we hadn't known about. The mistake turns out to be a blessing. The historian Samuel Eliot Morison tells of such a case in the early pages of *The Oxford History of the American People*: "America was discovered accidentally by a great seaman who was looking for something else; when discovered it was not wanted; and most of the exploration for the next fifty years was done in the hope of getting through or around it" (1965: 23). Alchian points out that a great deal of "pioneering and leadership" in the economic realm occurs by failed attempts at imitation (1950: 30). Because economic freedom presses entrepreneurs into contact and experimentation with their environment, it best conduces to socially desirable serendipity. Hayek remarks that economic freedom provides "a maximum of opportunity for accidents to happen" (1960: 29).

Serendipity differs from respondence in that serendipity involves a significant interpretive shift. Jed Clampett went hunting for some food, but the sight of the bubbling crude oil changes his interpretation of the conditions around him, of what he was himself up to that morning. Respondence, by contrast, entails merely new incoming bits of information, that is, new pieces of knowledge that fit pretty neatly into one's framework of activities. Respondence entails obvious new bits of information; serendipity is obvious new interpretation. In parallel fashion, search entails nonobvious new bits of information, while epiphany is nonobvious new interpretation. Later, we make a 2-by-2 typology using the distinction between whether what is new is information or interpretation, and that between obvious and nonobvious. The distinctions are continua, but we likewise distinguish "fat" and "thin." Standard economics downplays all four types of discovery, especially those involving new interpretations—namely epiphany and serendipity.

Compare Alchian's idea of shotgunning with Kirzner's theory of discovery based on interest. In his example of two individuals who walk

---

3. The genuine counterpart to Jed Clampett is James Marshall, a frontiersman who undertook to build a sawmill in the Sierra Nevadas in 1848. Instead, he struck gold and triggered the California Gold Rush.

down the same city block, Kirzner argues that each tends to notice things that he would best be able to make use of. But even if discovery is not led by interest and is merely random, there is a definite benefit to having two, rather than one, encounters with the environment, since with two it is more likely that at least one will serendipitously discover an as-yet-undiscovered opportunity. And Alchian's shotgunning idea is especially important if discovery depends not only on individual interest, as Kirzner maintains, but also on distinctive talents in perceiving the environment; thus, it has been argued that immigrant entrepreneurs sometimes succeed by virtue of their peculiar outlook on things. Each type of mind may have its own special propensity to have happy accidents.

Figure 2.1 summarizes things by listing types of discovery, a character illustration, and a representative economist. For the first column, where there is no discovery, we have maximizing economic man, who knows all the relevant conditions and knows his "utility function." Deirdre McCloskey usefully dubs this character "Max U.," for maximizing utility. The representative is the great but highly modernist economist Paul Samuelson. In the next column, I use respondence only, not search, to keep the display tidy. My listing of Coase as representative here is, admittedly, not a neat fit.

Returning to urban transit, market experimentation might mean new modes, new vehicles, new pricing schemes, new routes, new schedules, new aspects of service, etc. Those changes might come from within the industry, from newcomers, or from entrepreneurs initially based in other industries, perhaps in hotel services, delivery services, or even used-car dealing. A free-enterprise transit policy would invite all comers to take their shots in the market and let travelers select the most worthy. Depending on their discoveries, niche finders would survive, or prosper, or induce imitation.

Static choice	Respondence	Epiphany	Serendipity
Samuelson	Coase	Kirzner	Alchian
Max U.	switchboard operator	the verger	Jed Clampett
no discovery	small discovery within one's interpretive framework	discovery that alters one's interpretive framework	
More deliberate			Less deliberate

Figure 2.1: Facets of decision making, representing economists, and character examples

DISCOVERY AS POSITIVE EXTERNALITY

Within the neatly characterized settings of economic models, the opportunities are posited at the outset and often assumed to be common knowledge. When a producer enters a market or expands output, there is no consumer benefit associated specifically with that producer's activity, since the opportunity would have been filled by some other producer anyway. Consumers get their surplus regardless of the activities of any particular producer. The consumer surplus is virtually an *endowment*, embodied in the posited conditions.

Once we break free of equilibrium storytelling, we see that discovery is a lot like a positive externality. Discovery creates differentiated products, new markets, better consumer knowledge, and new cost conditions. If we must think in terms of supply-and-demand diagrams, discovery generates spontaneous outward shifts in the supply curve and wholly new horizontal axes over which to draw new demand curves (see Kirzner 1985: 143). Adam Smith said that new demands prompt producers to find "new divisions of labour and new improvements of art, which might never otherwise have been thought of" (WN: 748). Discovery steepens the *downward* slope of the so-called long-run supply curve. These gains are not ones that must happen in any event. Discovery generates whole regions of consumer and producer surplus previously unimagined by agent and by analyst. These fresh blocks of gain are like "public goods" (see Cowen 1985). As Hayek put it, "[T]here can be no doubt that the discovery of a better use of things or of one's own capacities is one of the greatest contributions that an individual can make in our society to the welfare of his fellows" (1960: 81). Michael Polanyi wrote, "A discovery, a work of art, or a noble act, enrich the mind of all humanity" (1963: 60).

We really know less about economic processes, transforming inputs into outputs, than we sometimes pretend. Too often, we mistake a thorough knowledge of the representations that other intellectuals make of a subject for a thorough knowledge of the subject itself (Schopenhauer 1851/1970: 199). To the extent that the economy is unknown and opportunity is hidden, hardy verities about the fount of discovery gain in importance.

ON GIVING EVIDENCE FOR DISCOVERY

If we are correct, we should observe the following pattern: Economists who neglect the discovery factors underpredict the harms of regulation and the benefits of deregulation. Clifford Winston reviews the deregulation experience for a number of industries, comparing the benefits as predicted beforehand by economists with the benefits as assessed afterward. The results are ambiguous but perhaps mildly supportive of our thoughts here. For the benefits arising from changes in service quality, which especially elude quantification, Winston remarks, "Most of these changes made deregulation more valuable to society. Economists effectively predicted lower bounds by not recognizing further adjustments by firms. These developments were not anticipated because economists' predictions generally rely on models that assume no technological change" (1993: 1277).

Discovery Factors and the Case for Freedom

Opportunity is very particular—to space, time, human experience, even humor and perspective. In coming to your knowledge of your conditions, you mind important details. You talk to people and to yourself. Your articulation gives new opportunity for examination and reconsideration. You interpret your conditions, and then you interpret your interpretations. Interpretation$_t$ is superseded by interpretation$_{t+1}$. The economy will remain a skein of particularistic affairs, half tacit, unknowable to so-called experts.

If we give more attention to the discovery factors, we might find ourselves to be stronger supporters of economic freedom. If, despite the best intellectual efforts, economic processes will remain largely unknown, it makes little sense for the regulator, aided by the academic economist, to try to improve matters, especially by restricting freedom.

Our appreciation of freedom is enhanced by seeing that knowledge is not merely information. If discovery were only informational, then government might attend to the accretion of new knowledge by managing search efficiently. New knowledge has public-good properties. If we know what to search for, and we know the searchable boxes to search over, then let's subsidize search with tax dollars!

The expert from the government talks from his interpretation of the matter. If he flattens knowledge down to information, he gives the impression that interpretation is final, that he can come to an authoritative understanding of the matter—after confirmation by panel or committee, of course. Such experts become dupes of their own pretensions. In government, inferior interpretations often prevail and persist.

At any rate, the interpretation of the expert is merely *some* interpretation, not The Authoritative Interpretation. We want a system that tends to retire any interpretation on offer. The economy doesn't exist for the benefit of intellectuals and regulators. The less that economic affairs are governmentalized, the less is there call for the pretension of mastery. I roller skate and you roller skate as equals. That is all. Interpretations are formed and assessed in the service of voluntary decision and action. Degovernmentalization delivers us from governmental interpretation.

As ordinary persons, we know that freedom carries a spiritual quality. Freedom goes with discovery beyond information, even a *becoming*. In reinterpreting my purposes and opportunities, I reformulate my alternatives, aims, intentions, aspirations—maybe my sense of self. I become a new "utility function." Kenneth Burke wrote, "If decisions were a choice between alternatives, decisions would come easy. Decision is the selection and formulation of alternatives" (1932/1966: 215). The selection and formulation come from higher knowledge and purpose, and they *precede* the "choice" told of by the storyteller.

We rightly associate freedom with the *spirit of enterprise*—the light bulb of epiphany, the happy accident of serendipity. The evolution of interpretation makes free enterprise an adventure, an experience in becoming. If we ignore epiphany and serendipity, if we flatten knowledge down to information, we leave out important discovery factors and fail to make the case for freedom.

About This Book

The next chapter is autobiographical. I narrate things from which the present volume emerged.

CHAPTER 3

༕

From a Raft in the Currents
of Liberal Economics

Nowadays, we see a trend toward disregarding disciplinary boundaries and admitting that in our policy judgment, as expressed, for example, in statements about economic efficiency, there is something akin to aesthetic judgment. There is a trend toward admitting that economics is inherently less precise and less accurate than some had thought.

I grew up in Bergen County, New Jersey, outside of New York City, in a family that was Jewish but not religious, and Democratic and "liberal" in the fashion common to such folk. My father, a pediatrician, is now retired. My mother, now deceased for some time, left the house after the divorce and turned entrepreneur when I was ten, but she by no means left her four sons.

At age thirteen, though not the least bookish, I was put in the smart eighth-grade class at the public school. Gradually, I became friendly with a classmate of very prodigious intellect. We shared interests in music and in our classmates and teachers. I read nothing, but I did know one thing: I disliked school. I had enjoyed kindergarten and first grade, but from second grade, I was not inspired by the teachers, and I resented being pressed into their programs. With each year it had gotten worse.

My friend's political inclinations were unconventional, but I scarcely knew how advanced he was in economics and philosophy. One day we were at his house playing ping pong in the basement, probably listening to the Beatles or Harry Nilsson or Queen, and he asked, "Have you ever thought about why school sucks?" I was puzzled and responded something like: "What do you mean? It's boring, they treat you like children, the teachers suck..." He cut in: "No, no, I mean *why* it sucks. Why is it like that?" I was still puzzled.

He explained that our school is a government operation, getting its money from taxpayers and its students from jurisdictional assignment. Our parents go along, because otherwise they would have to pay twice for schooling. The school itself is without private owners, so no one has much motivation to improve it. If schools were, instead, privately owned and had to compete for money by winning families in individual choice they would be much better. Those rules would give rise to a wholly different industry. You and your parents would have chosen the school. That would alter the whole ethic of the enterprise and your involvement. Each school would have to keep its customers satisfied, for otherwise they would go elsewhere.

The explanation was a revelation. It spoke to personal experience. It spoke of a trouble that loomed large in years of despair—the malaise and alienation of school. It only made sense. Moreover, the principles had application to many other issues, such as drug prohibition. That conversation awakened me to the idea, the hope, of making sense of the social world in a way that did not just knuckle under to whatever interpretations were dominant and official.

The ideas would upset my family's political sensibilities. Surely, I saw a daring, even heroic, radicalism in the ideas. I was convinced that the criticism of government schooling was sound. Yet my parents, my grand-parents, and officialdom all around us did not own up to the criticism and its sweeping implications. They did not give good counterarguments. The rust runs deep, and the young libertarian feels surrounded by a corrupt culture. He either keeps up the challenge or resigns and quietly submits. I kept up the challenge, along with that friend and others, forming a circle and finding validation from writers living and deceased, active intellectu-als, and leaders of libertarian outfits, especially in and around New York City, and soon networks beyond. I have made a career from the mode of thinking revealed over ping pong.

Why do I relate such matters? As we go through life, we develop com-mitments. It is useful of authors to disclose where they come from. Gunnar Myrdal (1969) argued for self-disclosure, saying it alerts readers to the biases apt to lurk in the author's discourse. Also, the story says something about my bearings. It is not as though I went to college, took an economics course, imbibed blackboard theory, became a proud economics major, and deduced that schooling should resemble perfect competition. Rather, the ideas that our circle pursued were discursive and argumentative: Frédéric Bastiat and Henry Hazlitt. The ideas helped me to see schooling as a pub-lic-policy issue and to distance myself from the immediate experience.

They proved themselves in things that mattered and made sense in human terms. The government school system is not merely inefficient; it is tragic. By the time I came to blackboard economics, I had already regarded it as dangerous in its artificiality and malleable to all bents.

So, blackboard economics never captivated me.

I did have some immersion in a different sort of modernist or proudly scientific economics. I have moved in libertarian circles that have had deep connections to the intellectual traditions that, especially from the 1970s, have been fashioned into a movement known as Austrian economics. This movement unfolded in two camps, one led by Murray N. Rothbard, the other by Israel M. Kirzner, both of whom during the 1950s were protégés of the Austrian émigré Ludwig von Mises. During the winter of 1979–80, I dropped out of high school and enrolled at Rutgers University in Newark, New Jersey, to join a program in Austrian economics. According to Mises, Rothbard, and, somewhat less emphatically, Kirzner, economics is based on axioms, such as "man acts," and, they say, the laws of economics are logically deduced from these axioms. Since the fundamental axioms are certain and the logic is valid, the resultant theories carry an "apodictic" and categorical truth. They call this style of reasoning *praxeology*. Shortly after I had joined the Austrian economics program in Newark, it moved to George Mason University in Fairfax, Virginia, and I moved with it.

As an undergraduate at George Mason in the early 1980s, my comrades and I dwelled deeply in Mises and Rothbard, and I certainly drew much from them that remains central in my thinking. It really was not long, however, before I was doubting the things most distinctive to their economics, namely, their image of economic science. I never warmed to Mises, and I have long felt that his argumentation exhibits crankishness. Early on with me, there were grave doubts and occasional raillery.

My reverence for them was—and remains—great. More than any other single person, Mises is the bridge from classical liberalism to modern libertarianism. More than any other single person, Rothbard set out for modern libertarianism an idea of liberty as an analytic fulcrum in the policy sciences and as an engine of inquiry, challenge, and debate. I felt, however, that they were overly ambitious, sometimes even ridiculous, in the claims they made for their core ideas, in their spirit of paradigm. I sensed that it was in those claims—and only in those claims—that they could claim to have a distinctive identity and brand of economics, and so I was never very comfortable in the corresponding "Austrian economics" identity. By the end of my undergraduate career, I was increasingly dubious of such identity, and had, in a quite conscious way, a merely "libertarian econo-mist" selfhood.

Next, I went directly to get a PhD. I had been admitted to a few programs, and I chose New York University, where I had been awarded entrance and support in the Austrian economics program conducted by the faculty members Kirzner, Mario Rizzo, and Lawrence H. White. The program, with its faculty, visitors, associates, and students meeting every Monday afternoon to discuss a paper in a ninety-minute colloquium, had been and still is the long-standing center of Austrian economics in New York and a legacy of Mises' instruction and seminars at NYU. I did not go to NYU to develop myself as an Austrian economist. My reasons for choosing NYU were that Austrians are libertarians, I was assured of funding, NYU was a reputable school from which to enter the academic job market, and the location was suitable to me (I moved back to Bergen County).

I think it was during my second year at NYU that the Austrian collo-quium hosted Donald (now Deirdre) McCloskey to present the "Rhetoric of Economics" article that had recently appeared in *The Journal of Economic Literature*. I was immediately taken with the paper and with McCloskey as a personality, thinker, and figure. I waxed about the book *The Rhetoric of Economics* (1985) in a review published by the Cato Institute, and I avidly mined the pragmatist tradition that McCloskey pointed to, especially William James and Richard Rorty. Meanwhile, two of my closest com-rades, then studying at Harvard, were reading W.V. Quine and auditing Hilary Putnam, so philosophical pragmatism had come to me and my pals. McCloskey's attitude of mere ethics, of broad learning, of candid purpose behind that better-organized conversation we might call science—with a small *s*—of indifference toward strutting methodological precepts, of aversion to sectarianism: all fit the selfhood I was working on. And he (now she) was even libertarian! It all fit! McCloskey validated my selfhood and richly instructed and provided for its cultivation.

At NYU I participated in the Austrian colloquium and took courses with Rizzo and White, but I concentrated on "normal science" and espe-cially game theory. My job-market paper was a game-theoretic model of credit reporting and promise keeping in the extended social order. I was fascinated by game theory, and I went on to teach it at both the undergraduate and graduate levels, but it never got in the way of my McCloskeyan attitudes. "Equilibrium" is meaningful only in reference to a specified model, and model building is itself a malleable art, so one can construe equilibrium in any phenomena under the sun. The model-building genre of creative literature has standards of elegance and, one hopes, relevance to problems discussed by concerned, purposive scholars. The stories were formally about machines, robots, but they can be useful as metaphors. My professors in game theory told stories laden with math; Thomas Schelling, whose works I especially admire, did it with less math and greater richness.

Thanks to the Institute for Humane Studies, I spent a year at Stanford University and then went on the market and accepted a job, starting in 1989, at the University of California, Irvine. I was making efforts in normal-science fields, such as game theory, economic history, and transportation economics. These efforts did not meet with complete failure. But I shared with both McCloskey and the Austrians the conviction that things were fundamentally amiss in establishment economics. I began to realize that I could never be embraced by a field community; I could not really be one of them. I would never be faithful to any such community.

I was isolated at Irvine. Searching for God, as it were, I took up teaching the introductory course in microeconomic principles and started a group called the Liberty Society of Irvine. When Friedrich Hayek died in the spring of 1992, I decided that I would give a lecture on his life and work, and I immersed myself in his writings.

My thoughts dwelled on the broad verities of liberal economics *per se*, their formulation and content. Hayek was foremost in my thoughts, but for additional points of departure and connections to living communities, I found myself returning to the work of my NYU professor Israel Kirzner, now with more interest and fascination as well as a better living understanding of the predicament of his tradition. At Irvine I increasingly departed from normalcy.

The Austrian economics movement is pretty uniformly libertarian, but there is an important division within the movement. Rothbard fashioned an Austrian economics in which, as it were, Mises was the great authority and Rothbard himself his apostle and interpreter. In lucid, intrepid prose, Rothbard reduced matters of social welfare to issues of voluntarism. Each person acts to better his condition, so restricting his action reduces the welfare of him and his trading partners, and hence reduced social welfare. He made it openly formulaic and categorical, giving little ground to aberrations of human folly, externalities, and the like. The praxeological laws of economics are deduced, yielding a science of economics. Many libertarians find Rothbard's axiomatic, formulaic approach refreshing, invigorating, and powerful. It would seem to coincide with the revelation that I experienced during the ping pong game in my friend's basement. Young libertarians naturally take to this approach and often buy into its precepts, image of science, heroes, narrative, and so on.

In Rothbard's view, Hayek was an intellectual cousin, but squishy, obscure, convoluted, and too conservative; not well aligned to Mises. To Rothbard, Hayek was something of a rival. Rothbard was often vigorous in criticizing rivals. He wrote that Hayek's eminence and influence might derail the science of liberty. The other camp of Austrianism, led by Kirzner, embraced Hayek along with Mises. The theory and historical intellectual narrative provided by Kirzner attempt to integrate Mises and Hayek, and, in suggesting that the integration is latent in both, to homogenize Mises and Hayek. Kirzner's influence within the Austrian realm is huge; he has often been called the "dean" of Austrian economics. Peter Boettke has been a leader of the Kirzner camp, and his own, often-repeated way of expressing Kirzner's view is: "The best reading of Mises is a Hayekian one and the best reading of Hayek is a Misesian one" (quoted in Horwitz 2004: 308).

I undertook explorations under the two rubrics stated in the title of the present book: knowledge and coordination. Under the knowledge rubric, I wrote of the discovery factors of economic freedom and offered a "deep-self" refinement of Kirzner's ideas about discovery, entrepreneurship, and error. The latter paper was published in *The Review of Austrian Economics* and even awarded a prize. I received warm letters about these papers from Kirzner, who also was writing recommendation letters in my behalf. By virtue of an invitation from Mario Rizzo, I contributed to a tribute on the occasion of Kirzner's retirement from NYU.

I also explored coordination. I distinguished two kinds of coordination, and I suggested that the distinction clarified some of the controversies surrounding the issue of whether successful entrepreneurial action disrupts coordination, as in "creative destruction," or enhances coordination, as Kirzner maintains. I was offering what I again thought was a useful refinement and clarification, ultimately affirming Kirzner's drift. I was invited to give the paper at NYU. At the seminar, Kirzner took demonstrative exception to the paper. He subsequently published a piece critical of that early paper.

My papers on knowledge and coordination were, to my mind, true to Hayek and useful as they connected to Kirzner, in refining and clarifying some of his ideas, and qualifying some of his claims. In time, however, it grew increasingly clear to me that those alterations, even though they affirm the importance of entrepreneurial discovery and its relation to coordination, threaten the Misesian aspects of Kirzner's doctrine, and hence his whole variety of Austrian economics. It seems to me that Kirzner grew to see that, too. He grew chillier toward my work. As the intellectual conflict grew more apparent, the Austrians of the Kirzner camp, too, grew chillier, without, I felt, giving good reasons. I felt that they were circling the wagons. Eventually I felt impelled to write (with Jason Briggeman) a lengthy and rather fierce critique of Kirzner, calling again for certain alterations. Kirzner replied, and I rejoined.

One alteration is to weaken our claims about the coordinative properties of entrepreneurial activity, and of liberalizing reforms generally. We should not even aspire to make them categorical. Rather, they are, by and large, presumptive—and, in consequence, less brittle, more robust. This attitude flies in the face of the Misesian approach of axioms and logical deductions.

Meanwhile, I pondered why all of us of the Hayek-Kirzner traditions seemed to carry two obsessions, namely, an obsession with knowledge and an obsession with coordination. The connection between the two rubrics remained unclear to me. I had the feeling that the two were connected in ways not adequately understood. The connection I eventually found comes from Scotland, from works written more than a century before Ludwig von Mises was born.

I was growing increasingly intimate with Adam Smith's works. I came to realize that Smith's ethical approach necessarily involves an allegorical spectator representing a conception of the social, and that the moral faculties of such a spectator are inherently like aesthetics—not precise and accurate, but, to use Smith's expression, "loose, vague, and indeterminate." I had adopted such a spectatorial approach in my papers on coordination. I came to see how Smithian allegory could be further deployed to give better formulation to economic talk of market communication, social cooperation, social error and correction, and other basic ideas in economics. Under the knowledge rubric, I had worked out an understanding of the richness of the agent's knowledge, involving the agent's information, interpretations, judgment, discoveries, plans, disappointment or fulfillment, regret or affirmation, and error and correction. Now, we may take that understanding and apply it to the Smithian allegorical being as the agent in question. It is precisely the applying of what is developed under the knowledge rubric to the allegorical being that gives meaning and coherence to a number of key ideas under the coordination rubric. To do so the allegory would have to be further developed, openly and unabashedly. We find Shaftesbury, Francis Hutcheson, Bishop Butler, and Smith writing of virtue as cooperation with the Deity (four quotations are appended at the end of this chapter), but the formulation can work for agnostics, atheists, and secularists, too, if they understand the beholder to be allegorical, socially shared and yet under contention, a cultural legacy and a work in progress.

In confessing the Smithian approach, we confess that economics is nested within ethics and that the composite involves aesthetics. We manage to develop some rules for our ideas of the social good, but they remain rather vague, like rules that might be offered for a good novel. There is disagreement over aesthetic rules. If our ideas of the social good conformed to precise and accurate rules, there would be less disagreement. They would be more like grammatical rules, about which we little disagree.

Thus, a second alteration to Kirzner is that our very notion of coordination is not precise and accurate but inherently somewhat loose, vague, and indeterminate, akin to our aesthetic sensibilities. This alteration, too, conflicts with the paradigmatic approach of Mises, and indeed with most any proudly scientific image of economic science. I am jettisoning what is really distinctive to Mises. In aligning my interpretations with Hayek, I am dehomogenizing Mises and Hayek.

I might concur with Peter Boettke that the most charitable reading of Mises is a Hayekian one. The most charitable reading of Hayek, however, is *not* a Misesian one. Arguably, the most charitable reading of both is a Smithian one. A principal aim of the present book is to give further development to the alternative centered on Smith.

All of this may seem like factional strife, but the viability of a discursive liberal economics, viability in terms of both the professional and the public cultures, would be significantly enhanced if more young liberal scholars, disenchanted with establishment economics and initiated to powerful insights, circumvented Austrian strictures and pretenses and found their way to Hayek and, especially, to Smith. The present formulations are sensibly discursive and human; they honor, credit, and preserve what is valuable in Mises, Rothbard, and Kirzner while avoiding some of their shortcomings. They strengthen our connections to the rich tradition of Smith and the original arc of liberalism.

"Heterodox" left economists often paint free-market economics as philosophically naive, as modernist or positivist. Some free-market economists are like that. More and more, though, they are like Adam Smith. I try to give expression to a character of liberal economics, an expression I hope serviceable to economists and others. The book expresses sensibilities highly congruent, I think, with those of Adam Smith. The present book, then, is a work in *liberal* economics. If one prefers to say "libertarian," that is OK, too, for libertarianism itself also grows more Smithian.

VIRTUE AS COOPERATION WITH THE DEITY:
SHAFTESBURY, HUTCHESON, BUTLER, AND SMITH

Shaftesbury, Hutcheson, Butler, and Smith make a warm tradition. I mentioned that these authors wrote of virtue as cooperation with the Deity. I thought it would be good to provide these quotations, because we are pursuing parallel ideas. I have added the underlining (the italics are in the original).

The Earl of Shaftesbury, Anthony Ashley Cooper (1671–1713), wrote:

> I consider, That as there is *one* general Mass, *one* Body of the Whole; so to this Body there is *an Order,* to this *Order* a Mind: That to this *general* Mind each *particular-one* must have relation; as being of like Substance, (as much as we can understand of *Substance*) alike active upon Body, original to Motion and Order; alike simple, uncompounded, individual; of like Energy, Effect, and Operation; and more like still, <u>if it co-operates with it to general Good</u>, and strives *to will* according to the best of *Wills*. So that it cannot surely but seem natural, "That the *particular* Mind shou'd seek its Happiness in conformity with the *general-one,* and endeavour to resemble it in its highest Simplicity and Excellence."
>
> (1709/2001 vol. 2: 201)

Francis Hutcheson (1694–1746) wrote:

> But if we have no other Idea of Good, than Advantage to our selves, we must imagine that every rational Being acts only for its own Advantage; and however we may call a beneficent Being, a good Being, because it acts for our Advantage, yet upon this Scheme we should not be apt to think there is any beneficent Being in Nature, or a Being who acts for the Good of others. Particularly, if there is no Sense of Excellence in publick Love, and promoting the Happiness of others, whence should this Persuasion arise, "<u>That the Deity will make the Virtuous happy?</u>" Can we prove that it is for the Advantage of the Deity to do so? This I fancy will be look'd upon as very absurd, unless we suppose some beneficent

(continued)

Dispositions essential to the Deity, which determine him to con-
sult the publick Good of his Creatures, <u>and reward such as cooperate with his kind Intention</u>. And if there be such Dispositions
in the Deity, where is the impossibility of some small degree of
this publick Love in his Creatures? And why must they be suppos'd
incapable of acting but from Self-Love?

(1726/2008: 109)

Bishop Joseph Butler (1692–1752) wrote:

We have then a declaration, in some degree of present effect, from
Him who is supreme in Nature, which side he is of, or what part he
takes; a declaration for virtue, and against vice. <u>So far therefore as
a man is true to virtue</u>, to veracity and justice, to equity and char-
ity, and the right of the case, in whatever he is concerned; <u>so far he
is on the side of the divine administration, and co-operates with
it</u>: and from hence, <u>to such a man, arises naturally a secret satisfaction and sense of security, and implicit hope of somewhat further</u>.

(1736: I.I.III)

Adam Smith (1723–90) wrote:

The happiness of mankind, as well as of all other rational creatures,
seems to have been the original purpose intended by the Author of
nature, when he brought them into existence. No other end seems
worthy of that supreme wisdom and divine benignity which we
necessarily ascribe to him; and this opinion, which we are led to by
the abstract consideration of his infinite perfections, is still more
confirmed by the examination of the works of nature, which seem
all intended to promote happiness, and to guard against misery.
But <u>by acting according to the dictates of our moral faculties, we
necessarily pursue the most effectual means for promoting the
happiness of mankind, and may therefore be said, in some sense,
to co-operate with the Deity, and to advance as far as in our power
the plan of Providence</u>.

(TMS: 166)

The Two Coordinations

If you look up the verb *to coordinate* in a dictionary, you will see that there is a meaning for the word as a transitive verb and a meaning for it as an intransitive verb.

The following three chapters expound on the distinction, dubbing one meaning "concatenate coordination" and the other "mutual coordination." I spell out the separate meanings; I illustrate the distinction with many examples; I test our understandings against passages from famous economists. I report the results of a textual analysis, which I did with Aaron Orsborn, to show how usage among economists shifted from concatenate to mutual.

These two meanings are distinct, even though, in a particular context, it is often the case that either can be seen if we put on the right set of lenses. Still, the lenses are distinct, and most statements about coordination are made with the understanding that we wear either one set of lenses or the other and will only make sense with the right set.

Each kind of coordination has certain familial ideas, so we explore the families of each. For example, concatenate coordination goes with the idea of social order. Mutual coordination goes with the ideas of focal points, coordination problems, and conventions.

I use the distinction to resolve some long-standing confusions and to formulate a definition of *cooperation* in terms of the two coordinations.

CHAPTER 4

༄

Concatenate Coordination and Mutual Coordination

Coordination has been said to be *the* economic problem that needs explaining (Knight 1951/1965: 6, Leijonhufvud 1981: 321–322). But what does *coordination* mean? Adam Smith addressed one form of coordination, first when describing the concatenation of factors producing a pin and second of a woolen coat (WN: 14, 22). Smith, however, never used the term *coordination*.

It was not until the 1880s that the term *coordination* appeared in economics. The history may be summarized as:

- Beginning in the 1880s, *coordination* was used to describe the effective arrangement of factors and activities within a firm. That array of factors and activities is, here, the referent concatenation.
- In the early twentieth century, *coordination* was extended beyond the firm, to describe the pleasing arrangement of activities within the entire economic system, like Smith's discussion of all that goes into the making of the woolen coat. Here, the referent concatenation would be a much wider skein of factors and activities, even the global economy.
- Beginning around 1960, with Thomas Schelling and game models, *coordination* took on another meaning: mutual meshing of actions, one to another. In the ensuring decades, the mutual idea of coordination caught on and became focal.

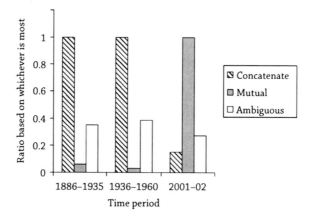

Figure 4.1: For a long time concatenate dominated, but now mutual does.
Source: JSTOR searches of *AER, Economica, EJ, JPE,* and *QJE*.

- Nowadays, the idea of mutual coordination overshadows concatenate coordination. Also, the two are sometimes conflated.

Figure 4.1 is based on JSTOR searches of five major general economics journals. Earlier, the dominant usage of "coordination" was concatenate, but in 2001–02 it was mutual. We will return to Fig. 4.1.

THE TWO COORDINATIONS

The dictionary gives two definitions of the verb *to coordinate*. One is transitive, taking a direct object; the other is intransitive, not taking a direct object.

An interior designer coordinates colors, patterns, and textures to make a pleasing look. The businessperson coordinates factors to make profits. An author coordinates the words of a sentence, the sentences of a paragraph, the paragraphs of a chapter, and the chapters of a book. The verb is transitive, and the result is an overall pleasure from the perspective of the coordinator or of anyone else like her. Components link one to another, forming a chain or concatenation. Call it *concatenate coordination*.

Then there is the intransitive verb: The Japanese drive on the left, and one *coordinates* to that convention (no direct object there). Call that *mutual coordination*. Mutual coordination is usually more or less manifest, like waltzing together. For the actors, the situation presents a coincidence of interests, as for two skaters on the floor of the roller rink. Actors might not be thinking about it, but they are potentially made aware that they are taking part in mutually coordinated action.

Concatenate coordination refers to a concatenation, and the referent concatenation depends on what we are focusing on—we can "zoom in" or "zoom out." Concatenate coordination can describe the skeleton of activities within a firm, where affairs are coordinated "top down," but it can also describe the pleasing quality of a wider skein of affairs lacking any top-down direction. In either case, improvements can be described as better coordination.

Mutual coordination describes mutually intermeshing behavior: Given what you are doing, my behavior is best for me (the Nash condition), *and*, given what I am doing, *your behavior* is best for me. Nash equilibrium requires only the first kind of condition: Every coordination equilibrium is a Nash equilibrium, but, as in a prisoners' dilemma, many Nash equilibria are *not* coordination equilibria. In a coordination equilibrium, there is a coincidence of interest, which is not necessarily the case for a mere Nash equilibrium. (Also, I would not say that coincidence of interest necessarily implies a situation of mutual coordination, for a coincidence of interest might exist across activities too disjointed to speak of in those terms.)

Mutual coordination is commonly depicted as a coordination game in which there are at least two coordination equilibria (Lewis 1969: 8), as in Fig. 4.2.

Suppose that because of the driver-seat location in our cars we both get higher payoffs by both driving on the right than by both driving on the left. Driving on the left, yielding payoffs (1, 1), is less pleasing in a concatenate sense—it is the lesser in *concatenate* coordination. In the *mutual* sense, however, everyone driving on the left is just as coordinated as everyone driving on the right. An inefficient coordination equilibrium generally holds a sort of intermediate position in terms of concatenate coordination: Though inferior to some other coordination equilibrium, it will generally be better than possibly relevant outcomes lacking mutual coordination—better that we suffer the inconvenience of driving on the left than that we run the risk of colliding.

One might say: "So, essentially, concatenate coordination is efficiency, right?" There are reasons to resist such translation. Terms like *efficiency* and *optimality* suggest a clearly defined maximand, or objective

	Drive on left	Drive on right
Drive on left	1 1	0 0
Drive on right	0 0	2 2

Figure 4.2: Mutual coordination: A coordination problem with two coordination equilibria

function or social-welfare function, while concatenate coordination allows considerations in the realm of the aesthetic. When discussing beauty or goodness in an aesthetic way—for example, after we have become familiar with a piece of music—we do not pretend to a well-defined standard or criterion. We do not invoke a specific "music excellence function," nor even entertain the notion of such a thing. Moreover, as we discuss the piece of music, we not only enhance our appreciation of that piece of music, we also cultivate our sensibilities of *what is beautiful* in music. Likewise, "coordination" talk (in the concatenate sense) readily allows the discussion to open up, explore, debate, and reform *our sensibilities* of what is good or beautiful in society, while "efficiency" talk restricts itself to instrumentalities, not questioning the maximand. With "coordination," we not only discuss instrumentalities, we excavate our respective notions of *the mind imagined to behold and to react aesthetically to the concatenation*. Both ends of the conversation are, in conjunction with one another, being explored and refined.

The two coordinations are conceptually and empirically distinct. Enhancements in concatenate coordination do not necessarily entail enhancements in mutual coordination. In fact, enhancement in mutual coordination might diminish a relevant frame of concatenate coordination—for example, when firms collude or predators conspire.

The two pervasively interrelate. In a relay race, one team's complete run is a kind of concatenation, but at just one moment, the baton pass, two of the teammates aspire to mutual coordination. Within a firm, the participants again are working on a "complete run," but the "baton passes" are pervasive. There is the boardroom "big picture"—the aspirational concatenation is called *"the* plan." Then, there are myriad instances of mutual coordination, both among workaday interactions and among longer-term habits, attitudes, and plans. The referent concatenation subsumes many instances of mutual coordination.

Also, the referent concatenation might, in the eyes of the chiefs, correspond closely to the mutual coordination among them. Suppose we have the owner of a golf course and the owner of a golf school. From the Schelling point of view, each has his individual interests, a situation of considerable coincidence of interest, and each mutually coordinates his own plans and actions with those of the other.[1] There is also, however, a

---

1. We said that mutual coordination derives from the intransitive usage of *to coordinate*, and yet it seems that the verb here is taking a direct object: "each mutually coordinates his own plans and actions." The direct object, however, is reflexive—it is oneself (or a part of oneself). This matter is treated in the next chapter.

sense in which *the two form a cooperative unit* (variously termed the *team*, *group*, *association*, *company*, *corporation*, *partnership*, *consortium*, *cartel*, *ring*, *cabal*, etc.), a supposedly unified agency that coordinates the set of activities (golf facilities and golf instruction) in the concatenate sense. Any such correspondence between the two coordinations may hold, however, only when the mutual coordinators may also be seen as *cooperating* in the larger, encompassing referent concatenation.[2] Consider a case in which such correspondence does not hold: On the floor of the roller rink, 100 skaters mutually coordinate to one another, but, allegory aside, we would not say that they cooperate in mapping out the coordination of the entire concatenation of skating.

Later, in other chapters, we further develop the distinction between concatenate and mutual coordination and clarify issues of great moment in political economy. Now we tell the history of *coordination* in economics. This establishes the lineages within economic literature of both concatenate and mutual coordination.

IN THE BEGINNING: CONCATENATE COORDINATION
WITHIN THE FIRM

Aaron Orsborn and I conducted a systematic search of five major economics journals. We also searched all English-language works online at the time of our investigation (during 2007) at the New School's history of economics website and the Liberty Fund "Library of Economics and Liberty" website, which together contain more than 100 works covering many of the main works of political economy. We supplemented the investigation with other sources. I am confident that our various efforts have coverage sufficient to establish the basic contours of usage of *coordination* in economic literature.[3]

Terms of "coord" or "co-ord" scarcely occur *anywhere* prior to 1880, and when they do, they often are used in ways not relevant. There are a few pre-1880 occurrences by Herbert Spencer in *First Principles* (1862), in which he extends biological ideas to social theory, by likening the coordination of parts of an organism to the coordination of parts or functions of a society.

---

2. On pages 63–64, I remark on a different aspect of the relationship between concatenate and mutual coordination—namely, the small gray area that lies between them.

3. Detailed results of our searches are contained in the Excel file at http://www.gmu.edu/departments/economics/klein/Assets/Coord5.xls.

Incidentally, the "coordination" chart generated by Google's Ngram viewer fits our narrative nicely. Usage of the term starts around 1880 and rises steadily.

Spencer was significant in advancing *coordination* in the social sciences. We find a small number of interesting occurrences shortly after 1880 in the Spencer-like biological line of thought, for example in Simon Newcomb (1886), Karl Marx (in works likely written years prior to publication), George Bernard Shaw, Sidney Webb, Franklin Giddings, and Max Hirsch (1901: 217, 267, 278, 282). This line does not jell in economics, however.

It is appropriate to highlight Simon Newcomb's usage of *co-ordination* as the first significant and squarely "economic" occurrence. Known more as an astronomer and mathematician, Newcomb brought a new perspective to economics. John Maynard Keynes (1930: 209, n. 1) described Newcomb's *Principles of Political Economy* (1886) as "one of those original works which a fresh scientific mind, not perverted by having read too much of the orthodox stuff, is able to produce from time to time in a half-formed subject like economics." Newcomb's book emphasizes the idea of the social organism, highlights Spencer's formulation of social progress (141), and, on a single page (138), uses the term *co-ordination* in the concatenate sense.

It is Newcomb's earlier usage that I wish to highlight. In "The Organization of Labor" published in the *Princeton Review* in 1880, the term *co-ordination* is introduced in the following passage:

> As society advances we find great changes both in the fundamental ideas on which organizations rest and in the objects for which they are intended. We must expect that, as a rule, each society will tend to the form best adapted to its preservation and efficiency under all existing conditions both internal and external. Now, in an advanced state of society these ends can be attained only by the formation of organisms having perfect co-ordination among the functions of their members, and there are certain conditions under which this co-ordination cannot be secured except by a system of subordination not in unison with the ideas of equal rights now prevalent.
>
> (Newcomb 1880: 395)

Activities must be coordinated top-down to produce a pleasing outcome. The members of an organization must be subordinate to the coordinator:

> With every increase in the number of persons co-operating, and in the delicacy of the material and instruments employed, comes an increased necessity for a precise co-ordination among the efforts of all. Thus there grows up an organization which in its outward form is more like a well-disciplined army than like a collection of individual producers of past centuries.
>
> (Newcomb 1880: 398)

In the decades after 1880, we find increasing occurrences of *coordination*. We have used JSTOR to search five lead journals: *Quarterly Journal of Economics* (begun 1886), *Economic Journal* (1891), *Journal of Political Economy* (1892), *American Economic Review* (1886/1908/1911, including precursor AEA publications), and *Economica* (1921). The results show that coordination meant concatenate coordination (with some occurrences of ambiguous or extraneous usage). During the early period, the focus is on the entrepreneur/owner/manager as the coordinator of activities and factors within the firm. Leading figures in the discussion are Newcomb, Frederick B. Hawley, John Bates Clark, Thorstein Veblen, Frank H. Knight, and Austin Robinson.

For example, John Bates Clark, in *The Distribution of Wealth*, had the following to say in discussing how income is divided up:

> The function of this natural law . . . causes the whole annual gains of society to distribute themselves into three great sums—general wages, general interest and aggregate profits. These are, respectively, the earnings of labor, the earnings of capital and the gains from a certain coördinating process that is performed by the employers of labor and users of capital. This purely coördinating work we shall call the *entrepreneur's* function, and the rewards for it we shall call profits. The function in itself includes no working and no owning of capital: it consists entirely in the establishing and maintaining of efficient relations between the agents of production.
>
> (1899: 2–3)

Like Newcomb, Clark is talking about top-down concatenate coordination within the firm. The discussion was joined by Frank Knight, who, in *Risk, Uncertainty, and Profit*, says, "The entrepreneur is the owner of all real wealth, and ownership involves risk; the coordinator 'makes decisions,' but it is the entrepreneur who 'accepts the consequences of decisions'" (1921: 45). Thus, leading economists focused on top-down coordination within a firm and debated how certain functions and corresponding remuneration should be distinguished.[4]

4. I should add that our investigation found two other types of early occurrences of *coordination*. First, there is a batch among transportation economists, who speak of the coordination of facilities and trips. Again, the meaning is concatenate; the discussion appears to have proceeded largely independently of that about the firm; for the most part, the transportation occurrences speak of a top-down process of transportation-system planning. Second, numerous economists used the expression "coordination of the laws of distribution" to describe the working out of compatible theories of economic value and earnings. Within our search results, this usage pretty much dies out by 1907. More detail is provided by Klein and Orsborn 2009: 179.

THE 1930S: LSE ECONOMISTS GO BEYOND
THE EYE OF ANY ACTUAL COORDINATOR

Up to around 1930, the primary economic talk of "coordination," aside from the transportation literature, concerned the concatenation of activities within the firm. In the 1930s, however, a new moment occurs, and it may be marked by a lecture by Friedrich A. Hayek in 1933 at the London School of Economics and published that year in *Economica* as "The Trend of Economic Thinking." Hayek takes *coordination* to the extensive economic cosmos. This step was not entirely novel,[5] of course, but it then becomes more salient in Anglo-American economics. The LSE during the 1930s seems to have bubbled with talk of coordination beyond the firm.

In the lecture, Hayek extends the idea of concatenate coordination beyond the eye of any actual coordinator:

> From the time of Hume and Adam Smith, the effect of every attempt to understand economic phenomena—that is to say, of every theoretical analysis—has been to show that, in large part, the co-ordination of individual efforts in society is not the product of deliberate planning, but has been brought about, and in many cases could only have been brought about, by means which nobody wanted or understood, and which in isolation might be regarded as some of the most objectionable features of the system.
>
> (1933a/1991: 129)

Hayek is describing independent actions that lead to outcomes beyond the actor's intention and comprehension. What Hayek is discussing is spontaneous order or, in our nomenclature, undirected concatenate coordination. Like the concatenate coordination within the firm, coordination means desirable arrangement or outcome. The question is, *desirable to whom?*

The matter, Hayek emphasizes, calls for great delicacy. He suggests that society has a "sense," like an "organism,"[6] yet he makes the suggestion with

---

5. I have mentioned some of the writers with Spencer-like biological analogies. Also, one may in the Excel worksheets find other scattered and fleeting occurrences of "coordination" meaning spontaneous concatenate coordination by Henry George, John Bates Clark, Philip Wicksteed, Ludwig von Mises, David Friday, Lawrence Frank, Raymond Bye, and Shorey Peterson.

6. On the matter of society as organism, Hayek cites the 1923–32 German-language editions of Mises' *Socialism* (1922/1981). Mises cites Spencer several times but never in connection with society as organism. Neither Hayek nor Mises cites Newcomb's *Principles of Political Economy* (1886), but it is noteworthy that Newcomb, like Hayek, articulates cautions while going forward with the organism metaphor (cf. Newcomb 1886: 7–8).

great caution. Classical liberals such as he dread metaphors of society as organism, for such metaphors bring hazards of statism when the organism's body is identified with polity and its brain, mind, head, or heart is identified with the polity's government. Hayek notes, "The limitations of language make it almost impossible to state it without using misleading metaphorical words" (130). The lecture is quite remarkable as an early expression of the dilemmas in opposing society-as-organization notions while trying to say that liberal processes are coordinative. Again, the big question is, coordinative to whom?

In the case of the firm, the answer is clear—the owners/managers—and the *criterion behind coordinativeness is honest profits*—a fairly precise and accurate rule. When the idea of concatenate coordination was extend *beyond the business enterprise*, however, there was no owner, manager, leader, or boss to occupy the spectatorial role, no tangible figure to provide the image of the beholder. Thus, the precision and accuracy of the criterion for coordinativeness melt away. For the vast polycentric spontaneous system, the imagined beholder is much less clearly defined. We enter a realm of goodness and beauty that is loose, vague, and indeterminate.

We imagine a fictitious impartial mind able to behold the extensive tapestry of social affairs, and we are inclined to judge that mind in a manner that the parties to the discourse situation are thought to find acceptable. This imagined beholder and judge is like that being whose hands, according to Adam Smith, are invisible. Alluding to Hume and Smith, Hayek, too, wants to talk about coordination beyond the eye of any actual human coordinator.

At about the same time, similar ideas were being explored by others at the LSE. Ronald Coase was writing his seminal article "The Nature of the Firm," drafted years prior to its publication in *Economica* in 1937. In it, he says, "An economist thinks of the economic system as being co-ordinated by the price mechanism, and society becomes not an organization but an organism" (1937/1988: 34). Coase is noting what Hayek had been discussing and emphasizes that at one level, prices help to coordinate economic activity. Coase makes another observation:

> Marshall introduces organization as a fourth factor of production; J.B. Clark gives the co-ordinating function to the entrepreneur; Knight introduces managers who co-ordinate. As D.H. Robertson points out, we find "islands of conscious power in this ocean of unconscious co-operation like lumps of butter coagulating in a pail of buttermilk." But in view of the fact that it is usually argued that co-ordination will be done by the price mechanism, why is such organization necessary? Why are there these "islands of conscious power"?

Outside the firm, price movements direct production, which is co-ordinated through a series of exchange transactions on the market. Within a firm these market transactions are eliminated, and in place of the complicated market structure with exchange transactions is substituted the entrepreneur-co-ordinator, who directs production. It is clear that these are alternative methods of co-ordinating production. Yet, having regard to the fact that, if production is regulated by price movements, production could be carried on without any organization at all, well might we ask, Why is there any organization?

(35–36)

Coase is seeing the two levels of concatenate coordination: the unplanned level mediated by prices and the planned level within the firm. On the heels of Hayek's step beyond the eye of any actual coordinator, Coase writes as though Hayek's formulation is commonplace and that the outstanding question is why there should be any planned coordination at the level of the firm. He adds:

In view of the fact that, while economists treat the price mechanism as a co-ordinating instrument, they also admit the co-ordinating function of the "entrepreneur," it is surely important to enquire why co-ordination is the work of the price mechanism in one case and of the entrepreneur in another. The purpose of this paper is to bridge what appears to be a gap in economic theory between the assumption (made for some purposes) that resources are allocated by means of the price mechanism and the assumption (made for other purposes) that this allocation is dependent on the entrepreneur-co-ordinator. We have to explain the basis on which, in practice, this choice between alternatives is effected.

(37)

Coase crystallizes concatenate coordination at two levels, the extensive economic system and the individual firm.

Coase may have treated Hayek's perspective as commonplace because it was so at the LSE. W.H. Hutt, who had studied at the LSE, published "Co-ordination and the Size of the Firm" in the *South African Journal of Economics* in 1934. He extended the domain of coordination beyond the firm, suggesting, decades prior to Coase's famous 1960 paper, that, under certain conditions, the coordination of factors would be the same regardless of whether the concatenation was planned by a single entrepreneurial authority or among a number of separate entrepreneurs (396–397). Likewise, Coase's mentor, Arnold Plant, in "Centralise or Decentralise?"

published in 1937, also extended coordination beyond the firm, speaking, for example, of firms submitting "to the co-ordination imposed upon their activities by the price mechanism of the market" (1937/1974).

One might take the two levels to correspond to "unplanned" and "planned," but a society's economic system is subject to degrees of direction, control, and planning, so an extensive economic system is not necessarily simply "unplanned." Moreover, firms might vary in their degree of central direction, so the concatenate coordination within a firm in not necessarily simply "planned." Both at the level of firm and at the level of the polity, we may think of there being *a degree* of planning, direction, or guidance of subordinate actors by superior actors who are supposed to imagine, "see," or at least concern themselves with the referent concatenation.

The two sources of coordination of the polity-wide concatenation, free enterprise and governmental regulation, were central to some of the most important debates in economics. The idea of central planning was to supersede the "anarchy" of production, making the economy essentially "one big factory" (Marx 1936: 391) in which managers make the production decisions, albeit in some schemes with surrogate pricing and feedback. The other major debate was whether the economy was self-coordinating, a debate brought forth particularly by the Great Depression and John Maynard Keynes.

MUTUAL COORDINATION EMERGES AND BECOMES FOCAL

Coordination meant concatenate coordination, but things started to change with Thomas Schelling, who developed what we term "mutual coordination," an idea that, prior to Schelling, seems to have had little place even in game theory.[7]

Schelling's *The Strategy of Conflict* developed and eventually established a meaning of *coordination*. He gives the example of a man and wife separated in a department store:

> What is necessary is to coordinate predictions, to read the same message
> in the common situation, to identify the one course of action that their

7. We inspected Von Neumann and Morgenstern (1953) and Luce and Raiffa (1957). Neither indexes *coordination*. A Google book search establishes that Luce and Raiffa use "coordinate" only incidentally, in the mutual sense, on but a single page (177). For Von Neumann and Morgenstern, the search gave only restricted results, but it appears that the book does not use "coordinate" (though both books use "coordinate" mathematically, as in the coordinates of a point in a graph).

expectations of each other can converge on. They must *'mutually recognize'* some unique signal that coordinates their expectations of each other.

(Italics added)

He adds:

People *can* often concert their intentions or expectations with others if each knows that the other is trying to do the same. Most situations—perhaps every situation for people who are practiced at this kind of game—provide some clue for coordinating behavior, some focal point for each person's expectation of what the other expects him to expect to be expected to do.

(1960: 57)

Here, coordination is understood as something we hope to achieve in our interaction with others. It is manifest in that the individuals are aware of the challenge and results.

Schelling also discusses situations with divergent interests:

If we ask what determines the outcome in these cases, the answer again is in the coordination problem. Each of these problems requires coordination for a common gain, even though there is rivalry among alternative lines of common action. But, among the various choices, there is usually one or only a few that can serve as coordinator.

(65)

So, even if interests diverge, as in Fig. 4.3, there are only certain strategy combinations in which actions are mutually coordinated.

Schelling argues that coordination is also important in bargaining: "The fundamental problem in tacit bargaining is that of *coordination*; we should inquire, then, what has to be coordinated in explicit bargaining. The answer may be that explicit bargaining requires, for an ultimate agreement, some coordination of the participants' expectations" (69–70). Schelling proposes that expectations may be brought into convergence with the help of a focal point (71–72). What is required is a kind of mutual assent or acceptance. "The coordination game probably lies behind the stability of institutions and traditions

	Meet at the pub	Meet at the park
Meet at the pub	2 / 1	0 / 0
Meet at the park	0 / 0	1 / 2

Figure 4.3: Mutual coordination: A coordination problem with partly conflicting interests

[or conventions]" (91). Schelling is acknowledging that this form of coordination is central to conventions. Subsequently, David K. Lewis, who studied with Schelling, developed the ideas of coordination game, coordination equilibrium, common knowledge, and convention, in *Convention: A Philosophical Study* (1969). The rubric of mutual-coordination concepts was also developed by Schelling's *Micromotives and Macrobehavior* (1978), Ullmann-Margalit (1977), Sugden (1986), Young (1996), Chwe (2001), and other works. All this was rooted in mutual coordination and mostly ignored concatenate coordination. In this literature, *coordination* meant mutual coordination.[8]

Schelling, Lewis, and others provided canonical formulation of the rubric of mutual-coordination concepts and proof of relevance. Game theory got legs in the 1970s and took off in the 1980s. With the rise of game theory, the word *coordination* was increasingly understood to mean mutual coordination, working with other components of the mutual-coordination rubric. Economists now consumed Schelling, "battle of the sexes," "cheap talk," and path dependence—all mutual.

Meanwhile, in matters of the social good, of the desirable, economists spoke instead of "social welfare," "social-welfare function," "optimality," or "efficiency." The older concatenate understanding of the term *coordination* was increasingly eclipsed, really, by two developments only loosely connected, one being those supposedly more scientific renderings of the social good, the other being the new developments in mutual coordination.

MUTUAL IS NOW DOMINANT

Since the 1980s and continuing today, the number of articles and books working in mutual coordination is simply enormous.

The switch in emphasis from concatenate to mutual can be found in a variety of areas. In the work on path dependency, *coordination* means mutual coordination: "Lock-in" is about society coordinating on an inferior standard (Arthur 1994). Building on Lewis, economists have refined

---

8. At the outset of *Micromotives and Macrobehavior* (1978: 20–23) Schelling discusses the extensive market process and uses the term *coordination* principally in the concatenate sense, endorsing the liberal order (22). He does so, however, to make clear what he is *not* focusing on: "I am interested here in how much promise the economist's result has outside of economics" (23), which he associates with markets, and the remainder of the book focuses on issues of *mutual* coordination.

the idea of convention, rooted in mutual coordination (Young 1996). Many articles now address how governments of different nations or jurisdictions coordinate their policy decisions with one another.

In macroeconomics, in which one would expect to find coordination meaning spontaneous concatenate coordination, we now find mutual coordination. New Keynesian macroeconomics, in particular, uses the coordination game to describe coordination failures in the macroeconomy (e.g., Diamond 1982, Bryant 1983, Cooper and John 1988, Ball and Romer 1991). In the past, a coordination failure would mean not reaching a pleasing outcome because of the failure of prices and institutions to promote beneficial production and exchange. Now, coordination failure means coordinating on an inferior coordination equilibrium—such as a group of producers failing simultaneously to lower prices even though they would all be better off if they all did.

FIVE MAJOR JOURNALS SEARCHED USING JSTOR

Reproduced immediately below is the same figure shown at the outset of the chapter:

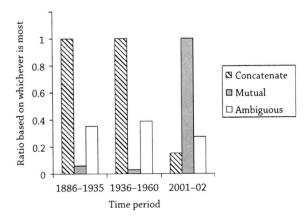

We used JSTOR to search five lead journals: *Quarterly Journal of Economics* (begun 1886), *Economic Journal* (1891), *Journal of Political Economy* (1892), *American Economic Review* (1886/1908/1911, including precursor AEA publications), and *Economica* (1921).

In September 2007, we sampled articles beginning in 1886, because that was the first year of publication of the *QJE*. We wanted to search through

1960, when Schelling's work emerged, decided to break the period in two, and used 1935 as a divider, yielding two pre-Schelling periods, 1886–1935 and 1936–60. We searched on "coordination" or "co-ordination" in full-text, and limited the search to articles. The items, as listed in the Excel sheets, are in the order displayed by JSTOR's "Relevance" option for displaying search results—the top fifty for each period. We also sampled articles of 2001 and 2002, because those were the latest years for which the five journals all had material loaded in JSTOR, yielding seventy-five results. Thus, the total raw sample represented in Fig. 4.1 is 175 articles. Each paper received a score of either 0 or 1 in the concatenate column, and either 0 or 1 in the mutual column; a small number of papers received a 1 in both columns. Many papers received a 1 in the ambiguous column, usually because the occurrence of "coordination" was brief and open to interpretation as either concatenate or mutual (as in our earlier example of the golf course owner and the golf school owner). Some papers were marked as not relevant, because "coordination" was used in an extraneous way, for example, only in the title of cited works. A skeptical reader can easily spot-check the Excel file. The bars in the figure are sized so as to represent a ratio of whichever type (concatenate or mutual) occurs most in the period.[9] The results show a dramatic change. Future research could chart the transition from 1960–2000 and expand the sample to a wider array of journals and disciplines.

Was Schelling's refocusing of *coordination* an irresponsible straying from well-established economic usage? Not at all. He simply pursued a meaning well established in the wider civilization, including the dictionary. That the economic literature so predominately used *coordination* in the concatenate sense, and that he didn't let that stop him, is testimony to his respect for common language and common experience, as well as to his intellectual independence.[10]

If a resuscitation of concatenate coordination is in order, the way forward would not be at the expense of mutual coordination, but rather by

9. The data are as follows: For the first period: thirty-four concatenate, two mutual, twelve ambiguous; for the second period: thirty-six concatenate, one mutual, fourteen ambiguous; for 2001/02: six concatenate, forty mutual, eleven ambiguous.

10. Schelling's remarkable intellectual independence is on display also *within* the field of game theory. From the start (1960: 21, 65–118, 163–169, 226, 246–248, 284–303), Schelling has emphasized and been sensitive to the importance of asymmetric interpretation (though not using that term), a condition that must be ignored or suppressed to assume common knowledge (or symmetric interpretation), which is generally used to ensure closure in a game model.

way of an awareness of the distinction between the two coordinations and a greater skepticism about the scientific status of "social welfare," "social welfare function," "optimality," or "efficiency" as conceptions of the good.

ECONOMIC SCIENCE OR PROTREPTIC DISCOURSE?

Concatenate came first, and it comes from the transitive meaning of the verb *to coordinate*, as in: The entrepreneur coordinates the factors of production within his firm. Spontaneous concatenate coordination extends the idea beyond the eye of any actual coordinator.

An appreciation of concatenate coordination informs the discursive approach to political economy exemplified by Adam Smith. That approach sees that aesthetic sensibilities regarding morals and culture play a large role in the craftwork of economists and, moreover, are themselves part of the economy, part of "well-being." Adam Smith explained that aesthetics are ineluctably "loose, vague, and indeterminate" (TMS: 175, 327). Talk of coordination will often entail, not only how best to please the mind imagined to behold the vast concatenation, but, to an inextinguishable degree, also an exploration of *what that mind's aesthetic sensibilities are.*

"As Frank H. Knight has so often emphasized, problems of welfare economics must ultimately dissolve into a study of aesthetics and morals" (Coase 1960/1988: 154). That is why we should resist translating concatenate coordination as *efficiency.* Talk of efficiency suggests a definitive characterization of the maximand (or of the "output" or "social welfare").

Concatenate coordination was done in, perhaps, by the desire to have an exact and separate science of economics. Many economists have tried to evade the loose, vague, and indeterminate part of the conversation by supplanting concatenate coordination with efficiency, optimality, and social welfare functions. Those concepts would enable economists to enclose economics within an exact grammar. Economists sometimes treat the actual living guts of those concepts as not their concern and at other times as much more exact and definite than they really are. As Peter Bauer (1981) put it: "[T]he use of mathematical methods has contributed more pervasively to inappropriate practices [including] the application of concepts which, even when they are capable of precise expression in the abstract, *are in practice necessarily vague*" (265, italics added). The desire for an exact and separate science of economics, along with the advance of mutual coordination, has pushed out concatenate coordination, particularly of the great skein.

In *Adam Smith and the Virtues of Enlightenment*, Charles Griswold writes that Smith's "work evinces a sophisticated awareness of the problem of the relationship between form, content, and audience" (1999: 41) and that his discourse "is intended to persuade us to view things in a certain light, to refine the ways in which we judge and feel, and perhaps to encourage us to act in a certain manner" (49). Griswold thusly characterizes Smith's discourse as *protreptic*—a term that refers back to Greek discourse that endeavored to persuade students, whose basic outlook and attitudes are still formative, to come to a favored way of viewing the whole matter, both "cause" and "effect" and their relations in one encompassing formulation, in preference to competing formulations, attitudes, and outlooks. Griswold views the "invisible hand" in just this way:

> Just as the 'invisible hand of Jupiter' was part of the vocabulary of ancient 'superstition,' the 'invisible hand' is part of Smith's philosophical and protreptic rhetoric whose purpose is likewise to establish order persuasively. The many 'teleological' or even, on occasion, 'religious' statements in *The Theory of Moral Sentiments* must be understood in connection with this aestheticized speculative outlook.
>
> (333)

All of social science has protreptic qualities, including "optimality," "efficiency," "social welfare function," and the like. I suggest, however, that the more discursive economics literature that used "coordination" in discussing the vast concatenation had a *more openly* protreptic quality, in that it addressed the aesthetic sensibilities that ponder the vast concatenation. The protreptic quality—addressed to edification of basic attitudes and outlooks—did not fit the "value-free" values of putatively scientific economics, however, and, hence, it was discouraged and displaced by more formal discourse, as "efficiency," etc. could be more neatly characterized within the terms—usually either very narrow or very abstract—that each article set for itself.

Concatenate coordination presupposes particular ideological sensibilities no more than the idea of beauty in music presupposes particular tastes in music. One may maintain, for example, that taxpayer subsidization of basic science improves concatenate coordination. It would seem that concatenate coordination can accommodate concerns about public goods, externalities, natural monopolies, distribution, addictive behavior, ways of life, identity, and the public culture.[11] Nothing about the idea of concatenate coordination denies that government intervention can improve the concatenation. In discussing the grand concatenation, the conversation is an exploration and negotiation of sensibilities about social betterment, especially in comparative terms and as regards alternative policy arrangements.

Coordination, in the concatenate sense, especially as applied to the great skein, may not be the all-encompassing term for bottomless goodness. In fact, it is meaning only in reference to a particular concatenation or set of potential concatenations. But whenever those concatenations grow complex and full of diverse human experience, concatenate coordination moves into realms loose, vague, and indeterminate.

11. Consider the following quotation from Friday (1922: 17): "we [must] scrutinize with the greatest care the assumption so complacently made by many economists that a set of market prices which brings about a proper coordination of the factors of production *effects an ideal distribution of product*" (italics added). Friday speaks of "a proper coordination" of factors on the basis of a mind of one type (interested in narrower productive efficiencies) imagined to behold the concatenation of production. We wonder, could he not then also speak of another mind beholding a larger or fuller concatenation of human experience and say that that concatenation is *wanting in coordination* because of its distributional aspects?

CHAPTER 5

꧁

Joy and the Matrix of Concatenate and Mutual

The previous chapter distinguished two kinds of coordination: concatenate and mutual. That distinction is closely related to another, namely the distinction between a social order and the rules/conventions by which that order functions (see Barry 1982: 11, 35). This chapter develops a taxonomy concerning social order and well-being. Among other things, it distinguishes between *spontaneous order*, which I associate with Smith, Hayek, and M. Polanyi, and *emergent conventions*, which I associate with Menger, Schelling, and path-dependence theorists.

OF WOOLEN COATS AND TIN TRADING: SMITH (WN) AND HAYEK

In an excellent article entitled, "The Tradition of Spontaneous Order," Norman Barry (1982) reviewed the development of ideas of undesigned social order. He discusses the work of many thinkers. I begin with some exploration of the most prominent three: Smith, Menger, and Hayek.[1]

In the opening pages of *The Wealth of Nations*, Smith expounds on the common woolen coat: "The shepherd, the sorter of the wool, the wool-comber or carder, the dyer, the scribbler, the spinner, the weaver, the

---

1. Other thinkers treated by Barry (1982) include Luis de Molina (1535–1600), Sir Matthew Hale (1609–76), Bernard Mandeville (1670–1733), Josiah Tucker (1712–99), David Hume (1711–76), Adam Ferguson (1723–1816), Frédéric Bastiat (1801–50), Gustave de Molinari (1819–1912), and Herbert Spencer (1820–1903).

fuller, the dresser, with many others, must all join their arts" (WN: 22). Thus it begins. He goes on to describe trades involved in producing the necessary equipment, in shipping the goods, in producing the ships, and providing all the necessary materials in turn—his description of concatenated activities runs an entire page of text.

The first sentence of the ensuing chapter states that this division of labor "is not originally the effect of any human wisdom, which foresees and intends that general opulence to which it gives occasion" (25). The undesigned social order that concerns Smith is *invisible*: It remains unknown, not only in its details, but even in its more general patterns.

Hayek posits the sudden elimination of a source of supply of tin. He describes how, by decentralized action, tin would be economized by users, and adjustments would occur in connected channels of industry. "The whole acts as one market, not because any of its members survey the whole field, but because their limited fields of vision sufficiently overlap so that through many intermediaries the relevant information is communicated to all" (1945/1948: 86). The spontaneous market order, which Hayek often calls a *catallaxy*, cannot "be perceived by our senses but can only be traced by our intellect" (Hayek 1964: 3). Whereas the emergence of a writing convention or the adoption of the HDTV standard is manifest to participants, the spontaneous, complex market order described by Smith and Hayek is "invisible."[2]

OF MONEY, LANGUAGE, LAW, AND LOCALITIES: HAYEK AND MENGER

Hayek explained that the free enterprise system, like other spontaneous orders, depends upon the participants acting in accordance with social rules. Unlike the spontaneous order itself, the rules—of language, of law, of manners, of money, of technological standards—very often *are recognizable* to the participants. These rules, nonetheless, might "manifest themselves only in their being obeyed" (1964: 7). Thus, the undesigned catallaxy depends on rules or conventions that in turn may be undesigned. Are these rules (or conventions or institutions or customs), when undesigned, also to be called examples of "spontaneous order"?

2. Along with Smith and Hayek, Herbert Spencer deserves mention for discussing the vast concatenation of economic activities as an undesigned order. Not only did he articulate its "invisibility" to the participants, he consistently described it as "spontaneous" (Spencer 1884/1892/1969: 135, 196, 274, 301, 326).

Carl Menger's 1883 work, translated most recently as *Investigations Into the Method of the Social Sciences* (1985), argues that, in Norman Barry's words (1982: 31), "[W]hile it is meaningful to talk of social 'aggregates,' the behavior of such aggregates is explicable only in individualist terms." Menger discusses at considerable length the evolution of money, the common law, the state, localities, language, market customs, and other social institutions that are often highly beneficial yet "organic," or undesigned. Menger (146) poses the following question as "perhaps the most noteworthy" problem of the social sciences: *"How can it be that institutions which serve the common welfare and are extremely significant for its development come into being without a* **common will** *directed toward establishing them?"* (Italics and bold in original.)

The notion of macropatterns emerging out of microbehavior puts Menger in the mutual-coordination rubric, in the company of Schelling and path-dependence theorists. That connection is strengthened by two additional common features. First, as Barry (1982: 32) notes, Menger "does not emphasize the *value* of undesigned institutions in quite the same way as other thinkers in the same tradition and does not assume that they are necessarily superior to pragmatic [or designed] ones." In Menger's discussion of what is today called agglomeration economies, he explains how a place will emerge organically as a locality, but he adds that "the common will...is more likely to produce...[its] perfection" (Menger 1883: 156). In discussing the evolution of the common law, Menger (233) declares that it is "erroneous in every conceivable respect" to suppose that the common law always performs better than any positive legislation could. Thus, Menger (233) notes the possibility of lock-in and the need for deliberate remedy: "[The] common law has also proved harmful to the common good often enough, and...legislation has just as often changed common law in a way benefiting the common good." As Louis Schneider sums up the point: "If there are institutions that may in a sense be regarded as 'storing' human wisdom...there is...nothing in Menger to suggest that there may not be institutions which 'store' foolishness or ineptitudes" (1963/1985: 12).

A second feature that Menger shares with Schelling and the path-dependence theorists is a focus on the undesigned emergence of conventions. He says very little along the lines of Smith or Hayek about the catallaxy at large. Menger studies the organic basis of the conventions by which the catallaxy works, but does not make a fuss over the catallaxy itself (see Menger 1883/1985: 146–147). He never marvels at the division of labor and knowledge that makes a woolen coat nor expounds on the importance of liberty to the felicity and beauty of such concatenations. Menger's principal work, translated as *The Principles of Economics*, talks about choice at the margin, price determination, and so on, but it too actually says very little about the grand concatenation and the social utility to which it conduces.

HAYEK IN RELATION TO MENGER AND SMITH (WN)

Menger focuses on emergent conventions and neglects spontaneous order. Smith, at least in the *Wealth of Nations*, focuses on spontaneous order and perhaps neglects emergent conventions. This fact might help us understand a rather remarkable passage in the *Investigations* where Menger denounces Smith:

> What Adam Smith and even those of his followers who have most successfully developed political economy can actually be charged with is...[a] defective understanding of the unintentionally created social institutions and their significance for economy. It is the opinion appearing chiefly in their writings that the institutions of economy are always the intended product of the common will of society as such, results of expressed agreement of members of society or of positive legislation. In this one-sidedly pragmatic view of the nature of social institutions, the sphere of ideas of A. Smith and his closest followers comes into contact with that of the writers of the French Age of Enlightenment in general and of the French physiocrats in particular. Adam Smith, also, and his school predominantly strive for the *pragmatic* understanding of the economy, even where such understanding is not adequate for the objective state of affairs. The result is that the broad realm of unintentionally created social structures remains closed to their theoretical comprehension.
>
> (1883/1985: 172; see also 176)

As Lawrence White (1985: xvi) points out in his Introduction to the *Investigations*, perhaps Menger's real target here is Jeremy Bentham, and he used Smith's name carelessly. I submit, however, that once we distinguish between undesigned conventions or institutions and undesigned social concatenations in the sense of the catallaxy, Menger's passage, though unfair to Smith,[3] becomes less puzzling.

---

3. It seems to me reasonable to say that Smith's *The Wealth of Nations* did not pay special attention to the "organic" or undesigned origins of social institutions and convention but unreasonable to say, as Menger does, that Smith strove for

Hayek (1994: 147) reports that the "conception of the spontaneous generation of institutions is worked out more beautifully there [in Menger's *Investigations*] than in any other book I know." Hayek's writings pay much attention to both the Mengerian and the Smithian, both emergent conventions—even lock-in![4]—and the catallaxy that, as if guided by an invisible hand, produces the woolen coat.

TOWARD A CONCEPTUAL SCHEME

The term "spontaneous order" is found in the work of Auguste Comte (1896: Book VI, ch. V) and the word "spontaneous" is used in corresponding fashion by Herbert Spencer (1884/1892/1969: 135, 196, 274, 301, 326) and Emile Durkheim (1964: 360 and elsewhere).[5] It was Michael Polanyi (1951), however, who used the term "spontaneous order" in a consistent way to mean polycentric order, or an undesigned concatenation of affairs. Hayek uses it in the same way (Polanyi is quoted at Hayek 1960: 160). Hayek uses it primarily to mean the catallaxy and other undesigned concatenations of social activities. He generally did not mean by it undesigned conventions or rules; for that he generally used the word "rules,"

---

an understanding of such institutions as being "pragmatic" or designed. Barry (1982: 27) construes Smith in the *Lectures on Jurisprudence* as viewing the law as organic in its origins. On the other hand, Smith makes remarks in the *Jurisprudence* (LJ: 337) about geometry, arithmetic, and writing having "all been invented originally to facilitate the operation of the severall arts." Beyond WN, Menger's accusation is groundless. In TMS, Smith explains how "the general rule...is formed by finding from experience that all action of a certain kind, or circumstanced in a certain manner, are approved of" (159), and his essay on the first formation of language speaks of simple rules for a complex system and contains various remarks such as that "The general rule would establish itself insensibly, and by slow degrees" (LRBL: 211). Menger probably knew little of Smith's writings beyond *The Wealth of Nations*. Menger described at length the organic emergence of money in both the *Investigations* and his *Principles of Economics* (1871/1994), and he probably felt that Smith's discussion of the origin of money (WN, 38ff) was not as organic as it might have been.

4. In *The Road to Serfdom*, Hayek writes: "It is, for example, at least conceivable that...the use of electricity for all purposes could be made cheaper than coal or gas if everybody could be made to use only electricity...[I]t must be admitted that it is possible that, by compulsory standardization or the prohibition of variety beyond a certain degree, abundance might be increased in some fields...It is even conceivable that a new invention may be made some day whose adoption would seem unquestionably beneficial but which could be used only if many or all people were made to avail themselves of it at the same time" (1944: 51). Also, Hayek (1973) says that even in a common-law state it will sometimes be necessary to alter judge-made law by legislation or deliberate redirection (88–89, 100, 105).

5. I am grateful to Lars Udehn for enlightenment on these matters.

although he did occasionally use the term "spontaneous order" to mean undesigned conventions or rules (e.g., 1964: 5–6).

Ambiguity in the meaning of "spontaneous order" closely parallels ambiguity in usage of the word *coordination*. A fine example of Hayek's usage is the following: In the market economy, we depend "on that division of knowledge between individuals whose separate efforts are co-ordinated by the impersonal mechanism for transmitting the relevant information known by us as the price system" (Hayek 1944: 49–50). Michael Polanyi writes in the same idiom in *The Logic of Liberty* (1951: 115): "[In] spontaneously ordered systems . . . persons mutually adjust their full-time activities over a prolonged period, resulting in a complex and yet highly adaptable co-ordination of these actions." As seen in previous chapters, Ronald Coase uses the word in the exact same way both when he explains his central aim in his famous 1937 essay on the firm and in his Nobel lecture (Coase 1992: 6), where he consistently refers to "the pricing mechanism" as a "method of co-ordination." Nowadays in economics, however, *coordination* usually means mutual coordination, wherein actors aim for mutually reinforcing actions. Mutual coordination is manifest.

Can the coordination of Hayek, Polanyi, and Coase be construed as mutual coordination? It is true that market participants achieve face-to-face coordination by sharing a common language, a common measure of time, and so on. Everyone at the office arrives by nine o'clock, and this mutual coordination enhances productivity. Indeed, every verbal interaction and every sharing of physical space is suffused by moments of coincidence of interest and mutual coordination.

But Hayek has more in mind. He means that when the blacksmith forges a pair of clipping shears, that activity is well coordinated to the activities of the weaver, who some time later works with the wool that was clipped from sheep with those shears. The blacksmith and the weaver do not even know of each other's existence, and one has no manifest sense of coordinating his actions with those of the other. If one were to visualize a "game" that included all of their relevant strategy alternatives, it would have to be a game that also included the relevant strategies of hundreds, or thousands, or even millions of other players alike. Hayek (1978c) even ventured to call it the "game of catallaxy" (60). Such an exercise would depart from noncooperative game theory, which draws up games with an understanding that *that is how the game is understood by the players*—the common-knowledge assumption of game theory. (Again, this is one reason why not every coincidence of interest represents a situation for mutual coordination; interests quite unaware of one another can still coincide in important respects, as do ours and certain ones of the Wright brothers.)

Hayek emphasized that understanding is local, situational, and purposive. The weaver sees only the manufacturer, not the blacksmith. The individual uses focal points to carry out interaction with others, but this is like the baton pass between members of a relay team. The individual confronts problems that differ from the problem of achieving manifest coordination, problems analogous to *running alone with baton in hand*. He pursues honest profit: He responds to price signals and local opportunities; he tries to gain lucrative insights; he works hard to keep his promises and to see that his trading partners keep theirs. He does not perceive himself to be playing a coordination game with myriad distant people. As Adam Smith (WN: 456) put it, each promotes "an end which was no part of his intention"—nor even of his knowledge.

There are other important points that suggest that Hayek's coordination is not mutual coordination. Hayek's coordination must involve myriad individuals. Shall the "catallaxy game" include one's *competitors*? Doing so would seem essential to a Hayekian framework, and it becomes plain that market outcomes are not ones of mutual coordination. Whether we think of coordination equilibrium in formal games or of resolutions in Schelling's parables, the outcome in which the two retailers compete is not a situation of coincidence of interest, not a game of mutual coordination. Retailer A, given his own action, is *not* best satisfied by the rivalrous actions taken by Retailer B. Retailer A is *not* best satisfied when the distributor supplies articles not only to him, but also to Retailer B. Most fundamentally, Retailer A is *not* best satisfied when the distributor raises his price, or when the customer departs without having made a purchase. Many different types of frames have myriad moments within the vast concatenation.

So, if Hayek's coordination is not mutual coordination, what exactly is it? In something of a paradox, Hayek, Polanyi, and Coase, the dedicated opponents of conscious effort to arrange society as a whole, meant, in fact, *pleasing arrangement*. The arrangement is abstract, and the pleasure is allegorical, but that is what they meant. In the Hayek meaning, the concatenation of affairs in cases like the catallaxy is not actually coordinated by a Great Arranger, but, as Smith's famous metaphor demonstrates, their idea of coordination is clarified by an allegory of the affairs being "led by an invisible hand."

The allegory goes as follows: There is a superior being named Joy who is invisible and who beholds the vast economic order. We cannot spell out what she values for society and hopes to witness, but it is not hard for us to understand. In her humanitarianism, she is basically like you and me, a genuine liberal, in the broad sense. Her pleasure increases when human society exhibits widespread prosperity, comfort, personal fulfillment, excellence, irony, and affection. In this regard she is like Smith or Hayek or Coase or Schelling. In the allegory in which Joy elicits our assent to her guidance, Joy coordinates the concatenation of our activities, like the way we coordinate colors in decorating our home. This is the allegory behind the meaning of "coordination" from the transitive verb.

Hayek's claim is the following: Liberal rules generate a dynamic, complex "spontaneous order" that Joy finds more pleasing than the order generated by the rather controlled or centrally directed economic system. The order of the catallaxy is like the naturally formed crystal, in which microscopic local conditions lead each element to settle into its place. Just as we enjoy a synoptic view of the whole crystal, Joy has a synoptic view of the concatenation.

We ought not speak of a "catallaxy game," however. The order encompasses all of the particular plans and activities of the individuals within that order; it is abstract, and beautiful only by way of an allegorical kind of cooperation. Figure 5.1 draws the distinction between the two coordinations.

Mutual coordination (From the intransitive verb)	Concatenate coordination (From the transitive verb)
Schelling, D. Lewis, game theory	Hayek, Polanyi, Coase, etc.
"Meshing" interaction within a situation of coincidence of interest	An arrangement or concatenation pleasing to beholder or spectator
Manifest from the interactor's point of view	In some cases, the concatenation and its coordination are only *abstract* or notional from the interactor's point of view ("invisible hand")
Of a rubric that includes: focal points, coordination equilibrium, coordination games, convention	A broad topic that includes features often out of step with the rubric of mutual coordination, features such as disjointed knowledge, asymmetric interpretation, discovery, innovation, entrepreneurship, competition, abstention, exit, shunning, and bargaining

Figure 5.1: Two concepts of coordination: some contrasts

THE CONTINUUM BETWEEN THE TWO COORDINATIONS

For the *transitive* verb *to coordinate, Merriam-Webster's Collegiate Dictionary* (1994) gives, "to bring into common action, movement, or condition." The etymology shows the Latin roots *co-* (a prefix for "joint") + *ordinare*, which means *to arrange.* Thus, one coordinates a class schedule, or one coordinates colors, patterns, textures, or motifs. The entrepreneur *coordinates* factors within his firm. Likewise, for bodily coordination—as when we speak of an individual being physically coordinated in his movement—we should think of the transitive verb, and we avoid reflexive objects by subdividing the being into the soul or will as something separate from parts of the body. Michael Polanyi (1963), for instance, writes of an animal's "active centre" coordinating the animal's "voluntary movements" (56). Thus, the "active centre" of a graceful athlete displays a pleasing concatenation of bodily movements.

For the intransitive verb, *Merriam-Webster's* gives, "to be or become coordinate esp. so as to act together in a smooth concerted way." This is mutual coordination; I coordinate *with* my friend; we coordinate *to* the drumbeat—no direct objects here. As for any intransitive verb, there can be a direct object only of a *reflexive* kind: I coordinate *my* doings, or *our* doing, or *our* plans, to meet this afternoon. In this fashion we could make the intransitive verb *to walk* superficially—and only superficially—transitive: I walk my body down the street.

We can see two extremes in the degree of reflexivity. There is no reflexivity in "I coordinate the colors," or in the allegory, "Joy coordinates the concatenation." There is complete reflexivity in "I coordinate *my* actions to the traffic light."

Between these extremes, however, is a continuum of reflexivity, and hence of the two coordinations. One might report, "I coordinate Charlie's action and my action to achieve (right, right) in the road game." The set of objects is heavily reflexive, although a significant part, namely, Charlie's action, is not. When the CEO of a company reports, "I coordinate the skeleton of activities of all 1,000 employees, including myself," the degree of reflexivity of the objects is, as it were, only one one-thousandth. Mostly, the CEO is coordinating the activities of others, so the verb is preponderantly transitive; the CEO is arranging a concatenation of activities. There is a small element of reflexivity, or intransitivity, however, in that his own normal responsibilities are also being arranged by him. All degrees of reflexivity are possible, based on *how large a part oneself is of the set of objects one coordinates.* The condition of continuum upsets the distinction between concatenate and mutual coordination no more than it does the distinction between transitive and intransitive verbs; there's a small gray area, but we nonetheless distinguish the two.[6]

MUTUAL COORDINATION GOES WITH CONVENTION

The distinction between concatenate and mutual coordination lines up with the distinction between conventions and social concatenations/orders. I have noted in loose terms how David Lewis defines a strategy combination, such as (left, left) in the road game (Fig. 4.2), as a coordination equilibrium, and the road game as a coordination problem. It is upon these coordination concepts that Lewis builds his definition of *convention*. The same connection is found in Schelling (1960: 91): "The coordination game probably lies behind the stability of institutions and traditions [or conventions]."

Put loosely, a convention is a behavioral regularity in a recurring social situation, in which the situation represents a coordination problem and the regularity is one of the coordination equilibria in that problem (cf. Young 1996). In the road game, a regularity of everyone driving on the left would be a convention, as would be a regularity of everyone driving on the right. Conventions are a regular manifestation of mutual coordination, and, by providing continual precedents, they generate the continual focal points that aid mutual coordination in the future. A convention is often self-perpetuating: The focal point for today's behavior is yesterday's behavior (or habit, practice, or experience). If we keep going back in time, however, we find that the convention grew from other focal points, or *precursive* focal points.

Lewis's convention is how we may read Hayek's "rules." Hayek (1948) said, "rules . . . serve as signposts to the individuals in making their own plans" (20). Rules generate focal guides to mutual coordination, and they usually qualify as conventions in Lewis's sense.

It is easy to see how many of the social institutions studied by Menger—such as language, a money standard, and localities—are conventions.

---

6. On pages 40–41, positing a golf course owner and a golf school owner, I remark on a *different* aspect of the relationship between concatenate and mutual coordination, namely as alternative *ways of seeing* those cases in which multiple mutual coordinators are also the joint chiefs of the relevant concatenation.

Smith's commutative justice, the "natural liberty" rules of ownership and consent, may also be interpreted as convention.

THE ELEMENTS OF CONVENTION IN THE NORMS
OF NATURAL LIBERTY

Scholars often think of ownership in terms of a prisoners' dilemma, which is not a coordination game. That perspective may make it difficult to see the elements of convention in ownership.

Schelling (1960) writes: "Trust is often achieved simply by the continuity of the relation between parties and the recognition by each that what he might gain by cheating in a given instance is outweighed by the value of the tradition of trust that makes possible a long sequence of future agreements" (134–135). Rules of property and contract may thus be seen as "conventions whose sanction in the aggregate is the need for mutual forbearance to avoid mutual destruction, and whose sanction in each individual case is the risk that to breach a rule may collapse it and that to collapse it may lead to a jointly less favorable [rule]" (260).

Conventions like respecting ownership can help actors avoid mutual loss. When one begins to transgress another's dominion, perhaps rashly, or inadvertently, or only apparently, "conventions...provide a graceful way out. If one's motive for declining [to compete] is manifestly no lack of nerve, there are no enduring costs in refusing to compete" (Schelling 1966: 120). The one who defends against a transgression of rights, such as one's rightful space on the highway, may find that "it may be safer in the long run to hew to the center of the road than to yield six inches on successive nights, if one really intends to stop yielding before he is pushed onto the shoulder. It may save both parties a collision" (124). Once transgression has begun or been suspected, ownership conventions help the potential aggressor and the potential defender to coordinate on peaceful disengagement.

David Friedman discusses the foundation of principles of natural liberty:

> I can control the motions of my body by a simple act of will. You can control its motions by imposing overwhelming force, by making believable threats to which I will yield, or in various other ways. Controlling it may be possible for both of us, but it is much cheaper and easier for me. In this sense, we may

describe my body as my *natural property*. The same description applies to my gun—because I know where I hid it and you do not.

(1994: 14, italics added)

It is natural for you to analogize from that human body you occupy to the other tangible stuff over which you especially have powers, and from you to everyone else. We observe such principles as focal points for co-existence and interaction.

Natural property makes for focal points that facilitate our coming together, and Friedman again applies focal-point thinking to contract or voluntary agreement. Our encounters form a cascade of yet more focal points:

> So far we have considered the Schelling point that generates an agreement. But the agreement itself, whether generated by a Schelling point or in some other way, is thereafter itself a Schelling point. It is a unique outcome of which both players are conscious. Once it has been made, a policy of "if you do not abide by the agreement I will revert to the use of force, even if the violation is small compared to the cost of conflict" is believable for precisely the same reason the refusal to pay tribute, or any insistence by a bargainer on a Schelling point, is believable. The signing of a contract establishes a new Schelling point and thereby alters the strategic situation. The contract enforces itself.

(1994: 8)

Even a prisoners' dilemma may be worthwhile to all players. It may be that every player finds the one-shot defection outcome *better than not being able to play the game at all*. To play the game and benefit from doing so, even if the outcome is less than optimal, however, the players must first come to some apprehension of the situation. In a sense, before playing the prisoners' dilemma, the players "play" a preliminary game of apprehending what the situation is. We exchange glances; we say hello—an encounter begins before choosing a strategy in the game as we come to apprehend it. Even on the Internet, we dwell within society and society dwells within us; we are not atoms bumping up against "game" matrices. Now, *that preliminary game may well be like a coordination game, and natural-liberty norms are likely to serve as focal points for coming to a workable mutual apprehension of the situation*. Natural-liberty norms may place us in situations of competition, bargaining, and misinformation, but they help us avoid paralyzing confusion, fear, and isolation. And, following a breakdown of voluntaristic conventions, they provide focal points for the resumption of voluntarism.

Natural-liberty principles are not the only focal points. In many ways, governments violate natural-liberty principles, but that condition rests on another focal point: *Government is the one kind of institution for which we make an exception to natural-liberty norms.* Government is the institutional apparatus of legitimized coercion. We follow a convention of governmental exceptionalism.[7]

David Hume had an uncanny appreciation of mutual coordination, focal point, and convention, and his writings support the points of this section (as confirmed by Haakonssen 1981, ch. 1). Though he never used the word "focal," he wrote of how a right of ownership "arises and perishes in an instant...by...the consent of the proprietor...without any of that insensible gradation, which is remarkable in other qualities and relations" (1740/1978: 530; see also 490ff, 522ff). He wrote that the will alone does not transfer property or oblige to duty, "but the will must be expressed by words or signs in order to impose a tie upon any man. The expression, being once brought in as subservient to the will, soon becomes the principal part of the promise" (1751/1902: 199, n. 5). The laws of justice evolved in ways that render them focal. Meanwhile, he also said that authority of government is based, not on social contract, but on convention arising from the focalness of established government. The two conventions— the principles of natural liberty/commutative justice, and government exceptionalism in *contravening* those principles—leave us with the signal understanding of Hume and Smith, that governmental contraventions of voluntarist principles will be considered, tolerated, and sometimes even endorsed, but that they will be understood *as exceptions*, as "politick" or "expedient"—that, by virtue of liberal semantics that recognize voluntarist principles as focal and honor them as presumptively proper, any contravention is made to bear the burden of proof. (For Hume's and Smith's ideas about political authority being a matter *of convention*, or acquiescence, based on utility and necessity, and *not a matter of social contract*, see Hume 1740/1978: 484–569, esp. 490, 548, 567, and in Hume 1987 the essays "Of the Original Contract" and "Of Passive Obedience"; Smith LJ: 315–319, 321,401–404; TMS: 80, 159–66, 252–253, 318, 340–342; WN: 416–417, 614, 710–714.)

---

7. Although David Friedman's 1994 paper does not make this point (about a focal point in governmental exceptionalism), I associate it with him (as well as Hume and Smith), partly because in an oral presentation of his 1994 paper he put the point clearly and related it to the focal point themes of that paper.

CONCATENATE COORDINATION GOES WITH SOCIAL ORDER

All of Menger's institutions, including norms of property and contract, therefore, can be regarded as conventions. Again, as both Menger and Schelling make clear, conventions may be unsatisfactory. There is nothing in Lewis's definition of convention to preclude the inferior coordination equilibrium as the social regularity. The ranking of coordination equilibria as "inferior" or "superior" is not a component of mutual coordination and convention. It is, however, germane to concatenate coordination. When Hayek and Polanyi write of coordination, they mean a pleasing arrangement of affairs. Hayek and Polanyi would say that in the road game in Fig. 4.2 the arrangement (left, left), though a coordination equilibrium, shows unsatisfactory coordination. They ask what kinds of social orders tend to generate, in games like that in Fig. 4.2, the superior outcome (right, right)? They evaluate the concatenation as a complex social order.

SUBSUMPTION OF MUTUAL BY CONCATENATE AND OF CONVENTION BY SOCIAL ORDER

Confusion arises from failing to distinguish between concatenate and mutual coordination, and from failing to distinguish between conventions and social orders. Confusion will arise again if, having made our distinctions, we think of the distinguished ideas as neatly partitioned. Again, concatenate coordination is not achieved apart from matters of mutual coordination. Concatenate coordination will usually subsume numerous narrower scenes of mutual coordination (in addition to other things, such as competition). Social orders do not function apart from rules and conventions; they subsume conventions. These relationships of *subsumption* are analogous to the point made by Hayek (1973: 46), Polanyi (1951: 134), and Coase (1937/1988: 35)—that an undesigned, spontaneous order will subsume pockets of conscious design.

TYPOLOGY

Figure 5.2 presents a typology of the topics I have discussed. It is based on three distinctions:

1. The distinction between conventions and social orders (or concatenations), which parallels that between mutual and concatenate coordination.

	DECENTRAL		CENTRAL	
Conventions (Mutual coordination)	EMERGENT CONVENTIONS		PLANNED CONVENTIONS	
	good for CC	bad for CC	good for CC	bad for CC
	(1) The principles of natural liberty Gold standard Superior languages	(2) British/American system of weights and measures Chinese writing	(3) Metric system	(4) American winter clock setting
Social Orders (or concatenations)	SPONTANEOUS ORDER		PLANNED ORDER	
	good in CC	bad in CC	good in CC	bad in CC
(Concatenate coordination)	(5) Catallaxy Roller skating The *process generating good language*	(6) Tragedy of the commons	(7) Skeleton of activities within most firms earning honest profits	(8) Centrally planned economy

Figure 5.2: Typology of conventions and social orders
Note: CC stands for concatenate coordination.

2. The distinction between whether the moving forces are central and "decentral" (a neologism I prefer to "decentralized"). This distinction calls for two clarifications. First, the distinction between central and decentral is often *a matter of degree*, of course, and may take on certain meanings depending on the discourse situation. *In matters of policy analysis or political economy*, "decentral" or "spontaneous" generally means free or voluntary, whereas "central direction" or "control" means coercive restriction. It is appropriate to say that a minimum-wage law, for example, makes a regime less spontaneous, more centrally directed than without such restriction on the freedom of contract. Second, for conventions, there is the issue of whether the standard (or rule) was intentionally designed, such as the QWERTY keyboard, and whether *its adoption or emergence* as a convention was centrally directed. Our focus here is the emergence of the convention, not the creation of the

standard. Thus, QWERTY represents a designed standard but an emergent convention.

3. The distinction between good and bad. For a convention, the issue is whether it is good or bad *for* achieving concatenate coordination. The assessment is based on comparison with *other* plausible or relevant conventions, not with the state of affairs where there is no convention at all. For a social order, the issue is good or bad *in* achieving concatenate coordination. Such judgment is comparative, rendered with some relevant alternative arrangement in mind, at least implicitly.

The 2 x 2 x 2 typology gives eight categories, numbered in Fig. 5.2. Here I comment on the cells numbered 1 through 8:

1. Emergent conventions that are good for concatenate coordination include the principles (or rules) of natural liberty, the gold standard, and superior languages.

2. Emergent conventions that are bad for concatenate coordination are the British and American system of weights and measures, and the Chinese writing system, which generally requires a distinct symbol for every word.

3. The metric system was designed in France in 1799, and *its adoption was centrally planned.* It is very good for concatenate coordination.

4. Compared to standard time, the daylight savings clock setting makes for less light at 6:00 A.M., when most people are asleep, and more light at 6:00 P.M., when most people are awake. In America, during World War II and during the winter of 1973–74, daylight savings time was enacted year round. In late 1974, however, America adopted, and has since maintained, a system of shifting during each year between daylight savings time for the eight warmer months and standard time for the four winter months. The current system may be a good example of a designed convention that is bad for concatenate coordination. Its badness would lie in its calling for two clock changes each year and its inferior clock setting during the winter months.

5. The leading example of a spontaneous order that is good in concatenate coordination is a free-enterprise economy, "the special kind of spontaneous order produced by the market through people acting within the rules of the law of property, tort and contract" (Hayek 1976: 109). A more visible example is the particular pattern of movements of roller skaters in a roller rink. Polanyi (1951: 162–165) applies the idea of spontaneous order to the *process of making* law and to the *process of making*

science. He is careful to speak of the process of making, as opposed to the distilled results. (Of course, not all such processes belong in the "good" cell.)

6. The fate of common or unowned resources shows that spontaneous orders need not be good in concatenate coordination. When a common pool is overfished, or a fraternity-house beer keg is overindulged, we see the functioning of a spontaneous order—or *disorder*. (It is useful to assume, nonetheless, that, *unless specified otherwise*, the term "spontaneous order" refers to concatenations or processes good in concatenate coordination, for the term is used mostly for such purpose.)

7. Planned order is never planned in full; there is always scope for decentral action within certain bounds. As Hayek (1964: 10) says, what distinguishes planned order from spontaneous order is that the *skeleton* of the pattern of activities is consciously designed. As Coase (1937/1988) argued, it will sometimes be good for concatenate coordination for owners and managers to create a planned order in creating and running a firm.

8. "As the area of unified planning is extended, particular knowledge of local circumstances will, of necessity, be less effectively used" (Hayek 1960: 352). Centrally planned economies score poorly in concatenate coordination.

CONCLUDING REMARKS

Modern economics has failed to bring the idea of spontaneous order into its grasp. The closest thing we have to a model of the complex process that makes a woolen coat is general equilibrium modeling, but GE models seem to miss something essential in spontaneity and seem to obscure, and even misrepresent, how the process actually works. Indeed, the models largely omit altogether *the process of* concatenate coordination.

We can better clarify the various social mechanisms at work, and the intellectual matters at hand, by distinguishing conventions and social orders, and mutual and concatenate coordination. There is a categorical difference between a set of emergent conventions and the concatenation of market activities that makes a woolen coat.

CHAPTER 6

⌘

Light Shed by the Two Coordinations

ere we put our distinctions to use: to clarify our language, to define cooperation, and then to resolve some confusions.

EMERGENT CONVENTION AND SPONTANEOUS ORDER

One can readily find examples of scholars speaking of the English language or certain local customs or a monetary standard as a "spontaneous order" (examples are given in Klein 1997). The English language itself is a distilled set of rules or focal points, a set that, to an extent, is captured by the dictionary and grammar books. To designate something of that nature, I suggest *convention* (or custom, rules, norms, institution). True, the convention emerges from a process, and that process is aptly termed "spontaneous." But the conventions themselves are not the process; rather, they are the rules or focal points. I suggest that they be called "emergent conventions" (or customs, etc.).

We also find discourse that crosses terms in the inverse way: Some scholars speak of spontaneous order as "emergent order." Here, I ask that we take "emerge" fairly literally. Baby sea turtles emerged from the sand. When something emerges, it comes into view; we see that which has emerged, like flotsam and jetsam emerging on the surface. Likewise, the English language emerged, and the gold standard emerged. As for orders (or concatenations or processes), in some settings, such as on the floor of the roller rink, we might say that the order emerges before our eyes; we have a synoptic view of it. But when we speak of "spontaneous order," and, also, typically, I believe, when scholars speak of "emergent order," the order referred to is not seen—it is often like the concatenation that yields the woolen coat or the pencil. It remains invisible, and any pretense of seeing it, or capturing it in a synopsis, is not credible. In sum, I recommend that we reserve "emergent" for conventions and "spontaneous" for orders (or concatenations)—of course, in each case, only where applicable: For example, the metric system is a convention in France, but for most purposes we would not call it an "emergent convention," because of the nature of its adoption process.

COOPERATION IN TERMS OF THE TWO COORDINATIONS

The Washington Redskins cooperate in winning the football game. Neighbors cooperate in keeping the neighborhood clean. Factory workers cooperate in producing bread—assuming, that is, that they do cooperate!

I define *cooperation* as the mutual coordinating of each person's actions in a context in which each cooperator perceives himself to be contributing *to the same referent concatenation*—a football victory, a clean neighborhood, a prosperous bread factory. There is mutual consciousness of each individual contributing to the pleasing concatenation. The *spirit* of cooperation is especially pronounced when there is not only mutual awareness of contribution but mutual sentiment: "We did it together!"

Hayek wrote: "Cooperation, like solidarity, presupposes a large measure of agreement on ends as well as on methods employed in their pursuit. It makes sense in a small group whose members share particular habits, knowledge and beliefs about possibilities" (1988: 19). There is a sense of common knowledge.

Some have depicted the free economy as a system of cooperation. Should we call the Smith-Hayek spontaneous order a system of cooperation? It entails *myriad instances* of cooperation, but it also entails myriad instances of competition. It entails myriad instances of rather impersonal exchange that, as cooperative moments, usually are only tiny and often are ambivalent. It also entails myriad instances of deception and misrepresentation. It entails a lot of things, not just instances of cooperation.

Adam Smith (WN: 23, 26) said the day laborer obtains his woolen coat by virtue of "the assistance and co-operation of many thousands," an expansive notion of cooperation reiterated by Thomas Hodgskin (1827/1966: 25) and Richard Whately (1832/1966: 98, 99), but when Smith observes that man "stands at all times in need of the co-operation and assistance of great multitudes," he says, "while his whole life is scarce sufficient to gain the friendship of a few persons," suggesting that it isn't simply cooperation that yields him the woolen coat.

Edward Gibbon Wakefield distinguished "simple co-operation," as with the Redskins or neighbors or factory workers, from "complex co-operation," a system of spontaneous concatenate coordination.[1] John Stuart Mill (1871/1909: 118f) followed and elaborated Wakefield's distinction.

Frédéric Bastiat exemplified the tendency to depict the free market system as a system of harmony and cooperation. In *Economic Harmonies*, he used "co-operation" recklessly and celebrated the market system as "a marvelous association" (1850/1996: 68). Another free-trade champion, Henry George, writes similarly: "But where the natural rights of all are secured, then competition...becomes the most simple, most extensive, most elastic, and most refined system of co-operation" (1886: 307). Philip Wicksteed likewise spoke of "a vast system of co-operation" and "one huge mutual benefit society" (1910/1967: 183). H.C. Macpherson wrote that Smith's division of labor unconsciously transforms "the selfish solitary worker into a member of a huge co-operative organization" (1899: 69). Milton and Rose Friedman take similar poetic license: "Cooperation is worldwide, just as in the economic system" (1980: 17).

At a different ideological pole, Karl Marx rightly emphasized that the capitalist system, *in the whole*, was not cooperation—and ultimately, he condemned it for that. "[A]ll labour in which many individuals cooperate necessarily requires a commanding will to coordinate and unify the process...much as that of an orchestra conductor" (Marx 1998: 382). As a matter of ethics and human fulfillment, Marx wanted the vast social concatenation to be a universal experience in mutual coordination—that is, he wanted everyone in society to be, in awareness and sentiments, mutually coordinated to the idea of the great concatenation as a cooperative project.[2]

Marx's vision forsakes the crucial liberal principles of achieving extended, complex, well-coordinated concatenations. As Hayek put it, "The 'moral equivalent of war' offered to evoke solidarity is but a relapse into cruder principles of coordination" (1988: 20).

1. Wakefield is quoted at length by Mill (1871/1909: 116–118). The citation given is "Wakefield's edition of Adam Smith, vol. I, p. 26." Wakefield's distinction also appears in Scott (1900: 237).
2. On Marx, see Tucker (1961: 188–223) and Klein (2005: 13–14).

I define cooperation as entailing a mutual consciousness among the cooperators. Yet, Max Hirsch made a distinction paralleling simple and complex, namely: *conscious* and *unconscious* cooperation. Unconscious cooperation? An unconscious mutual consciousness?

Drawing on Spencer and George, Max Hirsch, too, answered Marx: "The co-ordination of efforts may, however, take place consciously or unconsciously... [W]hile conscious co-operation utilizes only an insignificant part of the intelligence of the co-operators, unconscious co-operation utilises the whole sum of their individual intelligences. The latter, therefore, is a higher and more efficient form of co-operation, and its product must be superior to that of the former" (1901: 278, 282–283).

Is it semantically legitimate to regard Wakefield's "complex cooperation" or Hirsch's "unconscious cooperation" as cooperation at all? In defending the presumption of liberty, classical liberals need to distinguish mutual and concatenate coordination, so as to clarify the meaning of cooperation. If they wish to praise the free enterprise system as a system of cooperation, if they wish to talk like Hodgskin, Whately, Bastiat, George, Wicksteed, and the Friedmans, they had better be prepared to explain how two people who have no mutual consciousness, who know nothing of each other, can be said to be cooperating. We will return to this matter in Chapter 14.

RESOLVING CONFUSIONS OVER PLANNING AND "COORDINATION"

When Hayekians declare that free competition is the best method by which coordination can be adequately brought about (see Hayek 1944: 48), they mean concatenate coordination. Free competition generates the most pleasing arrangement. When "coordination" is read in the mutual sense, as a sort of manifest meshing of behaviors, Hayek's words become wrong.

A small group of musicians might sit down and spontaneously make pleasant music, but a large orchestra will certainly need a common sheet of music. A large complex system probably needs central direction or leadership to achieve mutual coordination. Imagine the symphony performance of only decentralized competing musicians.

In his book *Whither Socialism?* Joseph Stiglitz does not distinguish between concatenate and mutual coordination, and he repeatedly slips from one to the other: "Traditional discussions of market socialism focus on the lack of a coordinating mechanism"—that would be *concatenate* coordination. "Critics of markets" point out in real markets "the excess capacity that arises in some industries at some times and the shortages that arise in others...Each producer of steel not only has no incentive to share information about his production plans with other producers; he has incentives to hide information, or even to provide misleading information" (1994: 90–91). This he gives as an example of "coordination failure," but the example is foremost a matter of *mutual* coordination.

Once we train our eye to separate concatenate and mutual, we see that many writers point out that market actors do not mutually coordinate and on that basis imply that free markets do not concatenately coordinate. I believe that Hayekian claims about the coordinating properties of the free enterprise system have often been misunderstood because the word *coordination* is taken to mean mutual coordination. We will explore this point in Chapter 12 in the context of urban transit.

RESOLVING CONFUSION OVER WHETHER ENTREPRENEURSHIP AND INNOVATION ARE COORDINATIVE

The economist Israel Kirzner has highlighted the role of discovery. He has led an "Austrian" resistance to flattening knowledge down to information. He writes of the vital human faculty to apprehend opportunities for one's betterment or to re-interpret one's situation, calls it alertness, and integrates it into an understanding of market processes. He associates this alertness with entrepreneurship.

Kirzner has insisted that entrepreneurship is necessarily coordinative. Many, however, have taken issue with Kirzner's claim. Ludwig Lachmann (1986: 5) wrote, "Competitive market forces will cause discoordination as well as coordination of agents' plans...Schumpeter epitomized it in his phrase 'the perennial gale of creative destruction.'" Elsewhere, Lachmann wrote: "An institution provides a means of orientation to a large number of actors. It enables them to co-ordinate their actions by means of orientation to a common signpost" (1971: 49). Lachmann seemed to have mutual coordination principally in mind. Likewise, Jack High seems to have mutual coordination in mind when he writes, "Each new division of labor necessitates additional coordination somewhere in the social structure...Thus is the complexity of the market limited by the difficulty of coordinating actions" (1986: 117–118). Since coordination is commonly taken to mean mutual coordination, the entrepreneur's "creative destruction" and other forms of innovation may not seem particularly coordinating. When we think of the discovery of the chain-store concept, and its devastating consequences on mom-and-pop stores, or of entrepreneurs in Fig. 4.2 effecting a shift from (left, left) to (right, right), we see the disruption of established patterns of activity, of ways of life, of customs plied by *customers*, and a *prima facie* discoordination.

Since economic freedom tends to liberate and encourage entrepreneurship, Kirzner's claim figures into arguments for the liberalization of government controls. Confusion over Kirzner's claim may weaken liberal argumentation.

These matters are resolved by the distinction between mutual and concatenate coordination. If we interpret Kirzner to mean that entrepreneurial discovery, while not necessarily conducive to mutual coordinating, is, in general, conducive to *concatenate* coordination, then the claim makes good sense. Here, we adjust Kirzner's teachings in two ways. First, we must admit that the judgment of goodness inhering in the idea of concatenate coordination is not exact and grammatical, but instead is somewhat loose and vague, somewhat like an aesthetic. Second, we need to weaken the claim by admitting exceptions: Entrepreneurship is coordinative, not in every single case, but *by and large*—and yet quite often enough to make for a strong presumption.

By admitting the looseness of its judgments and the by-and-large status of its claims, laissez-faire liberalism makes its economic verities more robust and its presumption of liberty more viable. In this book's first appendix chapter, we explore Kirzner's teachings and call for adjustments.

Now we take leave of coordination, however, and turn to knowledge. In excavating the richness of knowledge, we will explore the meaning of such terms as *interpretation*, *discovery*, and *error*. Later, we take our knowledge ideas and apply them to Joy, the allegorical beholder of the whole concatenation, returning us to coordination, social order, and cooperation.

Asymmetric Interpretation

At the very beginning of this book, there appears a parable from Kierkegaard. In the story the husband and the wife had the open book before their eyes. We might say their sets of information were symmetric. Their interpretations, however, were asymmetric. He interpreted a dot as a printed vocalization; she interpreted it as a grain of snuff. Upon awakening to her interpretation, he readily judged it superior, bringing the couple into interpretational symmetry, at least as concerned the dot.

The four chapters that follow explore the richness of knowledge. I object to flattening knowledge down to information. Knowledge entails information, interpretation, and judgment.

In "Discovery and the Deepself," I make use of Marvin Minsky's *The Society of Mind* (1986) to mediate the impasse between the knowledge flatteners and Israel Kirzner. I use Minsky's text to unfold my resolution of the controversy and to develop "the deepself."

The next chapter reports on an experiment on entrepreneurial discovery. This time the joke was on me and my collaborator Henry Demmert, but perhaps not on us alone. It is not easy to design an experiment that puts the subject into a situation offering a nonobvious opportunity and that operationalizes motivation to discover such opportunity.

Next comes "Let's Be Pluralist on Entrepreneurship." I follow Kirzner's opportunity-discovery formulation of entrepreneurship, but other formulations of entrepreneurship are useful in other discourse situations, and all of them point up features that tend to go together.

The fourth chapter of this section contends that flattening knowledge down to information runs counter to liberalism.

CHAPTER 7

⚬⟊⟊

Discovery and the Deepself

Neoclassical economists—in a narrow sense of Max-U theorizing—have from time to time remarked on Israel Kirzner's theory of entrepreneurship. They have maintained that Kirzner says things that do not fit into normal economic theory, that conflict with normal theory, that are too speculative to entertain, and that contradict other things he says. Their criticisms tell us why Kirzner is rebuffed by Neoclassicism. The dialogue as a whole tells us why there is no place for Kirznerian entrepreneurship in Neoclassical economics: Anything that cannot be compressed into and sealed entirely within a pure logic of choice, that is, within an optimization framework of ends and means, is deemed to be nonscience and hence nonsense. In this chapter, I attempt to mediate the Neoclassical and Kirznerian views by borrowing ideas about the mind from Marvin Minsky. Minsky's ideas lead to a rich theory of mind, the "deepself," a theory that accommodates valuable features of both.

KIRZNER AND NEOCLASSICISM

Kirzner's Theory of Entrepreneurship

The simplest theory of the mind is a single-agent optimization problem, which posits a goal, or preference ordering, or objective function, and a set of alternative means. Much of the literature of Neoclassical economics is devoted to crafting models of optimizing agents, models that illuminate some real-world problem. Kirzner applauds such investigations and appreciates the fruits that they bear, but he insists that there is more to economics. He maintains that there are important facets of action that cannot be captured within the logic of optimization. Kirzner wants to probe the question of how the individual's optimization problem was arrived at, or how she arrives at a new one. Kirzner not only asks these questions; he maintains that there are important things to say about them.

Kirzner contrasts the optimization approach with a broader decision-making approach. In the broader approach, a decision "reflects not merely the manipulation of given means to correspond faithfully with the hierarchy of given ends, but also *the very perception of the ends-means framework* within which allocation and efficiency is to take place" (1973: 33). Entrepreneurship, he suggests, is that element of decision making that perceives and helps to formulate the ends and means that are to define the problem. It is also the element that enables the individual to transcend one framework and arrive at another. When the individual is abiding one optimization framework while a better one is readily available, if only the individual would notice it, there exists for that individual, according to Kirzner, a pure profit opportunity. Entrepreneurial discovery is the noticing (and, therefore, seizing) of such pure profit opportunities.

In Chapter 2, I referred to Somerset Maugham's short story "The Verger," which is about a man who, in seeking a cigarette, discovers the opportunity to open a tobacco shop. The story tells of a man who not only discovers something he isn't looking for, but who discovers something he quite possibly might not have discovered at all. The optimization framework seems to impel him to find a cigarette, and he engages in search. He comes to apprehend the street as a bad place to find a cigarette. Apprehending it as a good place to set up a tobacco shop is an insight lying outside the working (and obvious) interpretative framework. Kirzner would maintain that this discovery cannot be explained as the result of optimizing search, because the verger was not searching out career opportunities at the time. The verger had formulated neither what it was he would search for nor what set of searchable boxes he would search *over*. The experience of insight was a happening that scarcely conforms to what happens in Neoclassical search models in the tradition of George Stigler (1961). The opportunity could have been missed entirely or noticed only fleetingly.

Kirzner maintains that such entrepreneurial discovery is not, however, purely random and inexplicable. He maintains that "human beings tend to notice that which it is in their interest to notice"—they tend to notice opportunities for profit or betterment (1985: 28). He insists that interpretive discovery is not always the result of deliberate choice. The faculty of undeliberate noticing of opportunities for gain he calls *alertness*. Kirzner's concept of alertness is not an economic resource, like labor. Rather, it is a sort of propensity, a propensity that is exercised in the presence of available profit opportunities. Individuals do not decide to use their alertness: "Entrepreneurial alertness is not an ingredient *to be deployed* in decision making; it is rather something in which *the decision itself is embedded* and without which it would be unthinkable" (22). Were a bright and capable individual to deploy or rent out some of his attention to help solve a particular problem or to manage a firm, we would not describe such doings as the transacting of entrepreneurial alertness, but rather as the transacting of a designated sort of human labor, such as managerial effort or attention. Such activity would be undertaken deliberately. In contrast, entrepreneurial discovery is "undeliberate but motivated" (14).

Kirzner says that "a decision maker never considers whether to apply some given potential alertness to the discovery of opportunity A or opportunity B." If opportunities are already known to be out there, then they have already been discovered, and alertness has done its part. If options A and B instead represent alternative projects calling for cultivation or development, then it is not alertness that one allocates to them, but research or managerial effort. Unlike the consumption of a human resource, the exercising of alertness does not reduce its availability: "To recognize that opportunity A exists need not preclude simultaneously recognizing that opportunity B exists." Entrepreneurial alertness is, "in principle, inexhaustible." Kirzner says that "entrepreneurship is costless" (24–25).

With the notion of entrepreneurship comes a notion of error. Error occurs when an opportunity should be obvious to the individual yet goes unnoticed. Error is the missing of available opportunities that would be noticed with a modest or normal amount of alertness. Kirzner says, "[W]here ignorance consists not in lack of available information but in inexplicably failing to see facts staring one in the face, it represents genuine error and genuine inefficiency." Individuals who come to realize that they have made errors, that they have, *ex ante*, missed available opportunities, may, says Kirzner, *reproach* themselves for the actions they have taken (1979: 128–130). As Martin Ricketts notes (1994: 61), Kirzner maintains that in the narrow Neoclassical worldview there cannot be any role for self-reproach for decisions made at the *ex ante* position.

The chief practical use to which Kirzner puts his theory of entrepreneurship is to address the basic policy issue of freedom versus government regulation (1979: ch. 13; 1985: chs. 2, 6; 1992a: 51–54). Kirzner claims that Neoclassical theories tend to neglect the role of discovery in economic processes, instead focusing on issues of allocative efficiency. Once we admit that entrepreneurial discovery does play a big part in prosperity, Kirzner's ideas become especially pertinent to the basic policy issue. If, as Kirzner maintains, interest does stimulate discovery, then an important feature of any policy regime is the extent to which it gives people an interest in making such discoveries. By and large, laissez-faire gives people the widest and strongest interest in making socially beneficial discoveries. Kirzner argues that the discovery variable points up a very significant comparative virtue of laissez-faire, a virtue neglected by Neoclassical equilibrium studies that posit a neatly characterized framework of given ends and means.

Neoclassicals Contra Kirzner

Numerous Neoclassical economists—including Theodore Schultz, Benjamin Klein, Harold Demsetz, and Stephen Shmanske—have commented critically on Kirzner. Before visiting their comments, however, let us begin with George Stigler, who never commented explicitly on Kirzner but is the godfather of narrow Neoclassicism.

Stigler describes "the very logic of economic theory: we deal with people who maximize their utility, and it would be both inconsistent and idle for us to urge people not to do so" (1982: 6). He draws a hard line for the use of the terms *rationality, efficiency,* and *optimality,* a line that eradicates any place for the terms *irrationality, inefficiency,* and *suboptimality.* In his critique of Harvey Leibenstein's theory of X-inefficiency (Leibenstein 1966), Stigler maintains: "In neoclassical economics, the producer is always at a production frontier..." (1976: 215). Stigler seeks to eradicate any notion of X-inefficiency (which has parallels to Kirzner's theory of error). Any and every kind of limitation an individual faces must be regarded as part of the set of constraints, constraints that partly define the optimization problem but are separate from the act of decision making. In one of his most whimsical (and consciously self-contradictory) essays, Stigler insists that bad policies like rent control and import quotas should be described as "efficient," because they emerge from, and persist within, a setting in which everyone optimizes. In this manner of speaking, whatever *is* is efficient.

Stigler was a pioneer of the study of limitations in knowledge, but always he acknowledged only one sort of limitation: lack of information. He raises the question of the determination of technologies used by firms: "The choice is fundamentally a matter of investment in knowledge: the costs and returns of acquiring various kinds and amounts of technological information vary systematically…" (1976: 215). Stigler confined the idea of ignorance to lack of information. Ignorance, in Stigler's view, is nothing but an optimal response to information costs: "[I]nformation costs are the costs of transportation from ignorance to omniscience, and seldom can a trader afford to take the entire trip" (1967: 291).

Stigler's position was to have the discussion of human action sealed within a logic of optimization. He recognized that notions of "waste" and "error" could not be so sealed: "Waste is error within the framework of modern economic analysis, and it will not become a useful concept until we have a theory of error"—that is, a description of error as the deliberate outcome of optimizing behavior (1976: 216). Because notions of error, interpretation, and motivation (one of Leibenstein's variables) do not fit neatly into his scientific idiom, Stigler would treat them not merely as something different, but as utter nonsense:

> Potential motivation could indeed rewrite all history: if only the Romans had tried hard enough, surely they could have discovered America.
>
> (214)

> It is the most vacuous of "explanatory" principles to dismiss inexplicable phenomena as mistakes [read: errors]—everything under the sun, or above the sun, can be disposed of with this label, without yielding an atom of understanding.
>
> (1982: 10)

According to Stigler, once we entertain ideas that do not fit into the tight Neoclassical way of speaking, all of our scientific knowledge is subverted. Perhaps this is what McCloskey identifies as the positivist belief "that the only alternative to narrowly defined logic and fact is whim" (1994: 350; see also 354). My reading of Stigler suggests that he sees no place in economic theory for anything to be distinguished as "entrepreneurship."

Stigler's way of thinking is expressed by several economists who have commented on Kirzner. Benjamin Klein reviewed Kirzner's *Competition and Entrepreneurship* for the *Journal of Political Economy* (1975). Although Kirzner's book does not make a clear distinction between knowledge and information, it explores entrepreneurial insight, like that of the verger, that would seem to lie outside the bounds of Stiglerian information economics. Nevertheless, Klein reduces Kirzner's discussion to issues of information and the costs of acquiring information (some of Klein's words are treated in Chapter 17 of this book).

Theodore Schultz does ascribe to entrepreneurship a role in economic processes: "the ability to deal with disequilibria" (1975; 1990). Schultz regards this ability to be a specialized form of human resource. In perfunctory remarks on Kirzner, he says he loses sight of "the economic value of the costs of opportunity time that entrepreneurs devote to being entrepreneurs. Kirzner is patently wrong in his view that there are no expected entrepreneurial rewards that accrue to entrepreneurs as economic agents" (1990: 36). Schultz says entrepreneurship is a type of human capital, amenable to supply and demand and marginal productivity analysis.

Harold Demsetz (1983) and Stephen Shmanske (1994) have provided more discerning and more penetrating critiques of Kirzner. Their critiques run along very similar lines and may be treated as one. In assessing Kirzner's theory, Demsetz says that entrepreneurial discovery is the "only...truly distinguishing characteristic that separates entrepreneurship from maximizing behavior." He recognizes that discovery is a transcending from one optimization problem to a new one. It is "the stumbling onto a profit possibility without any intent (that is, without any deliberate, focused investment of time, energy, or other resources)...striking crude oil and recognizing its value while drilling for water." Both Demsetz and Shmanske are willing to accept the notion that the cost of making such a discovery would be zero or close to it, and they are open to the idea that such discoveries are an "important source of economic progress" (Demsetz: 278).

Shmanske sees decision making as "punctuated with discrete moments of planned and unplanned discovery" (219). As Demsetz puts it, however, "there is a more familiar name for it—luck." Such unexpected, serendipitous events may be important, but what are we to say about them? "[I]t is, in a sense, beyond the scope of scientific analysis. For luck by any name is the unexplainable occurrence" (Demsetz: 277). Demsetz and Shmanske read Kirzner as saying, essentially, what Alchian (1950) says in his famous paper on evolution: Sometimes behavior is matched appropriately to the circumstances not because the agent intelligently adapts his behavior to the circumstances, but because the circumstances adopt the behavior that, serendipitously, is appropriate.

Although Demsetz and Shmanske agree that such "luck" or "punctuation" can be a crucial ingredient to the perceiving and seizing of opportunity, they emphasize that there is a cost to being alert (Demsetz: 279; Shmanske: 218). Making a discovery in the instant may be virtually costless, but maintaining a state of mind that is loose and responsive to incoming opportunity does have costs, such as playing chess or taking a nap.

Thus, they maintain that the part of Kirznerianism that is amenable at all to scientific comment can be expressed within the Neoclassical idiom: Alertness is reduced to a form of investment under uncertainty, a form of search or responsiveness. Punctuating events may bring a true transcendence of optimization frameworks, but "[p]roblems of change associated with unforeseen and unforeseeable events are beyond the scope of analysis" (Demsetz: 278).

Were Demsetz and Shmanske to offer their own rendering of Somerset Maugham's story of the verger, it would run something like the following: The verger had a combination of short- and long-term goals, including finding a cigarette and finding a new career. He invested some of his time and attention in searching for a cigarette. In the course of doing so, he gained, purely by chance, new knowledge pertinent to his goal of finding a career. Subsequent to this punctuating event, he reoptimized. As Shmanske puts it, "the person is in disequilibrium but only for an instant" (208). The reoptimization takes place within a somewhat revised ends-means framework.

To sum up: Neoclassicals have rejected Kirzner's proposition that economics needs to think of human action as more than concatenated reoptimization within a punctuated series of ends-means problems. Stigler, Klein, Schultz, Demsetz, and Shmanske all would either eradicate entrepreneurship from economic theory or recognize it merely as a particular form of human resource to be called "search," "alertness," or "the ability to deal with disequilibria." Along with the eradication of Kirznerian entrepreneurship would come the eradication of error and any economic significance to regret or self-reproach. Demsetz and Shmanske recognize the existence or possibility of transcendence of one optimization framework to another, such as occurs with the serendipitous discovery. They say that such events might indeed be important in understanding the performance and evolution of markets, as explored by Alchian (1950), but can be part of an understanding of human action only insofar as they are guessed at, however vaguely, in advance, and thereby belong to a subjective stochastic backdrop within which optimization takes place. Other than that, the moments of transcendence are beyond the pale of economic theory.

Kirzner's Rejoinder to Neoclassicism

What would Kirzner say to the Neoclassical rendering of the Maugham story? The verger acquired information showing that on that street there were no stores selling cigarettes. The working interpretation within which this information was gained concerned the satisfaction of the verger's desire for a smoke. The alternative interpretation of the information— that the street represented an opportunity to open a successful tobacco shop—was not inherent in the information. The "event" that occurred was not only the arrival of information, but also a shift in the verger's thinking, a shift that permitted a different interpretation *of* the information. Kirzner is saying that, to be consistent, the Neoclassical view would have to include, as Shmanskian punctuating events or Demsetzian moments of chance, not only that external stimuli (facts, raw data), which translate, within the working interpretation, into a set of information, but also *internal changes*, cognitive changes that provide new interpretations (and, correspondingly, new sets of information).

Kirzner (1979: 161) offers an example. Robinson Crusoe catches fish day after day with his bare hands. One day, he realizes that he could catch fish better by making a boat. In this example, there is not even any external stimulus to be identified as part of the punctuating event (nor change in accumulated physical capital); the *only* change is a change in interpretation of information that Crusoe already has. In Shmanske's way of speaking, one would say that Crusoe was optimizing by catching fish by hand. Then, one day, his self-equilibrium was altered by a punctuating event: *an insight came to him*. This insight posed a new, revised optimization framework, and Crusoe immediately re-optimized and was in a new self-equilibrium. The insight can only be said to arrive by chance. Yet Kirzner rejoins: "[It] may not be arrived at deliberately, rationally, but neither is it arrived at purely by chance" (1979: 170). Shmanske's worldview would eradicate all of the following notions: that Crusoe might have had an entrepreneurial moment, that he might have been acting in error prior to that moment, that upon realizing his error he might reproach himself for having erred so long, and that there is economic significance in self-reproach or regret. According to Kirzner, Shmanske's view impoverishes our understanding of how people act and how markets function.

Yet Shmanske and Demsetz do take one step away from Stigler and toward Kirzner. The examples of the verger and Robinson Crusoe prove the claim that knowledge is more than just information. It also entails interpretation, and perhaps yet more. The point seems to be accepted by Shmanske and Demsetz in their acknowledgment of moments of "disequilibrium" and surprise. They move beyond the view apparently advanced by Stigler that knowledge is merely information.

Shmanske's piece provoked a response from Kirzner (1994). Kirzner emphasizes that he and Shmanske present different worldviews but that each of them is logically coherent and consistent. Shmanske would probably agree to this claim, were some pieces of Kirzner's theory expressed in Neoclassical idiom.

TOWARD A SYNTHESIS: THE DEEPSELF

Remarks on the "Costlessness" of Entrepreneurship

There has been much contention over Kirzner's claim that "entrepreneurship is costless." One way to interpret this statement is that entrepreneurship has a cost equaling zero. Indeed, Kirzner sometimes says things that suggest such an interpretation. Really, however, Kirzner does not mean that entrepreneurship has a cost equaling zero. He qualifies his use of the word *costless*:

> To describe the knowledge so acquired as having been costless or a free good is somewhat misleading. To be sure, the spontaneous learner has incurred no cost or sacrifice through his learning. But this is not so much because the knowledge was costlessly available as because the knowledge was simply not sought deliberately.
>
> (1979: 143)

What Kirzner means by the costlessness of entrepreneurship is not that the cost of entrepreneurial insight is zero, but that *the notion of cost does not apply to it*. Cost is a facet of choice, and Kirzner insists that entrepreneurial discovery is not an object of choice. Kirzner often states that people do not choose to be entrepreneurial. If it made sense to say that the degree of entrepreneurship that the individual actually possesses has a cost of zero, it also would make sense to say that any entrepreneurship beyond that degree has a cost of infinity. Indeed, Kirzner (131) says, "[W]e cannot conceive of one who lacks alertness making a decision to acquire it." The wiser idiom is simply not to speak of a cost of making entrepreneurial discoveries. Entrepreneurial discovery is not the result of choice, just as an earthquake is not the result of choice. Earthquakes do not have costs. They bring losses to people, but they do not have costs. Kirznerian entrepreneurship is costless in the sense that sound is weightless—not that sound weighs zero pounds, but that the concept of weight does not apply to sound (how do you put sound on a bathroom scale?).

Is Kirzner, therefore, surrendering to the Shmanske worldview? If the insights had by the verger or by Crusoe were not the result of choice, are we not forced to say that they are serendipitous events, governed merely by chance and punctuating one's existence? Kirzner objects to this as well. He refuses to play by the rules. When Neoclassicals claim that entrepreneurship is a normal human resource, Kirzner objects, saying it is not an object of choice. When they claim that it is a stochastic event, a matter of chance, again he objects. He says that, unlike chance, it is "motivated."

Then the question becomes: *Motivated by what?*

The Society of Mind

The motivation comes from a deeper level of self. There is a shallower agent, that often calls itself *I*, and then deeper agents. In the case of the verger or Robinson Crusoe, it is a deeper agent that deliberately searches for, or luckily finds, the alternative interpretation. The deeper agent conveys the results to the shallower agent, who receives it like money falling into its lap. This understanding of the matter relies on two basic premises: first, that there is a multiplicity of agents within the human being, and second, there is asymmetric knowledge between them—that is, they are not fully aware of each other's activities nor in mutual possession of each other's knowledge. These ideas are at variance with much economic discourse. The framework does however conform to the most fundamental premise of neoclassical economics: agents are optimizers. I propose that the mind be thought of as a layered society of interconnected optimizers.

The approach is unorthodox to economics[1] but not to the larger world of science. Research in psychology, philosophy, sociology, cognitive science, neuroscience, and computer science makes routine use of the notions of the multiple self, layers of thinking, imperfect self-knowledge, and so on. Indeed, such ideas are staples of everyday ordinary conversation. Our moments of wit, irony, and humor are messages designed to make ourselves aware of specific cases of these realities.

Consider the Abbott and Costello act "Who's On First," which provides an example of systematic misinterpretation; the act leads the audience to identify with the difficulty of juggling multiple ways of interpreting information and arouses the delight in seeing others (and, by extension,

---

1. Within economics, Thomas Schelling (1984: chs, 3, 4) is a notable exception, as is a small but steady stream of technical papers (an important early one being Thaler and Shefrin 1981). In social sciences more broadly, Jon Elster (1979) brought much prominence to the idea of the multiple self. For the idea of tacit knowledge, the major figure is Michael Polanyi (1962, 1963, 1966); see also Hayek (1952: ch. 8).

ourselves) struggle because they lack insight that we have. All humor seems to entail an element of asymmetric interpretation.

Marvin Minsky (born 1927) wrote a book, *The Society of Mind* (1986), that offers a great wealth of ideas highly pertinent to the Kirzner-Neoclassical debate. Minsky's degrees are in mathematics, from Harvard and Princeton. He has long been professor of electrical engineering and of computer science at the Massachusetts Institute of Technology. At MIT, he co-founded the Artificial Intelligence Laboratory, and he is former president of the American Association for Artificial Intelligence. He is a member of the National Academy of Science. Here I use ideas treated by Minsky to fashion a synthesis of Kirzner and Neoclassicism. I will quote him often and at length; unless another source is specified, all page references are to *The Society of Mind*.

The Multiple Self

Minsky's approach is to explain intelligence as a combination of simpler things called "agents." "This means that we must be sure to check, at every step, that none of our agents is, itself, intelligent...Accordingly, whenever we find that an agent has to do anything complicated, we'll replace it with a subsociety of agents that do simpler things" (23). Agents are the most fundamental unit; they are like simple machines.[2]

Agents, however, come in hierarchies and bureaucracies, or agencies. Minsky speaks, for example, of a child building towers out of wooden blocks. There is a *Builder* agent that turns on a hierarchy of subagents involved in building towers, such as "Find," "Get," and "Put," and each of these has subagents. Minsky says that we can think of *Builder* in two ways: as a panel of on/off switches for its immediate subordinates, in which case it is merely the top or chief agent in the hierarchy, or as a collection of all the subagents, and their subagents, and so on, in which case *Builder* is the entire hierarchy, or an "agency." To use a mechanical analogy, a steering wheel is an agent, whereas the entire steering apparatus, from steering wheel to tires, is the steering agency. It is the agency that may be said to contain knowledge. Each component senses activity of the other components and responds accordingly. "As agency, it seems to know its job. As agent, it cannot know anything at all" (23).

---

2. Michael Polanyi (1963) writes that "insofar as organisms are represented as machines, they have no appetitive-perceptive centre" (59).

Minsky views the mind as a community of agencies. They are not strictly hierarchical: They may cut across one another, sharing some of the same agents. He applies his ideas quite consistently: "Even the ideas we 'get' for ourselves come from communities—this time the ones inside our heads.... [T]o get a good idea, one must engage huge organizations of submachines that do a vast variety of jobs. Each human cranium contains hundreds of kinds of computers, developed over hundreds of millions of years of evolution" (66). To understand the mind, "We have to guard ourselves against that single-agent fallacy of thinking that the 'I' in 'I believe' is actually a single, stable thing. The truth is that a person's mind holds different views in different realms.... We each use many different views, and which we choose to use depends, from one moment to the next, upon the changing balance of power among our agencies" (302).

Asymmetric Knowledge

Minsky asks: "[W]hy do we so often embrace the strange idea that what we do is done by Someone Else—that is, our Self? Because so much of what our minds do is hidden from the parts of us that are involved with verbal consciousness" (50). Fundamental to Minsky's system is that the mind is not only a multitude of agencies, but that knowledge among these agencies is compartmentalized, divided, or, as economists might say, asymmetric:

> [Y]our agencies for locomotion, vision, and language may contain within their boundaries some processes that are quite as intricate as those "you" use for your own conscious thought. Possibly, some of those processes are actually more "conscious" than you are yourself, in the sense that they maintain and use even more complete records of their own internal activities. Yet what happens in those agencies is so sealed off that you have no direct experience of how "you" distinguish a cat from a dog, retrace "your" last few steps, or listen and talk without knowing how "you" do it... Several such agencies could have many agents in common, yet still have no more sense of each other's interior activities than do people whose apartments share opposite sides of the same walls. Like tenants in a rooming house, the processes that share your brain need not share one another's mental lives.
>
> (290)

Even within an agency, knowledge is divided: "The high-level agents... scarcely know which lower-level processes exist. Nor can lower-level agents know which of their actions helped us to reach our high-level goals; they scarcely know that higher level goals exist" (75; for similar comments see Hayek 1963/1967: 61).

A Spontaneous Order of the Self?

Economists have somewhat conflicting attitudes about asymmetric knowledge. On the one hand, it is celebrated as a great achievement. Smith said that the division of labor is limited by the extent of the market, and he might have said the same about the division of knowledge. The greater the market, the greater the division of knowledge. In the vast concatenation that makes a woolen coat, the division of knowledge seems to extend outward without identifiable limit. And within a firm, to have an extensive division of knowledge and still function effectively—or succeed in concatenate coordination—is testimony to good leadership, management, and teamwork.

On the other hand, asymmetric knowledge is often regarded as a kind of market imperfection. Models of asymmetric information tell of problems arising from shirking, adverse selection, moral hazard, and incomplete markets. "Lemon problems" and consumer ignorance are cited as a reason for various interventions.

The same sort of ambivalence over asymmetric knowledge exists in Minsky's work on the mind. On the one hand, one can see, in the spirit of Smith, Hayek, and Coase, a division of knowledge within the mind as achievement:

> Achieving a goal by exploiting the abilities of other agencies might seem a shabby substitute for knowing how to do the work oneself. Yet this is the very source of the power of societies. No higher-level agency would ever achieve a complex goal if it had to be concerned with every small detail of what each nerve and muscle does. Unless most of its work were done by other agencies, no part of a society could do anything significant.
>
> (169)

> How could any specialist cooperate when he doesn't understand how the others work? We manage to do our worldly work despite that same predicament; we deal with people and machines without knowing how *their* insides work. It's just the same inside the head; each part of the mind exploits the rest…It is enough for our words and signals to evoke some useful happenings within the mind. Who cares how they work, as long as they work!
>
> (169, 57)

Yet, on the other hand, a multiplicity of agencies means a degree of *conflict*, sometimes obstructing the flow of knowledge. Competitors might obstruct communication between teammate agents P and Q. P may send "a query straight to Q and hope that Q can get a truthful message back before other [competing] agents change Q's state—or change its message along the way" (61). What Minsky says about competing agents will sound plausible to public choice economists: "agents...suppress their competitors" (208):

> Asymmetric knowledge also arises simply from the lack of a common language: If a mind whose parts use different languages and modes of thought attempted to look inside itself, few of those agencies would be able to comprehend one another. It is hard enough for people who speak different languages to communicate, and the signals used by different portions of the mind are surely even less similar. If agent P asked any question of an unrelated agent Q, how could Q sense what was asked, or P understand its reply? Most pairs of agents can't communicate at all.
>
> (66)

For a mind, as for an economy, the more successful it is, the greater the division of knowledge; but the greater the division of knowledge, the more scope there is for rivalry, deceit, misunderstanding, errors, and mistakes.

The Verger's Story, Once Again

Let us consider a Minskian rendering of Maugham's story. Upon resigning his position, the verger faced the existential choice of how to occupy himself for the remainder of the afternoon. Figure 7.1 shows agents within the verger's mind. The verger could run errands, take comfort after his resignation, or try to find a new livelihood. Each of these agents would involve cascading sets of subagents, only some of which are drawn in Fig. 7.1. The verger chose to take comfort and to have a cigarette. This activated subagents beginning with *Search for Cigarette*. In searching for a cigarette, the active agencies acquired the information that on that street there were no shops selling cigarettes. This information was pertinent in an obvious way to each of the active agencies moving up through the hierarchy: It meant a direct frustration of effort of *Have a Cigarette*, *Take Comfort*, and *Occupy Oneself*. The information, however, also had a nonobvious pertinence to *Occupy Oneself*, in that the information was relevant to the *inactive* agent *Find a New Livelihood*. It is by virtue of the perceiving

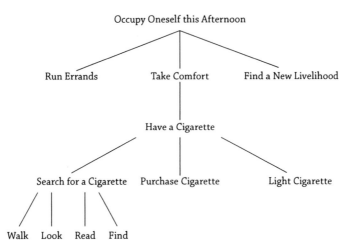

Figure 7.1: Structure of some of the agents within the verger

of this nonobvious new knowledge that the moment qualifies as an entrepreneurial moment.

Whence comes a second interpretation? It does not make sense to say that the agent *Have a Cigarette* saw the alternative interpretation and sent a special message to its superiors. Not only would *Have a Cigarette* not have any particular interest in doing so (even if it had the capability), it would have a definite interest in *not* doing so. The content of such a message could imperil its own life! The message might lead the superior agents to deactivate *Have a Cigarette* altogether. Each agent works to suppress any interpretation that competes with the interpretation that brings it life and success.

The second interpretation must spring from agents that do not appear in Fig. 7.1. Minsky explains that the mind can allocate some of its capacity to watching itself:

> Divide the brain into two parts, A and B. Connect the A-brain's inputs and outputs to the real world—so it can sense what happens there. But don't connect the B-brain to the outer world at all; instead, connect it so that the A-brain is the B-brain's world! . . . . Now A can see and act upon what happens in the outside world—while B can "see" and influence what happens inside A.
>
> (59)

The agency shown in Fig. 7.1 exists in the A-brain. In the mind, however, there is also a B-brain made up of agencies that are watching, reviewing, and evaluating the A-brain, and sometimes sending messages to influence the

A-brain. Minsky's book goes into detail about how agents can also be knowledge functions, agents called such things as *recognizers, memorizers,* and *knowledge-lines,* as well as other, unfamiliar names (*difference-engines, polynemes, pronomes, isonomes, perceptrons*). The point is that knowing, thinking, remembering, and communicating are, in Minsky's system, also the work of machine-like agents. Connected to agents of pure action are knowing agents, which in turn may have additional agents connected to them. In the story of the verger, the B-brain recognizes and evaluates certain features of what it sees in the A-brain. The A-brain has little or no awareness of what the B-brain is up to—indeed, for the two "brains" to have mutual full awareness would create a nonconvergent infinite loop that would immediately exhaust all mind capacity and bring everything to a stop.

It is agencies in B that recognize the second interpretation of the crucial information. B is engaged in an optimizing search for ways to improve what A is doing. Within B's search, the goal of finding a new livelihood looms large. The arrival of information about cigarettes being unavailable on that street may be considered a lucky accident for B, a sort of serendipity. Since B was engaging in a higher-level review of A, including its inactive agencies, the interpretation of this information as a career opportunity was, let us say, *obvious* to B. To B, the information was like money falling into its lap. Once B had gained this new knowledge, it now had to communicate with A.

The conveyance of knowledge from B to A is not a trivial matter. A's capacities are chiefly occupied, at the time, by *Have a Cigarette*, which not only does not see pertinence in anything B has to say but, indeed, may regard messages from B as imperiling its existence. It suppresses messages from B. To help A, B must *get past some of A's subagencies.* In the story, B's line to the superior agents in A were strong enough to succeed. The message got through. For A, this new knowledge did not arrive from the outside world. It came from within. The idea did not strike the verger as immediately obvious—quite the reverse. It was, to A, what I propose to call an *epiphany.* As far as A was concerned, the new knowledge was not inherent in the information.

Epiphany

Again, as discussed in Chapter 2, epiphany is a gaining of new knowledge (that is, a discovery) that alters one's interpretive framework and that comes, in a proximate sense, from within the mind. It brings an interpretive shift that, to the active agencies of the mind, is not obvious from the working set of information.

Minsky does not speak of epiphany, nor entrepreneurship, but the idea suits his system. Just as Kirzner emphasizes that entrepreneurship goes beyond mere optimizing, Minsky explains that thought goes beyond strict logic:

> I doubt that we often use logic actually to solve problems or to "get" new ideas. Instead, we formulate our arguments and conclusions in logical terms *after* we have constructed or discovered them in other ways.... [Logic] can serve as a test to keep us from coming to invalid conclusions, but it cannot tell us which ideas to generate, or which processes and memories to use. Logic no more explains how we think than grammar explains how we speak; both can tell us whether our sentences are properly formed, but they cannot tell us which sentences to make.
>
> (186)

In contrast to the Kirzner/Minsky view, George Stigler champions the unsophisticated view of knowledge: "Every failure of a person to make decisions which serve his self-interest may be interpreted as an error in logic" (1971: 144). Minsky suggests that we give up such hopelessly tidy notions: "We're always using images and fantasies in ordinary thought" (163). Creativity cannot be modeled as a *single-agent* optimization process, because it does not work according to any single-agent logic. As Minsky puts it: "Our best ideas are often those that bridge between two different worlds!" (131).

Kinds of Discovery

Kirzner writes of "entrepreneurial discovery," but he recognizes that not all discoveries should be described as entrepreneurial. As discussed in Chapter 2, there are different kinds of discovery. The kind of discovery that is most tractable within Neoclassicism is the realization of variables within a stochastic framework. The agent recognizes the framework and responds to realizations with contingent plans. This framework is very much like a search model in which laborers, for example, search over employment possibilities or car buyers search over offers. Economic actors, however, are often susceptible to stochastic variables without being engaged in any form of search (cf. Kirzner 1979: 142–143). I prefer to focus on the situation in which the realizations come to the agent rather than being the result of active search. This situational difference is not of great significance—the effort of searching can be separated from the responding to facts that come your way. In Chapter 2, I called responsive behavior within a stochastic framework *respondence*.

Search/respondence does not entail large interpretive shifts. Rather, it entails realizations that tell the agent *where he is* within a single interpretive framework. Each realization does represent a sort of discovery or new knowledge. The new knowledge, however, is merely new information. Respondence is what Shmanske (1994: 207) calls "contingent planning." Ricketts' characterization of neoclassical search puts the point nicely: "It is rather as if we are searching for something of which we once had full knowledge but have inadvertently mislaid" (1994: 60).

More significant discoveries are those that entail an interpretive shift. One kind is *serendipity*. Serendipity differs from respondence in that the discovery entails a major interpretive shift. Serendipity is utterly unexpected and leads one to rethink significantly what one is up to. Demsetz (1983: 278) gives the example of striking oil while drilling for water. Kirzner (1979: 159) gives the example of Robinson Crusoe "climbing a tree to look far out to sea—without realizing at all that his action will yield him fruit." Serendipity is not entrepreneurial. Serendipity entails a major interpretive shift that is *obvious* to the A-brain agencies active at the time.

Epiphany is the final form of discovery. It is a discovery entailing a major interpretive shift, a discovery that comes from inside the mind. Epiphany is nonobvious to the active A-brain agencies. As Kirzner (1992b: 86) says, the entrepreneurial "flash of light...lifts one out of the routine sequence of everyday experience." Kirzner (1979: 178, 1992b: 87) reserves entrepreneurship for this kind of discovery; he explicitly excludes what I call serendipity.

There are then two dimensions by which we can classify discoveries. One is whether the new knowledge entails a significant interpretive shift or is merely new information. The other dimension is whether the new knowledge is obvious or nonobvious to the active agencies. Figure 7.2 presents the typology. (In the upper right cell of the figure would come mere information of a trivial nature.)

The two dimensions are a matter of degree. In a sense, there is always a bit of surprise in what the world brings, and the interpretation is never perfectly obvious. In that sense, there is always an interpretive element in decision making. But we see, surely, that sometimes the distinguishing features are especially strong and noteworthy. Then we are especially inclined to identify entrepreneurship. Minsky discusses reformulation (or reinterpretation) and notes that distinctions come down to a matter of degree:

> Reformulation is clearly very powerful—but how does one do it? ... Does this
> depend upon some mysterious kind of insight or upon some magically creative

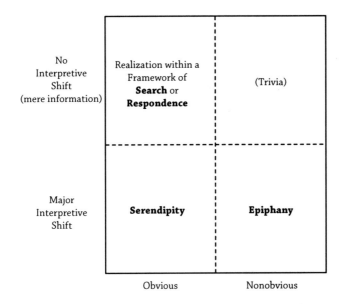

Figure 7.2: A classification of pieces of new knowledge (or discoveries)

gift—or do we simply come upon them by accident? ... [T]hese seem to me mere matters of degree, since people are always making reformulations of various sorts.

(133)

Although there is no sharp demarcation between respondence and serendipity, nor between serendipity and epiphany, the distinctions are meaningful nonetheless. Everyone has fat on his or her body, but we nonetheless distinguish between being "thin" and "fat." Of course, we may refine the categories: "thin," "average," and "fat;" or, "obvious," "average," or "nonobvious." Here, though, I keep with the simple dichotomy "obvious" and "nonobvious."

The Deepself

Figure 7.3 presents the basic structure of what I propose to call the "deepself" view of mind. Level A (or the "A-brain") is active at the surface of human existence, meeting the world and referring to itself as "I." Level A can get new knowledge in three ways. First, it can receive realizations from the outer world within a framework of respondence. Second, it can experience serendipity directly from the outer world. The meaning of these forms of new knowledge are so obvious that they need only a very basic level of

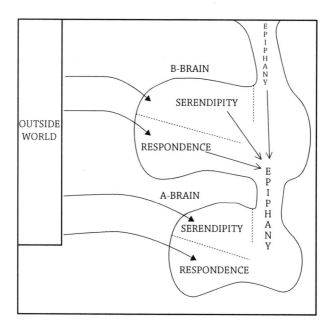

Figure 7.3: The deepself: Epiphanies occurring at one level come from a deeper level of mind

predigestion by the mind. The third kind of discovery is epiphany, which comes significantly predigested by the deeper Level B. B, in turn, can get its new knowledge in the same three ways, relying for *its* epiphanies on a yet higher level of mind. "[T]here is no reason to stop with only two levels; we could connect a C-brain to watch the B-brain, and so on" (Minsky: 59).

The morphology of the tangible world sometimes fails as analogy for the morphology of the self. I describe the more basic levels of mind as both "higher" and "deeper," yet as we stand on earth we think of deeper as *lower*. If we think of the human being (or deepself) as a sphere, we should think of the conscious, articulate selves as standing not on the surface, but within the center of the sphere, and, as depicted in Fig.7.3, looking upward for understanding. From that position, the deeper levels are higher.

Minsky's formulation of mind as a society of agents without full knowledge of one another may seem kooky. Yet, we find in Kirzner's writing some comments that neatly parallel the Minskian formulation:

A man decides to display behavior *a*. We may call the mental activity of making that decision activity *b*. Now the man *may* have decided (in the course of decision-making activity *c*) to engage in decision-making activity *b* (or he may have simply and impulsively engaged in decision-making activity *b*). But even if engaging in decision-making activity *b* (as a result of which behavior *a* was chosen) was itself the outcome of "higher" decisions, at some level our decision maker's highest decision was made quite unselfconsciously.

(Kirzner 1985: 48–49)

"[W]e can have a tacit foreknowledge of yet undiscovered things" (Polanyi 1966: 23). What is epiphany to Level A might have been respondence or serendipity to Level B. Similarly, the failure to make a discovery may be due to lack of respondence or serendipity at a deeper level. Thus, the deepself approach suggests that a lack of *knowledge* at Level A might be the direct result of weak *motivation* at Level B. Perhaps B lacks incentive to work hard at effective search/respondence, at listening carefully to epiphanies emerging from Level C or at conveying new knowledge to Level A. Ignorance at Level A is, at least in part, a *motivational* problem, and a motivational problem near Level A would seem to correspond to *incentive* problems at deeper levels of the mind.

Sometimes our A-brains overcome ignorance by way of epiphany. How exactly that happens is bound to remain somewhat mysterious. Minsky raises a related question about such breakthroughs: "[W]e usually see by hindsight that these were variants of things that people knew before that time. Then we have to ask, instead, for reasons why those reformulations were so long postponed" (133).

Error

Just as epiphany is the internal communication of new interpretive knowledge that is nonobvious, *error* is the failure to communicate new interpretive knowledge that is obvious. Error is like serendipity that fails to happen. Note that even in the case of serendipity the "outer world" must be digested by very basic realms of thought before reaching the A-brain; as Hayek (1952) says, "Every sensation, even the 'purest' must be regarded as an interpretation of an event in the light of past experience of the individual or the species" (166). Epiphany and error are theoretical inverses.

The deepself approach rejects the mono-agent view of mind. To build a satisfactory description of entrepreneurial insight and error, however, it is not adequate to move to a two-agent description. Entrepreneurial insight is essentially a conveyance of knowledge between two internal agents that are like teammates. We might expect communication between them to be very easy, but their communication is often difficult and faulty. To understand the difficulty we need to recognize the presence of a *third* agent.

Figure 7.4 provides a diagram of intramind communication. A's Friend might be a B-brain or another deep agency of the mind. A's Friend wishes to convey some new knowledge to A. The success of the message depends on three variables: 1) how clearly and loudly Friend sends the message, 2) how obvious and significant to A the value of the message is, and 3) how attentively A listens for such messages.

The third variable might come down to how yielding the active subagents of A are. An active subagent of A—for example, "Park the Car"—will be inclined to deflect, block, suppress, or even distort Friend's message to secure its own success. The active (and possibly hostile) subagents together form a sort of third agent positioned between Friend and (the core of) A. Different sets of subagents occupy this position as one set of subagents is deactivated and another activated. At one moment "Park the Car" is active, at another "Buy Groceries." Let us refer to this position, occupied in the instant by whichever subagents are most active, as *the gate* of knowledge conveyance. A gate can be either open or closed.

Just inside the gate are A's agents that listen for messages. Call these agents "listeners." (Minsky writes of "agencies whose job it is to learn" (77).) The success of Friend's message will depend in part on whether the listeners become active when the message is sent. If the currently active subagencies of A, such as "Park the Car," yield when a message arrives, they effectively step out of the gateway for a moment and let the listeners in. Then the message is likely to get through.

Given that Friend has a significant piece of new knowledge for A, we can classify such messages along two dimensions: whether they are successful or unsuccessful and whether they are obvious or nonobvious. Entrepreneurial discovery (epiphany) occurs when Friend, having a piece of new knowledge

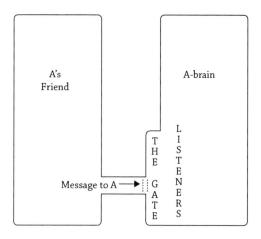

Figure 7.4: The structure of intramind communication. A's friend must get the message past "The Gate."

that is significant to A, gets it past the gate despite the fact that the new knowledge is nonobvious to A. That case is shown in Figure 7.5 in the upper right cell. The inverse (or diagonal) position in Fig. 7.5 is occupied by error. Error occurs when a piece of new knowledge had by Friend is significant and obvious to A yet does not get past the gate. The reason could be poor conveyance on Friend's part, poor attentiveness on A's part, or especially unyielding subagents occupying the gateway. *Entrepreneurial discovery and error are theoretical inverses.*

We might wonder whether we can dwell simply in the good cells and avoid error. Why can't we just keep our gates open? Why can't we get our active subagents to keep an open mind and be patient when messages arrive? That sounds nice, but it isn't that simple. The A-brain cannot constantly keep its gates open, because the subagencies currently occupying the gateway also have their regular specialized tasks to perform. Remember, agents occupying the gateway are *a part of A itself*, and if A is going to get anything done it cannot have its most active agents constantly yielding to competing agents (that is, to the listeners).

Scarcity and Mistakes

When a message from Friend comes to the gate, the message gets through only if the active agents yield sufficiently. That might seem like a small

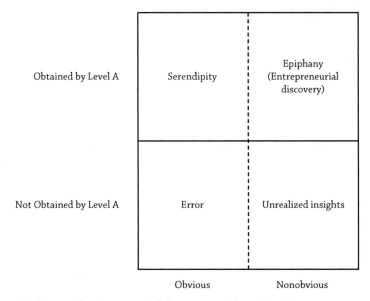

Figure 7.5: Error and entrepreneurial discovery are theoretical inverses

sacrifice, but actually it is not. The active agents follow certain programs. Once they are interrupted, there is the need to keep track of where they were. After the interruption, the yielding agents have to rely on short-term memory, or else they will go all the way back to the beginning of their program (Minsky: 159). If the short-term memory is imperfect, they might skip a step of what they were doing or otherwise foul up their execution—that is, they might make a *mistake*. Mistakes are different from errors. In keeping with Kirzner (1979: 122), we say that mistakes are simply slip-ups in carrying out a task; errors are the poor exercise of judgment resulting from one's overlooking something significant and obvious. Mistakes are made by active subagents of A; errors are made by the A-brain as a whole. When we make a mistake, such as hitting an adjacent car while parking, we say angrily, "God damn it!" as though reprimanding a subordinate. When we realize that we have made an error, we feel regret and sigh, "Oh Lord, what have I done?"

Minsky explains that when we are constantly interrupted, we incur high costs to avoid making mistakes:

> [W]e must have some way to store, and later re-create, the states of interrupted agencies. Behind the scenes, we need machinery to keep track of all the incomplete accomplishments, to remember what was learned along the way, to compare different results, and to measure progress in order to decide what to do next.
>
> (161)

There is a scarcity of mind capacity to allocate to such tasks. Hence, "the more things we think about, the harder it is to pay attention to them all" (224). In consequence, we cannot always keep the gate open: "No longer-term project can be carried out without some defense against competing interests" (163).

If active subagents yield constantly to the listeners, they will dissipate all their power on memory and make slow progress and many mistakes. On the other hand, if they keep the listeners suppressed, then A will receive fewer messages and suffer more errors. Thus, we see that one of the inherent trade-offs of the mind is how much it should train active subagents to yield to the listeners. Much yielding leads to mistakes and slow progress, but little yielding leads to errors.

The Trade-off Between Epiphany and Avoiding Error

Thus, there is a trade-off between making mistakes and suffering errors. Minsky explains that the A-brain also faces a trade-off among *different ways to listen to messages.* He explains why we cannot excel in epiphany while avoiding error. There is an inherent trade-off between those two goals.

Listeners can listen for different types of knowledge. One strategy is to listen for far-reaching chains of ideas that uncover a distant and substantial idea. Alternatively, one can listen for all the possibly relevant bits of knowledge nearest to the initial position. Suppose you were inside a square room, and in each wall there were two closed doors. The eight doors have misty hints as to what they lead to. Behind each door one finds another distinct room, perhaps containing some useful new knowledge and containing yet more doors. Suppose you have enough power or thinking capacity to open just eight doors. We can then imagine two extreme strategies. One is to pass into every newly opened room, going room to room, concluding in a room that is eight rooms removed from the initial one. The other strategy is to stay in the initial room, open all of its eight doors, and gain the knowledge of the eight adjoining rooms. The first strategy, proceeding room to room with some hunch about the best door to pass through next, leads to remarkable insights but suffers acutely from error. Sometimes one will overlook a major insight that is just one door away from the initial room. The second strategy is unlikely to achieve remarkable insights but is more likely to avoid major error. (The first strategy is sort of a "maximax" strategy, whereas the second is "maximin.") Minsky describes two types of thinkers that conform to our two types of listeners:

> [Those of the first type] disregard discrepancies in favor of imagined regularities. They tend to be perfectionists but also tend to think in terms of stereotypes. This sometimes leads to recklessness because they have to reject some evidence in order to make their [theories complete].

> [Those of the second type] are less extreme. They keep collecting evidence and hence are much less prone to make mistakes [read: errors]. But then they're also slower to make discoveries.

> (125; see also 161)

Hence, people face several trade-offs in how they manage their internal communications. First, they must decide the extent to which active agents should yield to the listeners. Second, they must decide the extent to which listeners should be epiphany maximizers as opposed to error minimizers.

These trade-offs suggest that for any level of discovery, if we can go deep enough we can make the occurrence depend on a choice.

Correction, Self-Reproach, and Learning

Minsky notes that "any problem will be easier to solve the more one learns about the context world in which that problem occurs" (177). The longer one dwells within a context, the less disruptive yielding to listeners becomes, and, over time, the more "doors" get opened. This simple insight concords with Kirzner's important premise that there is "a tendency to become aware of opportunities that do stare one in the face" (1979: 146). The natural tendencies for erring to be overcome and opportunities to be perceived are central to Kirzner's view that there are tendencies within the economy toward the solving of problems and the improvement of economic arrangements.

Consider an example provided by Kirzner (129): "A person [say, a maker of apple pies] walks along a street and sees a store with signs offering to sell apples for one dollar; but, perhaps thinking of other things, he enters a second store where he pays two dollars for [a great quantity of identical] apples." The first part of the overcoming of error is noticing the missed opportunity. Inasmuch as the situation is repeated or is continued, this noticing is the *correction* of error; it is the correction of an action that, to a deeper agency inside the pie maker, is a mistake.

With recognition of having forsaken an opportunity may come *self-reproach*. Kirzner (129) says the pie maker "will, when he realizes his mistake, reproach himself for having been so absentminded as to pass by the bargain." Kirzner uses the term reproach in this way seven times in three pages (see 128–130). Kirzner (146, 147) says, "one looks back at one's ignorance as upon a deplorable and embarrassing error," sometimes even as "a pity, possibly a tragedy." Elsewhere, Kirzner (1985: 56) seems to identify blaming oneself for having erred as essential to error. Although the scarcity of mind creates certain unavoidable trade-offs, we are nonetheless able to put mind resources into refining and developing our ability to listen to ourselves. We can reduce the trade-off between having epiphanies and avoiding errors, although doing so will come at a cost in some other dimension (such as taking up chess). To set ourselves the task of learning to listen better, learning to avoid error, that goal must prevail over others. It must scream and holler for the attention of superior agents and demand a reallocation of resources. As Minsky explains, "conflicts between agents tend to migrate upwards to higher levels" (32). Superior agents will redirect their efforts to resolve the conflict.

Self-reproach is a crucial part of the learning process. Self-reproach may be a matter of agents who watch agents who in turn watch yet other agents (see Minsky: 238), but it is, at the relevant level, simply another tendency toward the overcoming of error (or, at a higher level, a strategy to correct mistakes). If we have an economic theory that admits of entrepreneurship and error, and we believe in a tendency toward overcoming error, then we have an economic theory that admits of self-reproach. Self-reproach is one important mechanism in the machinery of economic development.

Note that matters of self-reproach and learning lie at the heart of the question of whether we should consider an opportunity to have been obvious. The pie maker reproaches himself and feels that apple-bargain signs should be noticed by him. The misfortune is an error only insofar as its correction elicits regret or self-reproach. Were the individual in the story not a pie maker, but rather a poet lackadaisically buying a snack, he will, upon recognizing the missed bargain, feel no need to pay greater attention in the future to apple prices, no sense of error, and no self-reproach. To one such as him, the apple-bargain sign was not obvious, because he would not feel that it should have been obvious. The pie maker, however, feels that it should have been obvious; hence, it was obvious, and not noticing it was an error.

Digression: A Reproach to Shirking Reproachers

The deepself approach to mind leads us to think of the human being as a sort of society. Notice that such an approach, by the same token, makes society more like an individual human being. Moreover, in our earlier talk of Joy, coordination, and so on, we pursued a kind of society-as-organism idea, and we will later take up the idea of Joy making errors to sustain talk like the following: America errs in sustaining policies like trade barriers, price controls, and certain "consumer protection" restrictions. Friends tell policymakers to overcome these errors, but the "gateway" is occupied by subagents who suppress the message. Such obviously pernicious policies may be deemed society's errors, because those subagents make a small portion of society. The persistence of the errors indicates that those positioned to reproach and persuade are neglecting the task. How tragic that the task often lies with those whose outlook, like George Stigler's, does not even admit of error and self-reproach (see Kirzner 1983/1999). Meanwhile, others who *do* accept and embrace a role as reproacher also warrant our reproach when they fail to recognize social erring or even promote it.

Does the Deepself Eradicate Kirzner?

The deepself approach enables us to see that what is epiphany to one level of mind results from serendipity or optimizing choice at a deeper level of mind. Have we then eradicated entrepreneurship by bringing it within the Neoclassical fold of optimization? Does Kirzner's claim—that there is something called entrepreneurship, something that lies beyond mere optimizing—therefore dissolve? I believe the answer is no. The deepself approach accommodates and, indeed, highlights Kirzner's contributions.

First of all, to look at the mind as a *society* of optimizers is itself beyond narrow Neoclassicism. Granted, we see each agent within the mind as a machine, as an optimizer, but they are *multiple*. Multiplicity within the self is a major departure from standard Neoclassicism. Along with multiplicity come the relations that take place between agents. It is within the newly found relations between internal optimizers that we find a secure home for Kirznerian elements.

A Neoclassical critic like Shmanske or Demsetz would perhaps respond with:

> "Okay, we can view the self as consisting of a multitude of optimizers. But the same might be said of the firm. Just because a firm has 100 employees does not mean that we can't talk about the singular optimization problem of *the owner*. In describing the owner's problem, the multitude of optimization problems faced by subordinates comes to characterize various *constraints* on the owner's choice set. Similarly, for the individual human being, there are multiple subagents, but their behaviors are not the optimization problem we focus on. Their behaviors belong, rather, to the set of constraints on the final optimization problem of *the uppermost agent*. That final optimization problem encompasses all the others. It is singular, and brings the whole deepself approach neatly into Neoclassicism."

The problem with likening the deepself to a firm is that in the self we never get to a definitive final "owner." The deepself approach does not come to a conclusion at the nth level of the mind. In knowing the self, we first meet certain lower agents, working, if you will, at the counter. We can try to infer what their superiors are like, and then theirs, and so on, *but we never come to an uppermost agent.* The deepself tells us that we cannot fully know even ourselves. As Minsky says, "[W]e never really know ourselves because there are so many other processes and policies that never show themselves directly in our behavior but work behind the scenes" (53). He says, "[T]he further back you trace your thoughts, the vaguer seem those causal chains" (196). It is, in fact, a contradiction in terms to say we can fully know ourselves, because, by the term "to know," here we mean to have a good description (or model), and we cannot have a description that *includes the describer*, including, that is, a description of the criteria for formulating the description. Even if such a metadescription is offered, we may ask for the criteria for formulating the metadescription, *ad infinitum* (cf. Minsky 1986: 88, Hayek 1952: 185, 189, 194 and 1967: 62).

Yes, for any level of discovery, if we can go deep enough, we can make the occurrence depend on a choice. Once we arrive at that deeper choice, however, we should still acknowledge discoveries and tacit contacts to yet deeper or higher levels and admit that we never come to a final level that would permit sealing the entire theory within optimization.

Minsky notes that his line of thinking gives rise to infinite regress.[3] "But when thinking keeps returning to its source, it doesn't always mean something's wrong. For circular thinking can lead to growth when it results, at each return, in deeper and more powerful ideas" (50). Infinite regress should not alarm us. Minsky points out what happens "whenever we try to probe into our own motivations by continually repeating, 'What was my motive for wanting *that*?' Eventually, we simply stop and say, '*Because I simply wanted to*'" (305). That final response is not answering the question; it is refusing to answer the question. It is confessing ignorance, but in a way that is acceptable within our culture. Human cultures evolve around the need to cope with this perennial problem:

Economics teacher: The price of Pat Boone records fell in the short run because the demand curve shifted back.
Student: But why did the demand curve shift back?
Economics teacher: Because consumers' tastes changed.
Student: But why did consumers' tastes change?
Economics teacher: Ask your cultural history teacher.

Minsky notes the parallel issue of infinite regress in the problem of "common knowledge": "*Did John know that I knew that he knew that I knew that he knew that?*" (305). David Lewis, who provided the seminal

3. See Minsky 49, 50, 59, 73, 88, 92, 150, 151, 174, 196, 219, 229, 238, 288, 305.

statement of common knowledge, explained that for the problem of whether John knew that...we simply cut it off at some point, figuring and hoping that the depth to which our knowledge does reach is *adequate for the human purposes at hand* (1969: 32). It is the particular human purposes in the discourse situation that determine the appropriate place to cut it off.

However deeply we excavate the mind, carrying our analysis to the nth level, there the Kirznerian elements exist in a state of unimpeachability. They exist there as relations to deeper-level agencies, but the deeper levels remain tacit, not articulated. At the nth level, we must admit of Kirznerian elements, notably discovery that is "undeliberate but motivated." As theorists, therefore, we find these elements to be perennial. "If, therefore," said Polanyi (1963: 12), "we are satisfied to hold a part of our knowledge tacitly, the vain pursuit of reflecting ever again on our own reflections no longer arises."

Roger Garrison commented on Shmanske and came to the same conclusion: "[A] cost-benefit analysis...pushes the positing of alertness one step back in the overall argument... An infinite regress can be avoided only by recourse to Kirznerian alertness or some effectively similar notion" (1993: 78); O'Driscoll and Rizzo say the same (1996: 70)). The Kirznerian elements, then, exist at the farthest reaches and are only dimly understood. (This relates to the "loose, vague, and indeterminate" in Adam Smith.) That does not mean that they are marginal, however. They are the farthest from "us" but therefore most fundamental *to us*, because they give origination to whole frameworks for action. Rather than call these elements marginal, we should call them *primordial*, as does Kirzner (1979: 131). How we think about these primordial elements is important. Consider the following words from Minsky:

> Our minds contain processes that enable us to solve problems we consider difficult. "Intelligence" is our name for whichever of those processes we don't yet understand.
>
> (71)

Nonetheless, we rely on the idea of intelligence. Although we do not understand its causes, we recognize some of its propensities and incorporate them into our explanations *of other things*.

At many points in Minsky's book, he flirts with the idea that the mind is a machine (see 160, 163, 171, 185, 186, 303, and especially 288, 323). He often leads the reader into suspecting that everything is either Cause or Chance—as the Neoclassicals maintain (with Cause corresponding to optimization or incentive). In the final pages of the book, Minsky makes good on this issue. The penultimate section is entitled, "The Myth of the Third Alternative." Minsky writes: "We imagine that somewhere in each person's mind, there lies a Spirit, Will, or Soul, so well concealed that it can elude the reach of any law—or lawless accident" (307). Minsky refers to this Third Alternative as a "myth," but not to derogate it. The label is apt. In the end, the MIT scientist affirms the worthiness of the myth, and related myths of "responsibility," because no matter how much progress science makes, we will always have to admit of a perennial, mysterious human element between Cause and Chance (see Hayek 1952: 193). Indeed, we can count on that element to transcend—willfully, if necessary—theories that purport to capture human existence.

CONCLUDING COMMENTS ON KIRZNER'S CONTRIBUTION

Kirzner has devoted much of his professional career to studying a component of economic theory that narrow Neoclassicism has worked to eradicate. By developing the idea of entrepreneurship and working out its role in fundamental questions of economic theory, Kirzner has helped to keep entrepreneurship a living, albeit marginalized, part of the economics conversation. In this chapter, I have suggested a deepself approach to the subject, an approach that supports Kirzner's line of thinking. I wish now to suggest some ways in which the deepself approach might offer specific clarifications to Kirzner's terminology and a restatement of his central conjecture.

Some Remarks on Terminology

Costlessness. Again, when Kirzner speaks of entrepreneurship as costless, one should read that to mean that the concept of cost does not apply to entrepreneurship (or, at least, not to the level of mind experiencing the epiphanies), not to mean that the cost of entrepreneurship equals zero.

Alertness. Kirzner calls the propensity to notice opportunities *alertness.* Yet, one must take care. In common language we use the term "alertness" in a way that often, even typically, does make it a matter of choice—choosing to sharpen our powers of respondence. The idea of making ourselves alert—during a lecture, for example, by drinking coffee—is natural enough, but it is not what Kirzner means. "Alertness" might be profitably replaced by "transcendence." We might talk of people's propensity to transcend their current way of thinking, but we would not say that they invest in being more transcendent. They do invest in being more alert (in the common-language sense of the term).

Discovery. Kirzner often uses the term "entrepreneurial discovery," and sometimes it gets abbreviated to just "discovery" (e.g., 1985: 78). Not all discovery is entrepreneurial, however. Even when we exclude pieces of new knowledge that are merely additions to a set of information (as occurs within a process of search or respondence), still not all discovery is entrepreneurial. Serendipity is interpretive new knowledge but is not entrepreneurial, as Kirzner points out (1979: 161, 165, 178; 1992b, 86–87). Rather, we should confine entrepreneurial discovery to what I have called "epiphany," nonobvious interpretational breakthroughs.

Profit Opportunity. Ordinarily, people think of profit as a pecuniary residual, but Kirzner means something broader. Kirzner (1992b: 88f) gives the example of a restless insomniac who comes to realize in the middle of the night that having some ice cream would better his situation. The ordinary person is surprised to hear that the insomniac found profit in thinking to eat ice cream. In the place of "profit opportunity" we might consider "betterment opportunity," a term that better accommodates the broad and often idiosyncratic character of entrepreneurial discovery.

Kirzner's Point on Freedom

With the deepself approach in mind, I offer a brief statement of Kirzner's most important contribution: the role of entrepreneurship in the intellectual case for liberty.

The justification for virtually any kind of government intervention, such as medical licensure or "pre-market approval" of drugs, is based on descriptions ("theories," "models") of how the world works, in one case with the regulation and in the other without it. The comparative virtue of the case with regulation is the justification for that regulation. Kirzner's point is as follows: In descriptions, each individual is understood by the theorist to be engaged in pursuing some goals subject to constraints. The description might have a general plausibility, but no matter how richly the theorist has described the problem, perhaps even to incorporate a deepself approach and stochastically incoming opportunities for serendipitous discovery, every individual in real life always holds the *further* capacity for epiphany. What the range or nature of these potential epiphanies might be cannot be written fully into the model, because the possibility of further epiphany *applies also to the theorist*. The individual subject's transcendence may come in any of innumerable forms—new ideas in pricing, production, organization, contracting, product line, marketing, customer service, and so on. The new ideas were previously imagined neither by the individual himself nor by the theorist. There will always remain, above and beyond the most complete description of a situation, a residual, uncaptured propensity for transcendence.

That the transcendence element works, especially over longer periods of time, to raise the comparative standing of freedom is Kirzner's key conjecture. The freer people are, the more scope and motivation there is for transcendent ideas. In the face of externalities, high transaction costs, monopoly power, ignorance—or *whatever* it is that the theorist perceives to be the *pitfall* of liberty—people never lie prostrate. Entrepreneurship is what brings them to their feet—it is "irrepressible and perennial" (Kirzner 1985: 92)—and it propels them towards discovery of a way to change the apparent framework. The pitfall itself generates betterment opportunities that spark entrepreneurial transcendence. The new level of entrepreneurial transcendence is *motivated by the pitfall*. By virtue of transcendence, *the pitfall fuels the overcoming of itself.* Compared to coercive regimes of governmentalization, Kirzner claims, liberty better exercises the transcendence element and channels it into activities that tend to be more socially beneficial.

Kirzner's point is not that the transcendence element seals the case for freedom. His point is that there will always be this transcendence element, and that usually, if not always, it works as a "kicker" for freedom: Kirzner helps to establish a presumption of liberty. The fact that scientists cannot compress the transcendence element into a model of optimizers, nor measure or quantify it meaningfully, does not mean that it does not exist. It always exists, and it is an important factor in economic understanding and judgment.

CHAPTER 8

⌒⌒⌒

Experiment on
Entrepreneurial Discovery

An Attempt to Demonstrate the
Conjecture of Hayek and Kirzner

In the previous chapter, on discovery and the deepself, I distinguished types of discovery based on whether the discovery involved an interpretative shift and, if so, whether the new interpretation was obvious. After formulating such ideas, I started to think about whether a researcher could construct an experimental setting in which there lay such an opportunity. At Santa Clara University, I pursued the idea with Henry Demmert. This chapter tells of the experiment we did.

In a famous article, "Competition as a Discovery Procedure," Friedrich Hayek (1978d) said that a chief virtue of the free enterprise system is its evocation of the discovery (and fulfillment) of opportunities for social betterment. As Hayek suggests, the discovery virtue is poorly featured in the two modes of discourse dominant in the economics profession: equilibrium model building and statistical significance. Equilibrium model building proceeds upon knowledge assumptions in which interpretation, if not information, is common and static. Within the paradigm, building in scope for discovery of new information is very cumbersome, building in scope for new partial interpretation is even more cumbersome, and building in scope for new fundamental interpretation, in equilibrium, is impossible.

The other dominant mode of discourse, statistical significance, also fails in addressing discovery. Across observations, the conditions for discovery are too particularistic to specify or control for. "If we do not know the facts we hope to discover by means of competition, we can never ascertain how effective it has been in discovering those facts that might be discovered" (Hayek 1978d: 180). A discovery that fails to happen is like the dog in the night that didn't bark. The investigator cannot know if it is a case of a silent dog or of no dog at all (Romer 1994: 26, Kirzner 1985: 146).

That the two formal modes of discourse are ineffectual at addressing the discovery conjecture throws researchers back on less paradigmatic methods, such as case studies, history, policy analysis, thought experiments, and introspection. In search of an empirical demonstration of the discovery conjecture, however, Hayek makes two suggestions (180). First, by comparing the economic performances of societies with different degrees of freedom, researchers might discern that the freer societies are the more prosperous. Hayek's suggestion has been carried out by research organizations that construct indices of economic freedom in countries throughout the world and correlate economic freedom and economic growth (Gwartney et al. 2010, Miller and Holmes 2010, Kreft and Sobel 2005). Their findings conform to Hayek's own impression of the historical record: Freedom correlates strongly with more growth. Hayek fails to note, however, that such historical/statistical findings do not necessarily bear out the discovery conjecture. It may be that freedom causes growth for reasons highlighted by mainstream economics: more competition, more efficiency in production and consumption, more certainty in investment, lower transaction costs, lower deadweight losses, less rent seeking, and so on.

Hayek's other idea for empirical illustration is offered as follows: "[W]e might conceivably test [a discovery conjecture] in artificially created real situations, where the facts which [may be discovered] are already known to the observer" (180). We pursued Hayek's suggestion. We designed a rather simple experiment that rewarded each subject in cash according to the amount of water he transferred from one plastic bucket to another. One method of transferring water was obvious and another, much superior, was nonobvious. By varying the rewards for transferring water, we sought to demonstrate that entrepreneurial discovery of the superior method depends on motivation.

Economic experimentalists have explored the relation between monetary rewards and search intensity (Schotter and Braunstein 1981,

Harrison and Morgan 1990), but, as far as we know, none has investigated *entrepreneurial* discovery, although our experiment was repeated by Kitzmann and Schiereck (2005) with similar results. Psychologists have done experiments testing whether creativity (which is akin to entrepreneurship) is affected by previous activities or changes in the setting (Dunker 1945, Adamson 1952, Scheerer 1963, Weisberg 1993: 96–102). In Dunker's famous experiment, for example, the creative act is to empty out a box of tacks and use the box as a candleholder. To our knowledge, however, such experiments have never involved variations in monetary rewards. It appears that ours was the first attempt to carry out Hayek's suggestion for demonstrating a discovery conjecture.

The results of our experiment were disappointing but instructive. A report on the experiment may help researchers formulate meaningful versions of the discovery conjecture and develop methods for testing. Our failure is useful for what it teaches about the difficulty of working empirically with the idea of entrepreneurial discovery. Not only is it very difficult to control the motivation for entrepreneurial discovery, it is difficult merely to identify discovery as *entrepreneurial* discovery, even when it happens right in front of the investigator.

ENTREPRENEURIAL DISCOVERY

A broad formulation of the discovery conjecture would be that the freer a society is, the better it discovers social opportunities. Another formulation would be as follows: Freedom causes prosperity *principally because* freedom generates discovery. Thus, the Hayekian conjecture is something like:

More freedom → more discovery of socially beneficial opportunities

Such formulations are impractical for experimental testing. To operationalize the causal factor, more freedom, the experimenter would have to vary and manipulate people's freedom, a dystopian notion, though one we have witnessed, in a sense, and with results supporting Hayek's conjecture (East versus West Germany, North versus South Korea). In our experiment, we instead treat of a different causal factor, namely, motivation, which we attempt to operationalize by varying monetary payments.

As for "more discovery," we find that we need to refine the ideas of the preceding chapter yet further, because we set people to *problem solving* and the deliberate search for *partial* reinterpretations of their situations. The reader may take the typological progression as demonstration of a key theme: There is always a next level!

Again, in stories of search or respondence to stochastic blips, agents discover new knowledge, but the new knowledge is merely new information. Such new knowledge fits into their wider interpretation. They obtain new information, but they do not discover new interpretations of what they themselves are up to.

Profounder sorts of discovery involve shifts in interpretation. An actor may puzzle over certain parts of his situation, seeking a better understanding or interpretation of those parts. Problem solving is engaged in deliberately by the self-conscious agency of the mind. When successful, it produces a partial interpretive shift, but partial interpretive shifts can occur in two other, undeliberate, ways. A person might stumble upon a new interpretation, obvious once he encounters the opportunity. Or he might arrive at a new nonobvious interpretation by virtue of efforts of the mind's other-than-self-conscious agencies. In this case, the insight strikes him with a certain epiphany and wonder. This sort of discovery may be associated with entrepreneurial discovery.

To complete a classification of discovery, we ought to consider also interpretive shifts of a more fundamental (rather than partial) sort. Fundamental interpretive shifts are not the result of problem solving or other deliberate efforts. They also, however, may be divided into cases in which one stumbles into an obvious opportunity and cases in which the discovery comes by virtue of the mind's other-than-self-conscious agencies.

A full classification is offered in Fig. 8.1. The rows express three grades of interpretive shift: no interpretive shift (mere information), partial interpretive shift, and fundamental interpretive shift. The columns combine different explanations for the occurrence of the discovery. The terms "obvious" and "nonobvious" refer to the following question: Is the nature of the opportunity obvious or nonobvious once the opportunity has been placed before the self-conscious agency of the mind? The nature of mere information is, by definition, obvious (hence the Xs in the top row). The term "deliberate" means that the work involved in realizing the discovery has been set by the mind's self-conscious agency as a task. It is a deliberate task. "Undeliberate" means that the discovery has not been the result of work by the self-conscious agency. "Undeliberate," therefore, may refer either to discoveries gotten by way of chance encounters (i.e., dumb luck) or to discoveries gotten by virtue of the work of the other-than-self-conscious mind. The processes that yield a fundamental

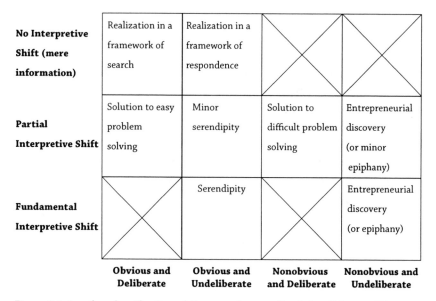

	Obvious and Deliberate	Obvious and Undeliberate	Nonobvious and Deliberate	Nonobvious and Undeliberate
No Interpretive Shift (mere information)	Realization in a framework of search	Realization in a framework of respondence		
Partial Interpretive Shift	Solution to easy problem solving	Minor serendipity	Solution to difficult problem solving	Entrepreneurial discovery (or minor epiphany)
Fundamental Interpretive Shift		Serendipity		Entrepreneurial discovery (or epiphany)

Figure 8.1: Another classification of discovery (more refined than 7.2 on p. 99)

interpretive shift are, by definition, undeliberate (hence the Xs in the bottom row).

The top row treats of mere information. We find realization within a framework of search, a deliberate task, and, in the next cell, realization within a framework of respondence to incoming pieces of information. The middle row, for partial interpretive shift, shows solutions to problem solving (which is "easy" when the solution is obvious and "difficult" when the solution is nonobvious), minor serendipity when the shift comes from stumbling upon an obvious opportunity, and entrepreneurial discovery (or minor epiphany) when the shift comes by virtue of work by the other-than-self-conscious mind. In the bottom row, we have fundamental interpretive shifts corresponding again to serendipity and entrepreneurial discovery (or epiphany).

In our experiment, it was the entrepreneurial sort of discovery—epiphany—that we sought to operationalize and evoke.

THE DISCOVERY CONJECTURE INVESTIGATED

When Kirzner speaks of discovery, he means specifically entrepreneurial discovery (or epiphany). Kirzner views human beings not as mere optimizers, but as creatures with both a deliberate faculty and a somewhat separate interpretive faculty. The interpretive faculty arrives at new formulations of the framework within which deliberate choice takes place. After arriving at a better formulation it attempts to communicate the insight to "us"—the deliberate faculty. The interpretive faculty is separate in the sense that at the deliberate or self-conscious level, we do not know what the interpretive faculty is up to or how it functions. We simply receive signals, experienced as insights. To us, the interpretive faculty appears as a mere propensity for epiphanies.

Although we cannot fathom the workings of the interpretive faculty, we may nonetheless maintain, says Kirzner (1985: 14), that it has motivation. The faculty is aroused in a setting of opportunity, as though opportunity gave off a scent (Kirzner 1979: 29). Kirzner (1985) maintains that "human beings tend to notice that which it is in their interest to notice" (28). Upon such reasoning, Kirzner offers an explanation for the epiphany virtue of economic freedom: Low taxes and freedom of contract put before the individual great opportunities that are well aligned to social betterment and that exercise and arouse the interpretive faculty. Under a regime of economic freedom, substantial and socially beneficial epiphanies occur more often not only because more opportunities exist but also because people's interpretive faculties are more advanced and more aroused.

Our experimental investigation attempted to demonstrate a core component of Kirzner's theory. We attempted to put a nonobvious opportunity before experimental subjects and vary the gain from discovering the opportunity. In other words, we sought to operationalize motivation of the interpretive faculty. We had hoped to observe that when the "scent" of opportunity was stronger, subjects would be more likely to discover the opportunity.

PROBLEMS OF DESIGNING A DISCOVERY EXPERIMENT

The experiment had to present an opportunity without actually telling the subject to search for such an opportunity. Were the subject explicitly cued to engage in a search or to solve a problem, any successful discovery would be the result of deliberate effort, not epiphany. For example, if the payment schedule offered a bonus for transferring an amount of water far exceeding the amount doable by the obvious method, subjects would be cued to look for another method.

We believed that the experiment should require the performance of some physical task rather than a written exercise. A written exercise could confound the experiment in several ways. Solving a written problem would have depended greatly on such things as the subject's reading and analytic aptitudes. Furthermore, intellectual puzzles and challenges offer a motivation of their own; our subjects, college students, naturally strive to prove themselves on any written test. Discovering the entrepreneurial insight under these conditions would more properly be classified as problem solving than entrepreneurship.

We considered several physical tasks. Some we ruled out because they relied on strength or other physical prowess, others because they might inspire heroic and possibly dangerous feats. We settled on moving objects from one location to another and decided that the interpretive breakthrough would involve recognition that a step stool, placed at the site, could be inverted and used as a carrier. We considered various movable objects, such as bricks, tennis balls, and golf balls. Finally, we settled on water, in the hope that the subjects might think their success would depend on avoiding spillage rather than on discovering a better way to transfer it.

Subjects would be taken to the site of the experiment, where they would see two plastic buckets, one full of water and one empty. Beside the full bucket would be a plastic step stool on which sat four plastic vessels of different sizes (see Fig. 8.2). Printed instructions posted near the bucket would encourage the subject to transfer as much water as possible

Figure 8.2: Water bucket and four vessels

to the empty bucket (about fifteen feet away). The instructions would indicate a simple payment schedule for the amount of water transferred. The instructions would specify that the subject could not move either bucket and that he could make only one trip from the full to the empty bucket. No other restrictions would be included in the instructions.

The obvious method of transferring the water was to use the four vessels, submerging each in the full bucket and then carrying all four, filled to the brim, to the empty bucket (see Fig. 8.3). The superior and nonobvious method entailed a novel interpretation of the equipment: The step stool itself could be inverted and used as a vessel—indeed, a vessel with capacity much greater than the other four combined. The best method to transfer water would thus be to invert the step stool, fill it with water using the smaller vessels, fill the latter, and then carry all five to the empty bucket (see Fig. 8.4). We would attempt to operationalize the causal variable, motivation, by varying the schedule of payments for water transferred.

To eliminate the possibility that gender differences might dilute our results, we decided to recruit only male students (Santa Clara University undergraduates). So as not to draw from the pool of potential subjects, we recruited mostly female assistants. Assistants were to be of two types: *attendants*, who would sit with waiting subjects in one of our classroom "holding pens," and *monitors*, who would escort subjects one at a time from a holding pen to her site and observe as he did the experiment. Each holding pen (five in total) would feed two or three sites (eleven in total). The experiment was

Figure 8.3: The obvious method of transferring water

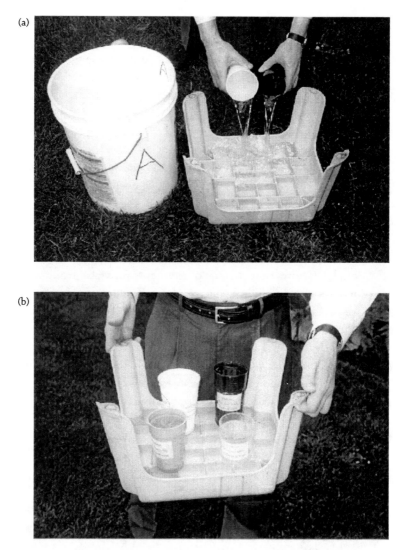

Figure 8.4: The nonobvious and much superior method of transferring water

to utilize a team of nineteen people, including us (Demmert manned the cashbox and I roamed around checking on sites).

REFINING THE EXPERIMENT: DRY RUNS

Experiments by economists typically are administered to numerous sub-jects simultaneously in a classroom or lab. Our experiment more closely resembles creativity experiments conducted by psychologists (Dunker 1945; Adamson 1952). In those experiments, as in ours, subjects must be taken in isolation, making the experiment time and labor intensive. Moreover, we would not be able to repeat the experiment because once word of the stool trick got out our entire subject population would be contaminated.

We refined the experiment through a series of dry runs (no pun intended). We conducted three such dry runs with teenagers off campus. Each dry run involved between five and eight subjects and used genuine and immediate cash payments. In the first, none of five subjects inverted the stool. We rewrote the instructions, altered the payment schedules, and changed the time allotted to each subject. In the second, five of eight inverted the stool. Again we tinkered. In the third, two of five inverted the stool. We were encouraged in that, taken together, the dry runs suggested that the inversion opportunity was neither so obvious that subjects were bound to see it nor so nonobvious that subjects were bound to miss it. We were discouraged, however, in that there was no evidence of a connection between discovery and monetary rewards.

The dry runs also revealed certain confounds. Some of the subjects missed or neglected the rule about making only one trip and raced back and forth between the buckets. In the final instructions of the actual experiment we placed substantial emphasis on a single trip. Evidently this was not enough, as this basic misunderstanding still plagued the experiment.

In one of the dry runs, a subject used a cup to cast water airborne from one bucket to the other, with considerable success. We subsequently put more distance between the buckets. Another subject filled his sneakers with water and carried them along with the cups we had provided. Hoping that small numbers were masking the validity of our conjecture (and running way behind in spending our grant money), we tinkered some more and planned for the big day.

THE PAYMENT SCHEDULES

We settled on four different forms, labeled 1A, 1B, 2A, and 2B. Each began by telling the subject that he would automatically receive a minimum $12 payment: "OUR APPRECIATION: For helping us in our study, we will pay you $12 in cash today." Beyond this, the schedules differed with respect to the opportunity they presented for *additional* earnings. Specifically, the marginal payoffs for cups transferred (where "cups" means the unit of volume, as in two cups to the pint) were:

Form	Schedule for Earning Additional Money
1A	If you do not transfer at least 7 cups of water, you receive **no additional money**. If you transfer at least 7 cups, you receive an <u>additional 10 cents for every cup transferred.</u>
1B	If you do not transfer at least 7 cups, you receive **no additional money**. If you transfer at least 7 cups, you receive an <u>additional dollar for every cup transferred.</u>
2A	Transfer as much water as you can.
2B	You will receive <u>an additional 50 cents</u> for every cup of water transferred.

Forms 1A and 1B create a threshold of seven cups. Provided that he transfers at least seven cups, the subject receives an additional payment per cup—10 cents for Form 1A, $1 for Form 1B. The purpose of the threshold was to lead the subjects to figure that the purpose of the experiment was to test how carefully they filled and carried the four plastic vessels. The combined volume of the four vessels was slightly more than seven cups, and the volume of each was prominently marked. We hoped that these details about volumes would help to anchor in the subject's mind the obvious (and inferior) means of transfer. With the obvious formulation anchored, Form 1B's higher rewards, we hoped, would induce a higher rate of interpretive breakthrough to the superior formulation.

Forms 2A and 2B are simpler, as they do not create a threshold. We had hoped that Form 2B's payment of 50 cents per cup would induce a higher rate of interpretive breakthrough.

THE ACTUAL EXPERIMENT

The experiment was set for Saturday, May 15, 1999. We advertised "$12 for 12 minutes of your time" to male students in the campus paper and by mass e-mails. The experiment, we said, would be "simple, pleasant, and uncompromising." We warned of a wait and suggested that they bring along a book or homework. We had recruited the assistants in advance but told them nothing of the experiment until we assembled them for instructions just prior to the actual experiment. We are confident that the subject population was not "contaminated" with knowledge of what was in store.[1]

---

1. The exit questionnaires asked the subject: "Had you heard anything prior to doing the experiment about the kind of tasks you would be asked to do?" One

The morning of the experiment, we deposited the equipment at each of the 11 sites. We convened the 17 assistants, explained the experiment, distributed and reviewed a set of guidelines, assigned positions, toured the sites and readied the equipment. The instructions for subjects were printed so that Form 1A and Form 1B appeared on opposite sides of a single sheet, and Form 2A and Form 2B likewise. At each site, either the 1A/1B or the 2A/2B sheet would be posted on a clipboard near the water bucket. To reduce the hazard that would arise if site-specific factors affected whether subjects made the discovery, we instructed the monitors to reverse their instruction sheet with each trial. Thus, each site would perform the alternating sequence A, B, A, B, A, B... Six sites used the 1A/1B sheet and five used the 2A/2B sheet.

The monitors were told to reset the equipment after each trial, escort the next subject to the site, indicate the instructions, and announce, once the subject finished reading the instructions, "I am starting the clock now"—for three minutes, as indicated on the instruction form. There was not to be any other communication between the subject and the monitor. The monitor was to observe casually from a distance and fill out an observation form (recording information on site, monitor's name, subject's name, instruction form, whether the subject inverted the stool, amount of water transferred, and open-ended observations). She would then fill out a payment chit, indicating the instruction form, cups transferred, and whether the subject inverted the stool. The subject brought the chit to the cashier for payment and answered one of two exit questionnaires, one for those who inverted and one for those who did not.

The basic logistics of the experiment ran fairly smoothly. To start, the student subjects—all male—arrived in ample numbers. They were briefed that they would go in groups to holding pens, fill out a registration form, wait to be escorted to a site, find instructions there, have three minutes to perform the experiment (but we did not tell them what it would be), and finally go to a specified room for payment. The monitors performed their tasks with a few mishaps and irregularities but basically as we intended. If the experiment was flawed, the flaws lay in experimental design.

---

student responded, "Yes, my friend described this exact experiment to me." We have expunged this subject entirely (he is not included in the 135 on which we report). Oddly, he did *not* invert the stool. He had instruction Form 1A, so excluding him weakens the result we desired.

BASIC RESULTS OF THE EXPERIMENT

Running simultaneously 11 test sites, we put 135 undergraduate subjects through the experiment in about two hours. The division of the subjects among the four different payment schedules was as follows: 35 subjects had Form 1A, 37 had Form 1B, 32 had Form 2A, and 31 Form 2B. The total expenditure on payments to experimental subjects was about $2,100 (including equipment, dry runs, and assistants, it was about $4,000).

Most of the subjects who completed the experiment transferred water in one of the two expected ways (carrying cups or inverting the stool). Many, however, did not read or understand the instructions and reacted in confounded ways. Using the monitors' observations, we identified the following sorts of *problem cases*:

The Problem: The Subject ...	Number of such subjects
Made more than one trip	22
Moved the bucket	1
Ran out of time	8
Transferred zero cups of water	5
(for reasons unknown)	
Other cases of basic misunderstanding[2]	1

Whether the problem cases ought to be expunged is not entirely clear.[3] As it happens, the problem cases do not much affect the results.

Retaining all 135 subjects, the results are reported in Table 8.1. We arranged the columns least to most additional money per cup. Because Forms 1A and 1B involve a threshold of seven cups, consider the pair-wise comparisons. The percentages inverting the stool of 1A subjects versus 1B subjects: 31.43% versus 35.14%. The percentages inverting of 2A subjects versus 2B subjects: 25% versus 32.26%. The differences are in the direction of the conjecture, but they are too small to provide a demonstration of anything.

If we expunge the 37 problem cases, leaving 98 subjects, we have the results reported in Table 8.2. Percent inverting the stool of 1A subjects

2. One subject misread the instructions to say that he could not lift or move the plastic cups; he transferred water in his mouth!

3. One might argue that attention to the instructions was a function of the cash opportunities, yet, since 57% of the problem cases had the high reward forms (1B or 2B), this does not appear to have been the case.

Table 8.1. ALL 135 SUBJECTS BY FORM (PAYMENT SCHEDULE) AND WHETHER THEY INVERTED THE STOOL

Form	Marginal reward (US$)	Subjects who did not invert (%)	Subjects who inverted (%)	Total subjects
2A	0	24 (75.00)	8 (25.00)	32
1A	0.10	24 (68.75)	11 (31.43)	35
2B	0.50	21 (67.75)	10 (32.26)	31
1B	1.00	24 (64.86)	13 (35.14)	37
Total		93 (68.89)	42 (31.11)	135

The χ^2 of Table 8.1 is 0.86, with three degrees of freedom and a P-value of 0.84. The χ^2 after merging the cell frequencies for forms 1A and 2A, and forms 1B and 2B is 0.47, with one degree of freedom and a P-value of 0.50, or a Fisher's exact test-value of 0.58 giving a P-value of 0.31 for a one-sided test.

versus 1B subjects is 34.62% versus 47.83%. For 2A subjects versus 2B subjects we have 28% versus 29.16%. The differences are still in the "right" direction, but they are not significant in any sense. For 1A subjects versus 2B subjects, the small difference is in the "wrong" direction.

REFLECTIONS

There are several reasons to doubt that the experiment tested the "motivation stimulates entrepreneurial discovery" conjecture. First, it is doubtful that we operationalized motivation. Economic experimentalists wrestle with the presence of nonmonetary factors such as decision-making costs

Table 8.2. THE 98 "PROBLEM FREE" SUBJECTS BY FORM (PAYMENT SCHEDULE) AND WHETHER THEY INVERTED THE STOOL

Form	Marginal reward (US$)	Subjects who did not invert (%)	Subjects who inverted (%)	Total subjects
2A	0	18 (72.00)	7 (28.00)	25
1A	0.10	17 (65.38)	9 (34.62)	26
2B	0.50	17 (70.83)	7 (29.16)	24
1B	1.00	12 (52.17)	11 (47.83)	23
Total		64 (65.53)	34 (34.69)	98

The χ^2 of Table 8.2 is 2.57, with three degrees of freedom and a P-value of 0.46. The χ^2 after merging the cell frequencies for forms 1A and 2A, and forms 1B and 2B into a 2 x 2 table is 0.52, with one degree of freedom and a P-value of 0.47, or a Fisher's exact test-value of 0.53 giving a P-value of 0.31 for a one-sided test.

and have sought to mitigate the problem by using larger monetary payments (Smith and Walker 1993). In our case, an impasse between potential monetary rewards and motivation is immediately indicated by the fact that some 25% of the subjects did not comprehend the instructions well enough to abide by them. The situation was highly artificial and peculiar. Many subjects may have acted under the general understanding of "the more water, the more money" (as one subject wrote on his exit questionnaire) regardless of the payment schedule.

More significant concerns about motivation stem from the fact that money is not the only motive. Form 2A offers no additional money and says, "Transfer as much water as you can." In writing the instructions, we had to walk the fine line between merely setting for the subject a deliberate task and offering our approbation for his having performed the task well. An imagined or implicit approbation—or, for that matter, the subject's own pride or sense of sport—would be a form of motivation independent of monetary rewards. Also, the admiration of the female monitor may also have motivated the male subjects. Indeed, the experiment seems to have evoked entrepreneurship in ways unintended. Although the instructions said, "Do not speak to the monitor," in two instances the monitor was asked out for a date!

The subjects were penned up for up to ninety minutes, talking freely with friends, classmates, or dorm mates. The advertisements said to expect a wait and to bring something to read, but almost none of them did. Although they did not know in advance the task of the experiment, they probably anticipated that after the experiment they would swap stories of their own performances (they had been told that they would "be allowed up to three minutes to perform your experiment task"). It is likely that peer rivalry was operating.

The presence of nonmonetary motivations might mean that the variations in monetary rewards generated only small differences in total motivation. Using the stool would increase one's water transferring ability by about twenty-four cups, which would mean an additional $24 for a subject with Form 1B. We cannot be sure, however, that in that situation even the promise of an additional dollar per cup significantly affected overall motivation. Adam Smith said: "In such games the stake is commonly a trifle, and the whole pleasure of the game arises from playing well, from playing fairly, and playing skillfully" (TMS: 279).

Besides teaching us subtleties of motivation, hindsight has taught us the *ineffability* of entrepreneurial discovery. The exit questionnaire for those who inverted the stool asked:

Which of the following two sentences better describes your experience? (Check one)

_____ I deliberately searched for the best way to transfer the water and came up with the idea of using the stool.

_____ The idea of using the stool just came to me.

The "deliberately searched" option was checked by 76%. It seems that many subjects approached the task in a mode of *problem solving*, exactly what we had hoped to avoid by making the task physical. Inasmuch as subjects deliberately puzzled over how to transfer water, the experiment did not test *entrepreneurial* discovery at all. The next question asked: "After thinking of using the stool, did you have any second thoughts about doing so?" The response of one subject perfectly depicts our failing: "None, I figured that it was the trick and I figured it out."

Those who did not invert the stool also answered an exit questionnaire. They were asked if they thought of turning over the stool, and 39% said they did! The next question asks: "If you did think about using the stool, why didn't you use it?" Answers included:

"I was lazy."

"I didn't feel any motivation to."

"I don't know, I guess I'm an idiot."

"I thought you could only use the cups."

"It just seemed a bit unorthodox."

"I didn't want to look like I was fumbling with all the equipment + spilling water everywhere."

Of the respondents who did not invert the stool yet said they had thought of doing so, 44% had high-reward opportunities (either Form 1B or 2B), so cash payoffs do not explain why they did not go through with the idea.[4]

It seems, therefore, that many came up with the idea of inverting the stool but did not judge the idea to be worthwhile (perhaps because they were unsure of its legality). In Kirzner's theory of entrepreneurial

---

4. It should be noted that subjects filled out the exit questionnaires in a hectic and noisy room where they conversed freely about the experience. It is possible that some subjects who had never thought of inverting the stool were ashamed of not having seen the "trick" and lied about having thought of it.

discovery, there is no impasse between perceiving an opportunity and seizing it: if the agent does not act on the idea, then he did not perceive it to be a *profit opportunity*. Only ideas that are indeed acted on are deemed to have been perceived as profit opportunities (1979: 169, 1985: 23). The experiment, then, besides having problems of controlling motivation and of separating entrepreneurship from problem solving, may have failed to make available a maneuver that, once noticed, would be considered by the subject to be a profit opportunity.

Our experience highlights the place of problem solving. Those who inverted the stool were "thinking outside the box," but inasmuch as they set out to solve a conceptual problem, they worked within a larger, more fundamental box, within which the subject's deliberate thoughts remained. Problem solving is the deliberate effort to get a new *partial interpretation* of one's situation. This description seems to fit the subjects' behavior better than either "search for information" or "entrepreneurial discovery."

Kirzner describes entrepreneurial discovery as "undeliberate but motivated." We have seen that in Somerset Maugham's short story "The Verger" he tells of a man recently put out of work looking along the street for a smoke. When he fails to find one, an idea comes to him—to open a tobacco shop. The experience is not a process of deliberate problem solving. Indeed, the man thinks to himself: "Strange 'ow things come to you when you least expect it." This tale of undeliberate discovery of a nonobvious new interpretation has undeniable intuitive appeal and relevance. And it may not have been absent in the experiment: Of the exit-questionnaire respondents who inverted the stool, 24% checked "The idea of using the stool just came to me" rather than "I deliberately searched for the best way to transfer the water."

Whether "undeliberate but motivated" discoveries are important in an economic system, and whether such beneficial discoveries are sensitive to public policy, seem to be questions that continue to frustrate formal methods of empirical investigation.

CHAPTER 9

✺

Let's Be Pluralist on Entrepreneurship

In the preceding chapters on discovery, I championed Israel Kirzner against those who would flatten knowledge down to information. For years I saw myself as refining Kirzner and clearing up some issues. Over time, however, I found that I was steering into deep conflicts. With this chapter, the move away from Kirzner becomes more explicit. I like his idea of entrepreneurship as discovery of opportunity, but I do not care to make that, or anything else, the essence of entrepreneurship. Many interrelated ideas are associated with entrepreneurship, and none is definitive. My disagreements with Kirzner are developed most fully in the first of the appendix chapters of this book.

My chief concern is justifying a presumption of liberty, and it seems to me that, in that, ideas of discovery are more elemental than entrepreneurship. In that sense, we do not need the term *entrepreneurship* to carry special meaning about discovery factors of free enterprise, for we can often just speak of discovery. We can take a catholic attitude toward the word *entrepreneurship*, accepting a cluster of the several important ideas associated with it.

The present chapter consists of remarks that clarify, extend, and apply our thoughts on the richness of knowledge. I discuss how several interpretations of entrepreneurship—those associated with Joseph Schumpeter, Frank Knight, Ludwig von Mises, Israel Kirzner, Arjo Klamer, and Deirdre McCloskey, and those associated with ordinary language—all relate to one another, and I suggest that none is really definitive. We should embrace the contextuality and pluralism of entrepreneurship talk.

Sherlock Holmes and Dr. Watson go on a camping trip. After a good dinner and a bottle of wine, they retire for the night and go to sleep.

Some hours later, Holmes wakes up and nudges his faithful friend. "Watson, look up at the sky and tell me what you see."

"I see millions and millions of stars, Holmes," replies Watson.

"And what do you deduce from that?"

Watson ponders for a minute.

"Well, astronomically, it tells me that there are millions of galaxies and potentially billions of planets. Astrologically, I observe that Saturn is in Leo. Horologically, I deduce that the time is approximately a quarter past three. Meteorologically, I suspect that we will have a beautiful day tomorrow. Theologically, I can see that God is all powerful, and that we are a small and insignificant part of the universe. What does it tell you, Holmes?"

Holmes is silent for a moment. "Watson, you idiot!" he says. "Someone has stolen our tent!"

Humor seems to depend on asymmetric interpretation. In this old chestnut, Watson offers five interpretations of the starry view, and Holmes proceeds to another. Yet the humor comes from another sort of interpretational asymmetry. We, the readers, know Holmes's talent for remarkable insight. We expect Holmes's brilliance, but instead we get Watson's dimness.

To one who went to sleep under a tent, its absence ought to be obvious. Watson fails to grasp an obvious insight. Watson errs, in that he failed to see an interpretation that he comes to feel he should have seen. Our distinction between obvious and nonobvious opportunity is as undeniable as the humor of this little story. Obviousness is indeed highly contextual, but it is meaningful and important, nonetheless.

OBVIOUSNESS IS CONTEXTUAL, YET MEANINGFUL

In a blog post, Jeff Ely wrote about the contextuality of compliments:

Let's say you hear someone play a difficult—but not too difficult—piece on the piano, and she plays it well. Is it a compliment if you tell her she played it beautifully? That depends. You would not be impressed by the not-so-difficult piece if you knew that she was an outstanding pianist. So if you tell her you are impressed, then you are telling her that you don't think she is an outstanding pianist. And if she is, or aspires to be, an outstanding pianist, then your attempted compliment is in fact an insult.[1]

The same contextuality applies to insightfulness. If you flattered Sherlock Holmes for his brilliance, perhaps he will insinuate that you should expect from him such "elementary" insight. The term *entrepreneur* is something of a compliment. But if you flatter an industrial swashbuckler for deeds that are obvious and ordinary *to him*, he might figure that you have no idea of his "real" entrepreneurship. Discourse is *situational*, and in two senses: the situation of the agent spoken of, and the situation of the speaker. The situational nature of discourse makes the words contextual.

Joseph Schumpeter knew this. He associated entrepreneurship with creativity, the introduction of "new combinations," and he understood that we draw lines appropriate to the discourse situation. "Similarly," he wrote, "we can assume that every healthy man can sing if he will," but "through a series of continually increasing singing ability and continually diminishing number of people who possess it, we come finally to the Carusos" (1934: 81–82). In some contexts, it is fair to say "Dan Klein can sing," but in others (most, in fact), it is not. Likewise, in each of the following very short statements from Samuel Goldwyn, we find two standards:

"We're overpaying him, but he's worth it."
"Let's have some new clichés."
"I'll give you a definite maybe."

Our finding humor in such statements, as opposed to sheer absurdity, depends on our sustaining multiple standards, each of which is meaningful.

When my daughter came up with the idea of selling her homemade bracelets on the Internet, I thought she showed entrepreneurial knack. The idea would not be obvious to most seven-year-olds. The obviousness of an opportunity, then, is not fixed in the stars. In some contexts, it will be fair to describe it as obvious, while in others it will not. It depends on the situation and context. As with singing, playing the piano, and being creative, whatever ambiguity there is may lie not in the quality but in achieving a common understanding of the discourse situation. We all know what "obvious" means. Confusion over context may lead you and me to situate the lines of "obviousness" differently. But the categories remain and the

1. Jeff Ely's blog post is found at http://cheeptalk.wordpress.com/2009/08/10/dont-link-to-this-post/. Accessed Aug. 10, 2011.

distinctions between types of discovery (and between error and merely unrealized brilliant ideas) go through nonetheless.

READING "OPPORTUNITY" SO THAT DISCOVERING AN OPPORTUNITY IMPLIES THE SEIZING OF IT

Minding the fine contextuality also helps with a common reservation with Kirzner. He says that if Jane comes up with an idea but does not act on it, then, in fact, she must not have seen an opportunity at all, for we say that one sees an opportunity *only if* she judges it worthy of acting on. Discovering an opportunity, then, implies seizing it. That seems to make sense, but Kirzner's auditors then scratch their heads. Suppose Jane discovered an opportunity, told a friend, and the friend then seized the opportunity. Doesn't that manner of speaking make sense? Do we not credit Jane with discovering an opportunity?

Here we may stick with Kirzner's manner of speaking but take pains to distinguish opportunity$_1$ and opportunity$_2$.

According to the "Velcro" entry at Wikipedia:

> The hook-loop fastener was invented in 1941 by Swiss engineer, George de Mestral who lived in Commugny, Switzerland. The idea came to him one day after returning from a hunting trip with his dog in the Alps. He took a close look at the burrs (seeds) of burdock that kept sticking to his clothes and his dog's fur. He examined them under a microscope, and noted their hundreds of "hooks" that caught on anything with a loop, such as clothing, animal fur, or hair. He saw the possibility of binding two materials reversibly in a simple fashion, if he could figure out how to duplicate the hooks and loops.[2]

George de Mestral pursued the idea, eventually patented it, and then sold the patents, presumably making some profits.

Now let's change the story. Suppose that George looked under the microscope, got the idea for Velcro, told it to a textile friend named Hans, and encouraged Hans to pursue it as his own idea. Suppose Hans, then, pursued, developed, and profited from the idea. George only gets a "thank you" from his friend. In this story, is not the opportunity discovered by George but seized by Hans?

---

2. "Velcro" entry at Wikipedia: http://en.wikipedia.org/wiki/Velcro. Accessed Aug. 26, 2009.

The story is pervasive. Someone comes up with an idea for a new product or a new way of doing something. She explains the idea to you, and you act on it—or vice versa. Is there not a separation between discovering and seizing?

We preserve the idiom within which discovering implies seizing by distinguishing two separate and highly situational opportunites, opportunity$_1$ and opportunity$_2$. In our story of George and Hans, George comes up with the hook-loop fastener idea, and he *does* seize an opportunity in this sense: *the opportunity of telling his friend something of potentially great interest.* George seized the opportunity of being of service and value to his friend Hans. That was the opportunity—opportunity$_1$—that George discovered and seized.

The opportunity that Hans seized—fabricating, developing, and selling the hook-loop fastener—was a related but separate opportunity—opportunity$_2$. Maybe George, who prefers traipsing about in the Alps, simply was not inclined to the business of product development. He was quite content to pass the idea on to his friend Hans and see him pursue opportunity$_2$. Opportunity$_2$ was an opportunity for Hans but not for George.

George gets the love and appreciation of his friend Hans—maybe that is George's "finder's fee." He gets it, though, only if his idea points to potential value for Hans. Opportunity$_1$ derives from opportunity$_2$, like a pool that feeds a waterfall down to George. We have cascading opportunities. In talking economics, we may think of there being a primary source opportunity, a pecuniary opportunity, where money trades for services in something like a marketplace, up the mountain, pouring down in multiple directions, creating cascading showers and pools. Perhaps the shower represents discovery, and the up-lying pool represents opportunity—opportunity gives off a spray. People, often in overlapping teams of cooperation, work their way up the fountain. Among the means used to discover the showers and up-lying pools are conversation and sympathy.

The seven virtues formulated by Deirdre McCloskey (2006) also rate a mention. The entrepreneurial experience calls especially on *faith* in one's own vision and judgment, *hope* for success, and *courage* in negotiating the uncertainties and challenges. Of secondary place are *love* for your fellow cooperators, *justice* to your partners and public, *prudence* in not neglecting your personally established interests, and, as always, *temperance*, or not being overly zealous in any of the other six.[3]

3. Jeremy Bentham (1787/2008) treats of courage (73) and hope (76).

Who, in the story of George and Hans, is the entrepreneur? Ordinary language would seem to side with Hans, the businessman, who actually went off and developed and sold a product. I admit that the opportunity Hans discovered and seized may have been quite obvious to Hans. After all, it was George who thought out the idea of the hook-loop fastener and in plain language simply explained it to Hans. In Hans's experience, there doesn't seem to be any "epiphany."

That's right, and one reason I do not insist that entrepreneurship be strictly defined in terms of epiphany (or nonobviousness of the opportunity). We should not insist on any strict definition of entrepreneurship. Many attempts have been made to infuse the term with strict meaning. I find that many have merit and tend to travel together. We should allow and appreciate many associations with "entrepreneurship."

In the matter of George and Hans, let me defend an opportunity-discovery take. First, consider Hans. True, he did not have any great insight about hooks and loops; he got that from George. Hans, however, does ascend the mountain and realize pecuniary gain, and that journey always involves novel situations, new challenges, and the need for original interpretation. In ordinary language, business creation or substantial ownership is the hallmark of "entrepreneurship," but a notable feature of such endeavor is coping with the nonobvious. After all, obviousness comes from routine and familiarity. In making fresh decisions about a new enterprise, or dealing with the changeful life of business, one cannot resort to what is merely obvious. In fact, it may be that no course is obvious. I am happy to call Hans an entrepreneur, but the discoveries that bolster the label simply do not include the hook-loop fastener idea.

Now consider George. One might pose the following challenge: George simply learns by investigating and passes an idea to his friend; he certainly does not seem like an entrepreneur; but it was he who discovered the novel idea of a hook-loop fastener. If "epiphany" were a sufficient condition for entrepreneurship, wouldn't that make George an entrepreneur?

First, I basically agree that it doesn't feel right to call George's actions entrepreneurial. I say "basically." Maybe George is keen for his friend's esteem, admiration, and gratitude. Maybe that is the betterment that motivates George. That motivation spurs him to wonder at the clinging burrs and dig his microscope out of the attic. George may feel great satisfaction in coming to the discovery and imparting the idea to his friend. In this, I see some sense in saying that George acted entrepreneurially, even that he reaped entrepreneurial "profit," albeit nonpecuniary.

Second, on a different telling, it may be that to George the discovery was less epiphany and more respondence or serendipity. Suppose that George's hobbies include botany, that his microscope is affixed to the kitchen table, and that he regularly examines bits of nature. Botanical examination is his routine. This day, he happens to put a burr under the microscope and sees that it clings by hooks and loops. At this point, the idea of mentioning the observation to his friend Hans, a textile merchant, might be rather obvious. In this story, George has discovered no great opportunity for himself, and by the time that the "scent" of opportunity was about him it was rather obvious. On this telling, the discovery was not an "epiphany."

Actual discovery is a story about what goes on within the individual. The story would seem to require first-hand interviews, and even those usually are not trustworthy. But the value of the idiom does not depend on empirical capture by the analyst. In a simplified story of private business, the parts played by George and Hans are likely to be collapsed into one experience. In such case, we see clearly why business creation/ownership will often involve discoveries of nonobvious opportunities, and hence why both aspects may be taken as highly, though not definitively, characteristic of entrepreneurship.

THE STREAM OF SELF-CONVERSATION

Just as the story of society among George and Hans is often collapsed into a single individual, the story of a single individual may be unfolded as a society of selves. Let's go back to the original and actual Velcro story, from Wikipedia, in which it is just George who discovers the idea and develops the product; there is no Hans. It may be useful to think of cascading opportunities and discoveries *within George*. George-today wants to feel that the day was one of accomplishment. George-today wants to be able responsibly to applaud himself *for passing a baton of insight to George-tomorrow*. George is a team, an institution—we could put subscripts on *George*. The team is dependent on the present George—George$_1$; we are prisoners of the present, and we salvage our future by developing the virtues, realizing a healthy cascade of opportunity, discovery, and reward within the society of mind.

We talk to ourselves and look for conversational opportunity each day to tell our day to ourselves. Many people find it important to talk daily to someone, a colleague, spouse, parent, sibling, or close friend. What the routine affords is the formulation of what has happened and what *can happen.* The formulation is then focal in your stream of self-conversation and cascade of discovery.

Each day I tell my day to my wife, who acts out a role of listener. I love her for maintaining a routine that enables me to tell it to myself. The most intimate, most situational, conversations are ones about the potentialities afforded by our fountains of opportunities.

As we converse, we explore what kind of source would be meaningful to us. We explore not only the relations of trickling knowledge but also the worthiness of our tracing our way back to the source. Is the pool really one for me to swim in? Who do I want to be? How do I best meet my higher duty? How do I best justify my existence? What "utility function" should I practice? Answers flow from sources higher up.

We hope it all traces back to a source opportunity. Honest pecuniary income is, by the invisible hand theory, a kind of validation of the whole internal fountain and the drama of tracing things back to the source. We want such validation of our worth, of our social value. Frustrations aggravate us because they upset this process of self-validation. Even minor frustrations seem to tell us that our internal cascade, or pursuit, is defective.

The cascade metaphor may be helpful in justifying economic liberalism. I believe that, if enterprise is private and free, in most cases honest pecuniary income is a rather sound validation of our efforts, interpretations, and judgments. If enterprise is private and free, honest income, arising from voluntary participation, validates our "actions as making a part of a system of behaviour which tends to promote the happiness either of the individual or of the society" (Smith, TMS: 326). Honest income validates our part in enhancing the coordination of the vast concatenation of resources, activities, and potentialities, and thus confirms that we make "becoming use of what is our own" (270). Sometimes we want income less for what it renders in purchasing power than for what it renders in moral validation.

In choosing terminology, I've opted for "epiphany" to designate discovery of nonobvious significant opportunity. I have reservations about the term, for its connotation of life-changing revelation. I don't find a good alternative, however. As for its connotation, think about applying what Michael Polanyi wrote about philosophical passion to the entrepreneur:

> These passions are powerful forces pursuing high hopes. Indeed, if the shaping
> of knowledge is achieved by pouring ourselves into new forms of existence,
> the acquisition of knowledge should be found to be motivated by the deep-
> est forces of our being. We see in fact that repeated frustrations in solving

a harassing problem can destroy the problem-solver's emotional balance... We know also that every increment in this process is induced by spontaneous acts of the growing mind. To a mind on the alert, whatever seems intelligible presents a problem and stirs it to the prospect of discovery. Thus will the active mind avail itself of ever new opportunities to undergo a change that will make it more satisfying to its modified self.

(1963: 34–35)

HOW DIFFERENT CONCEPTIONS OF ENTREPRENEURSHIP RELATE TO ONE ANOTHER

Several authors have criticized Kirzner for purportedly arguing that entrepreneurship is merely the noticing of opportunities out there waiting to be discovered.[4] Some of these authors prefer to emphasize, with Joseph Schumpeter (1934), the *creative* aspect of entrepreneurship. Kirzner posits the opportunity's existence prior to discovery. Schumpeter is more inclined to say that the entrepreneur creates something (a "new combination") that lacked prior existence.[5]

In addition to existence "out there," are there not also potentialities existing "in there"? Creativity is imagination made material. From no-telling where comes a grand image; to get there from here you forge in either direction, one by one, the necessary steps. Thus, Kirznerian entrepreneurship may be said to subsume inspired feats of creativity (cf. Kirzner 1985: 56, 58). In some discourse situations it will be better to emphasize creativity, not discovery, but there is no great divide between the two idioms.

In another turn, Peter G. Klein (2008) writes that "opportunities are neither *discovered* nor *created*, but *imagined*" (176). Klein emphasizes the feature highlighted by Frank Knight (1921: 276–281, 299–300), namely that the entrepreneur *bears uncertainty*. (Here, Klein also highlights Richard Cantillon and Ludwig von Mises.) Knight distinguishes between risk and uncertainty. A coin toss—supposing we have no doubts about it—represents mere risk. Uncertainty, however, is surrounded by doubts, and it is a matter of imagination and judgment. Thus, says Klein, the entrepreneur imagines opportunities, and, in acting, stands to make profits or

---

4. Authors who have made this criticism of Kirzner include Loasby (1983: 223), Ricketts (1992), and Gilder (1984: 260).

5. With a view to business strategy, Alvarez and Barney (2007) nicely elaborate and contrast the discovery and creation views of entrepreneurship.

losses, residuals that result after mere risk and payments to factors of production have been accounted for.

While Klein diminishes the opportunity-discovery idiom, I see much congruence between it and the Knightian conception he advances. Risk resides in settled interpretation, uncertainty in unsettled interpretation. Opportunities based on mere risk will be easy to communicate, to imitate—they will be obvious—and, in a free-entry environment, they will be quickly captured and closed. "Risk" seems to imply common knowledge, like our odds with a fair coin. But "epiphany" is typically the seeing of a new and better interpretation of things. Rather than common knowledge, it hinges on disjointed knowledge. Rather than symmetric interpretation, it hinges on asymmetric interpretation. A new, fruitful interpretation will be nonobvious to the extent that uncertainty, as opposed to mere risk, surrounds the circumstances and any opportunity lying therein. So, again, we need not exalt one idiom and reject the other, but embrace the pluralism surrounding entrepreneurship and use what best suits our discourse situation. Klein teaches in a business school and draws heavily on business-strategy literature; only incidentally do his works in this vein address issues of liberty. For business purposes it may be best, in exploring entrepreneurship, to emphasize uncertainty-bearing, imagination, and judgment.

Uncertainty-*bearing* means putting your resources in jeopardy—such as staking the payroll and other bills, and then hoping that the revenues yield you residuals that are positive, not negative. This relates to the point by Jack High (1982: 166) and Martin Ricketts (1992: 72) that Kirzner's system seems not to accommodate a place for entrepreneurial losses. It also relates to something else associated with entrepreneurship. As is the case with Klein, Joseph Salerno (2008), building especially on Ludwig von Mises and Murray Rothbard, sees "property ownership as central to the tasks that the entrepreneur characteristically performs in the real-world market economy" (189). Salerno contends that Kirzner—who says that "ownership and entrepreneurship are to be viewed as completely separate functions" (1973: 47)—departs here from Mises. For Kirzner, the key is discovery. If a person discovers a profit opportunity, borrows the necessary resources, and reaps a return, that makes him an entrepreneur.

Again, both make sense, and any impasse between them is not of great moment. Salerno acknowledges that Kirzner's pure entrepreneur appears in the writings of Mises, and is designated by Mises as a useful but "imaginary" construction (1966: 253, 306). Both Salerno (193, 203) and Mises (253) say that this character is "propertyless." But is he? Even this imaginary character is bound to own some resources and bear some uncertainty. Every soul owns its person and personal effects and, if only metaphorically, the social relations developed in existence. Nowadays scholars talk of "human capital" and "social capital." How, but by such capital, is this character to borrow the other necessary resources? He must put in jeopardy some of his energy, emotion, and other human faculties, as well as his reputation, image, relationships, good will, and sympathy. He is bound to make project-specific investment, if only in his human resources. In this sense, every soul is a capitalist. The *act of will*, which Salerno nicely highlights in Carl Menger, Eugen von Böhm-Bawerk, and Rothbard, and which he associates with the committing of and ultimate decision-making power over that will's property, is never the act of a disembodied spirit, but, rather, is the act of a will embodied in an individual, embedded in society.

Mises, Rothbard, Salerno, and Klein are right to underscore ownership as a core feature of entrepreneurship. That feature highlights some of the reasons that, as regards entrepreneurship, government agencies are thought to be deficient or even perverse—a line of discourse famously developed by Mises and Hayek in their criticisms of socialism. I see much affinity between the business owner and the seer of nonobvious interpretation. Again, business owners will generally encounter many situations where solution is nonobvious, challenging their decision-making faculties. Someone with a significant stake in a business, especially an owner-manager, will deal with change. As leader and executive, he is constantly catching as catch can, and needs to act on interpretations only half articulated or even only half conscious. As Kenneth Burke suggested, *decision* is the formulation and selection of alternatives, the set of which then frames *mere choice*. We may read "discovery" into the formulating and selecting, and "opportunity" into the alternatives.

Also, the business owner is immersed in an individuated world in which certain opportunities may be fairly obvious to him but not obvious to people without any such immersion. When the analyst speaks of an opportunity being nonobvious, it might be within the frame of what the rest of us would see. The business owner specializes in hitting on opportunities by searching in ways that are routine to him though foreign to others. When Samuel Goldwyn says, "I had a monumental idea this morning, but I didn't like it," we get a glimpse of his routine: He thinks up—searches for—opportunities that would be nonobvious to the layman. As analysts, it is often the layman's perspective that frames our standards for obviousness. Moreover, while resource ownership may be a salient feature, is it sufficient? Without some such element of discovery, mere resource ownership and investment do not make for entrepreneurship. Just as one may object to the merest discoverer as entrepreneur, one may object to the merest owner as entrepreneur. Salerno touches on this (195): "[T]he purchaser of an insurance annuity or of a share in a bond mutual fund acts entrepreneurially but is not an integral entrepreneur." He does not concede enough. I'd say that such a purchaser does not act entrepreneurially, except in the sense in which every action is entrepreneurial. In this sense, the term really becomes flaccid. Whereas it is vital to keep in mind that everyone owns some resources, just as everyone has some height and weight, it is not useful to say that every action has the quality of being entrepreneurial. That is like saying that everyone is tall, or that everyone is fat.

Deirdre McCloskey and Arjo Klamer have highlighted another salient feature of the entrepreneur: persuasion and rhetoric (McCloskey 1994: 370–372, McCloskey and Klamer 1995: 194). McCloskey and Klamer say yes to discovery, creation, imagination, innovation, and the like, but the entrepreneur inevitably must formulate and convey the vision and build trust among collaborators and backers. Another figure, by the way, who highlighted "the *benefit of discussion*" and evolving interpretation—"two wits, set to sift into the merits of the project"—was Jeremy Bentham (1787/2008: 75, his italics), in his glorious critique of Adam Smith on usury. This feature goes with discovery of nonobvious interpretation. The entrepreneur needs to talk, if only with herself, to work out her formulations and to clarify and confirm the sense of discovery. Going forward, rarely can she go it alone; she needs cooperators. Cooperation involves a sense of mutual contribution to the commonly envisioned goal or concatenation, the successful enterprise. A vision must be made common, and doing so will require talk, rhetoric, and persuasion. And the less obvious that the vision is, the more talk and persuasion will be required.

We've seen a number of things associated with entrepreneurship:

- Discovering (and seizing) a betterment opportunity
- Creating new products, methods, and improvements
- Bearing of uncertainty
- Owning the capital
- Creating and/or owning a business enterprise, especially as owner-manager

- Organizing and leading cooperation by engaging in speech, rhetoric, and persuasion

All of these features make sense and tend to travel together. The different idioms have their different advantages. I am interested particularly in arguing for liberty. Here, the idiom of opportunity and discovery, couched in terms of knowledge as information *and* interpretation *and* judgment, seems especially useful. Among Kirzner's works, my favorite is *Discovery and the Capitalist Process* (1985), which richly explores the merits of free markets using the opportunity-discovery idiom.

CHAPTER 10

✧

Knowledge Flat-talk

A Conceit of Supposed Experts
and a Seduction to All

If I were to list the *dramatis personae* of this book, I suppose it would be: 1) the character suggested by the ideas favored in this book, invoking Smith and Hayek; 2) Israel Kirzner and the more Hayekian of the self-identified Austrians; 3) George Stigler, or the modernist economists who generally favor freer markets; and 4) the less liberal economists such as Kenneth Arrow, who, like Stigler, flatten knowledge down to information. This chapter turns toward that final character.

I left out the self-identified Austrians who especially favor Mises and Rothbard. Living economists aligned more or less with that character would include Joseph Salerno, Walter Block, Robert P. Murphy, Hans-Hermann Hoppe, Mark Thornton, and Peter Klein, but Murray Rothbard, who passed away in 1995, remains the focal figure. They incline toward a dehomogenization of Mises and Hayek, and toward a candid authenticity that openly makes liberty a primary part of their economics, but, unlike me, they tend to favor Mises and the image of science further expounded by Rothbard. That character never becomes a principal in this book only because I do not directly engage the differences between us.

This chapter commences with some exposition of my general philosophy of knowledge, which is then used to criticize those who flatten knowledge down to information, a vice that lends itself to interventionist thinking, I think.

KNOWLEDGE AS ENTAILING INFORMATION, INTERPRETATION, AND JUDGMENT

In treating of knowledge, my approach is not foundational, but pragmatist, contextual, formulated in terms of levels of frame within which "we" are situated and our discourse embedded. In communicating, we generally proceed from some working interpretation of matters. "Information" is what we call the facts as seen within the working interpretation. Meanwhile, the "facts" reside in a more basic interpretive frame, in which "factual" statements are presumed acceptable to all parties of the communication. When Jane and Amy "argue over the facts," they are, as it were, revisiting what they propose to treat as factual for the purposes of the conversation. If the argument is unresolved, Jane may be deciding that she and Amy are not a "we," and may instead be drawing a circle of "we" with some of the auditors to her exchange with Amy, a circle that does not quite include Amy. (Although the facts remain unresolved between Jane and Amy, however, there is always the possibility that Amy will later reconsider matters and imaginatively enter the circle that Jane draws.)

Consider a situation in which we have no trouble agreeing to "we"-ness in our apprehension of the "facts." Suppose we sit down together with a telephone book. We call the ink markings on the page "the facts." Neither of us thinks to dispute statements about the printed letters and numbers on the pages. We then proceed to talk plainly of them as *phone numbers*. We often forget this working lens—interpreting the facts as phone numbers—because we see through it. One of us, however, may propose another interpretation: Might the list of "phone numbers" contain secret knowledge encoded by spies?

Thus, we have multiple interpretations of the ink markings that some understand as "phone numbers." Those quotation marks make it mean: what the facts are called when they are seen through the working interpretation. Quotation marks can be confusing, however, and we often just omit the quotation marks. We often, likewise, just speak of *multiple interpretations of the information* (as opposed to multiple interpretations of the facts). Rather than interpretively pivoting off the "fact"-level interpretation—that the line reads 678-3554—I formulate things so as to pivot interpretively off what I have called "the working interpretation"—that 678-3554 is a phone number—a level *up* from the factual, and there the pivot turns: "Maybe the phone number is a secret encoded message?" This works because I build universal acceptance among the "we" into "the facts." That is, by construction, at the factual level no pivoting is necessary—none of us disputes that the line says 678-3554. Put differently, wherever you want to accommodate interpretive pivoting, move "factual" to somewhere down from there.

Figure 10.1 shows a drawing that follows Ludwig Wittgenstein's discussion of a duck-rabbit illustration in his *Philosophical Investigations* (1953/2001). Working within the duck interpretation, we could cover up some of the pixels. Maybe you see only the "beak" and I see only the "back" of the head—asymmetric information. But beyond issues of information, there is another interpretation: Maybe what we need to see is not exposure to all the pixels, but the other interpretation of them: that they represent a rabbit.

The notable interpretations of the illustration are only two. But in human affairs, things evolve, and there is usually opportunity for further and better interpretation. Michael Polanyi (1963) noted the "peculiar opportunity offered by explicit knowledge for reflecting on it critically" (15). Interpretations evolve in dialectical fashion, each advance giving rise to further advance. New interpretations just keep coming.

Meanwhile, life rolls on. The pitch races toward the plate. If the batter waits for a better interpretation, he may be called out on strikes. The

Figure 10.1: Duck-rabbit illustration
Source: Gombrich (1960: 5).

action facet of knowledge is *judgment*, our taking stock in an interpretation by acting on it—though this "action" may be the act of *deciding* and not involve much muscular activity.

As speaker, we judge of judgments—those both of our interlocutors and of agents existing within the descriptions we give of things. We convey our judgments of their judgments using judgmental terms. Favorable, approving terms, or commendations, include *true, unbiased, right, better, superior, wise, good, enlightened*, and so on. Unfavorable, disapproving terms, or pejoratives, include *untrue, biased, wrong, worse, inferior, unwise, bad, unenlightened*, and so on.

Epistemologists sometimes say that a belief qualifies as knowledge only if it is true. I do not disagree, exactly, but my pragmatist approach deals with such concerns by way of the judgment dimension. If I think that one's judgments are inferior or unwise or cause for regret, and in that sense untrue, I express it by making my judgments of his judgments disapproving.

FLATTENING KNOWLEDGE DOWN TO INFORMATION

Suppose we are discussing some matter and working from a common frame of understanding. Now, suppose that someone brings a new and seemingly better interpretation to a matter, transcending our working frame. It may be true that the components of the previous frame can be recoded according to the scheme of the new frame. Thus, one array of information is transformed into a new array of information system. But it is pernicious to proceed in a fashion that suppresses an awareness of the pervasive potentiality of interpretive transcendence and of the dialectics of interpretational evolution. An example of such suppression is found in an extremely negative review of Kirzner's book *Competition and Entrepreneurship* (1973) by Benjamin Klein, who writes: "Although the problem of decentralized co-ordination of economic activity in an environment of transaction and information costs is complicated, there is certainly no reason why maximization techniques cannot and should not be used ... We just must assume a richer informational background under which individual maximizing decisions take place" (1975: 1307–1308).

Much of professional economics has made it a point of honor to flatten knowledge down to information—dubbed "flat-talk" in this book. The suppressive attitude is the following:

"Your pet terms like 'interpretation' and 'judgment,' your distinctions between decision and choice, between knowledge and information, between motivation and incentive, your notion of 'error,' do not really amount to anything, for any time someone brings a new true interpretation to a matter, we then make it scientific by recoding as necessary to bring it all into a system of information, probabilities, search costs, and optimization."

George Stigler, particularly in his last three decades, insisted on seeing all behavior as maximization and all knowledge as information; he insisted that the concept of "error" could have no place in economic theorizing. Since interpretation was effectively symmetric and final, economists were silly when they proposed to influence political tastes. He even chided Adam Smith for violating these organons. Part and parcel, he lent a hand in the subversion of the proper understanding of liberty.[1]

FLAT-TALK FLATTERS THE SO-CALLED EXPERT AS ABLE TO INTERVENE BENEFICIALLY

George Stigler and Benjamin Klein generally favored freedom of enterprise, but the strictures they practiced and promulgated are wrongheaded and unhealthy to liberty. Flat-talk gives the false sense that the theorist has or can have some composite master interpretation of things that subsumes the interpretations, present and future, of those within the system. Flat-talk is self-flattering, a hubris common in self-styled scientists and do-gooders. It also plays well with deep-seated yearnings for a sense of common knowledge and common experience, a universal human weakness. Intellectuals and politicians themselves are prey to this weakness, but they also consciously or unconsciously exploit it in their publics. Hayek wrote of a concurrence between the intellectuals' pretense of knowledge and certain primordial instincts of humans generally, a sort of tacit alliance against the enlightened norms and sensibilities of liberal civilization.[2] I take his and Adam Smith's view to be that liberal civilization

---

1. Here is a beginner's guide to the bane of Stigler: In Stigler (1976) he propounds that we are to construe all behavior as maximization, flatten knowledge down to information, and eradicate any notion of error, moves all of which, by the way, help to glorify the importance of Stigler (1961). In Stigler (1982) he whimsically sermonizes that it is folly to try to improve political "tastes." In Stigler (1971) he chides Adam Smith, based on an inversion of Smith's ethical teachings. In Stigler (1978) he subverts the sound notion of liberty.

2. See Hayek 1976, 1978c, 1979 and 1988.

should be a sort of project in teaching all to subdue and redirect certain primordial penchants and bents so as to accept voluntarism as a basic operating system, and to learn to accept, or make natural, its otherwise startling and upsetting exfoliations. More than anyone else, Adam Smith morally authorized voluntarism and its exfoliations, and that authorization probably figured significantly in the wealth explosion starting right about the time of Smith's death in 1790.[3]

An interpretation is "right" only in the sense that it is better than the relevant alternative interpretation. It isn't "right" in the sense of final or definitive. Once the government starts acting on an interpretation, it tends to become ossified. Even if the government seizes on a pretty good interpretation of what's going on "now," it is likely to cling to that interpretation long after it should have been superseded. Moreover, governmentalization of interpretation tends to regiment social affairs and repress the evolution of interpretation. Rather than fitting interpretations to the world, it tries to fit the world to its interpretations. If our expert understanding of things isn't common knowledge, well, we will see to it that it becomes common knowledge.

I should add, however, that even government operatives often do not really believe in and act according to official interpretations. The crumminess of government interpretation gives rise to all manner of interpretational falsification, dissonance, and confusion. By nature, government is Orwellian.

The renowned economist Kenneth Arrow is a knowledge flattener and a man of the left. As shown by the petitions he signs (Hedengren et al. 2010: 307), Arrow regularly supports interventionist causes. Speaking of his upbringing, Arrow writes, "my family was politically and socially liberal," and he describes himself as a "socialist sympathizer" in his youth (Arrow 1992: 43–44). A left-leaning family upbringing is common to many similar Nobel economists, including Paul Samuelson, Robert Solow, Joseph Stiglitz, George Akerlof, and Paul Krugman.[4]

---

3. Deirdre McCloskey (2010) expounds the view that the Industrial Revolution happened where and when it did in large part because of the cultural and rhetorical changes that expressed social approval of the pursuit of honest profit.

4. I have named six American left-leaning Nobel economists of Jewish background (I think). I wonder if there is some significance in the idea that American Jewish leftist intellectuals have often looked to enter and ascend American officialdom and cultural governance as a way of making themselves American, of overcoming their "other-ness" as Jews. Such would be only a particularistic manifestation of the more general conjectures about statism among intellectuals.

In a technical paper Arrow writes:

In this chapter I want to survey some aspects of the effects of information on the markets for contingent goods, by means of a toy example studied under different informational assumptions ... First, some definitions. By "information," I mean any observation which effectively changes probabilities according to the principles of conditional probability. The prior probabilities are defined for all events, an event being described by statements about both the variables that are relevant to the individual welfare and those that define the range of possible observations. Given an observation, there is a conditional or posterior distribution of possible values of the welfare-relevant variables.

(1984: 199)

In the "toy example," information means an observation that changes probabilities over a set of variables that matter. It all exists within a predetermined scheme neatly set out by the toy maker.

You might think that toy makers know the difference between toys and human society. Surely they do. Still, I believe that they fall back onto their mastery of toys, often their only claim to expertise, when treating of human society.

I edit a journal called *Econ Journal Watch*, and, to get people talking about the distinction between knowledge and information, I invited scholars to write essays on the distinction (the symposium appeared in the April 2005 issue of the journal). When I asked Arrow to participate, he replied in a letter that I published online with his permission:

Thank you for the invitation to participate in a symposium on the distinction between knowledge and information. I am afraid the topic does not inspire me. In my old-fashioned positivism, concepts have meaning only in the context of a model (which may be very general), and I can't think of one which will accommodate this distinction. Of course, there are many kinds of information and different modes of transmission and apprehension, e.g., tacit vs. coded knowledge (which is a very important distinction).

(2003)

I am inclined to concur that no model will well accommodate the distinction between knowledge and information, but what of the claim that "concepts have meaning only in the context of a model"? Is this itself a concept? If so, has this concept been couched within the context of a model? In the letter, Arrow does not provide a model, nor refer to one in the literature. I wonder what such a model would look like—that is, a model expositing the concept that a concept has meaning only in the context of a model.

If Arrow were to concede that there is no model contextualizing the claim, will he admit that his belief that "concepts have meaning only in the context of a model" is without meaning? If he did admit that, why does he make the claim in the first place? Why set down a string of words that is meaningless?

Perhaps Arrow would object to my identifying the statement that "concepts have meaning only in the context of a model" as a concept. Perhaps he would say it is not a concept, but rather merely a notion, idea, or belief. Then I may reply that a distinction between knowledge and information is a notion, idea, or belief. Notice that Arrow affirms a "distinction" between tacit and coded knowledge. Does he have a model for that distinction? Notice further how he switches from "information" to "knowledge." If there is no distinction between information and knowledge, why vary terms?

It seems that both he and I are practicing discourse beyond models, but Arrow declined to join the conversation. He added: "I realize you have asked for a weekend's reflection, but my general view is that it is easier to write a 25-page paper replete with formulas and footnotes than an expressive 5 pages."

Arrow knows that information is asymmetric—that is one reason why markets fail. Does he claim that the government can acquire the information? He once wrote:

> It will be necessary to increase the intensity of observation. Along the lines of the investment surveys of the Securities and Exchange Commission, it may well be possible to find out by direct interrogation to what extent investment and consumption projects have been curtailed by the interest rate changes.
>
> (1984: 51)

This kind of thinking helped to inspire the Sarbanes-Oxley Act.

But Arrow's chief error is not his confidence in government interrogation. He writes about government's inability to acquire information (1984: 159ff). Arrow's error concerns the asymmetry of interpretation. Economics ought to teach us to subdue our yearning for common knowledge of social life, a yearning both primeval and too often culturally inculcated. Rather than teaching to overcome it, economists like Arrow have been prey to it, and they have even worked to authorize it by promulgating a supposed science that gratifies it.

Their chief error is the one exposed by Smith and Hayek, the error of being too ready to believe that one knows well enough to intervene in a way that conduces to concatenate coordination. The classical liberal philosophy sees a nexus of verities that give strong presumption to liberty. Exceptions to liberty should be regarded as exceptional and bear the burden of proof. The liberal position is *not* that the powerful—rulers, politicos, and influential intellectuals—*never* know enough to intervene beneficially, but that they quite rarely do. Most of the interventions that we have gotten accustomed to do not meet the burden of proof. One reason that some intellectuals think otherwise is that they flatten knowledge down to information. They fail to admit the crumminess and arrogance of governmental interpretations, and the comparatively healthy interpretational dynamics of voluntary society—an open system of disjointed interpretations.

Consider the deliberations of the Justice Department's Anti-Trust Division in deciding whether a practice or merger is "anti-competitive." In many ways the issue turns on interpretation: how we define the good or service, how we define the industry, how we define the term *anti-competitive*, what we count as "evidence," and so on. Each of these matters depends on such things as how widely or narrowly we conceive the category—ballpoint pens, ink pens, writing implements, means of communication, and so on. Competition takes many forms; substitutes are everywhere. Every story of demand and supply depends, for example, on interpretations of hypothetical time-to-reaction ("long run" versus "short run"). Every thought experiment makes myriad assumptions about what happens (or doesn't happen) in the meantime. The stories vary with the interpretations. If you think that economists have anything like a standard for arriving at definitive interpretations, definitive stories of "the X market," much less a standard for estimating the parameters of such stories, you are gravely mistaken. In the end, "anti-competitive" may be nothing more than a loose, vague judgment that certain forms of government intervention would conduce to better coordination of the vast concatenation. Official anti-trust reports, rulings, and documents have a strong Kafkaesque quality, as does much of the scholarly literature, authored by supposed experts. Life within realms heavily governmentalized is often Kafkaesque.

In the matter of advertising, consider how flat-talk may breed illiberal thinking. Two flat-talking economists, William S. Comanor and Thomas A. Wilson, wrote in their book *Advertising and Market Power* (1974):

> If we could be assured that advertising provides no misinformation and thereby promotes consumer choices that are more in accord with those that would be made with full information, then we could argue that there

is a positive gain to the consumer associated with his revised preferences. Although this may be the case in many circumstances, we cannot rule out the prospect that some forms of advertising lead consumers further away from choices based on full information.

(250)

The authors write as though for each new model car or brand of shave cream there is a definitive set of qualities. When advertisements show some of them, the consumer comes closer to possession of "full information." When an ad shows few of the product's qualities, appealing instead to extraneous associations and impulses, it is persuading rather than informing, and it is wasteful. By departing from the true matrix of qualities, the advertisement might misinform.

There is no definitive interpretation of the product and its qualities. The advertisement is providing interpretations and may be creating value. With their "full information" talk, Comanor and Wilson mislead people about the economics of advertising.[5]

Officials and regulators know little about that which they are to regulate. For knowledge they can only turn to people with some knowledge. When such people exist, they often work in the regulated industries. When the government taps such parties, new absurdities flower. If the conversation is friendly and cooperative, commentators clamor against the influence of lobbyists and special interests. If the conversation is fearsome and demanding—as it generally is, surface pretenses notwithstanding—some complain that business withheld information or misled officials. Either way, interested parties, some in the government's chokehold, serve up descriptions of things, descriptions that are then received as official knowledge. Each politician, bureaucrat, respectable expert, and journalist has little choice but to play along.

FLAT-TALK FLATTERS THE VOTER AS FIT TO JUDGE

In *The Wealth of Nations*, Adam Smith speaks of people being "fully informed." What he says there speaks volumes about his understanding of knowledge:

But though the interest of the labourer is strictly connected with that of the society, he is incapable either of comprehending that interest, or of

5. Cf. Hayek 1961/1967.

understanding its connection with his own. His condition leaves him no time to receive the necessary information, and his education and habits are commonly such as to render him *unfit to judge even though he was fully informed*.

(266, italics added)

Unfit to judge even though fully informed. But if a person were fully informed, what could possibly make him unfit to judge? His education, his habits, says Smith. That is, his impoverished understanding of interpretations, his bad judgment.

In the *Journal of Political Economy*, then under the editorship of George Stigler, the economist Donald Wittman assures us that the citizen is fit to judge. Practicing flat-talk, he assures us of democratic efficiency:

> It would be foolish to argue that voters are perfectly informed about political markets. However, efficiency does not require perfectly informed voters any more than efficient economic markets require all stockholders to know the intimate workings of the firms in which they hold stock or all principals to perfectly monitor their agents. A voter needs to know little about the actions of his congressman in order to make intelligent choices in the election. It is sufficient for the voter to find a person or organization(s) with similar preferences and then ask advice on how to vote. For example, people who like to hunt are more likely to read the literature from the National Rifle Association than from an organization attempting to ban guns, and one can always ask advice from a more politically knowledgeable friend with similar tastes. Voters can also look at the list of campaign contributors (who typically make their campaign endorsements public) and infer the characteristics of the candidates' policies (pro or con). That is, interest group endorsements are like signals in the market and provide strong cues about candidates' preferences. Furthermore, competitors for public office need provide only the information when there are discrepancies between the voters' preferences and the political outcome, not all the unnecessary detail.

(1989: 1400–1401)

Wittman expanded the argument into an influential book, *The Myth of Democratic Failure: Why Political Institutions Are Efficient* (1995).

Were interpretation common and final and reasonably enlightened—were the common knowledge assumption to hold—the argument would have considerable force. The voter would know his preferences, and he may look to those people with "similar preferences" or "similar tastes" who are better informed. In this imaginary world, each of us knows wherein lies our well-being, and we all have a final and satisfactory interpretation of how things work. We need not mind the "unnecessary detail," for we leave the details to experts. They tell us which politician best advances our wellness, just as doctors tells us which medicine does.

The chief problem with Wittman's story is that, among us, interpretation is not common and final and reasonably enlightened. By instinct and by culture, people systematically take to unenlightened interpretations of how things work and what should be done—indeed, even of wisdom, of virtue, and of their own selfhood. In medicine, the system of expertise works pretty well, because the individual patient and the individual doctor have strong individual motivations to come to more enlightened interpretations, making for healthy dialectics in medical knowledge. Wittman, Arrow, and others act out and promulgate an unsophisticated image of social doctoring that elides the matter of interpretational dialectics by presupposing a condition of common knowledge, of symmetric interpretation, and by attributing it to officialdom—chosen by the people, led by politicians, advised by experts and university scientists—administering the great cooperative organization of the polity. It has a seductive appeal to intellectual and layman alike: Not only will we improve the coordination of affairs within this organization, we will have a sense of shared experience and sentiment in our jointly doing so.[6]

FLAT-TALK SUBVERTS LIBERALISM

Knowledge flat-talk creates a mirage of reducing the matter to information, search cost, probabilities, and incentives, all thusly amenable to beneficent expert intervention. It gives the illusion that political man is fit to judge, that governmentalization does not introduce great epistemic problems. It therefore subverts much of the basis for the call to degovernmentalize social affairs.

6. Bryan Caplan (2007) offers an extensive and influential critique of Wittman. Caplan's critique is one that I basically embrace and applaud, but rather than calling the median voter's positions "wrongheaded," "foolish," "unwise," "unenlightened," (or even "ignorant"), he calls them "irrational," which I find unhelpful. Then, by juggling several definitions of "rationality" (including a tacit one: what Caplan thinks enlightened), Caplan goes on to call this "irrationality" "rational." Also, Caplan leads the reader to believe that the extent to which professional economists share his judgments is greater than it really is. For my thoughts on Caplan, see Klein (2007); for an interesting four-part exchange between Caplan and Wittman, see Caplan (2005) and follow the links.

Meanwhile, in economic discourse, flat-talk keeps out the vocabulary of entrepreneurship, enterprise, discovery, insight, interpretation, and judgment. These rich words speak of comparative merits of freedom not well illuminated by the flat-talk. The defense of liberal verities is stronger when discovery, adventure, and the spirit of enterprise are accentuated. Such rich talk makes us mindful that articulate knowledge resides in tacit knowledge. As Don Lavoie (1985a) showed, such mindfulness makes the value of freedom more persuasive.

Studies in Spontaneous Order

In the preceding chapters, we developed understandings of knowledge and coordination to provide a new statement of an old liberal outlook. We will, in later chapters, bring those understandings together and attempt a fuller expression of the outlook.

Meanwhile, in this section's three chapters, we ramble in some public policy topics. The ideas developed earlier are used to justify a presumption of liberty in the matters discussed. Are these chapters persuasive?

CHAPTER 11

✃

Urban Transit

Planning and the Two Coordinations

United cooperative societies are to regulate national production upon a common plan, thus taking it under their own control and putting an end to the constant anarchy and periodical convulsions . . . of capitalist production.

Karl Marx (1871/1974: 213)

Much of the opposition to a system of freedom under general laws arises from the inability to conceive of an effective co-ordination of human activities without deliberate organization by a commanding intelligence.

Friedrich Hayek (1960: 159)

At Wikipedia, the entry on "Urban Planning" begins: "Urban, city, and town planning integrates land use planning and transportation planning to improve the built, economic and social environments of communities. Regional planning deals with a still larger environment, at a less detailed level."

Networks of researchers, officials, corporate officers, and academic programs and associations constitute the fields of "planning," represented by such organizations as the American Planning Association.

Many planners tend to believe in the necessity and desirability of urban planning. A pattern of thought among transportation planners has been noted by Donald Chisholm (1989: 13): "[C]oordination and centralization have become virtually synonymous. Where a need for coordination is perceived, the reflexive response is centralization." In a large urban society, it is thought, the transit needs of the people, and the schedules, routes, and modes of the vehicles that serve them, become so numerous and so complex that the only way to coordinate the pieces is by central administration.

This argument sounds a lot like the arguments on one side of the debate over economic calculation and planning in a socialist system. Advocates of central planning have long cited complexity as a *prima facie* argument against the "anarchy of the marketplace." Karl Marx said, "The capitalist mode of production... begets, by its anarchical system of competition, the most outrageous squandering of labour-power and of the social means of production" (1867/1967: 530). In the capitalist economy, "great disturbances may and must constantly occur." Under socialism, economic affairs would be organized like "one immense factory," "upon a common plan" (1885/1967: 315, 1871/1974: 213). Nicolai Bukharin criticized capitalism for being guided by "blind power... not by a conscious calculation by the community." He called for a "new society which is consciously planned and consciously executed" (1917/1972: 49, 1920/1971: 68).

In the early 1920s, Ludwig von Mises (1920; 1922) argued that only by the competitive forces of the free-market regime are the decentralized elements of the economy appropriately utilized. The system is indeed complex and beyond human comprehension, but that is no reason to attempt to replace it by a system of central direction. Price signals and the pursuit of profit lead the vast and varied lines of activity to be self-coordinating.

It was Mises' "powerful challenge," declared Oskar Lange (1938), "that forced the socialists to recognize the importance of an adequate system of economic accounting to guide the allocation of resources in a socialist economy." "[A] statue of Professor Mises," he said, "ought to occupy an honorable place in the great hall of the... Central Planning Board of the socialist state" (57). He argued that Mises' point was valid but not fatal. The solution that Lange and others[1] proposed was a scheme whereby the workings of the market economy, or, at any rate, the workings according to the model of perfect competition, would be simulated within the socialist system. Factory managers would be instructed to minimize average cost, set output to equate marginal cost and price, and so on. Prices would be dictated by the central planning authority. In each period, information about excess demands and excess supplies would be relayed to the central

---

1. Notably, E. F. M. Durbin, H. D. Dickinson, and Abba Lerner. I am drawing on Don Lavoie's study of the debate (1985b). My quotations of Marx and Bukharin are borrowed from his work.

authority, which would revise prices with the aim of making markets clear. In this procedure of trial and error, the system would coordinate itself by mimicking the self-coordinating forces of the market economy.

Talk about knowledge flat-talk! The standard blackboard story became the most stupendous quackery!

To this quackery, Hayek responded patiently, meticulously, and respectfully. His criticism (1940/1948) exposed many fundamental problems of the scheme: Without making the incentives genuine from the bottom up, and giving agents the freedom and flexibility to act on their hunches and expectations and special opportunities—their unique interpretations—nothing like a free-market economy would come from the simulation effort.

In *The Road to Serfdom* (1944), Hayek summarizes the view of the planners in this way: "What they generally suggest is that the increasing difficulty of obtaining a coherent picture of the complete economic process makes it indispensable that this should be co-ordinated by some central agency." Hayek, of course, dissents: "Any further growth of its complexity, therefore, far from making central direction more necessary, makes it more important than ever that we should use a technique which does not depend on conscious control" (50).

Hayek writes, "The more complicated the whole, the more dependent we become on that division of knowledge between individuals whose separate efforts are co-ordinated by the impersonal mechanism for transmitting the relevant information known by us as the price system" (49; cf. Epstein 1997). Hayek's talk of knowledge being "divided," "dispersed," or "diffuse" was unfortunate in a way, for it led some to see the matter was one merely of asymmetric information: Like a jigsaw puzzle, the knowledge is out there, but the pieces are scattered around. Beyond the adjectives "divided," "dispersed," and "diffuse," we need *disjointed*. People perceive and pursue their own overlapping jigsaw puzzles, and it is only in a very vague and abstract way that we propose to talk about all the jigsaw puzzles as a vast concatenation and judge its worthiness. A full appreciation of Hayek's oeuvre makes it altogether natural and proper to see Hayek as a "deepself" thinker and a critic of knowledge flat-talk. In his talk of the division of knowledge, Hayek was all along driving at asymmetric interpretation, but he did not always highlight the richness of knowledge.

The Hayekians won the socialism debate, but transit planning remains intellectually unimpeached. Hayek would maintain that the lessons do apply: "[P]lanners do not yet realise that they are socialists and that, therefore, what the economist has to say with regard to socialism applies also to them" (1933a/1991: 32).

Besides the problem of knowledge flat-talk, another reason that people often misunderstand Hayekian claims about "coordination through the price system" is the conflation of concatenate and mutual coordination. Distinguishing between the two coordinations helps us to clarify talk of planning.

"FREE COMPETITION" FOR URBAN TRANSIT

> We were the first to assert that the more complicated the forms assumed by
> civilization, the more restricted the freedom of the individual must become.
>
> Benito Mussolini (quoted in Hayek 1944: 43)

Electronic components are made in Korea, assembled into devices in China, shipped to Long Beach, California, and loaded onto trucks for delivery to distributors throughout the American West. The problems of mutual coordination are rather incidental. One of the simplifying features of the example is that electronic devices are not particular about the whens and wheres of the process. They are inanimate objects that will sit for days in dark, stuffy containers without minding a bit.

In urban transit, passengers are numerous, individual in their desires, and very particular about waiting. The problems of coordination are rather severe. Each passenger has his own preferred times and places to get on and off. Each day the individual's itinerary may differ or change on short notice. Vehicles usually follow schedules and routes to try to accommodate these desires. When making connections, passengers must coordinate with multiple vehicles, and the vehicles must coordinate with each other.

It is fair to say that a modern urban transit system, say in Los Angeles, achieves mutual coordination. Generally speaking, the system has settled into coordination equilibria. People know when and where to catch the bus and where it will take them. From the point of view of any particular bus rider, the actions of each of the parts of the system are satisfactory, given what he himself has gotten accustomed to doing.

But it is no great praise to say that the system achieves mutual coordination. The same may be said for prison life. The Hayekian challenge is: When placed within a broad view, is the current transit system conducive to concatenate coordination? To answer the question, one must, of course, compare the coordination of one concatenation to that of would-be concatenations.

Let us suppose that the government of Los Angeles closed down all its transit services and declared a "free competition" policy for all bus, shuttle, and taxi services. Also, private entrepreneurs would be welcome to construct rail lines, though it is unlikely that any would. All relevant levels of government sanctify this sudden transit *tabula rasa*.

Entrepreneurs both large and small would begin offering their services, just as entrepreneurs do in some cities today (sometimes even in defiance of law). We might expect the vehicles of many route-based services to be owner-operated vans, often operating under fleet brand names or associations. The variations and peculiarities of transit markets are many, and the vehicles, modes, and service options are impossible to predict. I will posit some general features of what might take place.

First consider door-to-door services. Taxis, shared-ride taxis, carpools, van pools, and subscription commuter shuttles would compete in the open market. The parties involved would mutually coordinate directly. Many services would use fancy dispatching or external display boards to aid on-the-spot coordination. Also we might well expect a spontaneous order of on-the-spot carpooling coordinated by real-time communication.

Then there is line-haul service on busy boulevards. One might envision a fairly steady flow of vehicles plying the boulevard, perhaps according to a fixed schedule, perhaps not. Finally, for secondary routes off the main boulevard or in the suburbs, let us imagine scheduled fixed-route service, every forty-five minutes or so.

PROBLEMS WITH "FREE COMPETITION" IN URBAN TRANSIT

Can we expect smooth and felicitous coordination from such a picture? On the floor of the roller rink, the skaters make moment-by-moment decisions, and it works out pretty well. With modern communications, maybe transit can be more like roller skating.

The door-to-door services would seem to pose no particular problem, but the line-haul and fixed-route services may experience trouble. Scholars have raised a number of concerns about the performance of free competition in transportation services:

1. One line of attack emphasizes *poor consumer information* about contending service providers. There are peculiar difficulties of price competition

in the transit industry. Many riders are nonrepeat customers traveling from airports, hotels, and resorts; nonrepeat customers are poorly informed and vulnerable. In communicating the fare, there is ambiguity about whether to express the charge per mile or for the complete trip. Either alternative might entail further ambiguities. There is an awkwardness in "shopping around," since the communication often takes place within the vehicle and causes delays for other passengers.[2] These problems might help to explain why there has been surprisingly little price competition in deregulated bus and taxi markets.[3] These problems also apply to some extent to competition in quality characteristics. Furthermore, there is the problem of trustworthiness, of "rip-offs" and crime in taxi markets. Because of the abnormalities of consumer information, there is an argument for alleviating the uncertainties and anxieties by having regulators control entry and set uniform prices.

2. A second argument is *economies of density*. Although it is agreed that bus service does not show economies of scale in production,[4] there are, nonetheless, systemwide gains from increased volumes. Part of the gains may come in the form of lower production costs, due to larger vehicles, but part accrues to riders in the form of higher frequencies, shorter waiting times, and a denser route structure.[5] Christopher Nash (1988: 118) argues that the free-market process of "piecemeal infilling of gaps" will not successfully achieve economies of density because some of the benefits flowing from volume-enhancing actions accrue beyond the calculus of piecemeal operators; they neglect consumer surpluses and other benefits that accrue in other pieces of the system. With density externalities, the incentives to advance concatenate coordination do not function properly.

3. Another criticism maintains that piecemeal operators in a free market will inevitably fail to coordinate schedules and to achieve smooth through-ticketing and interchange. Riders will be frustrated in connecting the pieces of their journey and will have to make a separate transaction for each piece. Nash (114) argues that there are systemwide benefits from through-ticketing schemes that the piecemeal operator would ignore. Nash combines this coordination argument and the

---

2. See see Frankena and Pautler (1986) and comments by Robert Samuels.

3. See Frankena and Pautler (1986: 3); Dodgson and Katsoulacos (1991); White (1995: 198); Moore and Balaker (2006).

4. See Viton (1981); Hensher (1988); Shipe (1992).

5. See Mohring (1972); Gwilliam et al. (1985).

density argument to make a case for transit "integration," or central planning.

4. Another issue is the provision of *passenger facilities* and *terminal capacity*, like benches, shelters, stations, and signage, which are an important complement to transit services. When carriers operate under laissez-faire, local authorities might have difficulty coordinating the provision of these facilities. The operators might lack an impartial representative to work with the local authorities, and the laissez-faire market might itself be in constant flux. Waiting passengers might begin to congregate at inappropriate locations, blocking sidewalks, driveways, or storefronts.

5. Another concern is that of *"cut-throat competition,"* an idea originally developed in the context of railroads and public utilities (see Keeler 1983: 22, 47). The argument maintains that in an industry with high fixed costs and low marginal costs, competition may drive firms to cut prices to such low levels that costs cannot be recouped. The argument is like the natural monopoly argument, except that there is no premise that the optimal number of firms, in a blackboard sense, is one. Bus service does not display the economies of scale associated with natural monopoly. Nonetheless, the cut-throat competition notion may be relevant on individual routes, or on a systemwide basis once the total costs of establishing schedules, consumer information, and public awareness are included (Savage 1986; Nash 1988: 112).

The storyline of the cut-throat competition argument is indefinite. Suppose Company A sets up a bus system. Perhaps there is call, in a blackboard sense, for a second firm. Company B enters, but the tendency toward price cutting is too strong, and both firms are ruined—thus, Marx's "periodical convulsions" and "the most outrageous squandering of…the social means of production." In reviewing bus service in Britain, Peter White (1995: 206) speaks of "instability and wasteful duplication found in deregulated areas" (although price cutting has not been common).

Variations on this story of cut-throat competition are, first, that Company B is smart enough not to enter, in which case Company A enjoys an unchallenged monopoly. Since it is free to revise its price downward in the event of entry, there in not much discipline exerted by "contestability," or hit-and-run entry. Another variation is that Company B enters and the firms recognize that there is neither profit nor sport in cut-throat competition, and manage to collude. In these cases, we get prices well above marginal cost and an inefficient contraction of ridership. Indeed, foes of free-market transit often argue that urban transit ought to charge very low prices and receive subsidies.

6. Then there is a final fateful argument against unrestricted competition: *interloping*. A company may take pains to establish some viable bus routes, but then interlopers in banged-up old vans—that is, *competitors!*—come around and collect the waiting passengers just before the scheduled service is due to arrive (Eckert and Hilton 1972, Roth and Wynne 1982). This will upset coordination in that the scheduled vehicle is harmed by the interloper activity, and, if such activity forces the scheduled service to give up the route, passengers for a time may suffer discoordination by waiting for buses that never arrive. Entrepreneurs might know that if they were to attempt to set up a bus route, the interlopers would only descend to "skim the cream" and destroy what had been created. In consequence, no one sets up a service, no one interlopes, and no one waits to be picked up. This would be a coordination equilibrium but obviously a poor result in terms of concatenate coordination. We can also imagine competing van drivers battling for customers on the line-haul routes, driving dangerously and becoming agitated (Grava 1980: 286). There might be ugly incidents such as fist-fights at the curb. A hot-tempered van driver runs down a pedestrian.

Having reviewed several arguments against free-market transit, we can see why such a regime is often rejected by urban transportation planners. It is particularly easy to reject Hayek's philosophy when the word "coordination" is read to mean mutual coordination. Urban planners can make a plausible case that free competition will *not* result in a smooth fulfillment of plans. As for concatenate coordination, they can well argue that Hayek's apparent prescription will be untenable because of poor consumer information and services, suboptimal route structures, disjointed pieces, destructive competition and interloping. On this ground, transportation planners opt for centralized integration, "taking [urban transit] under their own control and putting an end to the constant anarchy...of capitalist production" (Marx 1871/1974: 213).

IS "FREE COMPETITION" REALLY HAYEK'S MESSAGE?

A Hayekian faith would suggest that discoordination makes for opportunity for an entrepreneur to step in and make a profit by resolving the discoordination. In urban transit, in which information problems and network effects complicate every action, and where interlopers lie waiting to skim the cream, this logic simply may not hold. The pitfalls of free-market transportation are accentuated by Joseph DeSalvo in "The Economic Rationale for Tranportation Planning:"

> This faith in the free market has existed at least since the time of Adam Smith who used the term 'invisible hand' to describe its workings. It is only recently, however, that the 'invisible hand' theorem has been rigorously proved and the conditions under which the theorem holds spelled out carefully [i.e., general competitive equilibrium]. To the extent those conditions are not fulfilled in practice, the case against planning is much weakened, for decentralized deci-sionmaking cannot achieve desired economic goals when the conditions are violated. Some other method is then required.
>
> (1973: 22–23)

I have posited a "free competition" policy and some of its likely results, but is such a regime necessarily what Hayek would favor? Is Hayek instruct-ing us to choose policy to mimic the conditions referred to by DeSalvo? One of Hayek's chief missions as an economist was, in fact, to wean econo-mists away from equilibrium models and technical categories as ways of describing economic affairs. Those who would drape the ideas of Hayek and Adam Smith in a rarified notion of pure competition make a mistake much like that of Lange in proposing to mimic blackboard stories.

The first chapter of this book talked about roller skating. We focused on the skater on the floor of the rink. The coincidence of interest among skat-ers was used as an analogy for the coincidence of interest among actors in the economy. One such actor would be the owner of the roller rink. He gains honest profit by making the skating environment, including the house rules, conducive to experiences worth paying for. In advancing his own interests, the owner, like a roller skater, advances the interests of others.

In real life, deals are embedded in particularistic human contexts, and the money price may be only one part of the terms imposed on the "buyer." Commerce and industry are skeins of contracts, practices, understand-ings, and relationships—all particularistic, negotiated, and highly tacit. This view is what Hayek has in mind when he writes of the free competi-tive economy:

> It involves competition between organized and unorganized groups no less than competition between individuals...The endeavor to achieve certain

results by co-operation and organization is as much a part of competition as individual effort. Successful group relations also prove their effectiveness in competition among groups organized in different ways.

(1960: 37, cf. 1988: 37, 1944: 42)

The emphasis that Hayek places on local knowledge is not merely a recognition of the free market's function to distill dispersed knowledge into a price vector, in a manner like that of the New York Stock Exchange. Hayek also recognizes the importance of flexibility in private contracts: to sculpt private arrangements to fit the particulars, to cope with change, and to coordinate with others. Although concatenate coordination is distinct from mutual coordination, its process is not apart from mutual coordination. The process includes the practice of *voluntary planning*, by consent and contract, to achieve mutual coordination. Hayek (1973: 46) says, "The family, the farm, the firm, the corporation and the various associations, and all the public institutions including government, are organizations which in turn are integrated into a more comprehensive spontaneous order."[6]

This latter theme is prominent in the work of Ronald Coase and the law-and-economics tradition (to which Hayek (1988) pays tribute). In caricature, the firm is an island of planning, and the market is like a vector of prices. Yet, all voluntary activities involve contractual relations and elements of both jealous conflict and mutual planning. Armen Alchian (1969/1977 and with Harold Demsetz 1972/1977) writes of the competitive labor market within the firm. Other Coasians like Steven Cheung (1983) and Paul Rubin (1978) write of contractual relations making up an abstract and invisible firm within the market. It is not just speechless purchase but also the process of "truck, barter, and exchange"—"the necessary consequence of the faculties of reason and speech"—which was said by Adam Smith (WN: 25) to be guided by an invisible hand.

Marx saw a need to "regulate production" and looked for a solution in "united cooperative societies." But he would reject free enterprise as a basis for such cooperative societies, because he was unwilling to view "commodity" exchange as a process of cooperation between trading partners and fair play among competitors.

---

6. Elsewhere Hayek (1946/1948: 23) stresses that his philosophy "affirms the value of the family and all the common efforts of the small community and group,...believes in local autonomy and voluntary associations, and...indeed its case rests largely on the contention that much for which the coercive action of the state is usually invoked can be done better by voluntary collaboration."

Hayek's real message was the advancement of a legal order of private property and freedom *of contract*—not of "competition." With this understanding of Hayek's prescription, we might tell a quite different story of urban transit. The problems arising from information problems, poor passenger facilities, network effects, destructive competition and interloping may be described, not as the failures of free competition, but as failures arising from that part of the system that remains governmentalized.

THE HAYEKIAN PROPOSAL: PROPRIETARY GOVERNANCE

Imagine visiting a place that is just like Disneyland except for one thing: interloping food vendors were perfectly free to enter and roam the grounds. In this case, we might imagine some problems of "free competition" similar to those for urban transit. If a legitimate entrepreneur were to lease space at Disneyland and set up a large-scale restaurant selling barbecued ribs, the interlopers would strategically position their carts and wagons, perhaps also offering barbecued ribs, along the walkways leading to the entrepreneur's restaurant. In the face of the uncertainty about being able to appropriate the value of his investment, the entrepreneur might shrink from investing altogether. At the real Disneyland, we know, such "free competition" is not tolerated. Only a limited number of authorized concessionaires are permitted to operate, and they must operate according to contractual terms. These controls on competition are not, however, an example of intervention or socialism. They are practices of the private-enterprise system itself. As in the case of a shopping mall or proprietary community, the entire arrangement exists within a nexus of private property and contract.[7]

Just as we do not observe interloping problems at Disneyland, we do not find interloping problems at warehouses or private distribution centers. If thieves—interlopers!—were to descend on the distribution center and steal electronics equipment from the containers and warehouses, the private parties involved would find remedies. They employ security guards and the like because they recognize that otherwise shippers will take their business elsewhere. Like the concept of litter, the concept of interloping seems to be predicated on government property.

---

7. Diandas and Roth (1995) make the same point about urban transit using the example of shopping centers preventing unauthorized traders to set up stands on the walkways.

In American cities today, the sidewalks, passenger shelters, curbs, streets, roads, and highways are government properties. Access is free, and husbandry is fragmentary, clumsy, and lackluster. There is no one with both the flexibility and the authority to manage the resource, much less someone who *also* has the motivation to do so. There is no private owner. Authority to act depends on the concerted action of several inflexible and inert government offices.

The Hayekian proposal would be to bring the problem fully within the ambit of private property and freedom of contract. That means privatization of the sidewalks, shelters, streets, and highways. Private ownership of the streets would mean the existence of a party that has the ability and motivation to deal with information problems, passenger facilities, network effects, disjointed pieces, destructive competition, interlopers, and curb-side conflicts.[8]

Hayek's message has often been misunderstood. Christopher Nash, a supporter of transit planning, says: "Thus the argument over public transport integration really is the traditional one of central planning versus the market" (1988: 99). Yet, Nash's examination of these two regimes in transit is confined to equilibrium conditions within a rarified model. He compares benevolent central planning and atomistic private operators who pursue profits. In both regimes, actors are assumed to enjoy perfect, final, common interpretation! They've got everything figured out; now they just need to optimize. The atomistic regime is characterized as "the market." Yet, the private competition examined still takes place on *government* sidewalks, bus stops, stations, curb zones, and streets. Nash misconceives the traditional debate over central planning versus the market. He

8. Hayek never declared that all roads and streets should be privatized. He says that certain amenities cannot be provided by market mechanisms, including "most roads (except some long-distance highways where tolls can be charged)" (1979: 44). He says that market provision may be "technically impossible, or would be prohibitively costly." I wish to make four remarks. First, Hayek does not conclude that such amenities must be provided by government; he goes on to speak of the vitality and rich history of the "independent sector," which has provided amenities by voluntary, nonmarket, methods (49–51). Second, Hayek warns against the dangers of the government regulating "so-called public places," such as the "department store, sports ground or general purpose building," which are provided by private initiative (48). Third, even when amenities ought to be provided by government, he favors provision by local and competing government (45). Fourth, he explicitly notes the dependence of these matters on technology (47). There is good reason to believe that as powerful new technologies have become available, such as electronic toll collection, computerized payment methods, video monitoring, in-vehicle parking meters, and the remote sensing of auto emissions, Hayek would be increasingly supportive of road privatization.

associates "the market" with rarified concepts. One might instead read "the market" as entailing a set of legal rules giving much weight to private property and freedom of contract, and recognize that men and women acting within this legal framework can communicate and organize competing pockets of cooperation. Creatively, the system evolves, and with it people's interpretations of things.

A SKETCH OF THE HAYEKIAN ARGUMENT FOR URBAN TRANSIT

Owners tend to be mindful of the satisfaction of patrons, and visitors tend to be mindful of the norms and expectations of their hosts. Current practice at hotels gives us a clue as to what to expect. The hotel operates its own little transit station, where cabs, shuttle vans, and gratis hotel minibuses pick up and let off passengers. The hotel enters into agreements with certain carrier companies or associations and permits only those to take passengers. Contractual relations and private property guard against "interloping"—or trespassing. Private rules, reputational incentives, and ordinary virtues work against disorderly conduct at the hotel drive-up.

Imagine the city streets and roads divided up into segments or small districts. Each separate unit would be under the control and management of a private entity. Think of the city as a continuous patchwork of shopping-mall roads and hotel drive-ups. Just as shopping malls allow free parking, street owners might make road access gratis to visitors, residents, and businesses. Just as proprietary communities often provide minibus service gratis, the road owner might provide free bus service. Alternatively, the road owners might implement electronic road pricing.

If the owner of a piece of road were insane, he could foul things up in his neighborhood and beyond. He could write his street names in ancient Sanskrit. He could program the traffic lights to be green in all directions. He could refuse to participate in a regional billing service for electronic toll collection and instead make every car stop and pay a toll. He might invite a bus company to establish a route and then encourage interlopers to steal the customers.

Very few road owners would be insane, however, and few of those who were would also be wealthy enough to carry on long in such manner. The natural incentive is for the road owner to work with associations and agents that coordinate the interdependent parts of the road and transit system. In private industry, such standards for matters of technology, product design, product safety, and insurance emerge from voluntary machinations, both competitive and cooperative. We could expect the same for transit coordination. The natural incentive is for the road owner to form contracts that will enhance his road as a place to shop, work, and reside.

Road owners might permit only certain transit operators to serve their road, and only at properly designated places. These services would span numerous private districts. The road owners would jointly form their own association to confer over matters of common interest, such as security, sanitation, special events, and so on. The association would be an institution to reduce the transaction costs of coordinating collective action that spans several districts. It might happen that the owner of a particular piece of road would try to hold out for special terms in a transit arrangement, analogous to a holdout in a highway development project, but the road owner would be engaged in extended, repeated dealings with adjoining road owners and most likely such behavior would be checked by norms against demanding special treatment for oneself (Ellickson 1991). Sympathy, virtue, reputation, and norms are the glue of private agreement, and all are part of the voluntary process of concatenate coordination.

It may be contended that a road owners' association is a re-creation of local government, and in some respects that is right. Yet, in the case of actual municipal government, many types of service are bundled together over a very large geographic area. Choice and competition *within* the geographic unit has been supplanted by "the democratic process." Residents and businesses cannot exit the bundle except by departing the city altogether. The bundling of many services—libraries, museums, schools, parks, athletic fields, conference centers, hospitals, water, sanitation, power, homeless shelters, fire protection, security, streets, and transportation—all carried out by large municipal governments—might well reflect past conditions of technology and mobility, path-dependent government, and public-choice forces. If, instead of seeing private community as entailing government, we think of municipal government as a kind of owner, a city overlord, we see that it is a peculiar kind of owner, a fractured, incompetent, inert, capricious owner. It would be an owner that is not even publicly acknowledged as owner of the city.

In the case of private proprietary governance, services would tend to be broken down into separate and independent offerings. The owner of a private road who belonged to an association of roads could simply discontinue his participation in the association. If the association failed to satisfy its members, some would pull out and perhaps form a new, competing association. Like simply selling off one's shares in a declining corporation, this exit option generates incentives to keep up performance.

Proprietary governance would tend to debundle services, expand the number of nearby alternatives, and refine the variety of final packages one could create for oneself. Relatively easy exit by residents and businesses would discipline road owners, and easy exit by road owners would discipline associations, agents, and service providers (see Hayek 1960: 351f). These considerations point in the direction of James Buchanan's "club" model (1965), in which governance is best left to the market. The historian David Beito (1990) shows how nongovernmental planning built the private residential streets (known as "Places") of St. Louis, with complete infrastructure services. The economist Fred Foldvary (1994) presents numerous case studies and argues that private governance delivers the goods (see also MacCallum 1970). John Majewski and I tell of early nineteenth-century private builders mutually coordinating across tremendous distances so as to create great concatenations of turnpike infrastructure so as to traverse the mountainous terrains of upstate New York and of western Pennsylvania (Klein and Majewski 2006). The piece by Majewski and me appears in an anthology that richly explores many historical and living examples of exactly what this chapter is suggesting. *Street Smart: Competition, Entrepreneurship, and the Future of Roads* is edited by Gabriel Roth (2006), a longstanding leader in the Hayekian approach to transportation. The anthology's chapters show that the case has been demonstrated in the real world and articulated by researchers. A major book showing the same in the matter of parking issues is Donald Shoup's *The High Cost of Free Parking* (2005).

The role of competition in proprietary governance does not fit the model of perfect competition, but under a Hayekian regime it will be much more robust than it is in the case of municipal government. The debundling of social services and the reduction of geographic size would make it easier for residents and businesses to shop with their feet. Road owners would have to compete with other roads and districts. They would be led to utilize competition themselves to improve service and reduce cost. If transit services are granted on exclusive contracts, the road owners would naturally invite competitive bids for the contract. Also, road owners might permit multiple, competing carriers to operate on their road, but manage the particulars of that process.

A Hayekian will readily admit that certain coercive measures may be necessary, notably easements that enable crossing. This limitation on property has historically been placed on railroads, private toll roads, gas and oil pipelines and so on (Tullock 1993). Without such a limitation, road owners could prevent "trespass" by those wishing merely to cross their road. They could enclose or cut off vast areas and extract outrageous payment just for crossing. The road owners surrounding the residence of Bill Gates would be capable of extracting millions. The obvious solution is easements that permit free crossing at a sufficient number of locations. In similar fashion, it might be that attenuations of ownership control would be necessary to cope with the lately mentioned hold-out problem and perhaps for natural monopoly problems (Coase 1960/1988: 155; Tullock 1993). In these cases, coercive measures might conduce to concatenate coordination, but the outlook carries a very strong presumption against resorting to such measures.

We may now revisit Christopher Nash's criticism (1988) of free-market urban transit. He says that piecemeal operators will not take into account systemwide benefits, in particular consumer surpluses arising from density economies and smooth interchange. Once we put road owners into the story, however, we can see how they may be attentive to the consumers' demand for frequent and reliable service and smooth transfers. In fact, the road owners might *be* transit consumers, in that roads might be owned in joint-property arrangements by residents. With private, competitive road owners now part of the process, we can see that the decision-making process may not be terribly piecemeal at all. Rather than thinking of small transit operators roaming independently like myopic termites, we must think of players as creative, interpretive, sociable beings working within a responsive body of contract and private agreement, a nexus of voluntary planning among different road owners and service providers.

The workings of a proprietary metropolis are impossible to foretell. The contracts that are agreed to at any point in time may permit wide latitude in the action of piecemeal transit providers. What is especially frustrating to researchers who have a strong will to know is that the agreed contracts themselves—the rules of the transit game—too are evolving and somewhat piecemeal. They too are, as the model-builders put it, "endogenous." Pretending to model this system would be bound to be highly misleading. Hayek says that "the most important task of science might be to discover...[the] limits to our knowledge or reason" (1988: 62).

Yet, we may nonetheless invoke the general principle that each part of the proprietary system strives for a more profitable local coordination and in the process advances concatenate coordination. Freedom of contract gives authority and great flexibility in managing resources, and private ownership gives great motivation; together they make for a *system* that evokes and prospers joyful interpretations, activities, practices, and institutions. These claims may sound like hackneyed verities, but economic scholarship bears out their depth and power. There are no guarantees here, but it seems foolhardy to suppose that we could expect better from "the democratic process" and government officials, even ones with PhDs in civil engineering, urban planning, or economics.

CAN LOCAL GOVERNMENT MIMIC PROPRIETARY GOVERNANCE?

Since we cannot expect degovernmentalization of the roads any time soon, let us briefly ask: Could we hope to see local government manage the streets in a manner similar to our happy picture of proprietary governance? The local government would still be bound to face the rigidities and lack of incentives that prevent it from capitalizing on local opportunity, but we might encourage them to do the best they can and hope for decentralized competing efforts. Thus, we might develop a reform proposal of deregulation, privatization, and the devolution of full authority over service registration, safety requirements, insurance requirements, and curb rights to local government authorities. The local authorities would need to hammer out a system which effectively defined property rights in bus stops, curb zones, and other terminal capacity. Adrian Moore, Binyam Reja, and I have put forth a proposal for local governments to establish and enforce a system of curb rights appropriate to local conditions, aimed at remedying many of the problems arising from the street/curb/sidewalk being a commons (Klein et al. 1997).[9] We also call for lifting restrictions that hinder the emergence of terminal capacity on private property. The authorities might also need to facilitate the information flow between consumers and carriers, and they would still need to provide passenger facilities like benches, shelters, and stations on the relevant piece of government property not leased to private transit entrepreneurs.

CONCLUSION

The essential points of the liberal critique of government planning are that the economic terrain must always consist of conditions that are highly particularistic and constantly changing, and that an effective working of

---

9. Donald Shoup's proposals in *The High Cost of Free Parking* (2005) parallel our "curb rights" approach, but as I argue in Klein (2006), Shoup's argument really seems to point to full-on privatization.

the economic system needs to be taking these conditions into account. Knowledge of these conditions exists only in the minds of the dispersed individuals of the system. Thus the best way to utilize knowledge of the particulars is to let individuals respond flexibly to opportunity as they discover it.

The issue, says Hayek (1945/1948: 79), is not whether to have planning, but "whether planning is to be done centrally...or is to be divided among many individuals." Urban and transportation planners will agree that as planning becomes more centralized, "particular knowledge of local circumstances will, of necessity, be less effectively used" (Hayek 1960: 352). Some researchers have used this insight to make the case for decentralization of government authority (Chisholm 1989). Hayek's notion of decentralized planning, however, is essentially a proposal for a set of *legal rules* that give much weight to private property and freedom of contract. As Walter Block (1979) has argued, the plan of government action that would best induce the utilization of local knowledge is a plan to privatize the urban landscape and to enforce the contracts of private parties, although (and here Block would disagree) a few minor attenuations of ownership might be in order, for example if crossing really did turn out to be a big and persistent problem.

The invisible hand is without central planning, but not without planning. It moves by a web of voluntary planning. Because the web is voluntary, its elements must appeal to the people involved. Except in the case of systematic externalities like air pollution, the principles of property and contract generate incentives to bring the particularistic parts into an abstract concatenation that can be said to be well coordinated. Voluntary planning is usually better informed, more responsive, more intelligent, and more humane than government planning.

If concatenate coordination is thought of as mutual coordination, Hayek will be misunderstood. Yet, if Hayek's process of coordination is thought to involve only speechless, atomistic market purchase, as in the textbooks, again Hayek will be misunderstood.

It is often thought that urban transit is too complex to be left to the invisible hand and that the invisible hand would only create problems. Yet, Hayek's line of thinking may lead one to the conclusion that the problems really lie in the fact that the invisible hand has not had proper scope to function.

CHAPTER 12

⌀

The Integrity of You and Your Trading Partners

The Demand for and Supply of Assurance

The exclusive privileges of corporations [that is, town occupational guilds] obstruct [the free circulation of labour] from one place to another... The pretence that corporations are necessary for the better government of the trade, is without any foundation. The real and effectual discipline which is exercised over a workman, is not that of his corporation, but that of his customers. It is the fear of losing their employment which restrains his frauds and corrects his negligence. An exclusive corporation necessarily weakens the force of this discipline. A particular set of workmen must then be employed, let them behave well or ill. It is upon this account, that in many large incorporated towns no tolerable workmen are to be found, even in some of the most necessary trades. If you would have your work tolerably executed, it must be done in the suburbs, where the workmen having no exclusive privilege, have nothing but their character to depend upon, and you must then smuggle it into the town as well as you can.

Adam Smith (WN: 146, 151)

To illustrate concatenate coordination, I have spoken of an interior designer who coordinates the colors in a room. The colors appear in the furniture, rugs, wall paints, pillows, and pictures. Now, consider a second facet of the designer's task. Suppose the colors are prone to changing, perhaps because the room is exposed to sunlight or usage will darken the

(177)

rugs or fabrics. In addition to the matter of color coordination, there is the matter of color *integrity*.

Likewise, when an inventor contrives a machine, besides the smart coordination of parts, there is the issue of the integrity of the parts. Will this bolt or fastener hold up? Will it maintain its integrity?

Trade has sometimes been interpreted as an exchange of promises. Even in the mundane purchase of a gallon of milk there are promises on both sides, that the milk is not spoiled and that the bills are not phony. We have spoken of the vast concatenation of factors and activities. We might think of it as a concatenation *of promises*. We have discussed the coordination of promises. In this chapter we discuss the integrity of promises.

As society becomes more complex the integrity issue looms larger. As Hayek put it, "The more civilized we become, the more relatively ignorant must each individual be of the facts on which the working of his civilization depends. The very division of knowledge increases the necessary ignorance of the individual" (1960: 26). Increases in the division of knowledge imply greater dependence on things unknown to us, and hence on trust in economic affairs.

THIS CHAPTER'S POLICY MOTIVATION: QUALITY AND SAFETY RESTRICTIONS

Many agree that bread demand and supply are best left to free enterprise. But many who favor free enterprise for tangible goods oppose it for quality and safety. The economist Jerome Rothenberg says, "The market's myriad decentralized actions do not themselves ensure adequate safety. Centralized controls of various sorts are needed. These have been instituted in the form of regulations, constraints, information programs, licensing and certification" (1993: 172). Sometimes economists and others espouse quality and safety restrictions such as housing codes, occupational licensing, pharmaceutical approval, consumer product recalls, financial exchange regulations, and workplace safety regulations.

I suggest that the reasons we favor free enterprise in bread carry over to quality and safety. There is a demand for assurance, and this tends to elicit a supply of assurance. Assurance itself is a sort of interpretation, so we are here talking about a system of interpretations.

TRUSTERS AND PROMISERS

In a trade, there are usually promises on both sides. When payment is made in cash and counterfeiting is very uncommon, and in many other cases, the trust problem resides mainly on one side. Even when the problem resides on both sides, we can usefully break it down by examining the separate problems. That is how I proceed.

Many transactions involve promises of quality and safety that cannot be fully verified before the fact. One party decides whether to trust the other to deliver what is promised. A consumer decides whether to trust the grocer or pharmacist or mechanic to deliver the quality promised. A merchant decides whether to trust a prospective employee. A landlord decides whether to trust a prospective tenant.

The canonical example is a creditor deciding whether to trust a borrower who promises to repay the loan. The trust relationship is clarified by Fig. 12.1. *Truster* (the creditor) decides either to trust or not trust *Promiser* (the prospective borrower). If Truster decides to trust, then Promiser decides whether to keep his promise or to cheat. If he keeps his promise, then both parties achieve a happy outcome—each receives a payoff of 1. If Promiser cheats, he gets a payoff of W and leaves Truster with a payoff of –1. If Truster initially suspects that W is greater than 1, then she suspects that Promiser will cheat, and she decides not to trust in the first place. Deciding not to trust results in a payoff of zero for both players. A lack of trust is a social tragedy, because it prevents society from achieving outcomes in which everyone is better off.

I employ the following analytic scheme:

- Promiser communicates the content of the promise.
- Truster heeds any of a variety of *assurances* of Promiser's trustworthiness.
- Truster thereby forms a level of *confidence* in Promiser's trustworthiness.
- The parties make the decisions as depicted in Fig. 12.1.

The parties may deviate from this scheme in many ways. They may negotiate the promise or restructure the relationship. They may make fulfillment incremental

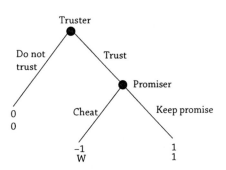

Figure 12.1: **Truster decides whether to trust promiser.**

rather than all at once, withhold payment until the promise is fulfilled, demand a security deposit, commit collateral, or attach a warranty or guarantee. But with suitable interpretation, every transaction that entails an element of trust may be viewed in the manner suggested above.

THE DEMAND FOR ASSURANCE

Truster owns a car, and the muffler is falling off. A local auto shop promises to do repairs honestly according to estimates. Truster seeks to produce for herself confidence in the promise, enough confidence to trust Promiser and to feel she has trusted responsibly. The inputs to her confidence production are any of the variety of assurances of trustworthiness. Thus, the entertaining of a promise ushers in a *demand for assurance*.

In the free enterprise system the demand for X tends to create opportunities for entrepreneurs to profit by supplying X.[1] When X is bread or toothpaste, we put a lot of stock in this dialectic. When X is assurance, some academic economists suggest that information asymmetries and externalities cause free markets to "fail." The Nobel economist Kenneth Arrow says: "Trust and similar values, loyalty or truthtelling, are examples of what the economist would call 'externalities'... They are not commodities for which trade on the open market is technically possible or even meaningful" (1974a: 23).

Too often, economists conceive of demand and supply in narrow terms—as the exchange or delivery of something the quantity of which can be measured along a horizontal axis. Equilibrium models such as textbook supply-and-demand blinker our understanding of that intangible and highly particularistic transaction cost, assurance.[2] The demand for assurance corresponds to particular promises, so in making the final decision about auto repairs, Truster assesses the combination:

(Thing-promised and its price, Confidence (Assurance), Other transaction costs**)**

---

1. The terms "demand," "entrepreneur," "profit," and "supply" are being used in broad senses.

2. Whether we ought to regard assurance as a transaction cost depends on how exactly we define transaction cost. If transaction costs are simply costs (other than price paid to the seller) of completing a transaction, assurance is not a transaction cost. If transaction costs are costs (other than price) of coming to, assessing, and completing an *ex-ante*-worthwhile transaction, then assurance is a transaction cost.

My contention is that the free enterprise system mobilizes an impressive, complex array of techniques to supply assurance, techniques which in one fashion or another potentially overcome or circumvent any of the particular pitfalls stressed by market-failure theorists and other pessimists. These assurances are themselves interpretations—the combination shown above and assessed by the consumer is an interpretation, and free enterprise tends to formulate and generate such combinations so as to appeal to voluntary trading partners. Even for assurance, then, the essential dialectic holds up well, and restrictions, which are often very costly, are typically unredeemed.

The supply of assurance uses many methods and takes many forms. I attempt to catalog the more important methods.

POINTED KNOWLEDGE CAN OBVIATE THE ROLE OF TRUST, OR PROVIDE A WARRANT FOR IT

The woman with the broken muffler seeks pointed knowledge. In inquiring about her broken muffler, the woman may come to apprehend the technical measures required; she may even find that she is able to fix it herself. If she can trace a good knowledge path, knowledge is less asymmetric, and she might circumvent the need for trust.

But knowledge that does nothing to advance her mechanical knowledge may be precisely what the woman needs. The woman may seek to discover not what is wrong with her muffler, but simply *who is an honest serviceman*. Her pointed knowledge may not provide a direct demonstration of quality but rather an assurance of quality. Similarly, in rhetoric, our warrant for an idea may be, not a direct demonstration of its validity, but its endorsement by a trusted authority. The knowledge she gains may tell her not about how her automobile operates but how the serviceman operates. Assurance itself becomes a valued input to the transaction, and those who can provide it will tend to prosper.

In any sort of personalized service, an important factor is face-to-face contact. By talking we may get a clearer understanding of the content of promises. Clarity, repetition, and publicness reinforce accountability. Sympathy and personal rapport is often part of the experience and necessary to informed treatment.

Even when trusters have little technical knowledge of the trouble, they can get an impression as to whether the promiser is trustworthy. It is always a good sign when the promiser takes pains to explain why the trouble is occurring and what the various options for remedy are. An understanding of the trouble usually comes down to a few basic relationships. Explaining the situation helps to inform the truster and creates a measure of accountability for the promiser.[3] In a wide range of contexts, the Internet and smart devices are making it easier to ask another question, to probe the content of promises and the integrity of promisers. Also, technology makes promisers more accountable, just as it reduces crime.

INFORMAL CHANNELS OF KNOWLEDGE SHARING

The housing development where I used to live has a homeowners association that issued a monthly newsletter. In one issue, there appeared recommendations for a plumber, a painter, an electrician, a Volvo mechanic, a window cleaner, a carpet cleaner, a piano tuner, a woodworker, a brick layer, a cabinet builder, a nanny, a handyman, a house cleaner, a furniture transporter, a floorer, two garage-door servicemen, and seven house cleaners. My neighbors provided the recommendations, acting individually and giving their own phone numbers for details. People in the neighborhood know each other well enough to doubt that anyone would take a bribe to recommend a lousy nanny or handyman. The recommended individual was quite likely to be an illegal practitioner, even an illegal alien.

The newsletter served as a sort of community concierge, steering members down happy knowledge paths. The newsletter column existed because there were knowledge problems to be solved. No one would get good-neighbor points or sympathy from the man in the breast for helping to solve a nonexistent problem.

Such a newsletter is a kind of local gossip. Gossip arises among family, friends, acquaintances, neighbors, and coworkers. It takes the forms of chatting, group meetings, correspondence, leaflets, bulletin boards, newsletters, local newspapers, websites, e-mail, Facebook, and Twitter. Anthropologist Sally Merry writes, "gossip can be viewed as a means of storing and retrieving information." "It forms dossiers on each member of one's community: who is a good curer, who can be approached for loans…who is a good worker, and who is a thief." In consequence, "the individual seeks to manage and control the information spread about him or her through gossip" (1984: 275, 279). In the marketplace, promisers do likewise by maintaining quality. If a promiser disappoints or cheats

---

3. Chatting might reveal the truster as naive, ignorant, or powerless, however.

a truster, she is likely to complain about it. Researchers have well documented that consumers are far more likely to spread knowledge about bad experiences than satisfactory experiences.

EXTENDED DEALINGS

Continuance, repetition, or knowledge sharing—forms of *extended dealings*—provide fertile ground for trust. Our power to reprimand a promiser, damage his reputation, or withdraw serves as a hostage that we hold against his promises.[4] Promisers build and protect their reputation, sensing the truth in the saying, "Time wounds all heels."

Gossip, letters of recommendation, newsletters, data banks, consumer survey literature, information reporting bureaus, referral agencies, electronic media all make for extended dealings. These practices serve not only those trusters who make use of them, but also those who do not. Although a promiser often knows whether a particular truster has frequent dealings, he rarely knows whether the truster has extended dealings, and nowadays must assume she does. The promiser must treat every truster as a conduit to others.

Lackadaisical trusters gain by the presence of persnickety trusters (except when they are being persnickety while we wait in line). Extended dealing exhibits positive externalities among the set of trusters, and there is an argument for government facilitation or performance of such services (Beales and Salop 1980). Even though this sort of free riding among the trusters does occur, the informed portion of the clientele does create a margin of punishment and reward, a margin that favors the trustworthy.

Extended dealings might benefit even trusters known to have isolated dealings. In the marketing of a standardized product, promisers cannot deal with trusters selectively. Protocol and the force of habit—including moral habits—usually keep the promiser honorable even when he knows that cheating would go unpunished (other than by his conscience, that is).

---

4. Common usage of the term "reputation" is sometimes at variance with my usage. In my usage, someone recognized for faithfully delivering the quality promised has a good reputation, even if that quality is regarded as low. My usage focuses on keeping the promise, not on what is promised. The content of the promise, however, is formed in large part by the quality that people come to expect, so my usage, in fact, addresses the broad notion of "reputation for quality" better than it might at first seem. Attached to every Nike product is the tacit statement "and we promise that it is of Nike quality."

TRUSTWORTHY PROMISERS CULTIVATE EXTENDED DEALINGS

Wary trusters share knowledge, but the practice is unwelcome only by promisers who are not trustworthy. Trustworthy promisers welcome knowledge sharing and, where permitted by law, tend to organize themselves to facilitate and expand the extension of dealings.

There are two ways in which a trustworthy promiser gains reputation by having a large base of trusters with extended dealings. First, when extended trusters are satisfied, they increase their own patronage and spread the good word. In his book *Industry and Trade*, Alfred Marshall (1927: 297) referred to "that highest form of advertisement, which comes from the recommendations of one customer to another; and from the inducements which dealings with one department offer to dealings with another." Second, promisers who enjoy a large extended base attract new, nondiscriminating trusters merely by the fact. Less persnickety trusters are attracted to a promiser with a large extended base, because they know that such a promiser has strong reputational incentives to make good, and that trustworthiness has probably been a means by which he achieved his standing.

THE UMBRELLA OF THE BRAND NAME

In the late nineteenth century, as transportation systems and mass production created a national market in America, consumers confronted "a profusion of unstandardized packaged goods... [and] unfamiliar selling and processing techniques," making it hard for them to judge such qualities as "the freshness of food or the durability of clothing" (Silber 1983: 3). The consumer historian continues:

> To ease the minds of customers about problems of quality, reliability, and safety, manufacturers and advertisers appealed to consumers to buy according to brand names. National Biscuit, Heinz Soup, Armour Meat, Standard Oil, and other companies placed one banner on many different products. The consumer who found one product of a brand to be satisfactory, those companies suggested, could assume that all other products also would be suitable.
>
> (3)

A brand name is a way of gathering together an array of services that make for frequent dealings. The array will be shaped by finding a fit with the tastes of the clientele (as well as by scope economies). Game theorists tell us that repetition makes for cooperation; hence promisers try to enhance repetition.

A machine-tool company such as Black & Decker makes hundreds of different products, but its customers will generalize to some extent about all of them based on their experience with only a few. By enlarging its product base the company creates frequent dealings with many of its customers, giving them a better opportunity to evaluate its trustworthiness. In this way, Black & Decker becomes a provider of assurance, as well as tools. The inventor-genius may contrive, *de novo*, in his basement workshop a fantastic new tool, but it is not a great *product* until it is combined with assurance. The inventor may find it advantageous to sell his invention to Black & Decker and let the firm offer it under the umbrella of its brand name. In a sense, Black & Decker is the expert that tells the truster that the new gizmo is trustworthy. Black & Decker is not merely a manufacturer, distributor, and advertiser, it is also a *knower* that grants its own seal of approval. A "knower" is anyone with valuable knowledge about the promiser's trustworthiness (in this case, the inventor's).

DEALERS MAKE FOR EXTENDED DEALINGS

Besides generating extended dealings with consumers, Black & Decker is at the center of a star-like pattern of dealings with scattered inventors. Consider the similar case of the used-car dealer. The used-car dealer might have only isolated dealings with the sellers of used cars. Although the dealer does not know the car's history, he knows how to inspect cars. He has broad parity, even superiority, in knowledge about the car, a parity or superiority that the ordinary individual would not have. By gathering up a stock of used cars from isolated sellers, the dealer produces a fixed lot of cars and a basis for extended dealings with buyers. Although he does not have many frequent customers, the dealer is a fixture in the community and a subject of gossip. A buyer gets to know her car intimately, and if disappointed will gossip. Also, the dealer can offer guarantees and warranties. The dealer, then, besides reducing transaction costs and upgrading the commodity, transforms a series of isolated dealings—many dyadic matchings between a buyer and a seller—into the star-like pattern shown in Fig. 12.2.[5]

---

5. Economist Eric Bond (1982) studied the market for used pick-up trucks, looking for lemons-market results, and found none. He reports: Pick-up "trucks that were purchased used required no more maintenance than trucks of similar age and lifetime mileage that had not been traded" (839). It would be interesting to learn whether used vehicles purchased from dealers require less maintenance than those purchased from isolated individuals.

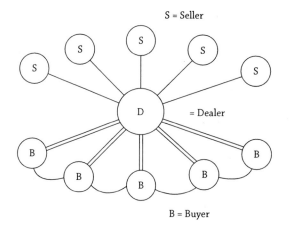

Figure 12.2: The dealer has a starlike pattern of dealings
With sellers, he deals on an equal knowledge footing. Once he has gathered the goods he has extended dealings with buyers.

Dealers often have credentials that enhance their credibility. The infrequent buyer feels that she can trust the credentialed dealer because the credential is a costly, irreversible investment. The truster is assured that the dealer has an incentive to protect his reputation, because he has the option of reaping the returns of honest and competent dealings.[6] Economist Gary Biglaiser says, "Coin and stamp dealers display to the public that they belong to dues-paying professional societies and are certified numismatists and philatelists... Many used-car dealers train mechanics to check and maintain car quality. If the dealers cheat customers and go out of business, then the investment in their employees' human capital is lost" (1993: 221).

REPUTATIONAL NEXUS AND THE MIDDLEMAN

My confidence in a handyman is strengthened by a neighbor's recommendation. My confidence is made still stronger by my neighbor's continued dealings with the handyman. The relationships form a *reputational nexus*, a constellation of extended dealings. In trusting the housecleaner, I become, in relation to my friend, *a potential knower*, and that enhances the housecleaner's motivation to keep her promises with me.

Reputational nexuses grow in the family, church, social club, neighborhood, workplace, and marketplace, creating a vast net connecting

6. See Marshall (1927: 270); Klein and Leffler (1981); DeLong (1991); Nichols (1998).

the social patchwork. Even in the days before the Internet and Facebook, social-network theorists figured that any pair of adult Americans could be linked by three or fewer intermediary acquaintances (Pool and Kochen 1978: 16).

The ordinary retailer demonstrates the reputational bridge. Many of the matches between consumers and producers are irregular—as when a consumer purchases an ulcer medication—but the consumer has extended dealings with the pharmacy, which in turn has extended dealings with the producer. As the economist Janet Landa says, "The middleman... mediates between traders... who do not trust each other but mutually trust the middleman" (1994: 125). The middleman creates a bridge of trust between two traders (see Fig. 12.3).

The liberal arts college is a middleman. It contracts with the promiser—the professor—and tries to build a reputation for general quality with trusters—students and parents. The firm, the chain store, and the trade association are all different species of contract nexus. Simple contracting can produce assurance in much the same way that a chain store does. The health care organization contracts with physicians and hospitals: the patient has extended dealings with the HMO, and the HMO has extended dealings with the physician. The reputational role of the HMO ranges over a contractual continuum, from employment within the firm (the staff model), through intermediate stages (group practice, individual practice associations), to selective contracting with health care providers (Wagner 1989).

THE MIDDLEMAN ALSO ACTS AS KNOWER

Besides straddling two extended relationships, the middleman also acts as a knower. The retailer specializes in knowing good products from bad—by recognizing brand names and seals of approval, studying the information on labels and packaging, keeping track of customer complaints and returns, conducting his own tests and investigations, hiring testing

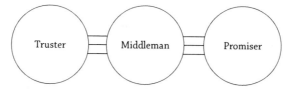

Figure 12.3: The middleman creates a bridge of trust between two traders

services, following trade or consumer literature, observing whether other retailers carry the product, and chatting with industry colleagues.

In his role as knower, the middleman works in knowledge that is often too costly for the consumer to gather and judge herself (Pashigian and Bowen 1994). In a sense, the premium she pays to the middleman, whether he is an established retailer, a brand-name manufacturer, or a contracting organization like an HMO, is a fee for the luxury of being uninformed yet assured.

No commodity is entitled to a strong market; it must concede its dependence on the services and institutions that produce recognition and assurance. Effective middlemen sell more of the product and at higher prices. Manufacturers respond by seeking to have their products carried by such middlemen. Like Landa (1994), I am using the term "middleman" in a sense that is much broader than the common usage, of the one in between a manufacturer and a retailer.

The two end points of the reputational link, the manufacturer and the consumer, both have an incentive to avoid the prisoners' dilemma outcome. Among the diverse, complex, and imperfect institutional experiments that take place in a free and open field, trusters and promisers will favor and sustain those experiments that produce assurance. Middlemen and knowers strive to produce it, because their cut comes from happy trusting outcomes.

KNOWER SERVICES: FEE FOR KNOWLEDGE

We might view gossiping as a sort of exchange. Sharing knowledge with acquaintances is one basis for our personal relationships. Knowledge sharing by gossip comes to be seen as a trade and as a source of profit. But the economist Hayne Leland says, "information on quality has many aspects of a public good: a consumer can give it away and still have it. Under such circumstances, inadequate resources will be channeled to providing information" (1980: 268).

Knowledge provision can be divided into generation and conveyance. Knowledge generation takes the forms of testing, inspecting, researching, interpreting, or evaluating. Consumers Union does all of these when generating product ratings in *Consumer Reports*. Consumers Union makes profits by selling its magazine to trusters. Is its information a public good? Once one person has the ratings, she can indeed share them with her friends and acquaintances—she may even sell her expertise in some manner. The law, however, forbids her from reproducing or selling the information. The information is proprietary and to a good extent excludable.[7] If you can protect information at the conveyance stage, then you can appropriate its value at the generation stage.

Excludability is often achieved in large measure by legal sanctions. Yet, often excludability is simply a matter of technical limitations on the part of would-be free-riders. Information conveyance requires the interpretive tasks of receiving, organization, storage, retrieval, and transmission. Credit bureaus such as Experian, TransUnion, and Equifax sell credit reports to trusters. They make profits by facilitating dealing, just as Manhattan parking entrepreneurs make profits by facilitating shopping. Experian releases valuable information to millions of parties every month, but that does not mean that they can appropriate the value of the information by reselling it. Experian provides highly individualized information. It makes information complete, speedy, and precise. For someone to free-ride on Experian by entering and competing, she would have to invest in vast data-processing systems. Kenneth Arrow jumps to conclusions when he says that in the absence of special legal protection, entrepreneurs cannot profit by sharing knowledge.[8] Like the private parking garage, the service performed by Experian is effectively excludable.

Consumers Union reports on standardized products, and its conveyance of information is uniform, not individualized. In consequence, it would be damaged by free-riding if its information were not protected by law. Experian deals in information of a more particularistic nature, namely credit records, and its conveyance is individualized. Its information is protected by the technical limitations of whoever might think of reselling the information, as well as by contractual protections and federal law. Whenever quality information is individualized, the opportunities for *re*conveying it are limited. Thus, knowers can make money by being hired by trusters to inspect customized security equipment, manufacturing plants, and used automobiles; to give second opinions on medical matters; and to evaluate prospective employees (Rees 1966). The beloved kibitzer can keep

---

7. *Consumer Reports* states its position in each issue: "Neither the Ratings nor the reports may be used in advertising or for any other commercial purpose. Consumers Union will take all steps open to it to prevent commercial use of its materials, its name, or the name of *Consumer Reports*." Silber (1983: 31) notes that in the 1950s, "Attorneys successfully protected the ratings of the magazine from unauthorized use by commercial interests."

8. "In the absence of special legal protection, the owner [of information] cannot, however, simply sell information in the open market. Any one purchaser can destroy the monopoly, since he can reproduce the information at little or no cost" (Arrow 1962/1971: 151).

up a steady trade in local gossip, because others cannot receive, interpret, organize, retrieve, and transmit information nearly as well as he can.

Kenneth Arrow has pointed out that trade in information is often hobbled by the fact that the "value of information is frequently not known in any meaningful sense to the buyer; if, indeed, he knew enough to measure the value of information, he would know the information itself" (1963: 946). In the case of *Consumer Reports* or Experian, however, the buyer does have a good idea of the value of the information she is purchasing, even though she does not know the information itself. Granted, the consumer cannot measure the value *perfectly* without in fact having the information, but she might know the range of the value, or the expected value. In this respect, *Consumer Reports* is like *The New York Times* or a novel or a movie ticket.

SEALS OF APPROVAL AND SELF-DISCLOSURE BY PROMISERS

When a knower generates basic quality information on a standardized product of interest to a wide class of trusters, reconveying the information might be easy, and he may go broke trying to sell information to trusters. In that case he goes to work for the promisers (Beales and Salop 1980). If a lack of parking spaces would prevent customers from coming to buy, and an independent parking entrepreneur could not exclude nonpayers, then the retailer would himself provide space for customer parking, at no charge. Similarly, if a lack of information would prevent trusters from entering into deals, the promiser provides the information. If his quality is high, he has every incentive to self-disclose far and wide.

Pauline Ippolito remarks on how sellers self-disclose:

> Low tar and nicotine cigarette sellers have been vigorous in distinguishing themselves from the higher tar brands (going far beyond the mandated disclosures in advertisements). High mileage automobiles often feature this fact in their advertisements. Lower calorie foods (especially in the diet soda and frozen food categories) have been very successful in conveying their superiority to higher calorie counterparts. The same is true for high fiber foods.[9]
>
> (1986: 23)

9. Ippolito and Mathios examine the effect of the removal in 1984 of a ban on health claims in the cereal market: "The evidence clearly demonstrates that fiber cereal consumption increased once the ban on health-claims advertising was removed. The development of fiber cereals also increased when producers were given the ability to advertise the health features of the products. Moreover, advertising appeared to reduce some of the differences across the population [of cereals], suggesting that

Sellers strive to demonstrate or indicate the uses, conveniences, durability, or special pleasures of their products or services.[10] They set up displays, employ salespeople to demonstrate and describe the product, advertise product characteristics, recruit referral agencies, and offer guarantees and warranties (which in Grossman's model (1981) lead to perfect disclosure). Assurance is a necessary input to the consumer's own production of confidence.

That the provision of knowledge may exhibit public-goods characteristics is not a curse to promisers but a blessing. An independent knower often evaluates quality or safety. If the word is favorable, the promiser broadcasts it. Computer and automotive advertisements tout "editor's choice" accolades, household products display the *Good Housekeeping* seal of approval, movie ads reproduce favorable excerpts from the critics, restaurants display favorable dining reviews. Gerald O'Driscoll (1976) argues that the American Express sticker on a merchant's window is a seal of approval.

Electronics manufacturers hire Underwriters' Laboratories to test and inspect their products and grant a UL mark upon approval.[11] Promisers assure trusters by advertising in media that police integrity—a strategy first employed against the quackery of patent medicine by *Ladies' Home Journal* (Calkins 1928: 49). Another class of knowers paid by promisers, particularly relevant to the issue of occupational licensing, is made up of professional schools, technical schools, institutes, and training programs that grant degrees and certificates. These credentials are then prominently displayed on office walls and listed in *curriculum vitae*. Transcripts and honors give a sort of rating system. Each of these organizations grants its own seal of approval.

Research on seals of approval has suggested that seals like the UL mark are not really understood by consumers and do not significantly enhance the consumers' confidence in the product (Parkinson 1975, Beltramini and Stafford 1993). Researchers show test subjects advertisements with and without seals of approval, and see if subjects have greater confidence in the ads with seals of approval. Such research is flawed for several reasons. First, assurances might gain meaning only

advertising may have had its effects by reducing the costs of acquiring information" (1990: 479).

10. Beales et al. (1981: 502f) offer a good discussion of self-disclosure, as well as of imperfections in the quality-information market generally.

11. Viscusi (1978) provides a model of quality certification that yields a happy outcome, in explicit contrast to the unhappy outcome of Akerlof's model (1970).

to consumers genuinely interested in the promise. Unlike genuine prospective buyers, test subjects do not have an interest in the particular products advertised, and hence do not have the incentive to gain pointed knowledge about relevant signals of quality. The research also says that consumers poorly understand seals of approval, because they do not know on what basis the seal is awarded. But again, pointed knowledge for the consumer is knowledge of whether products with the seals are more likely to be satisfactory, not formal knowledge of how seals are awarded. Knowledge of how seals are awarded might be known to only a few, but those few may provide the base upon which an inverted pyramid of divided knowledge is sustained, making the seal an effective signal to those farther up the pyramid who use only very limited pointed knowledge. In other words, advertising credibility may not be the relevant test of a seal's value: The seal may be most important to the distributors, retailers and other middlemen who decide whether to carry the product.

FRANCHISES AS A SYSTEM OF SEALS OF APPROVAL

When a motorist pulls off the interstate and into Joe's Garage for sudden repairs, she will have isolated dealings with Joe and feel vulnerable. The motorist would do better to pull into Midas, Shell, or Mobil, because if the local Midas franchisee cheats her, it faces the prospect of punishment. Punishment would come not from her (the motorist) but from the franchisor, which polices the service and probity of its franchisees using "mystery shoppers," audits, inspections, and complaint investigation. The franchisor *does* have to fear that the customer will harm the franchise by not returning or by injuring its reputation.

The franchisor is a knower who provides a seal of approval. When the serviceman wearing the Midas shirt and cap approaches us, he is not our connection to Midas. Midas is our connection to him. Midas is like a friend, and the serviceman is the friend of a friend. Although it is mutually understood that the motorist and the Midas franchisee will be interacting only once, the motorist has extended dealings (of an indirect sort) with the franchisor, who in turn has extended dealings with the franchisee. A franchise operation succeeds partly by capitalizing on product familiarity and low-cost replication of a successful formula, but also by producing that intangible input to mutual gains, assurance.

Knower is remunerated by

	TRUSTERS	PROMISERS
GENERATION	Hired inspectors (for buildings, automobiles) Letters of recommendation Doctors Financial advisors Hired investigators American Automobile Association	Credential givers (universities, institutes, training programs) Underwriters' Laboratories American Dental Association *US Pharmacopoeia* Good Housekeeping Security ratings (Moody's, Standard & Poor's) Securities underwriters Financial and accounting audits Notaries public Letters of recommendation Orthodox Union (kosher foods) Internet seals of approval (TrustE, Cyber Patrol, Safesurf, Verisign, BBB Online)
GENERATION AND CONVEYANCE	*Consumer Reports* Dun & Bradstreet Industry newsletters Hobby, product, and news publications Restaurant and movie reviews Employment agencies Brokers Internet chat groups (eBay)	Franchises Better Business Bureau Medical data banks Employment agencies Brokers (securities, real estate, produce, art, collectables)
CONVEYANCE	Gossip, e-mail, Facebook Consumer credit bureaus	Referral services Advertising firms Signs, labels, packaging, displays, sales help Web pages

Knower engages in knowledge

Figure 12.4: Classification of knower services

A CLASSIFICATION OF INDEPENDENT KNOWER ORGANIZATIONS

Two distinctions aid us in thinking about knower organizations. The first is whether the knower is remunerated by trusters or by promisers. The second is whether the knower is engaged in knowledge generation or conveyance, or both. Knowledge generation involves not only the collecting of information so as to make an evaluation, but, in the first instance, *the formulation or interpretation of quality and safety*. To attract voluntary trading partners, knowers must make and select *good interpretations* within which information is organized and given meaning. Knowledge conveyance is getting the knowledge across, and it is as much about communicating interpretation as transmitting bits of information. Using the two distinctions we get a classification scheme as shown in Fig. 12. 4.

Ways of Apprehending Untrustworthiness

Trustworthy promisers have every incentive to self-disclose. But the untrustworthy do not strive to self-disclose; in fact, they have a special incentive to deceive. How do trusters apprehend the untrustworthy?

One way is to ask for a public elucidation of the content of the promise. If they fudge and prevaricate, you get suspicious. Perhaps even more telling are the accolades, coveted seals of approval, and glowing endorsements that are not. When we view a curriculum vitae, a meagerness of distinctions will make itself evident and lead us to doubt outstanding ability. Similarly, trusters remain wary when they do not hear any of the wide variety of horns that trustworthy promisers blow in self-disclosing. It is precisely because the horns are unavailable to untrustworthy promisers that they are effective signals of quality.

One sort of evidence is the demonstration of traits distinctive to trustworthiness, such as announcing "Established in 1924," or promotional efforts lucrative only for a worthy promise (Klein and Leffler 1981). Before the Federal Deposit Insurance Corporation was created to bail out banks, banks had traditionally used large pillars and heavy marble in their architecture to signal permanence. Another way to apprehend untrustworthiness is to hire knower services. Hired inspectors, *Consumer Reports*, Dun & Bradstreet, Experian, Roger Ebert, and the neighborhood gossip all report on the trustworthy and untrustworthy alike.

A third way of apprehending untrustworthiness is forged by competitors. Promisers expose the poor characteristics of competitors' products, if only by insinuation, in advertisements, sales demonstrations, and marketing literature. Before the imposition in 1971 of restrictions on cigarette advertising, advertisements for low-tar brands sometimes pictured rival brands and listed the tar content beside each. Many researchers think that the restrictions have inhibited the market for low-tar cigarettes.[12] Competitive advertising is a great service to trusters, as it helps them discover product differences and the validity of product claims.

In his 1928 book *Business the Civilizer*, advertising executive Earnest Elmo Calkins wrote of an early case of competitive exposé:

> Dr. Lyon's Tooth Powder and Colgate's Dental Cream are both using their advertising space to offset undue claims instead of stretching them further. That is one of the values of advertising. It will correct itself. The lying advertisements will find themselves surrounded by truth and will be forced back in line by the weight of public opinion.
>
> (284)

Of the sixty-five advertising challenges resolved by the Better Business Bureau's National Advertising Division in 1992, almost all of which dealt with the truth and accuracy of advertising claims, 72% were brought by competitors.[13]

In the areas of health care and pharmaceuticals, competitive exposé is restricted—drug manufacturers are not permitted to report findings about their own products, much less their rivals'. A robust arena of self-disclosure and competitive exposé, also known as free speech, would help trusters gain the opportune, pointed knowledge they can really use (Ippolito and Mathios 1990: 479, Russo et al. 1986). In his famous paper on the market for lemons, George Akerlof (1970: 495) suggested that sometimes "dishonest dealings tend to drive honest dealings out of the market." Freedoms to engage in self-disclosure and competitive exposé—and, first of all, to enter and compete as a trustworthy alternative to the lemon—are what best ensure that honest dealings drive dishonest dealings out of the market.

---

12. "[T]he ban substantially increased the cost to firms of introducing new low-tar brands and the cost to consumers of obtaining information about these newer brands, thus slowing down the movement to these lower-tar cigarettes" (Schneider et al. 1981: 610).

13. BBB annual report for 1992 (2).

A FEW WORDS ABOUT THE FINANCIAL CRISIS OF 2008

Figure 12.4 includes "Securities ratings" and cries out the need for some qualification, especially in light of financial crises of 2008. In this chapter, the storytelling is simplified and meant to illuminate general tendencies of free, private enterprise in the demand and supply of assurance. The optimism of the chapter is not meant to deny that private enterprises—free or otherwise—often misrepresent product characteristics and omit knowledge that would be of interest to the truster. Sometimes private enterprise acts in ways—voluntarily, knowingly, and profitably—that injure concatenate coordination. I am interested in arguing that the dynamics of laissez-faire assurance are generally healthy, not that they are perfect. It is obvious that in the crises of 2008 private knowers did not keep up with actual conditions of quality of financial assets. But, at the end of the day, we are less interested in confidently describing how a system works than in comparing and judging alternative systems. Just about everything that can go wrong with laissez-faire assurance systems can go wrong with governmentally restricted assurance systems.

More specifically, there are things that are quite special about financial matters. First, contrast the finance example with the other examples given in this chapter. In medical services, building certifications, product quality, and pharmaceuticals, there is little if any interdependence between promisers. That is, the safety and efficacy of one ulcer medication is not interdependent with another, or with a flu vaccine, or with a heart medication. One auto mechanic's trustworthiness does not become degraded because another auto mechanic's trustworthiness becomes degraded. Even if all n-1 auto mechanics badly lose their trustworthiness, that will not keep the nth auto mechanic from maintaining his trustworthiness. It is very different with financial securities when lenders turn around and borrow, and borrowers turn around and lend, so they are all holding each other's promises. That's one thing that gives rise to *systemic risk*. There is no systemic risk in the matter of ulcer medications, auto repairs, or, it seems safe to say, *any* of the cases apart from financial interconnections. I concede that we should acknowledge systemic risk in interlocking financial systems, but that concession does not speak to the other kinds of goods and services treated in this chapter.

Second, in the finance example government intervention plays huge roles on all sides of assurances, as Jeffrey Friedman tells in his article "A Crisis of Politics, Not Economics: Complexity, Ignorance, and Policy Failure" (2009). A player of any kind can goof badly, and when it is a big player, the fallout can be big. Governmental institutions and governmentally privileged private institutions, including cartelized rating agencies, act as promisers, trusters, knowers, and middlemen. Assurance practices became systematically confused and degraded in part by the many large roles that government agencies, government guarantees, and restrictive policies played in the lead up to the crises of 2008. Assurance dynamics were operating in a highly governmentalized context. In the case of pharmaceuticals, by contrast, while government acts in the name of assurance to restrict the introduction of new pharmaceuticals, it does little to degrade the functioning of the private demand and supply of assurance of safety and efficacy. In the case of financial services, however, government interventions significantly confused and degraded both the supply and demand of assurance, because highly governmentalized institutions were acting not only as suppliers of assurance, but also as irresponsible *demanders* of assurance. Finally, there is the moral hazard and uncertainty of government bailouts.

There is yet another very important way in which financial assets differ from the examples of this chapter. The seller of an asset does not, in fact, promise that the asset will hold its value. When I buy a home or a mortgage-backed security and its value collapses, that does not mean that the seller broke a promise. I admit that my talk of "assurance of quality and safety" gets blurry here, but nonetheless there is a relevant difference between promising that your service has certain characteristics (or *qualities*) and promising that its future market value will be high. This chapter is focused on the former.

All told, I say that the failures in the financial arena do little to undermine the ideas of this chapter.

INTEGRITY AND HAYEKIAN DIALECTICS

What explains promise integrity? The answer turns out to be, excepting the tort-enforcement explanation, a special instance of the answer to the original question: *What explains promise coordination?* People truck, barter, and exchange, utilizing their local knowledge. To assure that promises will be kept, other promises are made. There is a demand for and supply of assurance:

> In actual life the fact that our inadequate knowledge of the available commodities or services is made up for by our experience with the persons or

firms supplying them—that competition is in a large measure competition for reputation or good will—is one of the most important facts which enables us to solve our daily problems. The function of competition is here precisely to teach us *who* will serve us well: which grocer or travel agency, which department store or hotel, which doctor or solicitor, we can expect to provide the most satisfactory solution for whatever particular personal problem we may have to face.

(Hayek 1948: 97)

But doesn't the "assurance industry," while supposedly solving one trust problem, simply create other trust problems? The manufacturer contracts with Underwriters' Laboratories, but how do we know we can trust UL? Do we not have a problem of assurance "regress"? UL would stand to lose much if, by compromising integrity, its reputation were injured. Hence it would be incorrect to say that the division of knowledge implies a constant amount of vulnerability, or constant amount of doubt. No such conservation principle holds, because in the competitive processes of voluntary affairs, assurances tend to be shifted to the ground where they are strongest. Voluntary mechanisms—abstention, shunning, exiting, free competition, individual contracting—deal with the regress problem much better than do the involuntary impositions of government. Just as government itself creates free-rider problems in purporting to solve free-rider problems (Tullock 1971), government creates assurance problems in purporting to solve assurance problems.

Telecommunications are vastly expanding all forms of knowledge exchange and assurance. When critics find some fault in e-commerce, such as doubts about privacy, security, or trustworthiness, entrepreneurs invent an e-solution, usually taking the form of a middleman service or a knower service.

Intellectuals and regulators working on quality and safety regulation should seriously consider how resourceful middlemen, expert knowers, trustworthy promisers, and wary trusters find ways to overcome shortcomings of the free enterprise system. The demand for assurance calls forth a supply of assurance.

CHAPTER 13

ᴄᚢᛉ

Outstripped by Unknowns

Intervention and the Pace of Technology

As the social machine becomes more complex and interdependent, it becomes increasingly easy for an aggressive group to disrupt it. The need for discipline is greater, the necessity more pressing. Individual freedom, always circumscribed, from the clan up, by the necessity of consideration of the rights of others, becomes inherently narrowed.

Vannevar Bush, "The Engineer and His Relation to Government,"
Science (July 30, 1937: 91)

From one fruitless care [the attention of government] was turned away to another care much more intricate, much more embarrassing, and just equally fruitless.

Adam Smith (WN: 434)

In the "Rinkonomics" chapter, I said that a central planner would make a mess of tracking, planning, and instructing the skating of 100 people in the roller rink. What if, however, the planner had some extraordinary new technologies? What if he had super capabilities in seeing what each skater sees, of integrating the patterns of the skaters, of formulating instantaneous plans and of relaying instruction to each skater? Maybe then central planning—in real time, as opposed to choreographed performance—would be more effective, perhaps even superior to the anarchy we know and love. Maybe technology can enable the central planner finally to conquer the knowledge problem and harmonize the skating of 100 people.

Suppose there are such extraordinary advances in technology. Does that undo our argument against central direction and control? That argument was based largely on the difficulty of dealing with complexity. Will technology someday catch up?

I think not. The skaters, are they not also equipped with these marvelous new technologies? Are their potentialities not also enriched and expanded? The central planner may have better powers of knowing, but do those powers keep up with the growing complexity of all that is to be known?

Here, I argue that the advance of technology actually bolsters the case against intervention and control. The main argument, treated later in the chapter, is the argument just sketched, that the pace of unknowns will tend to outstrip the pace of knowledge capability.

There is another kind of argument that also supports our contention about technology and the case for intervention: Technological advance often dissolves the momentary rationale for the particular intervention, and the more that technology has such potential, the less sense it makes to get locked into a regulatory apparatus based on some obsolete justification for intervening. (Fred Foldvary and I edited a book (2003) in which both arguments were developed in specific public-policy areas, including those touched on in this chapter.)

TECHNOLOGY WORKS TO RESOLVE MARKET IMPERFECTIONS

> Laws frequently continue in force long after the circumstances which first gave
> occasion to them, and which could alone render them reasonable, are no more.
> Adam Smith (WN: 383)

Writers have occasionally noted that a policy's appropriateness depends on the current state of alternative technologies and that technological changes make old policies obsolete and new policies worthwhile (Hayek 1979: 47, Rosen 1992: 68). Most market failure arguments boil down to claims about invisible-hand mechanisms being obstructed by some kind of transaction costs. If technology trims transaction and production costs, the invisible hand works better.

When technology advances, government, too, may become more effective; they too can run highways as toll roads. Or, consider a common argument against regulation: that it introduces noncompliance problems and requires costly enforcement. Insofar as technology facilitates government monitoring and enforcement, the case for government regulation gains strength. But if both free enterprise and the government are technically capable of, say, producing tomatoes, the sheer incentive argument recommends free enterprise. Good government itself is a public goods problem (Tullock 1971); government often fails to do the good that it is technically capable of. The free enterprise system, on the other hand, generally creates for its participants incentives to pursue what is good for society. Hence, the incentive advantage recommends free enterprise, given technical and institutional workability.

Technology Enables Metering, Excluding, and Charging

New technology is making it easier to define and enforce property rights, and to charge for use. The following are examples of this expanding capability:

> **Highways and parking.** Traditionally, highways have been publicly provided without explicit user charges. In the past, toll collection entailed significant transaction costs, such as delays and inconvenience for motorists, handling and securing of cash, and costly or unsightly toll booths or parking meters. Technology has greatly reduced the transaction costs of toll collection. Electronic tolling allows highway users to pay highway tolls as easily as they pay a monthly phone bill, weakening the case for operating highways as "freeways" and strengthening the case for privatization. Technology has also reduced the costs of charging for parking. Anyone with curb space to rent could do so without even erecting parking meters. One could well imagine turning on-street parking space over to private entrepreneurs or adjoining land owners, to rent by the minute using high-tech metering.

> **Marine resources.** New technologies are enhancing the ability to define, secure, trade, and enforce private property in marine resources. Just as ranchers and cattlemen in the American West secured and built up their property by virtue of such innovations as branding and barbed wire, today entrepreneurs can do likewise in oceans with the technologies of livestock herding, "fingerprinting," tagging, sonar, satellite tracking, creation of habitat, fencing, gating, and guarding. Technology has reduced the cost of private aquatic farming and ranching.

Technology Facilitates Quality and Safety Assurance

As discussed in the previous chapter, many government interventions in markets have a "consumer protection" rationale: Assurance of quality and safety cannot be adequately provided by voluntary practices and the court system. The argument is that accurate quality and safety information is costly or impossible for consumers to obtain. As consumers demand assurance, however, voluntary market processes find ways of supplying it. Service providers assure quality and safety by building and conveying a good reputation. They obtain certifications and seals of approval, seek affiliations with trusted sources, and develop a brand name. Consumers, for their part, also look to rating or recommending agents to ascertain reputations. All these methods and media depend on the generating, collecting, interpreting, formatting, storing, retrieving, and transmitting of information about service providers.

Medical services and products. Information technologies are enhancing quality assurance in medical care. Computer technology coupled with practice review and monitoring have given hospitals, clinics, health organizations, and insurers new means of evaluating practitioner performance. These institutions function as knowers and certifiers. Consumers themselves are more able to gain pointed expertise, by learning of available therapies, tapping knowledge of fellow patients, and checking the credentials and affiliations of practitioners. The Internet provides consumers with both technical knowledge and assurances. Also, rating organizations can develop a good reputation for conveying accurate assessments of sellers and manufacturers. Consumers may read detailed reviews online or look merely for the seal of approval. If assurance is inadequate the consumer may, with a click of the mouse, turn to another vendor.

Money and banking. Critics of free-market unregulated banking argue that such a system would be marred by bank runs and panics, hyperinflation, embezzling and counterfeiting. Such phenomena may be thought of as lapses of quality. Can banks meaningfully assure quality? Would a free banking system—without government guarantees and bailouts—prevent such problems? Managing solvency and providing assurances of solvency are especially viable today by virtue of technology. Up-to-the-moment financial statements and assessments can be generated and made widely available. Contractual arrangements giving banks options to delay redemption or withdrawal could be more easily posted, managed, and conveyed to worried depositors. Inflation and counterfeiting can be discouraged by rapid feedback mechanisms, such as adverse clearing. In an information age, reputation keeps more current and counts for more.

Technology and Natural Monopoly Arguments

The so-called public utilities—water, sanitation, electricity, natural gas, telephone, and cable television—are characterized by large fixed and low marginal costs. Such industries, it is said, cannot sustain competition, and, thus, they become natural monopolies. Monopoly providers charge higher than efficient prices, produce less than efficient quantities, and earn excessive profits. Potential competitors do not enter and bid down prices, because they understand that if they did invest in a competing system, the incumbent firm would reduce prices to marginal costs, resulting in losses for both firms. To prevent natural monopolies from charging more than marginal costs, many have argued, government ought to supervise such utilities and control their prices.

Technological changes provide alternatives that undermine the traditional cost assumptions about natural monopolies. Even if the engineering efficiencies of large-scale production improve in proportion to the engineering efficiencies of small-scale or decentralized production, it is important to realize that as the latter become increasingly viable, it becomes, in principle, increasingly possible to avoid altogether the *nonengineering* issues of being dependent on and enmeshed within a large-scale grid—which is nowadays a heavily governmentalized affair. The technological viability of small-scale alternatives could mean the opportunity to dodge many of the social and political costs of depending on "the public infrastructure."

> **Electricity.** Large central-station electric generators linked to consumers through monopoly transmission and distribution systems have been thought to have lower costs than decentralized generation systems. Thanks to technological advances, however, smallscale generation, powered by diesel, natural gas, or other fuels, and small local-distribution grids are now increasingly viable. Also, computer-controlled drilling and line laying allow workers to snake

under streets and buildings without above-ground disturbance and reduce the costs of entry.

Water and sanitation. Technological change is also reducing the cost of decentralized water-treatment systems that can compete against traditional public sector water and sewer monopolies that move massive amounts of water via the grid, both to and from users. An alternative is to develop on-site systems. Such systems would inventory a quantity of raw water, treat water according to a quality hierarchy for local uses, and then recover raw water from the waste for inventory and reuse. So-called gray water could be treated and used for landscaping, cooling, fire fighting, and sanitation. The small amount of water for sensitive human uses, such as bathing, cooking, and drinking, would be distilled to a purity and a safety that the current one-quality-fits-all water systems could not hope to match. The "black water" from toilets and kitchen-disposal units would be treated and disposed of via sewage, vacuum truck, or other method. Depending on recovery rates, the system would need replenishment from rainwater catchments, trucked water, or other sources. Combining on-site utilities may yield economies of scope (the heat from an electricity generator could warm and distill water, for example).

Postal services. Postal service has been a government monopoly in the United States, and most countries, despite the lack of good economic rationales. Technological advances have further undermined the rationales for the postal monopoly; postal communication now competes with myriad electronic alternatives. Express mail is already provided by private competitors, and the Internet provides for electronic payments and the transmission of documents with electronic signatures. For those who are concerned that rural service could not exist in a competitive market, the removal of monopoly protection for the U.S. Postal Service would allow a firm to carry newspapers, packages, and mail in one delivery.

Telecommunications. Telephone line and television cable networks have been regarded as natural monopolies because laying down multiple grids would duplicate great and uneconomical fixed costs. Long ago, J. Maurice Clark (1923: 321) concluded, however, that telephone companies showed no economies of scale, "but rather the opposite." The monopolization of telephony in the United States resulted chiefly from government policy that restricted competition and mandated regulated telephone rates. Technology has further weakened any claim of natural monopoly. Fiber-optic line and drilling technologies make competing lines more viable than ever. Wireless telephones and satellite television transmissions provide expanding dimensions of competition. Technology is blurring the lines of telephony, cable television, and Internet service. Change is rapid, and the hazard of regulatory fossilization is greater than usual.

THE COMPLEXITY/UNKNOWABILITY ARGUMENT

While admitting some symmetry in the effects of technology, I think that there is an important asymmetry that goes against governmentalization. Any form of government intervention or enterprise depends for its justification on an understanding of what the private enterprise economy would otherwise be lacking or failing to achieve. Justification for occupational licensing depends on consumers being unable, in a regime without licensing, to obtain quality and safety assurance. Utility regulation depends on theories of natural monopoly. Government activism is predicated on a belief that regulators or planners can *know the economy well enough* to restrict, manipulate or supplement it beneficially.

Yet, like the skating in a roller rink, the more complex the system, the more mischievous is the notion of centralized control. After all, even if the rink is without bound, the increased complexity does not pose a comparable problem for the individual skater. He does not interpret the whole; he utilizes pointed knowledge in pursuing opportunities of his particular time and place. The world economy is like a vast global roller rink. The complexity of that whole does not upset the individual actor, because the opportunities that he pursues are interpreted within his local view, from the few pieces and signals he learns to manage for himself. The individual is little concerned with global complexities; if it rains in his locale, he takes his umbrella. He does not try to know global meteorology.

Technology enhances government's ability to gather, collate and convey information; to monitor actions; to identify transgressions; and to enforce compliance. Technologies expand the informational capability of government. Improved technology, as previously mentioned, might improve regulators' knowledge of particular sets of activities, and might seem to recommend more interventions such as anti-trust restrictions. Decades ago, Kenneth Arrow wrote: "Indeed, with the development of mathematical programming and high-speed computers, the centralized alternative no longer appears preposterous. After all, it would appear that one could mimic the workings of a decentralized system by an appropriately chosen centralized algorithm" (Arrow 1974b: 5). Even though few today advocate "the centralized alternative," many still feel that by virtue of information technology government can actively manage or guide significant portions of the economy.

But technology accelerates economic change and multiplies the connections among activities. It integrates dimensions, connects multitudinous variables, and, moment by moment, alters constraints and opportunities. To know market arrangements—either those current or those that would exist under alternative policy—such fundamentals would have to remain unchanged for the time being. Yet technology makes the whole economy —that which is to be known—far more complex. It brings fundamental upsets, now and again, to even our best interpretations of current arrangements and of their shortcomings. After all, society includes the thoughts and potentialities of private individuals and organizations, each of whom has likewise enjoyed vastly expanded informational capabilities.

In *The Lexus and the Olive Tree*, Thomas Friedman relates comments from a friend that illustrate the contest between informational capability and complexity. He quotes Leon Cooperman, former director of research for Goldman Sachs:

> "When I joined Goldman Sachs in 1967...I was the head of research and I hired analysts. In those days, a typical analyst covered seventy-five companies...I was recently talking to one of the analysts I had hired back then and he told me he was terribly overworked now because he had to cover twelve companies. I just laughed. Only twelve companies? But you have to look into those twelve companies so much more deeply now in order to get some edge that it takes up all of his time."
>
> (Cooperman quoted in T. Friedman 1999: 101–102)

One might imagine that, because of today's high-speed data access, computation, and so on, the analyst would have been able to cover *more*, rather than fewer, companies. But his informational capabilities do not keep up with the complexity of the world to be analyzed.

In 1879, Cliffe Leslie, an Irish economist and expositor of Adam Smith, wrote: "[T]he movement of the economic world has been one from simplicity to complexity, from uniformity to diversity, from unbroken custom to change, and, therefore, from the known to the unknown."[1] In later years,

---

1. Leslie (1879/1888: 224). He writes also: "And just in proportion...as industry and commerce are developed, does the social economy become complex, diversified, changeful, uncertain, unpredictable, and hard to know, even in its existing phase" (223).

Friedrich Hayek took the point further: the economic world has moved not merely to the unknown, but to the *unknowable*. The effect of technology is asymmetric in the epistemic situations in which it leaves, respectively, private actors versus social planners (such as those at the FDA or the Anti-Trust Division). Technology's heightening of society's complexity outstrips its heightening of the social planner's informational capabilities.[2] As David Hume said, in order to recommend narrow limitations of our inquiries, "it suffices to make the slightest examination into the natural powers of the human mind, and to compare them with their objects" (1748/1902: 163).

Like Hume and Smith, Hayek drew a lesson for policy: Except in the most clear-cut cases of systemic harm, like air pollution, the supposition that government officials can figure out how to improve upon the results of decentralized (i.e., voluntary) decision making becomes more and more outlandish. In his Nobel lecture, Hayek (1974/1978) called that supposition the *pretense* of knowledge. As intellectuals who ponder the complex workings of the social world, we really know little aside from the hardy verities, such as that if those who participate in an activity do so voluntarily, each is probably bettering his or her own condition. The more complex the system, the more skeptical we ought to be about claims to knowledge that go beyond and against the hardy verities.

There are, then, two ways in which technological advancement enhances the case for free enterprise: 1) It reduces the costs that had obstructed (actually or supposedly) invisible hand mechanisms, and 2) it makes the economic system ever more complex, and makes the notion that interventionists can meaningfully know and beneficially manipulate the system ever less credible.

POLICY AREAS IN WHICH THE CONCLUSION MAY BE DOUBTFUL

Some cases seem to go against the general tendency. Technology might make it especially difficult to secure and appropriate the value of one's intellectual products, such as basic scientific research, ideas, inventions, software, music, and writings, because current technology vastly facilitates the replication of "knock-offs" and sharing without authorization. The situation might call for stepped-up government enforcement of patents and copyrights (whether one considers that government intervention or

---

2. See Roger Koppl, who writes, "The level of complexity is likely to outstrip our analytical engine" (2000: 105).

property-rights enforcement), or more interventionist measures, such as subsidization of knowledge and cultural products. On the other hand, unauthorized replication might, too, have a short technological half-life, as new technologies develop methods to foil unauthorized replication.

It may be argued that technology favors expanded government control of pollution, because it enhances the effectiveness of detection, measurement, impact assessment, and enforcement. Common law, however, traditionally treated air pollution as a nuisance, and direct polluter-pays policies keep to that spirit. If government uses new technologies to define and enforce property rights in water, airs, or animal resources, those might be seen as "nightwatchman" functions compatible with the principles of free enterprise.

Security is another area in which technology might suggest certain expansions of government activity. Capabilities to create advance quickly, but, alas, so do capabilities to destroy. New destructive capabilities in arms, biotechnology, and, eventually, nanotechnology might recommend certain security measures. Depending on the measures, we might not deem them "government intervention" but rather to be "nightwatchman" functions.

Finally, it might be argued that technology will make government more transparent and, hence, more accountable. We may put more trust in government because any abuse or outrage will be more readily exposed and investigated (Brin 1998). This optimistic factor surely has some validity; there has been a profusion of websites supplying information about candidates, their positions, their voting records, their contributors, and so on. One may argue that technology will facilitate public discourse, public understanding, and participation in direct democracy. Perhaps government can be made more accountable and reliable through "electronic town meetings," in which each citizen may delegate their voting rights to proxies (as in shareholders' meetings). If government were thereby improved, the case for activism might be strengthened. On this matter, it is useful to remember that knowledge entails not merely information, but also interpretation and judgment. A profusion of new information does not necessarily mean improvement in interpretation and judgment.

CONCLUSION

The appropriateness of alternative policies depends on the state of technology. The case for specific policies changes as technology changes. Thus, the pace of technology imposes on policies and their justifications what may be called a half-life. The faster technology advances, the shorter will be the half-life of policy rationales.

More specifically, technological advancement usually favors the effectiveness of free enterprise over government intervention. If that is the case, interventionists especially need to concern themselves with the intellectual half-life of their positions, lest they promote policies appropriate yesterday but no longer appropriate tomorrow.

Just as policy depends on the state of technology, so technology depends on policy. The technological advancements help solve social problems. In doing so, they bring participating parties some kind of betterment. Technological advancement is itself a member of the invisible hand, tending its current shortcomings. Voluntary social mechanisms and technological advancement enjoy a complex dialectic of mutual improvement.

Rethinking Our Way

The following chapter, "Unfolding the Allegory behind Market Communication and Social Error and Correction," further spells out the allegory of Joy, in particular as her leading a voluntary cooperation through the vast concatenation. The chapter takes ideas about an agent's knowledge and applies them to Joy as the agent in question.

Then comes "Conclusion: Liberalism These Past 250 Years," which spins up two fabrics and weaves the two together. One is a sketch of the liberal philosophical outlook hinted at throughout this book. The other is a historical narrative about the fortunes of that outlook since the time of Adam Smith.

CHAPTER 14

✺

Unfolding the Allegory behind Market Communication and Social Error and Correction

This opinion or apprehension, I say, seems first to be impressed by nature. Men are naturally led to ascribe to those mysterious beings, whatever they are, which happen, in any country, to be the objects of religious fear, all their own sentiments and passions. They have no other, they can conceive no other to ascribe to them. Those unknown intelligences which they imagine but see not, must necessarily be formed with some sort of resemblance to those intelligences of which they have experience.

Adam Smith (TMS: 163–164)

The only difference between [the system which places virtue in utility] and that which I have been endeavouring to establish, is, that it makes utility, and not sympathy, or the correspondent affection of the spectator, the natural and original measure of this proper degree.

(306)

Adam Smith enumerated not one but four sources of moral approval. What they were does not concern us just now—the paragraph (326–327) is reproduced here as an appendix. Though underplaying the tensions among the four sources, Smith nonetheless showed awareness of the tensions, as well as of the difficulty in distinguishing them. Smith did not pretend to any integration of the four sources. He did not pretend to solve for overall moral judgment. In fact, he scoffed at the pretense or aspiration of definitive resolution. Overall moral judgment, rather, is in the realm of the "loose, vague, and indeterminate," like "the rules that critics lay down for the attainment of what is sublime and elegant in composition" (175, 327).

The vague rules are explored by way of figurative or allegorical reasoning.[1] Smith invokes or sketches beings who judge the action or conduct. The rules of their judgment are vague but not empty or arbitrary. The figurative beings have ethical sensibilities, the sensibilities imparted by Smith's discourse. Conjuring the judges, Smith explores overall moral judgment in terms of what aspects of human conduct they regard as beautiful or becoming. Overall moral judgment is an aesthetics of human agency.[2] The judges are like the panel of judges of a figure-skating competition. They score performances; they indicate which they like and why. But they do not pretend to any determinate formula or precise grammar for figure-skating aesthetics. Their scores are rarely in exact agreement.

By marking their judgment in particular instances, enabling us to surmise their sensibilities,[3] Smith enables us to react to the judges, to discover whether we comfortably "enter into" their interpretations and attitudes, whether our sentiments "beat time" with theirs. We judge the judges. We do so by appealing to higher judges; we proceed, as it were, to the even sketchier panel that assesses the panel that assesses figure skating. Smith sketches the spectator not as a purely austere and inscrutable authority who issues an exact code of righteousness, but, in essential respects, as a being close to ourselves and to whom we morally respond. As Fonna Forman-Barzilai (2005) has explained, there is a dualism in spectating impartially: To spectate knowingly, one must be somewhat close/warm/soft toward the individual and his express part in the matter, but

---

1. I find one dictionary definition of *allegory* as: "an expressive style that uses fictional characters and events to describe some subject by suggestive resemblances; an extended metaphor."

2. Indeed, Smith could pass seamlessly between science and aesthetics. He narrated the history of astronomy as a quest for successively more beautiful or satisfying systems, and in treating music he spoke of the mind enjoying "not only a very great sensual, but a very high intellectual, pleasure, not unlike that which it derives from the contemplation of a great system in *any other science*" (EPS: 205, italics added; see also 212).

3. Charles Griswold beautifully highlights that for Smith an aesthetic sensibility is surmised from points or moments, not given as algorithm or formula: "Just as we do not know what nature is in and of itself, so too we do not know what the imagination in and of itself is, but we can describe its works in all of the ways that I have specified. Since we lack a theoretical account of mind *qua* mind, we seem to be largely left with an account of mind in terms of *how it comes to see nature in this or that particular way, and that is just the kind of account Smith aims to provide*" (1999: 343, italics added).

to judge impartiality one must be sufficiently distant/cool/tough toward that part, so as to do justice to the other parts touched by the matter (not just of other people but also of the first individual). The inherent dualism evokes Smith's (occasionally gendered[4]) dialectic of amiable and respectable virtues (TMS: 23, 306).

Smith says:

> All such sentiments suppose the idea of some other being, who is the natural judge of the person that feels them; and it is only by sympathy with the decisions of this arbiter of his conduct, that [the individual] can conceive, either the triumph of self-applause, or the shame of self-condemnation.
>
> (TMS: 193; see also 46 (fn), 165)[5]

Throughout Smith's work, figurative beings, though only sketchy, even subconscious, mediate social affairs and moral conduct. We relate to each other, and to ourselves, by way of substantive yet figurative beings and how they would feel about the matters in view. In Smith's 1761 essay on the first formation of languages, he comes to the following sentences:

> The word I, does not, like the word *man*, denote a particular class of objects, separated from all others by peculiar qualities of their own. It is far from being the name of a species, but, on the contrary, whenever it is made use of, it always denotes a precise individual, the particular person who then speaks. It may be said to be, at once, both what the logicians call, a singular, and what they call, a common term; and to join in its signification the seemingly opposite qualities of the most precise individuality, and the most extensive generalization.
>
> (LRBL: 219)

The precise individuality is clear enough, but the word *I* also always carries "the most extensive generalization," for we always conjure general, albeit tacit, perhaps unconscious, even instinctual, sensations of a being, sensations that mediate our understanding of the person who writes *I*.

---

4. Humanity, which "consists merely in the exquisite fellow-feeling," "is the virtue of a woman, generosity of a man. The fair-sex, who have commonly much more tenderness than ours, have seldom so much generosity" (TMS: 190). Also, Smith makes contrasting terms of "resolute" and "effeminate" (TMS: 187); see also "masculine firmness" (TMS: 209).

5. Likewise, in a letter Smith affirms "my Doctrine that our judgements concerning our own conduct have always a reference to the sentiments of some other being" (Corr.: 49).

We glean the general being that that person is like. For Smith, sympathy could be morally compelling even though "illusive" or "imaginary" (see, for example, 19, 21, 71, 78, 317). It is the nexus of such inchoate imaginings that enable us to relate to one another.

I believe that economists practice the Smithian way but are reticent, even unconscious, about doing so. One cause of the reticence is that the figure does not conform to images of science as precise and accurate, or "positive" and "objective." The Smithian awareness declares that economic judgment involves aesthetics, but popular images of science say that aesthetics are not supposed to play a role in scientific judgment.

Economists often hold up the idea of *economic efficiency* as precise, accurate, positive, and objective. I say that such claims are overdone and again invoke Coase (1960/1988: 43): "As Frank H. Knight has so often emphasized, problems of welfare economics must ultimately dissolve into a study of aesthetics and morals." A number of points argue that efficiency is much vaguer than often thought.[6]

I unfold the allegory in important economic tropes. One is the market process as "a system of telecommunications" (Hayek 1948: 87). In the literal sense, prices, profits, inventories, and so on communicate very little. In a figurative sense, however, prices may communicate how to advance the vast concatenation. When skeptics declare: "What communication

---

6. Some points one might make about why efficiency/willingness-to-pay concepts are often ambiguous would include: 1) The diminishing marginal utility of wealth; 2) The hypothetical nature of propositions, giving rise to ambiguities in, for example, the time-to-adjustment in deciding one's willingness to pay; 3) The collective action problems that might matter to the individual's contemplation of how much he would be willing to pay; 4) The issue of deeper, truer preferences, as opposed to unenlightened preferences, which is especially relevant in considering policy reforms; 5) Identity factors involved in changing policy; 6) Inasmuch as a policy reform would alter future preferences, perhaps of the new and future generations, we have to consider what preferences are worth fostering; 7) The Smithian distinction (TMS: 68, 83, 137, 188–192) between passive experience of the effects of a change and moral agency for the change; and 8) Economists often, perhaps usually, do not have good data on the willingnesses to pay that are most pertinent to their theoretical arguments.

And, where "economic efficiency" is confined in such a way as to make it relatively precise and accurate, it really is a lower-level criterion for overall judgment. That is, narrower, more precise notions of economic efficiency are not a final arbiter of the social good.

The following sentences appear at the very end of I.M.D. Little's book *A Critique of Welfare Economics* (1957): "Economic welfare is a subject in which rigour and refinement are probably worse than useless... It is satisfying, and impressive, that a rigourous logical system, with some apparent reality, should have been set up in the field of the social sciences: but we must not let ourselves be so impressed that we forget that its reality is obviously limited; and that the degree of such reality is a matter of judgement and opinion" (279).

are you talking about?" the economist—if unprepared to supply the allegory—can only offer explanations incorrect or nonsensical.

Another is the idea of market, social, or policy *error*. We often say that society or policymakers have erred. When we get out the microscope, however, we might find that no one erred. How do we have social error without any agent error? Lying behind the social error is allegorical error. Similarly, we often speak of *correction*, as in the claim that governments do not correct themselves as well as markets. We can make sense of it by unfolding the underlying allegory.

There are other economic tropes, not treated here, such as "social cost/benefit,"[7] and even "the economy," that may be clarified by bringing out the allegory behind the text. In a number of ways, important economic discourse is made clearer, more correct, and more accountable by seeing the allegory behind the text.

THE ALLEGORY BEHIND CONCATENATE COORDINATION

As shown in Chapter 3, what economists up to 1960 principally understood by *coordination* was a quality of a concatenation of activities and factors, here dubbed concatenate coordination. It invoked a judgment imputed to a mind imagined to behold the referent concatenation. If we refer to the concatenation within Adam Smith's pin factory—"placed at once under the view of the spectator" (WN: 14)—it is natural for the beholder to correspond to the owners, and to assume that the criterion behind coordinativeness was honest profits, a fairly precise and accurate rule. But when Hayek, Coase, and many others took the idea of coordination beyond the firm, just as Smith promptly took it to the global concatenation yielding the woolen coat, the precision and accuracy melted away. For the concatenation of the great skein, the imagined beholder is much less clearly defined. That did not stop them, however, from talking about coordination of the vast concatenation. Concatenate coordination invokes a Smithian sort of beholding, a figurative being. In talking about concatenate coordination, we develop ideas of the sensibilities proper to such a being. The circle of "we" tempers us to draw or entertain a being agreeable to the circle. We explore not only certain causes and effects narrowly conceived, but attitudes about the whole. We do so by discovering

7. James Buchanan's work often speaks of the allegorical basis behind talk of social costs and benefits, and of the economy.

and cultivating our sympathetic reactions to figurative "arbiters." Smith, Marx, Veblen, Keynes, Hayek, Myrdal, and Friedman symbolize figures that are relatively focal in the culture. How finely we delineate the being depends on the discourse situation and the circle of "we."

Adam Smith never used the word *coordination*, but the idea of concatenate coordination figures very prominently in his work and is plain enough, as when he wrote:

> Human society, when we contemplate it in a certain abstract and philosophical light, appears like a great, an immense machine, whose regular and harmonious movements produce a thousand agreeable effects. As in any other beautiful and noble machine that was the production of human art, whatever tended to render its movements more smooth and easy, would derive a beauty from this effect, and, on the contrary, whatever tended to obstruct them would displease upon that account: so virtue, which is, as it were, the fine polish to the wheels of society, necessarily pleases; while vice, like the vile rust, which makes them jar and grate upon one another, is as necessarily offensive.
>
> (TMS: 316, see also 165, 185)

As Smith turns to market forces, he uses analogy to illuminate their marvels. He sketches an aspect of concatenate coordination: "It is the interest of the people that their daily, weekly, and monthly consumption should be proportioned as exactly as possible to the supply of the season." In the pursuit of profit, the grain dealer adjusts price in ways that conduce to such concatenate coordination:

> Without intending the interest of the people, he is necessarily led, by a regard to his own interest, to treat them, even in years of scarcity, *pretty much in the same manner as the prudent master of a vessel is sometimes obliged to treat his crew.* When he foresees that provisions are likely to run short, he puts them upon short allowance. Though from excess of caution he should sometimes do this without any real necessity, yet all the inconveniences which his crew can thereby suffer are inconsiderable in comparison of the danger, misery, and ruin to which they might sometimes be exposed by a less provident conduct.
>
> (WN: 525, italics added)

The analogy of the prudent ship master is a miniature of the allegory of the being whose hand is invisible.

Unfolding the allegory behind concatenate coordination helps us to address some big questions in economics. Unfolding the allegory helps us to clarify what it means for entrepreneurship to be coordinative, and to assess whether it is *always* coordinative or only *usually* coordinative (or, perhaps, not even usually). Unfolding the allegory helps us to clarify what we mean if we say free enterprise is a system of *cooperation*. Unfolding the allegory might spare one from misrepresenting or overstating the case for economic liberalism. Meanwhile, it may *embolden* liberals and economists—by and large, entrepreneurship *is* coordinative, economic freedom *does* conduce to coordination, free enterprise *is* a system of cooperation—for we can justify those claims by virtue of, and *only* by virtue of, cogent allegories natural to human understanding.

THE MARKET SYSTEM AS A COMMUNICATION SYSTEM

One way to explore the free-enterprise system is to liken it to a system of benevolence working by communication. That is what Friedrich Hayek did in his famous essay "The Use of Knowledge in Society" and elsewhere. He posited the elimination of a source of tin, such as the collapse of a tin mine, traced out market adjustments, and said: "The whole acts as one market...so that through many intermediaries *the relevant information is communicated to all*." Further: "We must look at the price system as such a mechanism for communicating information if we want to understand its real function." And: "It is more than a metaphor to describe the price system as a kind of machinery for registering change, or a system of telecommunications" (1945/1948: 85–87, italics added). In his Nobel lecture, Hayek spoke of "a communication system which we call the market" (1974/1978: 7; see also 1955: 99, Lachmann 1956/1978: 62).

Hayek mostly avoided simile in speaking of the market system as a system of communication, just as Adam Smith did in speaking of the invisible hand.[8] God aside, Smith's "invisible hand" is fictitious. I think

---

8. There are varied interpretations of Smith's "invisible hand." My view is of a traditional classical-liberal sort, broadly in line, I believe, with a great many including F.W. Maitland, William Smart, Edwin Cannan, F.W. Hirst, A.L. Macfie, Jacob Viner, Friedrich Hayek, Ronald Coase, E.G. West, D.D. Raphael, Ian Ross, Norman Barry, Ronald Hamowy, Karen Vaughn, Jerry Muller, Peter Minowitz, Jeffrey Young, James Otteson, Craig Smith, and N.E. Aydinonat. My view takes exception to those who diminish its importance, see it as very specific to the textual neighborhoods in which it appears, or treat its referent to be behavior that is merely "self-interested," for example, variously, William Grampp, Emma Rothschild, and Gavin Kennedy, as well as to those, like Joseph Stiglitz, who would interpret the invisible hand narrowly in terms of "perfections" obtaining in certain equilibrium models.

that Hayek's "communication" is no less fictitious. Indeed, the two are basically the same (at least as we confine Smith's invisible hand to the matters addressed by Hayek). If, when we say that the market system communicates knowledge we are not prepared to elaborate the allegory, we can only speak falsehood or nonsense, for the statement is unsound save for the allegory.

Hayek writes as though market signals—prices, profit and loss, inventories, etc.—are forms of communication telling people how to advance the general interest. We should, however, mind the element of communion, or community, in communication. In its literal sense, communication is *a meeting of minds*. The knowledge communicated passes through us as commonly experienced ideas, images, or notions. It is much like the beat or melody of the music that Smith says we share. It passes through us in a common experience, neither mine, nor yours, but ours. An idea, image, or notion communicated is understood commonly by us, we feel the beat commonly or symmetrically.

At the supermarket, where a carton of eggs bears the price $1.89, there is *only one bit* of communication in a literal sense: the supermarket telling you, "Yours for $1.89." As for the entrepreneur computing her profit or loss, there really is *no* communication in the literal sense, no meeting of minds—whose mind would she meet? In no literal sense is the market system or anyone within it telling you to forgo tin or buy eggs.

From knowledge communicated, each party makes inferences, and inferences may be closer or farther from the basic knowledge communicated. If the price of tin is $5, a close inference might be "the price is higher than last month." As inferences get farther from the basic knowledge, it becomes less correct to say they have been communicated.

Crucial to Hayek, in fact, is that people's inferences are highly asymmetric, that, contrary to the common-knowledge assumption, all information is not commonly interpreted. Different people have different circumstances and perceive different opportunities in prices, etc. They interpret asymmetrically. Even "the price is high" might fit your interpretation but not mine. It makes little sense to say that inferences as to how one should respond to prices are matters of literal communication. We talk to merchants of their advantages, ready payment, said Smith, not our necessities, and even less our schemes.

Hayek means an allegorical communication. Hayek addresses the allegory most explicitly in his 1933 lecture at the London School of Economics, "The Trend of Economic Thinking":

Unfortunately, this oldest and most general result of the theory of social phenomena [viz., the spontaneous coordination of individual efforts] has never
been given a title which would secure it an adequate and permanent place in
our thinking. The limitations of language make it almost impossible to state
it without using misleading metaphorical words. The only intelligible form
of explanation for what I am trying to state would be to say—as we say in
German—that there is *sense* [*Sinn*] in the phenomena; that they perform a
necessary *function*.

(1933a/1991: 27)

We must work in a zone between embrace and rejection of such
allegories:

But as soon as we take such phrases in a literal sense, they become untrue.
It is an animistic, anthropomorphic interpretation of phenomena, the main
characteristic of which is that they are not willed by any mind. And as soon
as we recognize this, we tend to fall into an opposite error, which is, however,
very similar in kind: we deny the existence of what these terms are intended
to describe.

(27)

During the remainder of his career, Hayek wrote only fleetingly of a
"social mind" in his own theorizing. It may be that, launching as he did
so fully into attacking collectivist thought, he underplayed the allegory
behind his own text. James Buchanan is another thinker who notably
struggles in the zone between embracing and rejecting the allegory—
mostly rejecting but not always convincingly (see, e.g., 1999: 193–196).

The figure was hardly unknown. For example, Edwin Cannan—an
ardent Smithian and editor of *The Wealth of Nations* (1904)—wrote in
1902: "The reason why it pays to do the right thing—to do nearly what
an omniscient and omnipotent benevolent Inca would order to be done—are to
be looked for in the laws of value" (461, italics added). The free-enterprise
system, Cannan suggests, leads to patterns of activities that please a
benevolent being.

In Chapter 5 I posited a beholder and gave her the appellation Joy.
That beholder corresponds to the impartial spectator in *Theory of Moral
Sentiments* (though Smith wrote of the impartial spectator as a "he"). The
allegory in Cannan's remark is that Joy's knowledge encompasses what
Knud Haakonssen (1981: 79) distinguishes as system knowledge and con-
textual knowledge. Joy has system knowledge and contextual knowledge

for every individual. The allegory, to continue, is that Joy issues instructions, or requests, cooperatively, to each market participant spelling out "the right thing" to be done.

Joy tells Bridget the baker that perhaps she should buy new ovens, look out for better deals in flour, and advertise her confections. Within the allegory, Joy communicates these instructions to Bridget. Within the allegory, there is a meeting of Joy's and Bridget's minds regarding these instructions. Within the allegory, Bridget, who is sensible to Joy's benevolence and ethical wisdom and who feels entrusted to advance what Joy finds beautiful, follows not market signals, but Joy's communications, embraced voluntarily by Bridget from what Smith would call her *sense of duty*—she "enters, if I may say so, into the sentiments of that divine Being" (TMS: 276)—and those communications tell her to take actions rather like the actions that the market signals would lead her to take. Cannan suggests that the market conduces to socially beneficial actions much as a benevolent system of superior knowledge, communication, and cooperation would.

The allegory fits Smith's vision of virtuous behavior:

> But by acting according to the dictates of our moral faculties, we necessarily pursue the most effectual means for promoting the happiness of mankind, and may therefore be said, in some sense, *to co-operate with the Deity*, and to advance as far as in our power the plan of Providence.
>
> (TMS: 166; italics added)

The pervasive modifiers "nearly," "much as," and so on, are necessary and important. If interests coincided neatly and perfectly (as Bastiat in *Economic Harmonies* (1850/1996) seems to have suggested save for evil and error), then we would have much less trouble getting everyone to sympathize with a common, universal moral system. Morality would be a snap. Smith used *harmony* often but meant only a coarse or tolerable harmony. He writes, for example, that the sentiments of two people "may, it is evident, have such a correspondence with one another, as is sufficient for the harmony of society. Though they will never be unisons, they may be concords, and this is all this is wanted or required" (TMS: 22). As Maitland put it, "we cannot appeal to him as the father of those who see *nothing but harmonies* in political economy" (1875/2000: 132, italics added). Following Klamer et al. (2007), we may say that the central claims of Smithian political economy are *enthymemes*—meaning, claims that hold by and large, but not 100 percent of the time.

The figurative being exercises judgment, and we demand that its character or sensibilities be fleshed out. We want to know what kind of being we are being asked to go along with. We may well argue over the character of Joy. We distinguish multiple characterizations of Joys, perhaps as Joy_1, Joy_2, Joy_3, etc., and highlight and contend over the differences. Some are similar and form a family that we recognize and label. Sometimes, we downplay the family bickering and work with the more generic family representative, highlighting differences among separate families—"socialist," "liberal," "conservative,"—though also aware that all the Joys are of the broadest human family. The judging never ends, so we have to get used to the idea that any characterization of Joy invites a further one.

The game, however, is played by the rule that in some ultimate sense there is only one, universal Joy.

Consider some generic person Joe. According to Smith, the grand, allegorical impartial spectator, whom I call Joy, is not Joe's conscience. Joe's conscience, or "man in the breast," is only a *representative* of the impartial spectator (TMS: 215). Rather, Joy is Joe's conscience's conscience's conscience's...conscience. Joy is universal in that she is also Mary's and everyone else's conscience's conscience's conscience's...conscience. Each person's series is unique, but every series leads to Joy—which is not to say that everyone's conduct and sentiment conform to Joy. It is only a ground rule for the discussion.

Once we get comfortable, once a sense of Joy's character is sufficiently shared, once the circle of "we" is mutually coordinated, the allegory opens up a fruitful way to think about institutional quality. What institutional arrangements generate the "signals" that best "communicate" what to do? Such talk gets us to focus on what the relevant signals are. It gets us to focus on how well they conduce to the general interest. It helps us appreciate how "communications" adjust when practices go wrong. If the signals start "telling" people to go in the wrong direction, will the system correct itself? Will it tend to correct errors? Will it tend to keep up with changes? Also, will it dig up new opportunity, new matters for "communication"? The allegory of Joy communicating instructions is useful because it enables one to reason from the perspective of someone who has superior knowledge and purposes that we go along with.

Many writers in the "Austrian" tradition have acknowledged that prices do not literally communicate knowledge. In his presidential address to the Society for the Development of Austrian Economics, for example, Steven Horwitz (2004) offers the felicitous "knowledge surrogates" and references others who likewise seek to salvage Hayekian market communication despite the fact that, in a literal sense, prices communicate almost nothing. My residual dissatisfaction with Horwitz and others writing in the same vein is that they neglect—even stubbornly resist!—explaining the allegory of knowledge surrogacy. If they were to unfold the Smithian sort of allegory embedded in knowledge surrogacy, they would upset "Austrian" strictures concerning social aggregation and social welfare and the particular modernist image of scientific economics expounded by Ludwig von Mises (for whom economic theory was axiomatic, categorical, apodictic, deductive, *wertfrei*, etc.). They might become as much "Scottish" as "Austrian" economists. If latter-day "Austrians" were to open themselves up to Smith, see his paramount place in the great conversation, and see that Hayek is closer to Smith than to Mises, they would face the choice of either shedding the "Austrian" identity or withdrawing into the styles of reasoning distinctive to Mises, Murray Rothbard, and those associated with the Ludwig von Mises Institute.

UNFOLDING THE ALLEGORY MAKES IT INNOCUOUS

A.L. Macfie (1967a) noted, "the theory and politics of the eighteenth century did not permit of any explicit theory of *society* as in some sense a *living human organism*" (69), and Hayek (1955) was probably right to criticize social-organism thinking as misleading or worse. But unfolding the allegory is no slippery slope to grief. Cannan makes the being an Inca, to make sure that his readers do not start looking around for a benevolent, omniscient, omnipotent being. Making the allegory explicit makes it clear that it is a fiction. There is no being telling Bridget to replace her ovens. And to the extent that moral norms exist within living society, they do not make a social organism. If Joy were a god, she would not have any powers over the individual save that of conveying her approbation or disapprobation, sensed within one's own breast. The more the allegory is spelled out—in particular, as Joy being *knowing*—the less it seems to correspond to any external being or institution, perhaps least of all government. Smith was right that we work by sympathies with figurative beings, and rejecting such awareness is not sensible. But by embracing the insight, and by explicitly developing a figure with certain sensibilities, and explaining how different institutional arrangements appeal to those sensibilities, liberals and economists may advance a spirit or ethos that contends for recognition and understanding.

AGENT ERROR

Agent error is not merely risk that turned out badly. A poker player who makes a good bet but draws a "bad beat" did not make an error. One identifies an action as "error" from an imagined perspective *ex ante* to the play-out but wise to other potential interpretations of the hand. At the agent level, error entails a sense of regret. That is absent in the case of the poker player drawing a "bad beat," who so often afterward graciously says, "That's poker." Smith put it this way: "If notwithstanding all his skill, however, the good player should, by the influence of chance, happen to lose, the loss ought to be a matter, rather of merriment, than of serious sorrow. He has made no false stroke; he has done nothing which he ought to be ashamed of" (TMS: 279).

Israel Kirzner tells of a person walking along the street, seeing *and reading* a sign offering apples for $1, yet proceeding to buy apples elsewhere for $2. Kirzner writes: "[S]urely, in an important sense he will, when he realizes his mistake, reproach himself for having been so absentminded as to pass by the bargain, *which he saw*, for the more expensive purchase. In this sense he *did* commit an error, the error of not acting on the information available to him or not perceiving fully the opportunity before his very nose" (1979: 129–130). Kirzner repeatedly associates error with regret and self-reproach.[9]

Actual regret occurs when you acted on one interpretation of the situation ("apples will cost me $2"), and later you reproach yourself for not having had the insight and judgment instead to see and act on another superior interpretation ("apples will cost me $1"). But, also, the sense of regret or self-reproach can be only vicarious or potential. You might speak of an individual, such as your brother-in-law or any of a class of people caught in a familiar syndrome, acting in error because under a not fantastic counterfactual—a counterfactual made more relevant and possible by your discussing the error—he could see, or could have seen, the better interpretation.

---

9. This regret/self-reproach-based definition agrees neatly with *some* of Israel Kirzner's expositions of error. In my view, however, Kirzner is inconsistent, at times holding a broader conception that would not necessarily entail any kind of regret or self-reproach. Kirzner rightly notes that the obviousness of the missed opportunity, and hence the basis for regret or self-reproach, "must be a matter of degree" (1992a: 22). The issue, then, becomes how one draws the lines to delineate error. At times Kirzner, as in the quoted passage, seems to draw the lines, as I do in Chapter 6, such that error is the missing of obvious opportunities and entails a sense of regret, but at other times (e.g., 1992a: 21–23) he draws the lines much wider, at not-totally-unobvious, and drops the necessity of any regret or self-reproach. For further discussion of the difference, see Chapter 16 of this book.

In discussing affection as habitual sympathy, Smith brings up the syndrome of family members who have grown up in absence: "The absent son, the absent brother, is not like other ordinary sons and brothers; but an all-perfect son, an all-perfect brother; and the most romantic hopes are entertained of the happiness to be enjoyed in the friendship and conversation of such persons...Time and experience, however, I am afraid, too frequently undeceive them" (TMS: 221).

Such syndrome is an example of error based on regret that may be only vicarious or potential. If someone you know lays plans to reunite with a previously absent and supposedly perfect relative, you might say that he acts in error, because you see vicariously, or he sees potentially, the badness of the interpretation he acts on. His interpretive lenses are rose-tinted. A better interpretation is available—he can find it in on page 221 of *The Theory of Moral Sentiments*.

Smith noted that the word *I* simultaneously carries two significations, one of "the most precise individuality," the other of "the most extensive generalization" (LRBL: 219). These two significations are only "*seemingly* opposite" (italics added), for human individuality is not all that individual. We put ourselves in each other's shoes, relate to the apparent situation, and judge each other's actions. Just as Hayek indicated a zone in which we carefully invoke a notion of social sense or function, we work in zones of generalization in which we feel we know the individual's purposes and situation well enough to judge his action. The zone is a sort of overlap region, an intersection of *closeness to the individual*, to understand his partial view of things, and *distance from him* so as not to be entangled in his partialness. As Forman-Barzilai puts it, "for Smith, the sympathy model is effective for producing impartial moral judgments because the spectator is *at once* both involved and detached" (2005: 193). Further: "[A]n ideal Smithian perspective will be that of a spectator who is essentially Janus-faced: near enough to access the meaning and vicissitudes of a particular situation but distant enough not to be entangled within them—both hot and cool" (204).

Self-reproach is reflexive, entailing a sort of multiplicity of selves. It is useful to think of an actor calling on internal subagents or routines. When the subagent or routine messes up in the instant, spilling a drink or mistyping a word, the mishap is best called a *mistake*. The actor curses angrily, as though reprimanding a subordinate. But the actor saying *I* in the situation is itself an agency embedded in a larger being, and sometimes it comes to doubt itself, it feels that it employs the wrong routines, it suspects that it has made an *error*. It feels regret, not anger. The actor resides in a hierarchy. Error, for him, relates to what is above, mistakes to what is below. Erring is poorly interpreting the situation; making a mistake is slipping up within the situation. Error is regretting the path one embarked on; mistake is slipping up along the path. Likewise, on the happy side, affirmation of the plan may be distinguished from fulfillment of the plan. Plan affirmation does not imply plan fulfillment, and plan fulfillment does not imply plan affirmation. Although the terms *mistake* and *error* are often used interchangeably,[10] economists have found it useful to distinguish them.[11] Also, it should be noted that it is impossible to eradicate a theoretical domain for error, for any agent that says *I* must emerge from and be subordinate to higher (or deeper) levels. The uppermost articulated level carries hints, understandings, questions, and aspirations relating to a lowermost nonarticulated level, and it is fatal to deny the tacit contacts to higher matters.[12] As a practical matter, there is always a realm above the articulated *I*, there is always a *yet* superior character (cf. TMS: 137), a *yet* more exalted propriety (cf. 192).

We see the difference also when we turn to correction. Correcting a mistake is revising the instant. A typing mistake is corrected by retyping the word. Correcting an error, however, involves more significant reform of the actor and of how he manages his sub-routines.

In his economics, Smith gave too scant attention to these matters.[13] In the morals, however, he linked error and remorse. For example, he tells

10. One reason that *error* and *mistake* are often used interchangeably is that mistakes alert us to possible error—if a student's paper is filled with mistakes, maybe he needs to rethink his idea of having done his homework. Another is that action is situated, such that what is to one agent an error may be to a higher agent a mistake, just as the fifth floor of a building is up to some and down to others. Yet another reason may be that there is no verb for *mistake*, and hence we resort to using the verb *to err* even for mistakes.

11. Our distinction between mistake and error comports with Kirzner (1979: 121–122) and with the distinction made by Polanyi (1963) between "faults committed within an acceptable framework" and "rational applications of an unacceptable framework" (87).

12. See Polanyi 1962, 1963, 1966; Hayek 1952: 185, 189, 194; 1955: 89; 1963/1967: 62; Chapter 6 of this book.

13. Smith's deficiency was picked up on by others including Jeremy Bentham (1787/2008), J.B. Say (see quotes in Hodgskin 1827/1966: 54–57), Thomas Hodgskin (1827: 34, 45–99, 120), James Maitland Lauderdale (1819/1966: 265–304), and John Rae. Regarding the last two, Macfie writes: "[Lauderdale and Rae] thought Smith's theory should give more weight to the importance of invention, novelty, new arrangements in history. Smith, of course, did much here, but to Lauderdale and Rae invention is picked on as the core of economic growth, and this is suggested as the central issue in theory and practice. One cannot say this of the *Wealth of Nations*" (1967a: 35).

of characters in Voltaire who, faced with conflicting interpretations of their moral duty, commit a crime and then "discover their error, and the fraud which had deceived them, and are distracted with horror, remorse, and resentment" (177).[14] Smith's thought is suffused with appreciation of knowledge's richness.[15]

ERROR AND CORRECTION AS APPLIED TO AN ALLEGORICAL BEING

The preceding section supplied a formulation of *agent* error and *agent* correction. When it comes to the pervasive talk of "*market* error," "*social* error" or "*policy* error," we find statements that are best expounded by way of a figurative being. The statements are meaningful fundamentally as agent error *applied to an allegorical being.*

Israel Kirzner has much to teach humankind, but, his protestations notwithstanding, many of his teachings make sense only by virtue of Smithian turns and qualifications. In the case of market error, Kirzner writes:

> Except in the never-attained state of complete equilibrium, each market is characterized by opportunities for pure entrepreneurial profit. These opportunities *are created by earlier entrepreneurial errors* which have resulted in shortages, surplus, misallocated resources.
>
> (2000: 16; italics added)

Consider an example raised by Kirzner (250f), the invention of the automobile. Kirzner suggests that it devastated the livelihoods of many who had built their entire careers around the horse-drawn-carriage industry. Kirzner's writings would suggest that the malinvestments were a result of error. Such unfulfilled plans were based on "an erroneously imagined decision framework" (17). Kirzner links the earlier error with a process of correction. He writes that "earlier entrepreneurial errors have created profit opportunities which provide the incentives of entrepreneurial corrective decisions to be made" (31). Elsewhere Kirzner (1985) writes that

14. Also, in discussing self-deceit, Smith mentions error and regret (TMS: 158).

15. Again, a prime example is when Smith, in *The Wealth of Nations*, says that, in the matter of judging how society's interest relates to his own, one may be "unfit to judge even though he was fully informed" (266).

"To act entrepreneurially is to identify situations overlooked until now because of error" (52).

Speaking historically, surely some of those in the horse-drawn-carriage industry had erred. The invention of the automobile, however, was a highly exceptional event. It is possible that only some, it is conceivable, in fact, that *none*, in the horse-drawn-carriage industry actually looked back on their undertakings with a feeling that they had acted foolishly, that they should have been more aware than they were. They may not have erred. They may have all felt like the poker player who made a good play but drew a "bad beat." Similarly, it is conceivable that no individual undertook any correction of a foregoing error.

The general interpretation of the market correction is best expounded as analogous to how a figurative being who gives instructions might have felt about it. As we look back on the economic history, we know things that our predecessors did not, and we attribute such knowledge to our figurative being. If Joy knew what was coming—and surely some inventors had early anticipations of what was in fact coming—and she nonetheless communicated instructions to build and expand livery stables and stage-coach lines—undertakings that subsequently did not pay off socially— Joy would be erring. Her giving of such instructions is something that *she* would look back on with regret or self-reproach. She would feel she erred. As those bad instructions were reversed and she reconsidered whatever had impelled such a faulty plan, *she would be correcting her error*. Like the metaphor of market communication, the talk of market error and correction is fundamentally understood by way of allegory.

If we deny the allegory, if we confine our thinking and talk to *agent* error and correction, we may fall into statements that are not justifiable in those terms. But the point here is not to avoid talk of market communication, error, and correction. Kirzner's theorizing, indeed, may help us see how Joy error and correction relate to agent error and correction, and thus to justify the figurative theorizing. The theorist typically invokes a perspective that no one in the story quite possesses, a perspective attributed to some enlarged beholder. Again, the Joy-like being is not a glinty inscrutable figure, but a being that understands and sympathizes with us, a being in the zone of both intimate knowledge and less partiality. Her benevolence is such that what makes a set of instructions issuing from her erroneous will tend to correspond to vicarious or potential errors for people in the story of the market process. Kirzner is right that equilibrium modeling provides no scope for human error or human imagination (2000: 59); his brilliance lies in seeing the need and doing the work to get such things into economic theory. But our endeavor gains by unfolding the Smithian elements—a turn vehemently rejected by Kirzner (2000: Ch. 7; 2010). Behind the will of the individual as he goes about his market activity, there are figurative beings, perhaps only inchoate or unconscious,[16] and behind the theorizing of the economist, there are figurative beings seemingly appropriate to the discourse situation, *and the two are related.* The error of the individual may be only vicarious or potential—in that it invokes an onlooker who reinterprets what he does. That onlooker is related to the onlooker invoked by the theorist who talks of market error and correction. Lon Fuller, an eminent legal scholar whose work drew in a fundamental way on *The Theory of Moral Sentiments,* wrote:

> The economist may not care what the consumer wants, but he cannot be indifferent to the process by which the consumer reaches his decision as to what he wants. If he is to understand that process, the economist must be capable of participating in it vicariously and have an understanding of its terms.
>
> (1969: 18)

The relatedness between theorizer and theorized, like that between judge and judged of, may draw on Kirzner's insights and help give them power, for, if Kirzner is right, and I think he is, that in *most* (though not all) market moments there is a tendency for the individual to correct his errors and there is no tendency for him to make errors (2000: 31), then the suggested relatedness helps to sustain the general idea that there are tendencies for market processes to avoid and correct Joy errors.

The being with an invisible hand is an allegory invoked in theorizing about spontaneous order, a being that sees the particulars of what to us remain only abstract generalizations, abstract theoretical tendencies. Meanwhile, the impartial spectator—or, rather, his representative (TMS: 215)—is the ordinary individual's moral counselor, especially sensitive to commutative justice and established propriety but also to the becoming virtues. Perhaps Joy corresponds in some way to both. Perhaps we have a duality, or at least a potential duality. Smith says that religion "gave a sanction to the rules of morality, long before the age of artificial reasoning and philosophy" (TMS: 164). In the age of artificial reasoning and philosophy, perhaps common understandings of vast social coordination and com-

---

16. James Otteson stresses that our moral bearings may be unconscious (2002: 21, 104–106, 116, 123–124, 264).

mon understandings of mundane propriety evolve along paths potentially roughly parallel, depending on the cultural ecology.

SOCIAL OR POLICY ERROR

Adam Smith favored separation of church and state but was concerned that little sects might breed morals "disagreeably rigorous and unsocial" and suggested "remedies" by which the state might "*correct* whatever was unsocial or disagreeably rigorous in the morals of all the little sects" (WN: 796, italics added). Does Smith mean to say that the state corrects the agent error of the individual sectarian? I think not, at least not primarily. The correction and implied error are social, which is to say allegorical. Smith's talk is perfectly natural, but the allegory is rarely spelled out. Consider a matter in which economists often diagnose the existing interventionist policy as error and prescribe correction in the form of liberalization.

Economists who study the U.S. Food and Drug Administration are accustomed to analyzing its decision of whether to permit a new drug as one involving a trade-off between two possible bad outcomes, as shown in Fig. 14.1.

Economists say the FDA apparatus is faulty because the FDA officials are overly prone to Type-2 bad outcomes and are too stingy with permissions. Economists who publish judgments on the matter really do very

	Permitting would be beneficial	Permitting would be harmful
The FDA reviewers . . . permit the drug	Good outcome	Type-1 bad outcome: Permitting a bad drug. Victims are identifiable, traceable and might appear on television.
do not permit the drug	Type-2 bad outcome: Not permitting a beneficial drug. Victims are not identifiable and scarcely even acknowledged in the abstract.	Good outcome

Figure 14.1: Two types of bad outcomes for an FDA permit decision

preponderantly say this.[17] I should note that economists' judgments are based significantly also on the suppression of drug development—that is, restrictiveness discourages researchers and drug makers from generating many would-have-been drugs from ever being in a position to enter into the context of Fig. 14.1.

In the literature, bad outcome is often called "error," but I want to focus on the higher-level managing of the trade-off between the bad outcomes. I suggest that standard discourse implicitly projects the allegory of Joy running a benevolent and super-knowledgeable system of communications and cooperation. We confine her possible communication to instructions about the general stance the official should take, that is, his stance with respect to permissiveness.[18] Every outcome involves an element of luck: Just as in poker a lost hand does not necessarily indicate bad play, an unfortunate outcome does not necessarily indicate error. Joy's communication tells the FDA official how permissive to be, what "cut points" to use, in deciding whether to permit drugs.[19]

FDA officials are too stingy. It is said that "the FDA is erring" or "society is erring" or "we are erring." But the "error" talk is best understood by way of an allegory involving a being like Joy. If the FDA's actions flowed from Joy's communications, then we would deem Joy's communications to be in error, for her communications would in that case have FDA officials too often withholding permission. The definition of agent error is being applied to Joy, as the agent in question.

But Joy's point of view stands in contrast to that of the FDA official as the structures actually exist and function. Economists, including Stigler (1966: 74–75) and Coase (1975/1994: 59), have been quick to explain that the individual FDA reviewer does *not* necessarily err when he is stingy with permission, because the consequences of permitting a bad drug loom much larger for him personally than do the consequences of not permitting a good drug. Although it is possible that the human agents involved

17. See D. Klein (2008: 319). Meanwhile, Klein and Briggeman (2010a) summoned over 44 economists to a questionnaire on the policy of banned-till-permitted, yielding a bona fide enlargement of conversation (Briggeman et al. 2010).

18. If we, instead, allowed Joy's instructions to be specific to each individual drug decision, so that Joy might use her super knowledge of the particular case, we would weaken the affinity between the agent's context and Joy's framework for issuing instructions.

19. Conceivably these "cut points" would otherwise become so permissive as to run into further issues of the FDA abiding by the legislation that it is charged with executing, but it is clear that there is ample scope for relaxation without running into such issues.

in the process do err, the more central point is that they need not: *The high rate of Type-2 bad outcomes (and the associate suppression of drug development) does not necessarily reflect any agent error.* The human agents do not necessarily feel any regret or self-reproach, even of only the vicarious or potential sorts. Perhaps the error told of in the familiar analysis is *only* figurative.

The figurative dimension does not hinge on assuming no agent error. Even if we assume that some of the agents did err, it is the figurative that is more fundamental. The vicarious or potential regret can be said to fall back on some notion of a generalized being the actor could have sympathized with, could have seen himself as like. Indeed, Smith's internal arbiters—he speaks of the conscience, the inhabitant, inmate, or man within the breast, the impartial spectator, the *supposed* impartial spectator, the *representative* of the impartial spectator—are all usefully interpreted as allegorical or metaphorical figures. Smith even lets on: "The real *or even imaginary* presence of the impartial spectator, the authority of the man within the breast, is always at hand" (TMS: 292, italics added).

I suspect that the conclusion that there is social error without any agent error rubs us, as human beings, the wrong way. I suspect that we are programmed[20] to think that if there is social error, somewhere along the line there must be agent errors. If, as some allege, our instincts are rooted in the Paleolithic small band, a society so simple that any sense of social error would plausibly be amenable to correction by the alphas, it would make sense that we instinctively feel that social error implies agent error.

I suspect that we are programmed to think that Smith's fourth source of moral approval, particularly the aesthetic beauty in the social system writ large advancing happiness, tends to go with the other three sources, which have to do with the propriety of the microbehaviors in terms of the actor's intentions, the moral responses of those affected, and how those microinteractions fit customs or established rules of conduct. Indeed, there are cultural dynamics that may give rise to such consonance among the four sources of moral approval: When some analyst, at 100,000 feet up, notices failings at the grand fourth source, she tends to voice them and challenge the sense of propriety that has till now inhered in the baneful microbehaviors. In a book like Thomas Schelling's *Micromotives and*

---

20. Programmed, that is culturally or genetically, though, as Hayek argues, culture plays such a large role in both genetic selection and genetic exfoliation that the distinction is dubious.

Macrobehavior (1978), someone explains how erstwhile blameless micro-motives spell bad macrobehavior, people read the book, and the trouble-some microbehavior *becomes less blameless*. Smith, who rode a position of cultural royalty, tended in *The Theory of Moral Sentiments* to play up such consonance, at least in affairs among "equals."

In a world checkered with baneful policies that enjoy official propri-ety and the assent or even approval of the cultural elites, and are awfully impervious to challenge, the presumption of consonance seems much less assured. We should allow that even very persistent Joy error does not nec-essarily entail any agent error of the *actual* sort (as opposed to the vicari-ous or potential sorts). If humans tend to overestimate the traversability of the impasse between Joy error and agent error, that could help explain why they are disinclined to bring out the allegory behind social error, for they feel they can make do by indicating agent errors.

Humane aspiration certainly goes along with supposing that some-one on the ground could feel self-reproach in his helping to establish or preserve what, from 100,000 feet up, is seen as a baneful arrangement of practices. At any rate, the culture tends to welcome such humane opti-mism. Presuming agent error, focusing on agent error, then, signals one's rejection of the disagreeable, fatalistic view of no agent error. Indeed, to embrace the fatalistic view, to surrender hope for potential agent regret and efforts at vicarious agent regret, would be to give up engagement and fundamentally to reject Smith's Solonic outlook. Signaling against the fatalistic view might help explain why the allegory remains as tacit as it does.[21]

SOCIAL OR POLICY CORRECTION—OR LACK THEREOF

Hayek, Kirzner, Armen Alchian (1950), and others have stressed that the fertility and flexibility of an economic system lie in its propensities to cor-rect its own errors—that is, Joy errors. Consider what happens when an FDA-permitted drug is found to be harmful. Patients suffer and actors

---

21. Incidentally, among the ways that the great economist George Stigler in his last three decades distinguished himself was by propounding the fatalistic view (e.g., 1982), as well as by championing the related views that knowledge should be flattened down to information and that the concept of liberty was nugatory. His inconsistencies and absurdities in these matters were often so immediate that sympathetic onlookers tend to see his sermons as arch irony. Less sympathetic onlookers may see them as irresponsible whimsy.

in the private nexus adjust rapidly, as the patients, doctors, pharmacies, health institutions, the manufacturer, lawyers, journalists, and others quickly stop the harm; they act quickly to correct the Joy errors.

How well do Joy errors located in government self-correct? Permitting a bad drug leads to identifiable sufferers and public outcry. Not permitting a beneficial drug, however, leads to little public outcry. The suffering is relatively neglected, *unseen*, overshadowed by what is officially intended. FDA critics who identify the Joy error in FDA stinginess—who, that is, do the analysis at Smith's fourth source—seem to have very little political or cultural traction; they too seem to be largely ignored. That is why the FDA official may feel secure and just as regards Smith's first three sources of moral approval. Moreover, each person tends to get locked into basic beliefs and outlooks[22]—"I may become more deeply entrenched in my historical context, progressively less capable of understanding myself and others" (Forman-Barzilai 2005: 208)—a fact that dims our hopes of her coming to feel regret. Within the socio-politico-cultural ecology, therefore, the evolution of the links between Joy interest and agent interest, the process for correcting Joy errors, is often extremely bad.

Smith and Hayek taught that libertarian arrangements tend to align Joy and agent interest. In the free context, most Joy errors tend to be self-correcting. In a highly governmentalized context, many of the most grievous Joy errors do not have similar tendencies toward self-correction. Buchanan says, "There is no political counterpart to Adam Smith's invisible hand" (1999: 458).

AGENT ERROR IS A MATTER OF CULTURE

The FDA official may pretend to be deciding with the general interest in mind—he may pretend to be following the communications that would flow from a benevolent figurative being. Yet often he does not, either because the pretense is fake or because he misunderstands the general interest and how to advance it. Perhaps his figurative beings differ quite fundamentally from others'.

---

22. On the lock-in of ideological views by the age of twenty-five or thirty, see for example Jennings (1990: 347–348), Alwin et al. (1991: 60), and Sears and Funk (1999: 1). La Rochefoucauld, Smith (TMS: 158), Kierkegaard, and Schopenhauer also make pertinent remarks.

One reason that the microcontexts of bad policy often feel just is that, by procedure and by taboo, political culture has cordoned off certain aspects and consequences, particularly those on coercees and their would-be trading partners, into seemingly separate moral contexts or, indeed, into docility, acquiescence, silence, and invisibility. Whether the FDA official would reproach himself for being stingy depends on his moral qualities, intellectual understandings, and cultural pressures. As Forman-Barzilai says, rendering an enlarged cross-cultural judgment "requires that the spectator be able to question and sometimes subvert the very measure by which he has become accustomed to judging himself and the world" (2005: 207). Lauren Brubaker expresses similar concerns:

> The desire to receive the sympathy or approval of others, however, leads us to conform to the opinions of others. When the actual spectators and the impartial spectator are in conflict, as is almost always the case when there are divisions or disagreements in society, the desire for sympathy is corrupting. Under most political conditions, then, the natural desire for sympathy leads us to adopt the partial opinions of our religious, ethnic, political or economic peers at the expense of impartiality.
>
> (Brubaker 2006: 200–201)

What is so saddening about governmentalization is that it not merely suppresses the fruits of voluntary actions but breeds cultures that make the bonds of candid and natural discourse, sympathy, and approbation so clouded, conflicted, and weak. Smith writes:

> The great pleasure of conversation and society, besides, arises from a certain correspondence of sentiments and opinions, from a certain harmony of minds, which like so many musical instruments coincide and keep time with one another. But this most delightful harmony cannot be obtained unless there is a free communication of sentiments and opinions.
>
> (TMS: 337)

Governmentalization sometimes perversely tends toward the disjoining of one source level from the next, yielding cultural confusion, degeneracy, deep disharmonies, and unhappiness. For many people, these moral and cultural consequences are quite central in judging policy and politics—more central, in fact, than they usually manage to communicate. We want a better world materially, but, more important, we want a better world culturally. Indeed, when we read Smith's descriptions of the "superior stations," where unlike "the middling and inferior stations" honesty is not the best policy (TMS: 63–66), when we notice Smith's confidence in and favor for active agency rather than passive bystanding (TMS: 68, 83, 137, 188–191), and when we heed his emphasis on the love and esteem of "those we live with,"[23] we feel that Smith is concerned primarily with the moral and cultural, as opposed to the material. "What can be added to the happiness of the man," Smith asks, "who is in health, who is out of debt, and has a clear conscience?" (TMS: 45).

In addition to the officially superior stations, things are difficult also when it comes to cultural figures. One must judge the wisdom and scruple of the scholar and the pundit. He may be very eminent and, by well established standards, satisfy moral norms at the first three sources of moral approval, but his ideas may be nefarious and fail in the matter of the fourth source, although he does not think so.

Some measure of correction may come by directing understanding, criticism, and judgment to what is being done and what should be done. These efforts help to align Joy error and agent error. After all, what actually keeps government and political culture from being much worse is not any democratic accountability but rather the fair measure of decency and enlightenment nestled within each agent within those structures. It is primarily as lattice of not-too-terribly-unenlightened despots that politics works as well as it does.

CONCLUDING REMARKS

Most of the morality plays in *The Theory of Moral Sentiments* are of a private nature—interaction among neighbors or "equals"[24] in which the broad social view plays little role. That is why the impartial spectator is usually thought to be a personal moral advisor, not a political economist. *The Wealth of Nations*, however, was an annex of *The Theory of Moral Sentiments*, making together a more extensive system of moral sentiments. *The Wealth of Nations* explores the broad view in *The Theory of Moral Sentiments'* fourth source especially as concerns commercial behavior and

23. TMS: 116, 122, 166–167, 200, 213, 253–254, 272, 295, 297, 298, 307.
24. As noted by editors D.D. Raphael and A.L. Macfie from the fourth edition (1774) on the title page: "The Theory of Moral Sentiments, Or An Essay towards an Analysis of the Principles by which Men naturally judge concerning the Conduct and Character, *first of their Neighbours*, and afterwards of themselves" (italics added).

public policy.[25] In that sense, contrary to what Alec Macfie (1967b: 10) and Vivienne Brown (1994: 46) observe, perhaps the impartial spectator *does* appear in *The Wealth of Nations*—as its author (suggested by Bitterman 1940: 520).[26] For, if the inmate within the reader's breast is its representative, and if "To direct the judgments of this inmate is the great purpose of all systems of morality" (TMS: 293, see also 329), then the author of such a system, if edifying and properly so, would be akin to the impartial spectator.

When people espouse "the most abominable maxims of conduct," and "we are eager to refute and expose such detestable principles," Smith says (TMS: 89) we cannot appeal directly to the "intrinsic hatefulness and detestableness" of those principles. Rather, we try to show why they should be hated and detested, and, as we "cast about," "the consideration which first occurs to us, is the disorder and confusion" that follow from practicing such principles. "We seldom fail, therefore, to insist upon this topic"—such as by writing *The Wealth of Nations*.

Smith was culturally tops in his day, but times have changed. In the worst cases, totalitarian cases, Hayek suggested, the worst get on top. The situation today in the United States and elsewhere is not nearly as bad as that, but still, many of the positions of greatest political and cultural power tend to attract, breed, or prosper people who are less than attuned to Smith's moral and economic sensibilities. Those more attuned may criticize them, but such criticism may smack up against the simpler sources of moral approval. It is obnoxious and offensive, at least to those criticized and all who go along with their sentiments and eminence. One consequence may be dismissal and freeze-out of our enlightened critic, reducing the good he does.

In a letter to David Ricardo, James Mill (1818/2005) urged Ricardo to follow "the plain rule of utility which will always guide you right, and in which there is no mystery." Quoting the passage, Macfie adds: "No mystery for James Mill; but for Adam Smith there was always mystery" (1967a: 146). For those who heed moral guides like those heeded by Smith and

---

25. My remarks about *The Wealth of Nations* as an annex of *The Theory of Moral Sentiments* comport with Stewart (1794/1982: 310–315); Haakonssen (1981: Ch. 4); Young (1997: Ch. 8, esp. 192–193, 201); Macfie (1967a: 61–62, 75f); and Otteson (2002).

26. The phrase "impartial spectator" does not appear in *The Wealth of Nations*, but in the closing pages Smith writes that a union between Great Britain and the colonies would put the colonists at a great distance from "the center of the empire"—London—and would render "them more indifferent and impartial spectators of the conduct of all" (WN: 945).

Hayek, the mystery may seem to grow ever more perplexing, but, still, there are helpful answers and less partial resolutions. There is sense in the liberal cultural project. That sense is well served by bringing implicit figures more clearly out into the open.

APPENDIX

Adam Smith's Paragraph about the Four Sources of Moral Approval

Here, Smith is criticizing Francis Hutcheson's doctrine of a moral sense. Smith writes that in his own system the four sources of moral approval leave no place for a further moral sense.

> When we approve of any character or action, the sentiments which we feel, are, according to the foregoing system, derived from four sources, which are in some respects different from one another. First, we sympathize with the motives of the agent; secondly, we enter into the gratitude of those who receive the benefit of his actions; thirdly, we observe that his conduct has been agreeable to the general rules by which those two sympathies generally act; and, last of all, when we consider such actions as making a part of a system of behaviour which tends to promote the happiness either of the individual or of the society, they appear to derive a beauty from this utility, not unlike that which we ascribe to any well-contrived machine. After deducting, in any one particular case, all that must be acknowledged to proceed from some one or other of these four principles, I should be glad to know what remains, and I shall freely allow this overplus to be ascribed to a moral sense, or to any other peculiar faculty, provided any body will ascertain precisely what this overplus is. It might be expected, perhaps, that if there was any such peculiar principle, such as this moral sense is supposed to be, we should feel it, in some particular cases, separated and detached from every other, as we often feel joy, sorrow, hope, and fear, pure and unmixed with any other emotion. This however, I imagine, cannot even be pretended. I have never heard any instance alleged in which this principle could be said to exert itself alone and unmixed with sympathy or antipathy, with gratitude or resentment, with the perception of the agreement or disagreement of any action to an established rule, or last of all with that general taste for beauty and order which is excited by inanimated as well as by animated objects.

> (TMS: 326–327)

CHAPTER 15

⌒∿⌒

Conclusion

Liberalism These Past 250 Years

But, while it is easy to show the absurdity of most concrete attempts to make the social sciences 'scientific,' it is much less easy to put up a convincing defense of our own methods, which, though satisfying to most people in particular applications, are, if looked at with a critical eye, suspiciously similar to what is popularly known as 'medieval scholasticism.'

Friedrich Hayek (1948: 58)

If you don't know where you are going, you could end up somewhere else.

Yogi Berra

It is fitting to end a book by reiterating its key ideas in relation to our larger purposes. I here relate our ideas to certain currents since the time when *The Theory of Moral Sentiments* was new. To contextualize the discussion, I state a series of facts about *The Theory of Moral Sentiments*:

- As a Glasgow professor, Smith had had local prominence, but his first book established him as a leading Scots thinker. Upon its appearance in 1759, *The Theory of Moral Sentiments* was a success. It appeared in "no fewer than twenty-six editions in English between 1759 and 1825, together with six editions of three separate translations into French and two editions of two separate translations into German." It "was read by a fairly comprehensive sample of the leading philosophers during this period" (Reeder 1997: vii). In 1776, *The Wealth of Nations* raised the stature of an already pre-eminent moral philosopher.

- *The Theory of Moral Sentiments* was mysterious and difficult to fathom. Moreover, its author had a stately persona, and he continued to revise to the sixth edition of 1790. It took time for critics to develop criticism and put it before the public. The critics included Scotsmen Lord Kames, Thomas Reid, and Adam Ferguson, all in private unpublished materials, and, after Smith's death in 1790, then in print by Dugald Stewart and his students Thomas Brown and James Mackintosh, as well as by several Frenchmen. These authors (whose critiques are neatly gathered in Reeder 1997) all explain their dissatisfactions with TMS, and none embraces it. Stewart would advance to intellectual leadership in Scotland, and he preferred the "common sense" teachings of his professor and friend Reid. Stewart wrote:

> It is only to be regretted, that, instead of the metaphorical expression of '*the man within the breast* [etc....]' [Smith] had not made use of the simpler and more familiar words *reason* and *conscience*. This mode of speaking [that is, "man within the breast," etc.]...has the effect, with many readers, of keeping out of view the real state of the question, and...to encourage among inferior writers a figurative or allegorical style in treating of subjects which, more than any other, require all the simplicity, precision, and logical consistency of which language is susceptible.
>
> (Stewart 1828/1997: 125–126)

The influential Alexander Bain (1868: 642) wrote: "It is not without reason that Stewart warns against grounding theories on metaphorical expressions." Within a few generations after Smith's passing, TMS is effectively set aside.

- After 1830 or so, there followed about 150 years during which TMS was scarcely read. In 1873, James F. Stephen asked: "Did anybody, except perhaps Mr. Buckle, ever feel any enthusiasm about [Smith]?" (22). Buckle himself says that TMS "has had no influence except on a very small class of metaphysicians" (1861/1904: 895). TMS is treated rather scornfully by Walter Bagehot (1876/1915: 12–15, 24) and Leslie Stephen (1876: 71–78). In 1927, the exceptional Glenn Morrow wrote of TMS resting in "oblivion": "Few people ever read it now, except antiquaries of thought and persons celebrating the sesquicentennial of the *Wealth of Nations*" (336; see also Morrow 1923). As late as 1985, Samuel Brittan said that TMS "would not be studied today except by a few specialists in the period if Smith had not gone on to write the later work" (51–52).

- The disregard of TMS is particularly noteworthy in the classical liberal/libertarian tradition. My searches, fairly extensive, show virtually no engagement with TMS by William Godwin, Jeremy Bentham, James Mill (a classroom pupil of Stewart), and John Mill, nor by David Ricardo, Nassau Senior, and J.R. McCulloch (another classroom pupil of Stewart); nor by Richard Cobden, John Bright, Lord Acton, John Morley, Auberon Herbert, Henry Sumner Maine, F.W. Maitland, A.V. Dicey, Isaiah Berlin, Michael Oakeshott, and Ernst Gellner; nor the Frenchmen Destutt de Tracy, J.B. Say, Alexis de Tocqueville, and Frédéric Bastiat; nor the Germans Alexander Rüstow, Rudolf Rocker, and Wilhelm Röpke; nor the Americans William G. Sumner, H.L. Mencken, Albert Jay Nock, Ayn Rand, and Robert Nozick. Individualist thinkers have often hailed from economics, but practically nothing about TMS is said by Henry George and his followers; by Frank Knight, Milton Friedman, George Stigler, and Chicago and UCLA economics; by Carl Menger, Friedrich von Wieser, Eugen von Böhm-Bawerk, Mises, Rothbard, and their followers; by James Buchanan, Gordon Tullock, and public-choice economics. Even Hayek scarcely references TMS.
- "Oblivion" is confirmed, though qualified, by listing the English-language attention that TMS did receive prior to 1976 (the Glasgow/OUP edition) or even 1982 (the Liberty Fund reprint). TMS is mentioned and quoted by Richard Whately (1832/1966: 44f), Herbert Spencer (1851/1970: 89; 1871/1901: 346), Henry Hazlitt (1964: 56–57, 110, 113, 118), and Lon Fuller (1969: 6), but without deep engagement. Edwin Cannan wrote little about TMS and said that WN "was of incomparably greater importance than" TMS (1896: xv). Several authors in specialized studies draw on TMS, including Glenn R. Morrow, Jacob Viner, Joseph Cropsey, Ronald Coase, J.R. Lindgren, and E.G. West. Perhaps the scholar who dwelled most deeply in TMS was Alec L. Macfie (1967a; 1967b; 1971), who, while noting that TMS "is read by few" (1971: 595), aided the later revival by co-editing with D.D. Raphael the Glasgow/Oxford University edition of TMS (1976). A few biographers and others along the way would include J.A. Farrer, John Rae, H.C. MacPherson, F.W. Hirst, Albion Small, Eli Ginzberg, and W.R. Scott, and surely another dozen or two. But all such references to TMS appeared in rather isolated works. A favorite of mine, Haakonssen (1981), fits both the specialized monographs and the beginnings of a new period.
- For some 150 years, then, Smith was known chiefly as the author of *The Wealth of Nations*, with TMS just something else he had written. And

yet, according to a 1790 letter by Samuel Romilly, Smith **"always considered his *Theory of Moral Sentiments* as a much superior work to his *Wealth of Nations*"** (Romilly 1840: I, 404; bold added).

- But from 1990 the interest in Smith grew rapidly, and it continues to grow. Especially hot is TMS. Every year brings an outpouring of new books and articles, in many fields and disciplines, and extending well beyond the academy. It is as if our culture had finally "cracked the code," or found relevant something that had been deemed irrelevant, or permissible something that had been impermissible.
- The burgeoning interest in Smith is ideologically diverse. The left, conservatives, and libertarians all seem to want to dwell in Smith, embrace him, and lay claim to him.
- I find particularly noteworthy the interest on the left. Several prominent Smith scholars, sometimes writing in a voice more or less openly leftist, have suggested that Smith would favor many, if not the general run, of today's familiar interventions and extensive welfare-state programs, including progressive taxation. Such a notion is now aired by prominent left intellectuals and is not uncommon among Smith scholars. A left-oriented "reclaiming of Smith" is now well established and increasingly popular throughout left-leaning discourse.

Our interest is betterment going forward. To understand where we are today, we need to interpret the paths traveled and where things went wrong. My puzzlings about what went wrong these past 250 years revolve around matters of science and of political ideology. I declare for philosophical pragmatism in the one and pragmatic libertarian liberalism in the other. Those two attitudes combine and interact. They dovetail in a sturdy outlook.

"To the sceptical eighteenth succeeded the fervent, dogmatic, to us rather credulous nineteenth century" (Macfie 1967a: 149). The first thing that went wrong, I suggest, was that leading figures took themselves to be working toward *doctrine* or *science*, that is, something, whether in moral theory or political economy, that was analogous to, say, Newtonian doctrine, something that had first principles or clear foundational formulations, and that boasted categorical descriptions, the epistemic conquering of the cosmos, a depiction of things, an aspiration of prediction and control. Perhaps this very aspect of their doings was necessary to make such thinkers *leading* figures, so perhaps the story is as much one of the culture and institutions that prospered those aspects and those thinkers rather than other ones. But whatever the reasons, the aspiration toward, or pretense of, definitive doctrine is much less pronounced in Smith than in

Stewart, Bentham, James Mill, Ricardo, Say, Senior, Torrens, and John Stuart Mill.

Nicholas Phillipson (2010) maintains that from when Smith was a young man he conceived his overarching project to be *a science of man*. I go along with that to some extent, but incline to say rather that Smith's over-riding purpose was to further *a culture of liberty, a liberal civilization*. There is no need to put one ahead of the other, but I think that a culture of liberty is at least on a par with a science of man. Also, the best way to advance a culture of liberty might be to advance a supposed science of man.[1]

If Smith was advancing a science of man, what was the nature of that science? Did it make for a progressive research program, the progressive depicting of the cosmos? Did it enhance our powers of prediction and control? Does it gratify the will to know, the pride of knowing? Was it grounded in certitudes? Were its rules of investigation and reasoning pre-cise and accurate, like grammar and mathematical technique? Were its pronouncements definite and categorical? Also, did it observe a demar-cation between *is* and *ought*, fact and value, "positive" and "normative," according to later fashions?

I read Smith as highly congruent and Hayek quite congruent with an idea of moral philosophy (subsuming political economy) not altogether well described as a science, as a doctrine, or as a method for the progres-sive discovering and establishing of truth. Rather, it is a complex that for-mulates certain central statements on important issues, that develops the most important arguments for those statements, and that holds certain attitudes about discoursing throughout. I will call such a complex an *out-look* (cf. Lindgren 1969: 899). For the outlook articulated in this book, the central statements and the attitudes are related: Some of the statements concern the disjointedness of knowledge, and the attitudes reflect sensi-tivity to that disjointedness. The outlook is one among outlooks, but it is *sui generis* in the sense that its facets are complete only in the whole of the outlook. I call this particular outlook *the S outlook*—a name that suggests Smith but hedges on the issue of just how well it fits him.

What are the central statements of Smith? He seems to affirm an ethic of universal benevolence. He seems to enshroud all moral judgment in sympathy. He seems to see our wellness as residing in the love of those

---

1. I should note that while Phillipson makes a science of man the overt theme of his characterization of Smith's purpose, he also peppers the book quite consistently with tidbits that pointedly support a culture-of-liberty theme. Also, Phillipson's clos-ing words suggest a pragmatist attitude on Smith's part about a science of man.

we live with. He seems to presuppose that his readers naturally aspire to wisdom and virtue. In the realm of government policy, however, I see the affirmation of a presumption of liberty, a presumption against further governmentalization of social affairs and for degovernmentalization. Put differently: Smith wanted to advance, as a social operating system, the equal-equal relationship, parsed according to the principles of voluntarism, and to minimize the superior-inferior relationship, parsed according to the contravention of those principles by institutionalized authority. Such are the strong undercurrents in TMS. I see TMS and WN as a single performance in two acts. What, besides the presumption of liberty, might be the moral of the story? TMS teaches the extreme disjointedness of knowledge of affairs beyond the very local; the particularism of propriety in our doings, and hence the particularism of their meaning; the ineffability of happiness. Such teachings, indeed, lead Smith to criticize the casuists, "generally as useless as they are commonly tiresome," for cataloguing specific counsels for people in their personal affairs: "That frivolous accuracy which they attempted to introduce into subjects which do not admit of it, almost necessarily betrayed them into those dangerous errors [chicaning with our consciences, evading the most essential articles of our duty], and at the same time rendered their works dry and disagreeable" (TMS: 339–340). In John Robertson's view, the Enlightenment in Scotland (and in Naples, he says) was "dedicated to understanding and publicizing the cause of human betterment on this earth. In both cases, the terms in which this objective was articulated were those of political economy" (2005: 377). In TMS, Smith opens several lessons, establishes his moral authority, and says that "political disquisitions, if just, and reasonable, and practicable, are of all the works of speculation the most useful" (TMS: 187). In WN, he develops some of those lessons and morally authorizes the pursuit of honest profit and a presumption of liberty in policy. (And then came the industrial revolution.)

At the center of the S outlook is a statement that involves *the liberty principle*. The liberty principle says: In a choice between a pair of policy reforms (one of which may be no reform at all), the reform that ranks higher in liberty is the more desirable. Thus, the liberty principle says, for example, that abolishing the minimum wage is more desirable than keeping it as instituted at present.

Now, what actually constitutes the S outlook's central statement is the following, which may be dubbed *the liberty maxim*: *By and large the liberty principle holds*. The "by and large" does not qualify the statement but inheres in it, and thus the statement is about the full range of meaningful policy reforms. The "by and large" is strong enough to give a presumption to the liberty principle; that presumption places the burden of proof on those who would favor the less-liberty choice (such as preserving the minimum wage). In Smith, the presumption is plain—for example: "In general, if any branch of trade, or any division of labour, be advantageous to the public, the freer and more general the competition, it will always be the more so" (WN: 329).

The present occasion is not suitable for my expounding the liberty maxim and even less for defending a reading of Smith, so I just press on: I have called the liberty maxim the "central statement," but better still is "central *verity*," a term that maintains its hardy soundness, importance, and venerability, yet allows us to avert demands of exactitude, completeness, and categoricalness. "One of the chief attractions of Adam Smith as a philosopher is the fact that he generally eschews universal, exceptionless claims" (Otteson 2008: 304). Rhetoricians and logicians might associate "verity" with *enthymeme*, a statement that is qualified, vague in parts, not necessarily complete. The S outlook entails a web of statements, some of greater centrality, thereby graduating to "verity," with the liberty maxim being the verity that is most central within the web.

The S outlook lives in its participants. A participant in the outlook dwells in it by exploring, for example, facets of the central verity, the meaning of its constituent parts and its interdependence with other propositions of the web. To assess a "by and large," for example, one must survey enough of the web so as to assure oneself of the warrants and extent of the "by and large." A cultivator of the outlook may fine-tune the web, especially some of its more central verities, perhaps thereby clarifying the limitations and delimiting the exceptions; or he may develop further illustrations of those verities, or teach the verities to wider publics, or engage detractors by taking up their challenges to the web or any of its statements. An exponent may meet in debate or even obtrude upon the discourse of rival outlooks and serve up criticism informed by his own. And so on.

But during the last 200 years, many aspects of the S outlook and its cultivation and promulgation have been at odds with currents in both the scientific and the political cultures. An "outlook" attaches to a looker, a spectator. A spectator is a being, such as Adam Smith, with a history, commitments, sensibilities, purposes, and character; the community of that outlook develops and advances that character. Moreover, the outlook sees and enters into the purposes of the beings looked at. Thus, *ises* and *oughts* intermingle throughout, easily and naturally translatable the one into the other. Attuned to the normativity of every statement, and, similarly, the consequence in every ethical consideration, the S outlook did not sit well with dichotomies between "positive" and "normative," "deontological" and "consequentialist," and so on.

The liberty maxim entails the idea of a reform being *desirable*. Economists might instead speak of (concatenate) coordination and argue that the reform conduces to better coordination. Either way, people naturally ask: What is the standard? Here, the S outlook must confess that its standards are often akin to aesthetics—loose, vague, and indeterminate. That again offended against modern dogmas (Booth 1974). Science was supposed to be precise and accurate; talk of "efficiency," "optimality," and "social welfare" seemed to satisfy the demand.

What's more, the S outlook confesses also that it is not merely invoking certain vague sensibilities about the desirable. In virtually any context of discourse, the purposiveness in applying those sensibilities also carries an espousal of them. The S outlook teaches to see as it sees. Moreover, it not only invokes but also simultaneously *explores* the sensibilities, admitting that characterizations of them among us may be under dispute and in progress. But according to modern dogmas, we scientists are not here to explore and cultivate ethical sensibilities; we are value-free.

This book has treated of the richness of knowledge. As we candidly face the disjointedness of knowledge, we see further tensions between the S outlook and modern dogmas. In discussing types of discovery and the idea of error, we find intense particularism in defining an opportunity, in the insight that illuminates it, and in the basis for saying whether the opportunity was obvious. These matters depend on the agent's interpretive frames in the moment and context, like the skater acting moment-by-moment on the floor of the roller rink. The idea of error entails a sense of having missed something that should have been seen. This again, along with correction, is highly particular. If, in ordinary life, we use the words *discovery, opportunity, obvious, regret, error,* and *correction* without great difficulty, it is because a context is drawn and a discourse situation is clear. As theorists we must generalize, perhaps before multiple publics, and we respect particularism by formulating statements with by-and-larges and with elements admittedly vague or incomplete.

Yogi Berra once said, "If you don't know where you are going, you could end up somewhere else." I think of Israel Kirzner and his followers, who principally share the S outlook but also lean on modern dogmas. They often pretend that coordination is precise and accurate, and they declare a supposed value-freedom. Regarding the idea of entrepreneurship, Kirzner claims to have a definitive theory that supposedly affords the fashioning of categorical statements. I have suggested a pluralist approach to entrepreneurship and more robust, by-and-large alternative statements concerning coordination, honest profit, and policy liberalization.

I hope that the people who are pursuing the tradition of Mises, Rothbard, and Kirzner turn toward a more knowing embrace of the *S* outlook. To do so, they would need to overcome certain resistances. To highlight one in particular, I expound on the *S* outlook a bit further.

The *S* outlook entails a web of statements. A statement may speak of "the economy" or "the drug industry" or "the drug market," and perhaps of only certain effects of, say, a policy change, with the effects themselves being comparative in nature, as in, "the restrictions tend to suppress drug development." A statement, then, refers to certain concatenations, which themselves are doings unfolding through time, as we might refer to the patterns of skating that take shape during a two-hour session of roller skating.

If one sits and observes a session of roller skating, one gets a sort of synoptic view of the whole. One could even write a sort of synopsis of the concatenation, by, say, recording the number of skaters, the average speed of the skating, and the number of falls and injuries sustained by skaters. In that sense the spectator enjoys a synoptic view of the concatenation. We have spoken of the roller rink as a "window" on spontaneous order.

For Smith, with his ethic of universal benevolence, the concatenation that concerns him is, in principle, all of humankind; he speaks of the Chinese unknown to the "man of humanity in Europe" as that man's brethren (TMS: 137). Smith postulates an ideal spectator, called the impartial spectator, whose view of the vast concatenation is single and universal; I have called this spectator Joy. The circumstances, situations, traditions, and histories surveyed by Joy are myriad and individuated, but her perspective sees all the nodes on all the branches. On this postulation, Joy surveys all communities, even if they have not formed connections. Universality is one of Smith's ground rules for the conversation. The universality of Joy is rather like the universality presupposed by monotheism.

A statement, then, entails Joy's synoptic view of the concatenation discussed. So there is, within the *S* outlook, an element of synopticism. That synopticism, however, is of a peculiarly anti-synoptic sort: We do not claim to see what Joy sees. In that sense we do not claim to know the economy, the industry, the market, or whatever happens to be the concatenation discussed. We do not even aspire to see what Joy sees. Rather, we posit things that she might see, though we do not, and we speculate on her sentiments about them.

Indeed, we research corners or factual accounts of the concatenation rather directly, to help us create or fashion the things that we posit and then discuss. Borrowing words from W.V.O. Quine, we might say that the web "is a man-made fabric which impinges on experience only along the edges," or, it "is like a field of force whose boundary conditions are experience" (1961: 42). Quine continues:

> A conflict with experience at the periphery occasions readjustments in the interior of the field [or web]. Truth values have to be redistributed over some of our statements. Reevaluation of some statements entails reevaluation of others... Having reevaluated one statement we must reevaluate some others, which may be statements logically connected with the first or may be the statements of logical connections themselves. But the total field is so underdetermined by its boundary conditions, experience, that there is much latitude as to what statements to reevaluate in the light of any single contrary experience.
>
> (1961: 42–43)

Thus, within the web, the ancillary statements serve as the warrants or arguments or guts of the more central statements, with the most central statement being, in the case of the *S* outlook, the liberty maxim.

As I say, however, the *S* outlook's synopticism is of a peculiarly antisynoptic sort. Thus Smith, immediately following the paragraph in which he speaks of an invisible hand:

> What is the species of domestick industry which his capital can employ, and of which the produce is likely to be of the greatest value, every individual, it is evident, can, in his local situation, judge much better than any statesman or lawgiver can do for him. The statesman, who should attempt to direct private people in what manner they ought to employ their capitals, would not only load himself with a most unnecessary attention, but assume an authority which could safely be trusted, not only to no single person, but *no council or senate whatever*, and which would nowhere be so dangerous as in the hands of a man who had folly and presumption enough to fancy himself fit to exercise it.
>
> (WN: 456, italics added)

In TMS, in the brief chapter entitled "Of Universal Benevolence," which is the culmination of Smith's section on what has been termed his "social distance" theory of sympathetic inclinations, Smith says, as it were: Friends, neighbors, do not trouble yourself about distant affairs. "To man is allotted a much humbler department, but one much more suitable to the weakness of his powers and the narrowness of his comprehension; the care of his own happiness, of that of his family, his friends, his country" (237). Centered on a respect for liberty, the spirit of Smith and Hayek is, then, one of humility.

Wisdom in economics resides principally in know-how in explaining that we do not know how to intervene in a way that conduces to concatenate coordination. Field expertise resides principally in knowing enough to show that interventionists do not know enough.[2] These two competencies correspond to the two central and interrelated intellectual tasks of the *S* outlook: 1) Developing and expounding the central verities; and 2) showing the error, perhaps the "folly and presumption," of erroneous departures from them. The spirit of humility is captured in one of the definitions in Ambrose Bierce's *The Devil's Dictionary*:

> **Education, *n*.** That which discloses to the wise and disguises from the foolish their lack of understanding.
>
> (1911/1993: 28)

When Smith reproves the pretense of knowledge, however, there is no rejection of the ethic of universal benevolence. On the contrary, such reproofs invoke that ethic in morally authorizing each to focus his efforts where they are most likely to do good for the whole. Thus, when we discuss the effects of a new Wal-Mart, when we defer, as it were—and I speak of a deference strongly presumptive but not absolute—to the entrepreneur and *his* synoptic view of his own firm, when we defer to the individual and *his* synoptic views of his own voluntary affairs, and, hence, to his course in making certain commutatively just interests *his* interest—which we then call his "self-interest," not because it is likely selfish but because knowledge of it resides in his self and not ours—or to what Smith with his chessboard metaphor might call *his* principles of motion, *we are not jettisoning Joy.* We are positing his actions, analytically framed in terms of property and voluntary agreement, as viewed, not by us, but by Joy, and we allegorically describe or explore Joy's sentiments about those actions. Our statements about market signals, about market coordination, about social

---

2. "Is it not proper to...perceive the necessity of carrying the war into the most secret recesses of the enemy?" (Hume 1748/1902: 12).

cooperation, and about the social good are, if only implicitly, still statements about Joy, about *her* synoptic view and her universal benevolence.

From the anti-synoptic tendencies of its teachings, the individualist traditions of liberal economics have often expunged the allegorical synopticism that underlies statements of the Smith-Hayek tradition. The Mises-Rothbard-Kirzner tradition, in particular, takes an essentialist turn wherein certain theoretical claims about Wal-Mart, entrepreneurship, and the free market supposedly inhere in the activities independently of their nature as parts of a larger whole. That tradition has often scorned any invocation of allegory, much as Dugald Stewart does in the quotation given early in this chapter.

Here a textual specimen is worthy of attention, not as commentary on its author specifically, but as a platform for commenting on individualist thinkers quite broadly. In his magnum opus *Human Action*, in a section entitled "A Critique of the Holistic and Metaphysical View of Society," Ludwig von Mises wrote:

> Many economists, among them Adam Smith and Bastiat, believed in God. Hence they admired in the facts they had discovered the providential care of 'the great Director of Nature.' Atheist critics blame them for this attitude. However, these critics fail to realize that to sneer at the references to the 'invisible hand' does not invalidate the essential teachings of the rationalist and utilitarian social philosophy. One must comprehend that the alternative is this: Either association is a human process because it best serves the aims of the individuals concerned and the individuals themselves have the ability to realize the advantages they derive from their adjustment to life in social cooperation. Or a superior being enjoins upon reluctant men subordination to the law and to the social authorities. It is of minor importance whether one calls this supreme being God, Weltgeist, Destiny, History, Wotan, or Material Productive Forces and what title one assigns to its apostles, the dictators.
>
> (1966: 147)

Mises sets up a simplistic dichotomy and champions "rationalist and utilitarian social philosophy." What is most significant about the passage is that anyone who strays from what Mises (41–46) calls "methodological individualism" is regarded as an abettor of dictators. In the present book, in the preceding chapter, I spelled out an allegory of Joy leading a *voluntary* expansive cooperation. Being voluntary, the affairs traverse, on the one side, the intrapersonal sense of duty—as, for Bridget the baker, Joy becomes like "the man in the breast"—and, on the other side, the grand cooperation. Such allegory is not allowed by Mises: Either individuals engage in simple/conscious cooperation or "a superior being enjoins upon reluctant men subordination to the law and to the social authorities." Many liberal economists similarly failed to work out the tensions that Hayek raised in 1933, and they scorned constructs beyond the kind of voluntary affairs we know in simple/conscious cooperation.

In denying the allegorical, individualists invite three kinds of problems. First, they play into the role that they are so often accused of, namely that of someone unattuned to the social. Second, they nonetheless proceed to speak of coordination, of market communication, of social error and correction, of an invisible hand, and of cooperation through the vast concatenation, thereby violating the tenets of "methodological individualism," thus falling into inconsistency and self-contradiction. Third, they relinquish the allegorical to those who too often are inclined to take it in illiberal directions.

As I see it, liberals need to fight illiberal allegory, not with denials of allegory, but with liberal allegory. Just as Shaftesbury, Hutcheson, Butler, and Smith spoke of virtue as cooperation with the deity—making them, according to Mises, abettors of dictators—liberals today need to speak allegorically of virtue as cooperation.

When Smith says something as commonplace as that the legislature should direct its deliberations "not by the clamorous importunity of partial interests, but by *an extensive view of the general good*" (471–472, italics added), he is being allegorical, for, in a literal sense, no human being has any such extensive view. The allegorical being Joy has such an extensive view. Smith is saying that we should scrupulously develop and mind our thinking about Joy's sentiments about what *she* sees. As one aspiring to wisdom and virtue, you want to sympathize with Joy's best representatives, not with partial interests. Upon such allegory we develop the scruple to overcome the errors of partiality.

I have been discussing what has happened to Smith during the last 250 years. Another way to approach the matter is to imagine how, at some past point, a proponent of the *S* outlook would have fared in the world of ideas and academe. One can imagine that anyone attracted to the *S* outlook, with its peculiar anti-synoptic synopticism, would have felt impelled to submerge the allegorical, with its candid relationship to ethics and its confessions of vagueness, to such a point as to deny it altogether. I think that the anti-synoptic element has led some strands of individualist liberal economics to end up somewhere other than where they were originally going.

But the situation was particularly unenviable for the rare intellectual with an affinity for the S outlook during the first half of the twentieth century. No matter how he fashioned his discourse he would be engulfed by feelings of tragedy and hopelessness, and any efforts would likely be doomed to grief and isolation. We have discussed the snares of modern dogmas in science. We must also consider the currents in political ideology.

At the end of the nineteenth century the intellectual currents turned sharply against liberalism and toward statist collectivism—notably, social democracy, whether in its more or less aggressive forms—which, in the Anglosphere, would then upset the semantics of liberalism, and even arrogate to itself the name "liberalism." Within just two or three generations, authentic liberalism was utterly devastated as an intellectual enterprise. I wonder how things may have been different if in 1820, say, some keenly attuned minds had dwelled in TMS and had worked to integrate its wisdom into the current of liberal thought. Tragically, none did.

Whether they admit it or not, intellectuals organize themselves around larger purposes and outlooks. The decades of the rising of the social-democratic tide were, especially in the United States, also the decades of the formation and rapid expansion of academia and its disciplinary associations and organizations, jelling across campuses into the lattices of disciplinary settlements called departments. And the subdividing proceeded within each discipline, with still narrower research areas constituting various "fields." But, despite diligent specialization, there was a pervasive spirit of social science in the service of improvements to be implemented, not by independent private enterprises and voluntary associations, but by government. The spirit was that of social engineering and the rule of experts, serving the people by guiding the officials who have, by democratic processes, ascended to positions of authority. This statist spirit of cooperative meliorism was not shared by all, but it was pervasive enough to make any proclamation for the S outlook, with its epistemic humility and veneration of old principles, seem like the prepossessions of a bygone age—consider the speaker in the accompanying cartoon. What mattered was advancing a progressive research program, not meditating on "verities" now anachronistic.

But the greatest liability of the *S* outlook was not its unsuitability to generating specialized progressive research programs. That can often be feigned. The most deadly characteristic of the *S* outlook was that its core formulations were liberal. The heart of the outlook is a presumption of liberty. But as early as 1887 the economist Herbert Foxwell would write in *The Quarterly Journal of Economics*: "Every one can see that *laissez faire*, formerly a forgone conclusion, is now scarcely even a presumption" (101). Indeed, it was not just liberty's favorable regard that offended, but liberalism's very semantics. The social-democratic tide saw the polity to be, not a configuration of myriad things each the property of some individual owners—and, by the way, in *this* the liberal philosophy *is* individualistic— but as one collective operation managed under democratic governance now deemed voluntary, as would be the case with a collectively owned property or, and more fittingly, with a collectively owned envelope within which all encompassed tenants are under contract as to what contracts they may make with each other and in how they may use their private property. The social-democratic tide busied itself in making the corresponding changes to the meanings of the central words of liberal civilization. Referring to the highly influential English Hegelian philosopher Thomas Hill Green, the progressive American economist Richard T. Ely heralded the new thought: "As Adam Smith's philosophy of liberty is an expression of the eighteenth century, Thomas Hill Green's view may be looked upon as an expression of the philosophy of liberty with which the twentieth century opens" (1903: 403).

It is the presumption of liberty that predicates the *S* outlook's humility: Beyond the presumption of liberty, we are humble about our ability to know how social affairs should be arranged or rearranged. During the first half of the twentieth century the outlook was vanquished, its sympathizers few and marginalized. In a 1960s essay, Alec Macfie closed with the following call for a return to humility: "In the scepticism, yet faith, of the eighteenth century we may recover the humility and caution which specialization does the reverse of fostering, but which we so need, and lack, today" (1967a: 151).

Before proceeding, I must acknowledge that, today, libertarians, often fervent to abolish contraventions of the liberty principle, may seem anything but humble. Smith's parable of the man of system, who rearranges institutions as though they were pieces on a chessboard, draws from the presumption of liberty but also from another important presumption, namely, *the presumption of the status quo*—the status quo, that is, in the constitution of society's morals, culture, and institutions. When the reforms would newly contravene liberty, the status-quo presumption *reinforces* the liberty presumption. But when the reforms would repeal, abolish, or liberalize existing contraventions, the status-quo presumption obstructs and moderates the liberty presumption. Then we acknowledge a humility attaching to the presumption of the status quo, and it tempers liberty's alacrity—a temperance that permeates Smith's writings and finds explicit recommendation (cf. M. Clark 2011). These considerations would lead us to refinements (cf. Klein and Clark 2010), but here I simply declare that the wisdom in according some presumption to the status quo does not fundamentally upset our drift, and press on.

The second half of the twentieth century saw the continued intensification of specialization. But other changes were also taking place. The sins and failures of statism were becoming apparent. Classical liberalism had been marginalized and driven underground, but in epoch-bridging figures like Mises it had never quite died out, and the stream of liberalism was revived, led by people like Hayek, whose rehabilitations of liberalism most closely fit the *S* outlook. Clarence Philbrook, a rather obscure economist who kept the faith, wrote in 1953 of "idea force":

> The force at work changing attitudes is, then, 'idea force'... [H]owever an idea may get into a mind, it is capable of dying there or of gathering immense force. Moreover, a number of minds can be seeded with one expression of the idea.

Potentially, then, the force may grow at an astronomical rate. All the determinants of whether it dies or gathers strength in a particular mind, we simply do not know. We do know, however, that which is believed to be true has an appeal to the mind believing it, over and above the attraction it may have on other grounds: truth has a positive appeal in its own right. Although other appeals may swamp this one, there is no limit to the possibilities of its breaking through and causing action. The degree of apparent influence of the person holding an idea is, therefore, no measure of the potential effect of his giving utterance to it. If there is one belief fundamental to, and universal in, our culture, it is this notion that truth as such has power. Such justification as may exist for the hope of a better world lies here and here only.

(Philbrook 1953: 856–857)

Even though it was up against the modern dogmas of science and antipathetic ideological tendencies, the *S* outlook found footholds—in part, simply because growing wealth afforded the nurturing of diverse seeds, each with potential to become a tree of idea force.

The discipline of economics has always been especially important. Only within economics had classical liberalism retained any significant numbers, energy, and standing. There the skepticism and humility of the *S* outlook still lingered, serving as a conscience within economics, and thereby making economics something of a conscience of the others—a conscience that still nagged, since the civilization was, after all, still liberal in much of its sensibility. In the postwar period, many questioned the statist trends. Individualist ideas found new idea force.

By the 1960s, the writings of the liberal age had been so forgotten that the ideas could now be reinvented and received as fresh, original, and exciting. Scholars developed ideas altogether original, of course, but also they plucked the low-hanging fruit of orchards that had been harvested in works now forgotten. They made an epic era of forwardness in liberal thinking, say 1960 to 1990, and emerged within economics as major figures, some to win Nobel prizes, including Friedrich Hayek, George Stigler, Gary Becker, James Buchanan, Ronald Coase, Douglass North, Vernon Smith, and the especially remarkable Milton Friedman. Many others, such as Armen Alchian, Gordon Tullock, Murray Rothbard, and Israel Kirzner, have also been major figures within traditions of liberal economics and the wider discourse.

But many of the free-market economists were strongly attached to modern dogmas. George Stigler was particularly influential, and he championed many of the modern dogmas and made himself into the Anti-Smith in everything but the disposition toward free markets. As noted, the leading liberal economists showed little familiarity with TMS.

Meanwhile, the modern dogmas were growing tiresome. Lost in specialization, people asked: *Knowledge for What?* (Lynd 1948). The virtue of specialization depends on the specialized activities being coordinated within a larger whole. What mechanisms are assuring any such coordination? Faith in the melioristic cooperation was waning. Besides the criticism of classical liberals, such as Hayek and Michael Polanyi, the left also protested the modern dogmas, in part because they perceived them as prophylactics guarding established interests and mentalities and as constraints on leftist discourse and aspirations. Postmodernism, philosophical pragmatism, rhetoric, cultural studies, and related movements challenged modern dogmas, such as the banishment of the normative, the pretenses of exact and separate sciences, and the demands of formalism. Overcoming taboos, scholars asked: What is it all good for? Whose interests are being served? By what mechanisms does modern social science work toward the social good? Such questioning of basic purpose led to the crossings of disciplinary boundaries, and the more people crossed the more they discovered the good sense in crossing, in overcoming the taboos. It became fashionable to be interdisciplinary, even if the academic apparatus formally retained specialization. Within economics, Deirdre McCloskey emerged as something previously unknown, a postmodern libertarian economist. For her, Stigler personified the modern dogmas, and she mounted a powerful critique of them.

I suppose that people are always searching their soul, but I wonder whether the opening of the twenty-first century is notable in that respect. I have suggested that Yogi Berra's dictum might apply to individualist economics. I think it may also apply to many left-leaning people who, searching for the soul of liberalism, dwell in Smith. That both free-market people and left-leaning people are turning to Smith is an exciting conjunction, one that, under Smith's gaze, is apt to be more genial than usual.

To folks of the left, I say: Search your soul about just how compatible the social-democratic intellectual turn of 1880 is with Smith. We understand the dream:

All the members of human society stand in need of each others assistance, and are likewise exposed to mutual injuries. Where the necessary assistance is reciprocally afforded from love, from gratitude, from friendship, and esteem, the society flourishes and is happy. All the different members of it are bound together by the agreeable bands of love and affection, and are, as it were, drawn to one common centre of mutual good offices.

(TMS: 85)

Smith seemed to see man as, in some respects, not fitted for life in a "great" or commercial society, as though man must subdue, temper, and channel certain primeval yearnings he has for a visible, encompassing "common centre." Smith called for a society of equals, a society of commutative justice, with each "abstaining from what is another's" (TMS: 269), a society in which each person's practice of distributive justice, "the becoming use of what is our own" (270), would be "the ornament which embellishes" (86). The invisible-hand philosophy authorizes the pursuit of honest profit. It validates hard work and the income earned in honest, productive employment. It authorizes a presumption of liberty. And it gives rise to an incredible system of mutualities, one that yields woolen coats and positive capabilities but is quite devoid of any common center.

Can its incredible system also afford at least a vague, imagined communion through the great global society? Perhaps it can afford an imagined chain of beings, a "we" of humankind, in the knowledge of what Wakefield and then Mill called "complex co-operation." Smith invites us to imagine the synoptic social beauty, as when he says that the many different products of a great diversity of talents are "brought, as it were, *into a common stock*, where every man may purchase whatever part of the produce of other men's talents he has occasion for" (WN: 30; italics added). The invisible-hand outlook might provide our best surrogate for a "common centre of mutual good offices." In living by liberal principles, we practice a beautiful albeit allegorical kind of cooperation.

Beyond that, does Smith speak to our search for meaning in ordinary life? Recall Smith's rejection of the casuists. In the lived context of meaning, little can be gotten from liberal intellectuals. Aside from the broad authorizations and validations just mentioned, the chief value of liberal intellectuals consists in telling the individual where *not* to search.

The Wealth of Nations is famous for debunking interventions to augment holdings of gold and silver. While demonstrating that those interventions were bad, Smith suggested certain images of the good. Holdings of gold and silver are limited by the use that there is for them, he says, just as the number of pots and pans "is in every country necessarily limited by the use which there is for them." To attempt to increase the wealth of any country by tampering with gold and silver flows "is as absurd as it would be to attempt to increase the good cheer of private families, by obliging them to keep an unnecessary number of kitchen utensils" (WN: 439–440).

————————⌒\⌒————————

Appendix Chapters

The following chapter is a critical examination of Israel Kirzner's writings on coordination and discovery. I thought it unsuitable as a regular chapter because it is long and intricate, and because my attitude toward Professor Kirzner is chiefly admiring and appreciative, not critical. The chapter draws on an article that I coauthored with Jason Briggeman, in *The Journal of Private Enterprise* 25(2), Spring 2010: 1–53 (to which Professor Kirzner replied, in the same issue). For this chapter a full abstract might be particularly useful:

In Kirzner's rendering of the Austrian school, one finds a marriage between Friedrich Hayek's discourse with Ludwig von Mises' deductive, praxeological image of science—a marriage that seems to us somewhat forced. The Misesian image of science stakes its claims to scientific status on purported axioms and categorical, 100-percent deductive truths, namely: (1) gainful entrepreneurship is *always* coordinative; (2) the *only* coordinative force is entrepreneurship; (3) entrepreneurial gain *always* implies preceding error. In keeping with that style of discourse, Kirzner claims that his notion of coordination can be used as a clear-cut criterion of economic goodness. We contend that Kirzner's efforts to be categorical and to avoid looseness are unsuccessful. We suggest that Hayek is closer to Smith than to Mises, and that Kirzner's invocations of Hayek's discussions of coordination are spurious. In denying looseness and trying to cope with the brittleness of categorical claims, Kirzner becomes abstruse. His discourse erupts with problems. Kirzner has erred in rejecting the understanding of coordination held by Hayek, Ronald Coase, and their contemporaries in the field at large. Once we give up the claim that voluntary profitable activity is *always or necessarily* coordinative, and once we make peace with the aesthetic aspect of the idea of concatenate coordination, the basic claims of Kirzner can be more robustly affirmed and sustained. Voluntary profitable activity is *usually* coordinative, and government intervention is *usually* discoordinative. Thus, beyond all the criticism, we affirm the basic thrust of Kirzner's central substantive statements. But our critique casts doubts on his project in Austrianism.

Next comes a chapter entitled "Some Fragments," a collection of apothegms that amplify some of our ideas.

The final chapter assembles passages from Michael Polanyi's little book *The Study of Man* (1963). The passages suggest that "we need reverence to perceive greatness, even as we need a telescope to observe spiral nebulae." Polanyi defends our dwelling in great minds, an activity that relates to the ideas in the Conclusion of this book, ideas of our developing judgments about the spectator's synoptic view, whether it be Adam Smith's view of the "web" discussed in the Conclusion or Joy's view of the vast social concatenation.

CHAPTER 16

✧

Owning Up to and Properly
Locating Our Looseness

A Critique of Israel Kirzner on
Coordination and Discovery

Israel Kirzner is best known for his work on the role of discovery and entrepreneurship in economic affairs. He sees entrepreneurial alertness as the vital human faculty for apprehending opportunities for one's betterment. Entrepreneurial discovery entails interpretive shifts and awakenings. It goes beyond the deliberate search for or mechanical response to new information. Kirzner's insights about discovery make a contrast to the kind of economics that regards human beings as interpretively flat and fixed. If economists confine their thinking to stories of final and symmetric interpretation, they will underappreciate the role of discovery and entrepreneurship in economic affairs, and fail to do justice to laissez-faire (Kirzner 1985).

Kirzner strives to integrate his discovery ideas into theories of market coordination. Refining ideas at both ends—discovery and coordination—Kirzner works to maintain that, *in market activity, successful voluntary entrepreneurial action necessarily enhances coordination*.

Our attitude toward Kirzner is great admiration mixed with frustration and regret. We embrace the central teachings—notably, that successful entrepreneurship and voluntary activity more generally usually enhance coordination, and, even more typically, that restrictions on voluntary activity diminish coordination. We are thoroughly supportive of those broad themes developed and expounded by Kirzner.

We feel, however, that Kirzner has made errors. Our impetus is to strengthen the central teachings by identifying and correcting the errors. Greater robustness of the central claims—that entrepreneurship, that freedom conduces to better coordination—is achieved by two sorts of changes. First, in certain respects, the claim must be weakened. Kirzner makes "always"- or "necessarily"-type claims—categorical claims—when, rather, the claims should be "usually" or "by and large." Second, changes are needed in the formulation and semantics. Suitably tailored, the chief messages still ring out but become looser. Broadly speaking, our approach is *greater robustness through greater looseness.*

If we basically agree with Kirzner's teachings, why the disagreements? We begin by offering a broad interpretation of why Kirzner would develop the ideas in ways we deem erroneous.

MISES, KIRZNER, AND TWO WINGS OF AUSTRIAN ECONOMICS

Kirzner has been a leader in building an Austrian identity within economics. The narrative makes Ludwig von Mises the central figure of the Austrian tradition, although the tradition is said to originate with Carl Menger. In Kirzner's view, Friedrich Hayek also looms large, but Hayek is thought to develop the economics of Mises. Kirzner and his followers tend to homogenize Hayek and Mises.

Although Mises and Kirzner declare their economics to be "value free" (or "*wertfrei*"), it is clear that they believe that economics ought to address the most important things, notably major policy issues, and that they believe that the economics profession and the public culture poorly appreciate laissez-faire. It is clear that Mises, Hayek, and virtually all self-described Austrian economists are motivated to advance classical liberalism, but that impetus is not distinctive to Mises, Hayek, and the self-described Austrians. If there is to be a distinctive Austrian identity, it must draw on other elements.

Kirzner sees Austrian distinctiveness in the praxeology of Mises, who propounded a view of economics as a science built on fundamental axioms of human action. Mises ascribes to his praxeology a truth status like that of mathematics:

> The theorems attained by correct praxeological reasoning are not only perfectly certain and incontestable, like the correct mathematical theorems. They refer,

moreover, with the full rigidity of their apodictic certainty and incontestability to the reality of action as it appears in life and history. Praxeology conveys exact and precise knowledge of real things.

(1966: 39)

It is upon a supposed status of axiomatic foundation, logical deduction, and apodictic certainty that Mises and those who have promulgated an Austrian identity, led by Kirzner and Murray Rothbard (1926–95), stake their claim for a distinct science of economics, a science that happens to support libertarian conclusions.

Hayek, however, never embraced Mises' approach and never promulgated an Austrian identity. Compared to Mises, Hayek is considerably looser and more pragmatic—and pragmatist. We think Hayek is closer to, say, Adam Smith and Edwin Cannan than to Mises. Hayek sees economics not as an exact or deductive science but as part of the civilization's general cultural purpose, and, hence, as framed by the civilization's notions of the good. Hayek (1978a) said: "Mises himself was still much more a child of the rationalist tradition of the Enlightenment and of continental, rather than of English, liberalism...than I am myself."[1]

"[T]he diverging interests of [Mises and Hayek]," suggest Keith Jakee and Heath Spong, "is potentially relevant to the disunity that has surfaced within the Austrian school since the 1970s" (2003: 473). They relate that divergence to tensions in Kirzner's discourse, particularly between the Misesian image of science and the theories about entrepreneurship.[2]

The wing of Austrianism associated more closely with the ideas of Murray Rothbard and with the Ludwig von Mises Institute elevates Mises (and Rothbard) clearly above the squishy Hayek. In "Mises and Hayek Dehomogenized," the Rothbardian Austrian Joseph Salerno (1993) argues that Hayek is importantly different than Mises. The wing more associated with Kirzner and Peter Boettke, however, tends to homogenize Mises and

---

1. Hayek made related remarks about Mises' undue rationalism and emphasis on the a priori in an interview published in *Hayek on Hayek* (1994: 72–73) and in his foreword to Mises' *Socialism* (Hayek 1978b: xxxiii).

2. There is much congruence between the views of Jakee and Spong (2003) and ours. They are skeptical of the homogenization of Mises and Hayek and would seem to favor Hayek. Also, they repeatedly make an issue of a distinction that seems to track ours, presented below, between plan fulfillment and retrospective plan affirmation (477: n. 24, 480–481, 482, n. 32). They, however, seem to enter into the dubious practices of speaking of equilibrium, equilibration, etc., without reference to a model (e.g., 474–478), and of speaking of equilibrium and coordination apparently as though they were interchangeable (e.g., 480).

Hayek. Many of Kirzner's followers seem to subscribe to the homogenization and to Kirzner's writings on coordination (for example, Ikeda 1990, Thomsen 1992, Sautet 2000, Boettke 2001).

While earning an MBA at New York University during the 1950s, Kirzner encountered Mises and his private seminar. Kirzner was captivated and, along with Rothbard, became a leading protégé. Working under Mises, Kirzner earned his PhD in economics at NYU in 1957. Throughout his career, Kirzner has remained loyal to Mises' conception of "the pure, universal truths of economic theory" (Kirzner 2001: 56), or Mises' image of science. We contend, like Jakee and Spong (2003: 470–473), that Kirzner has been committed to building a distinctive Misesian science of economics.

Kirzner has produced extensive discourse, in which a central word is *coordination*. Kirzner writes that coordination is "a clear-cut, objective criterion... which may satisfy the intuitive conviction of economists that their science does objectively demonstrate the economic 'goodness' of some economic policies" (2000: 133). Thus, for Kirzner, coordination signifies economic goodness. He claims to show that voluntary, successful entrepreneurial action in the market necessarily advances coordination or is coordinative. Notice the two important features: First, the claim is categorical, or 100%—that is the nature of praxeological truth and, to Misesians, the mark of economic science. The matter of a claim being "100%" concerns the coverage of the claim, as in "all swans are white," not the speaker's level of confidence in the claim. Second, the claim lends support to (though does not seal the case for) libertarian policy, for to obstruct such entrepreneurial action, as with government restrictions, would be to prevent coordinative actions.

To our thinking, Mises, Rothbard, and Kirzner are alike in their image of science. *Coordination* does not play a large role in Mises and Rothbard, but Kirzner makes great efforts to develop the concept of coordination in order to integrate teachings of economic liberalism with Mises' image of science. In contrast, Smith and Hayek may be said to advance the teachings of economic liberalism in ways that better avoid modernist conceptions of such discourse.

CONCATENATE COORDINATION: HAYEK, COASE, ETC.

Along with other economists of their times, Mises and Hayek used the term *coordination* in the sense of concatenate coordination explained in

Chapter 3: A concatenation of activities and resources is coordinated to the extent that the concatenation would be satisfying, pleasing, or even beautiful to a mind imagined to behold it. Hayek's usage of *coordination* nicely fits this understanding, but Kirzner (2000: Ch. 10) contends that his coordination is true to Hayek's. We wish to disentangle concatenate coordination from some of Kirzner's characterizations of coordination.

As discussed in Chapter 3, Hayek writes of a social "sense" or "function," notes that we then balk at any kind of anthropomorphism, but then warns that we may consequently fall into an "opposite error." He writes that a notion of social organism is necessary to economics: "The recognition of the existence of this organism is the recognition that there is a subject matter for economics" (1933a/1991: 27). Yet he makes these suggestions with great caution. Classical liberals dread the hazards of any society-as-organism metaphor.[3] The lecture is quite remarkable as an early expression of the dilemmas in opposing society-as-organization notions while trying to say that liberal processes are coordinative.

The way to interpret the "sense" of the social "organism" of which Hayek spoke is to think of a fictitious mind able to behold the extensive tapestry of social affairs, in principle including future generations, and inclined to judge it in a manner that parties to the discourse are presumed to find acceptable. This imagined judge is like that being whose hands, according to Adam Smith, are invisible. Alluding to Hume and Smith, Hayek, too, wants to talk about coordination beyond the eye of any actual human coordinator. This understanding of coordination comports perfectly with the dictionary definition of the transitive verb *to coordinate*, to put things into a pleasing order or arrangement. Necessarily embedded within such understanding are aesthetic or moral sensibilities relevant to the interlocutors. The understanding thus involves deep dimensions that are, in Adam Smith's words, "loose, vague, and indeterminate" (TMS: 175, 327).

In writing of society as organism, Hayek cites the 1923 and 1932 German-language editions of Mises' *Socialism* (1981), which not only affirms the notion of the social organism but uses it very extensively (as may be easily confirmed by electronic text search). Interestingly, in Mises' later magnum opus *Human Action* (1966: 589) there is but a single, insignificant instance of such usage. The disappearance reflects deep changes in Mises' intellectual enterprise; as Kirzner notes, "Mises' distinctiveness had *not* yet been firmly established by 1930" (2001: 54). Further, it should

---

3. Like Hayek, Simon Newcomb (1886: 7–8) articulates cautions while going forward with the organism metaphor.

be recalled that Hayek entered intellectual maturity as a mild socialist and a pupil of Friedrich von Wieser, whose works burble with notions akin to social organism (Shearmur 1996: Ch. 2). Hayek (1978a) noted that he had come from Wieser and that Mises "gradually, but never completely, won me over." It is true that Mises converted Hayek on economic policy, but there is no reason at all to suppose that Mises drove organism metaphors from Hayek's mind, particularly as at the time Mises himself was expounding on them. Hayek said that "[Mises'] *Socialism* told us [young idealists] that we had been looking for improvement in the wrong direction" (Hayek 1978b: xix)—not that the book transformed their idea of improvement.

Hayek's idea of coordination was apparently no different from that of Coase and many other economists. Yet Kirzner develops claims about coordination that he presents as true to Hayek and part of a distinctively Austrian sort of economics.

KIRZNER'S COORDINATION OFTEN SEEMS LIKE CONCATENATE COORDINATION

A great many of Kirzner's statements about coordination read fine as concatenate coordination. Early in his career, he described the price system as a coordinative force in society: "Clearly, with innumerable producers making independent decisions as to production techniques, the economy must *coordinate* these decisions so as to ensure that each producer uses those resources least needed elsewhere in the economy... An efficient system will provide sufficient reward to each participant to enable all participants to enjoy the benefits of the widest possible range of resource services" (1963: 38). Elsewhere, Kirzner writes: "Within the firm, activities are co-ordinated by central direction, not by market competition via a price mechanism" (1992a: 161).

Indeed, we find Kirzner articulating the construct of a mind imagined to behold the vast concatenation and its potentialities, as when he writes that the actions of buyers and sellers who have not noticed certain profit opportunities "are, *from the perspective of omniscience*, uncoordinated and inconsistent" (1985: 59; italics added), or when speaking of coordinating traffic flow: "Were *an omniscient single mind* to make the decisions for *all* the drivers, that mind might arrange the drivers' actions in a smooth and safe fashion" (1992a: 140; first italics added).

Because we believe that concatenate coordination conforms to the coordination discussed by Herbert Spencer, Simon Newcomb, Mises, Hayek,

Coase, and many others, we think it is significant that a great many of Kirzner's utterances about coordination might be read that way. It gives the reader the impression that Kirzner is adhering to conventional usage, and it allows Austrians to speak to wider audiences. Our view, again, is that the coordination talk among Austrians ought to become sensibly about concatenate coordination—but, again, doing so would upset their claim to distinctiveness in the matter. In earlier work, I proposed that Kirzner's basic claims be understood as by-and-large claims about concatenate coordination, but this proposal was vigorously resisted by Kirzner (2000: 132–148, 199).

KIRZNER'S TROUBLED CLAIMS ABOUT COORDINATION

Kirzner's discourse has come to center around "coordination." Kirzner introduces and attempts to reconcile a jumble of claims about coordination. Before addressing the problems, we lay out the pieces that Kirzner attempts to fit together.

Two background conditions should be clarified. In speaking of whether economic actions are coordinative, Kirzner does not mean burglary, fraud, and other coercive actions (e.g., Kirzner 1992b: 93); he confines the discourse to voluntary action. Second, Kirzner means entrepreneurial action that is successful, in the sense that the agent does not feel that his entrepreneurial action was an error but rather that it was gainful. Kirzner acknowledges that actors may make losses and feel regret, and that such voluntary acts might be discoordinative. His statements concern the coordinative aspects of the successful entrepreneurial seizing of gainful opportunities (e.g., Kirzner 1992a: 21–31). Kirzner is on solid ground in supposing that markets do *not* tend toward specific agent errors, and *do* tend to weed out each loss-making activity and to correct agent errors (2000: 31), so it is appropriate to focus on successful entrepreneurial action in characterizing market tendencies. Although there are issues about which actions are to be deemed entrepreneurial, we, too, mean such actions that are voluntary and successful.

'Every Entrepreneurial Gain Is Coordinative'

The great virtue of Kirzner's coordination discourse is the emphasis he places on discovery, on the idea that new discoveries of gainful activities represent advances in coordination—a point too often neglected by formalistic economists and by interventionists who presume that regulators can know the economy and its potentialities well enough to manipulate it beneficially. We salute Kirzner (1992a) when he writes that entrepreneurial discoveries constitute "steps through which markets tend to achieve co-ordination, gradually replacing earlier states of widespread mutual ignorance by successively better co-ordinated states of society" (151). Concatenate coordination will typically recognize such discovery as coordination: A humane liberal mind imagined to behold the vast tapestry and its potentialities normally will smile upon the discovery of such opportunities.

The Misesian image of science, however, leads Kirzner to make strong claims about the relation between coordination and the discovery of such opportunities. He maintains that every instance of discovering and seizing gainful opportunity advances coordination, and, inversely, every unexploited opportunity represents a failure in coordination, as instanced by the following quotations:

- "to identify absences of coordination among the plans of market participants *it is sufficient* to identify profit opportunities" (1973: 222; italics added).
- "where an unexploited mutually beneficial exchange opportunity for A and B exists, the resulting 'inefficiency' can be described as an absence of coordination" (1973: 216).
- Kirzner suggests that *all* profit opportunities are "created by initial discoordination" (2000: 21).
- Kirzner asserts that market entrepreneurship *always* advances coordination when he refers to "a possibly faulty functioning of the market" as "a possibility we have denied" (2000: 86).

So, Kirzner frequently says that market entrepreneurship is always coordinative. There is another issue worth clarifying before proceeding: In assessing whether an entrepreneurial action enhances coordination, what is the comparison? What is the hypothetical alternate concatenation? How do we characterize the concatenation *without* the entrepreneurial event? Like Kirzner, we focus on the discovery of opportunity. We suggest that usually the most relevant alternate concatenation is to imagine that for some adventitious reason the actor misses the opportunity. Imagine that an extraneous, unwelcome distraction interrupted the moment of discovery, preventing (or perhaps delaying) the actor's discovery of the opportunity, and, in consequence, after getting past the distraction he goes about his affairs without any really useable apprehension or formulation of the opportunity—without any sense of having "gotten an idea." In the case of distraction, we don't know exactly what would happen or how coordinative that world would be—possibly, the entrepreneurial action in question would itself have been a distraction to an *even better* discovery, which is now *realized* by virtue of the adventitious distraction that blocks the lesser discovery—after all, there is usually an even better opportunity out there. We resort to supposing, however, that without discovering the opportunity in question the actor instead carries out actions that are more obvious, closer to routine. With Kirzner, we say that there is no tendency to experience one discovery when a merely adventitious distraction would have brought one to an even better discovery—otherwise people would invite random distractions. It could happen, of course, but it would be somewhat aberrant. Accordingly, for our perspective as social analysts, the "expected" concatenation of the world without the discovery is more commonplace than the world with the discovery, more like "the day before" in the relevant context. It is a world without the "development" of the new discovery.

'The Only Coordinative Force Is Entrepreneurship'

Kirzner asserts that coordinative enhancements come *only* by entrepreneurial actions: "What *alone* tends to introduce a modicum of consistency and coordination into this picture, preventing a situation in which even the slightest degree of coordination could exist only as a matter of sheerest chance, is market entrepreneurship, inspired by the lure [of] pure market profit" (1973: 59, italics added; see also 1992a: 151, 171).

'Coordination Is the Fulfillment or Compatibility of Plans or Expectations'

Kirzner characterizes coordination "as the state (or the process leading towards the state) in which the individual plans of independently-acting persons display mutual compatibility. Such compatibility may be couched, as in the preceding sentence, in terms of plans, or it may be couched in

terms of decisions, or of expectations" (2000: 190). He adds, "The fundamental idea in this coordination concept is that we (the economic or social
scientists) are interested in the extent to which the decisions made by an
individual correctly anticipate (and take advantage of) the decisions in
fact being made by others" (191).

Elsewhere, Kirzner offers the following characterization: "A fully coordinated state of affairs, for our purposes, is one in which each action
taken by each individual in a demarcated set of actions, *correctly takes into
account* (a) the actions in fact being taken by everyone else in the set, and
(b) the actions which the others might take were one's own actions to be
different" (136, italics added).

Kirzner inversely characterizes discoordination as involving discor-
dance, disappointment, or regret: "disappointment and/or regret...must
ultimately ensue from patterns of action which incorrectly anticipate and
depend upon the actions of others in the system" (145); "The entrepreneurial-competitive process becomes visible...as discovering and correcting discordant individual plans and decisions" (1973: 218).

Kirzner makes use of two different perspectives, each entailing a different sets of sentiments. One perspective regards how things go along
a chosen plan (or projected path of action), the positive sentiment there
being fulfillment and the negative being frustration or disappointment.
The other perspective regards retrospectively the chosen path as opposed
to some could-have-been alternate path, the positive sentiment being
affirmation of the choice one made and the negative being regret or
self-reproach. For example, an employer hires Meg, and it all goes fine
and as expected, the plan is fulfilled, but once the action is irreversible,
the employer realizes that he could have offered the job to Valerie, who
likely would have accepted and been better, and he feels he *should have*
thought of that. This would be a case of fulfillment of the plan but nonetheless regret and an introspective sense of error. Our distinction seems
to correspond to ones presented by Jakee and Spong (2003: 477 n. 24,
480–481, 482 n. 32 referring to High 1982), who argue that Kirzner's
idea of entrepreneurial alertness "becomes *overly elastic* and therefore
must carry too much of his argument." We, too, contend that Kirzner
blurs the distinction, which is elaborated in Fig. 16.1. While it is true that
Kirzner himself has recognized a distinction similar to the one we make
here (e.g., 1992a: 169), it is nonetheless also true that he has often run
the two perspectives together, or shifted from one to the other, when
they needed to be kept separate.

	Positive	Negative
Sentiment along the path pursued	Fulfillment	Disappointment, frustration
	Compatibility	Discord
Sentiment looking back on the path pursued, as opposed to some alternate path	Affirmation	Regret, self-reproach
		(Error, according to Ch. 7 here and *sometimes* Kirzner)

Figure 16.1: Two perspectives about a plan: fulfillment vs. retrospective affirmation

Kirzner also uses the term "dovetailing" to express the positive aspects of coordination, as when he says: "Co-ordination does not refer to the well-being achieved through its successful attainment; it refers only to the dovetailing character of the activities that make it up" (1992a: 185; see also 191; 2000: 183, 196). He even says that "dovetailing" is the "earmark" of coordination (2000: 190). Later we discuss Kirzner's usage of the term "dovetailing."

'Coordination Makes No Resort to Social Aggregation'

Kirzner insists that the coordination criterion "relies not at all on any notions inconsistent with subjectivism or with methodological individualism" (1992a: 185); "The coordination criterion does not purport to say anything whatever about aggregate well-being" (2000: 144); "It is possible to evaluate a system of social organization's success in promoting the coordination of the decisions of its individual members without invoking any notion of social welfare at all" (1973: 216).[4]

4. Hayek at times invokes aggregation quite readily, for example: "[T]he ordering and productivity enhancing function of prices, and particularly the prices of services, depends on their informing people where they will find their most effective place in the overall pattern of activities—the place in which they are likely to make the greatest contribution to aggregate output" (1978c: 63).

I	II	III
Concatenate coordination	**A notion of fulfillment or compatibility**	**A notion of opportunity-exploitation**
HAYEK'S (and Mises') statements about coordination.	Kirzner holds that coordinative actions necessarily entail the resolving of problems in fulfillment or compatibility of plans or expectations (or the correction of error).	Kirzner holds that *every* entrepreneurial gain is coordinative.

Figure 16.2: Kirzner has projected III onto Hayek by attributing II to Hayek and equating II and III.

DIAGRAM OF THREE RUBRICS

In Kirzner, there is a two-step process at work, by which Kirzner asserts that Hayek (and Mises) really meant what Kirzner means by "coordination." Let us explain with reference to Fig. 16.2:

Rubric I: Here is concatenate coordination, and here is where Mises and Hayek properly belong. When they spoke of coordination, they almost always meant concatenate coordination. As shown in the Excel file, the occurrences of *coordination* are few in Mises and abundant in Hayek. The meaning is clearly concatenate. Note that "coordination" did not play a significant role in Mises' propounding of praxeology, so, while we reject that propounding, we see no particular problem in Mises' usage of coordination.[5]

Rubric II: Here is a Kirznerian coordination wherein expectations/plans are fulfilled, compatible, or affirmed. We noted earlier that there is actually quite a lot floating around in Kirzner's utterances

5. Kirzner (2001) writes: "Now Mises himself never did focus explicitly on plan-coordination in all of his work; he never did focus on the dispersed character of knowledge, and on the consequent coordination problem. (This does not mean that Mises's seminal insights in each of the above two areas cannot be faithfully articulated in plan-coordination terms; it merely means that Mises himself never explicitly recognized this possible articulation.)" (198).

about fulfillment, compatibility, and affirmation, or—to take them in their negations—disappointment, incompatibility, and regret. The variations here have to do with the distinction between what happens along a path of action (or plan) and how one regards the entire path in retrospect. The variations here give rise to different versions of the claims under rubric II, and we shall see that the versions have differing implications.

Rubric III: Here is a Kirznerian coordination wherein every entrepreneurial discovery is coordinative.

Kirzner projects III backwards onto Hayek (and Mises), first, by attributing II to Hayek's meaning of coordination, and, second, by equating II and III. We feel that both steps are unacceptable.

KIRZNER'S INVOCATION OF HAYEK

Hayek wrote a few passages about expectations or plans being fulfilled, realized, or mutually compatible. In every such instance, however, he was speaking of either equilibrium or order, *not coordination*. In 1937, Hayek wrote: "For a society, then, we can speak of a state of equilibrium at a point of time—but it means only that the different plans which the individuals composing it have made for action in time are mutually compatible" (1937/1948: 41). Perhaps one may read Nash equilibrium into Hayek's idea of equilibrium. Hayek later (1978d: 184) says he prefers the term "order" to "equilibrium," and in trying to clarify "order" he writes of plans being realized or expectations being correct (1973: 36, 44–55, 103, 106f).[6] The important thing about these passages is that "coordination" is nowhere to be found. Hayek never equates equilibrium and coordination and never defines or characterizes coordination in terms of plan/expectation fulfillment or compatibility.

Indeed, in "Economics and Knowledge" Hayek first writes of equilibrium and then emphasizes that such a position of equilibrium "is not an equilibrium in the special sense in which equilibrium is regarded as a sort of social optimum" (1937/1948: 53)—this special sense being coordination, though he does not use the word. Thereafter in the article, Hayek

---

6. In Hayek's order, plans "can be *mostly* realized" (1978c: 184; italics added) and that expectations "have *a good chance* of proving correct" (1973: 36, italics added), showing philosophical departure from the categorical approach of Mises.

talks in a way highly reminiscent of his 1933 lecture. He speaks of a "social mind" (54) that sees opportunities unknown to actors in the position of equilibrium. In no way does Hayek affirm usage of the term "equilibrium" for the "social mind" concept. Hayek's primary point is that "equilibrium analysis can really tell us nothing about the significance of such changes in knowledge" (55). Thus, Hayek's point is that important coordination claims cannot be derived solely from "the pure logic of choice." Decades later, Hayek (1983) said he wrote the piece "to persuade my great friend and master, Ludwig von Mises, why I couldn't accept all of his teachings."

It is clear that Hayek used coordination with a connotation of economic goodness. Kirzner concedes that "at least sometimes" Hayek used coordination to mean "some desired overall patterned outcome" (2000: 189). Referring to Klein (1997),[7] Kirzner concedes (199) that such usage in Hayek conforms to my idea of concatenate coordination, and Kirzner himself provides several excellent Hayek quotations in which coordination means concatenate coordination. Kirzner concedes that these occurrences of coordination do not coincide with his own notion of coordination: "such coordination is certainly not defined in terms of the mutual compatibility of independently made plans or independently held expectations" (189).

Kirzner then insists "that, *at least part of the time*, Hayek was using the term 'coordination' not in the sense of Klein's [concatenate] coordination, but in the sense of the achievement of mutual compatibility among independently made individual plans (without regard to any overall desirability of this outcome)" (199, italics in original). The evidence is thin, however. At the top of page 191, Kirzner quotes two essays by Hayek, but the quotations by no means clearly involve Kirzner's notion that coordination hinges on plan/expectation fulfillment or compatibility. In one quoted passage, Hayek says that in a decentralized system "some method must be found for coordinating these separate plans which does not depend on conscious central control" (Hayek 1941/1997: 144). The grand concatenation of course entails individuals' plans, and of course a good concatenation must entail good coordination of such plans. The other quotation has Hayek speaking of a decentralized system "with prices conveying to each the information which helps him to bring his actions in relation to others" (Hayek 1939/1997: 194). The phrase is brief and "in relation to others" is vague, but it is appropriate to read the "helps him" in the following

7. Kirzner refers to Klein (1997), where concatenate coordination was originally and regrettably dubbed by Klein as "metacoordination." That regrettable term also appears in Klein (1998).

allegorical invisible-hand sort of way: Free prices conduce to individual actions corresponding in a rough way to those actions individuals would take if they were cooperating in the commonly valued project of making a good overall concatenation. Thus, the "helps him" is allegorical—prices help individuals do their part in the imagined cooperation. Hayek is contrasting the effectiveness of the decentralized approach to that of central direction which, in the very next sentence, is said to entail the construct of "some individual mind." Hayek is yet again grappling with the problem of his 1933 lecture, in which he affirmed the need to speak of some such "sense" of the social "organism" even in argumentation against central control.[8] The passages that Kirzner invokes are but further instances of Hayek speaking of concatenate coordination.

Similar interpretation should be applied to the single occurrence of the term *dovetail* in Hayek's *Individualism and Economic Order*. We enter into consideration of "dovetail" because Kirzner and his followers have used this somewhat mysterious term to signify the distinctive Kirznerian notion that coordination hinges on plan fulfillment/compatibility. As noted, Kirzner (2000: 190) says that "the dovetailing of individual purposive efforts" is the "earmark" of such coordination.

The "dovetail" terminology appears to be twice removed from the tail of a dove.[9] The "dovetail" talk alludes to the woodworking joint (see Fig. 16.3), and that alludes to the tail of a dove.

As I see it, the woodworking joint suggests both concatenate and mutual coordination. First, one may aptly interpret it as concatenate coordination. The way the wood fits neatly together makes for a strong joint and a solid wall—a pleasing concatenation of parts in erecting a sturdy house. David Hume and Adam Smith both said that considerations of utility are central to aesthetic pleasure (though Smith varied from Hume in this matter only by putting utility at one remove from pleasure or approval, behind, as it were, the immediate sense of taste or propriety). A neat dovetail joint is useful to the owners and users of the building, and it comes to be regarded as beautiful or proper.

But the dovetail joint also has a flavor of mutual coordination. There is a mutual reinforcement of one wall by the other, analogous to the conditions of coordination equilibrium. In a coordination equilibrium, player

8. Further, note that talk of prices "conveying" or "communicating" information—as Hayek famously writes elsewhere—also is metaphorical or allegorical (see Chapter 15).

9. I am grateful to Israel Kirzner (2010) for making us aware of the derivation of the "dovetail" terminology.

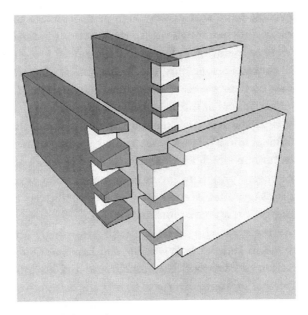

Figure 16.3: A thorough dovetail joint
Source: Wikipedia "Dovetail joint" entry; accessed 7 Sept 09.

A's action is best given what player B is doing, *and*, player B's action is best *for A* given what player A is doing. (And vice versa.) Similarly, if we think of each wall as *a sentient creature* choosing its own shape or position and preferring a snug fit, then we say wall A's shape/position is best given wall B's shape/position, and wall B's shape/position is best *for A* given wall A's shape/position.

The dovetail joint has nice connotations of both concatenate coordination and mutual coordination. It is indeed a wonderful metaphor to indicate the coincidence of both coordinations and an affinity between them. Kirzner, however, says that his coordination is neither concatenate nor mutual coordination. I do not see that the dovetail joint does anything to bolster or clarify his coordination, the coherence of which is being challenged here.

An extensive electronic search of Hayek's writings finds but three occurrences of the word *dovetail*, most notably in the essay "The Use of Knowledge in Society" as the essay appears in *Individualism and Economic Order*:[10]

10. We notice that as "The Use of Knowledge in Society" was originally published in the *American Economic Review* in 1945, Hayek had *fit* in lieu of *dovetail*. The other occurrences of *dovetail* in Hayek's writings are found in his essay "The Mythology of Capital" (Hayek 1936: 220) and *The Pure Theory of Capital* (1941/2007: 293).

> Which of these systems is likely to be more efficient depends mainly on the question under which of them we can expect that fuller use will be made of the existing knowledge. This, in turn, depends on whether we are more likely to succeed in putting at the disposal of a single central authority all the knowledge which ought to be used but which is initially dispersed among many different individuals, or in conveying to the individuals such additional knowledge as they need in order to enable them to *dovetail* their plans with those of others.
>
> (1948: 79; italics added)

Once again, we see Hayek's main concern as concatenate coordination, and we would interpret "enable them to dovetail their plans with those of others" as describing the allegorical need to guide individual efforts in ways that improve the concatenation. Hayek is considering which system is "more efficient" and how "fuller use" may be made of knowledge. We recognize that "dovetail" does carry a connotation that, in their situations, individuals experience a kind of *mutual* coordination with their partners. But that connotation does not detract from the larger concatenate-coordination interpretation, for one core value of the moral community that Hayek is participating in is that individuals should normally experience a sense of purpose, fulfillment, and local cooperation (or mutual coordination) in their lives. The Hayek passage just quoted indeed dovetails beautifully with the following that comes a few pages later: "[P]rices can act to co-ordinate the separate actions of different people in the same way as subjective values help the individual to co-ordinate the parts of his plan" (Hayek 1945/1948: 85). To me, this passage, itself tacitly suggesting an allegorical super-being, screams out concatenate coordination.

Kirzner (2000: 191) next tries to show that Hayek is Kirznerian by providing two quotations in which Hayek writes of plan/expectation fulfillment or compatibility, but in those passages Hayek is speaking of equilibrium, not coordination. In fact, the two papers that Kirzner quotes (Hayek 1933b/1939 and 1937/1948) contain no occurrence of the term *coordination* or its cognates.[11]

---

11. Similarly, elsewhere Kirzner (2000: 79) writes of how Austrian economics "has dismissed the idea that the function of the market is to allocate resources efficiently" and instead embraces the idea that the function of the market is "one of coordinating the plans" of participants, and then says how this coordinative function "has been interpreted as that of promoting" discovery, and cites, aside from his own work, Hayek's "Competition as a Discovery Procedure" (1978d). The term *coordination*, however, does not occur in Hayek's piece.

The *only* proper location of Hayek in Fig. 16.2 is under rubric I, concatenate coordination. Kirzner locates him "at least part of the time" under rubric II. Then, in equating II and III, Kirzner implies that Hayek is therefore with him under rubric III. Now, we turn to the problems of equating II and III.

THE DISPARITIES BETWEEN KIRZNER'S TWO PIECES

As we have seen, Kirzner makes strong claims about coordination in relation to plan fulfillment/compatibility and in relation to the discovery of opportunities. These are represented in Fig. 16.2 as rubrics II and III. To maintain his categorical system, these two pieces must fit neatly together. Here we argue that those two pieces do not fit neatly together. Our own understanding leaves open the distinct possibility that weakened versions of the claims may be vitally important, as elaborations on concatenate coordination, but we think that the categorical versions should be jettisoned.

Entrepreneurial Discovery Need Not Entail Any Experience of Correction (or, III Does Not Imply an Error Version of II)

Kirzner writes, "To act entrepreneurially is to identify situations overlooked until now because of error" (1985: 52),[12] and he holds that error necessarily entails disappointment and/or regret: "The entrepreneurial-competitive process becomes visible...as discovering and correcting discordant individual plans and decisions" (1973: 218). Our objection can be couched within an example offered by Kirzner (1979: 161). Robinson Crusoe stands on shore catching fish day after day. One day, he realizes that he could better catch fish by making a boat. Kirzner writes: "Nothing has changed since yesterday except that Crusoe has discovered that his time is more valuably spent in building the boat than in catching fish. He has discovered that he had placed an incorrectly low value on his time. His reallocation of his labor time from fishing to boat-building is an entrepreneurial decision, and, assuming his decision to be a correct one, yields pure profit in the form of the additional value discovered to be forthcoming

---

12. Similarly: "The opportunities that market entrepreneurs perceive and exploit are created by earlier coordination failures by market participants" (Kirzner 1992b: 91).

from the labor time applied." In this story, does Crusoe *necessarily* experience feelings of disappointment or regret? In our view, it is possible that he would experience regret in not having come to the boat-method sooner. Kirzner says that Crusoe "has discovered that he had placed an incorrectly low value on his time." That telling suggests regret; it suggests that Crusoe feels that he had erred in not previously seeing the boat-method opportunity. With a slight change in the story, though, we may have Crusoe entrepreneurially discovering the boat-method opportunity without any such feeling of regret—indeed, the term "entrepreneurship" would seem to suggest an insight that was not obvious. At any rate, it is perfectly natural to have Crusoe one day seeing the boat method without his experiencing any sense of previous error, feeling neither regret nor disappointment. Indeed, if Kirzner maintains that every entrepreneurial discovery implies preceding error and, hence, disappointment and/or regret, then humanity must be a lugubrious lot, for they often look back on their preceding actions with a better interpretation of the information they had had. By making his claims categorical, Kirzner boxes himself into identifying error (and hence disappointment and/or regret) in any previous action that one would revise based on one's *later* interpretation of the information. Such talk will often simply do violence to our language. One day a light bulb—illuminating how he may fashion a boat—goes off in Crusoe's head. This entrepreneurial moment is, quite plausibly, one of gleeful pride. Crusoe looks back on yesterday with neither disappointment nor regret; rather, today he feels a sense of improvement and forwardness. Entrepreneurship does not necessarily entail preceding error or any sense of disappointment or regret. As for the coordinative aspect of the story, it is natural enough to say that Crusoe's discovery is coordinative, for a mind imagined to behold the potentialities would smile on Crusoe's advancement. That mind would see a better concatenation of resources and efforts in Crusoe's world. The story is one of coordinative entrepreneurial discovery, but Kirzner's strict coordination claim involving error, disappointment, or regret must be dropped.

It is straightforward to take the point beyond Crusoe to the normal economy. Entrepreneurial actions in the economy simply need not entail any disappointment or regret about preceding actions. A story of entrepreneurial discovery is Somerset Maugham's verger who, unable to satisfy his urge for a smoke, is struck by the notion of opening a tobacco shop in the lacking area. In Maugham's story, the verger feels neither disappointment nor regret in not having come to the idea earlier, nor does anyone else. There is no reason to insist, as does Kirzner, that there was any prior error. If in Kirzner's system entrepreneurial discovery necessarily entails "correcting discordant individual plans and decisions" (1973: 218), then there is something very wrong with the system. If prior to the verger's discovery some being had a feeling of discord, that being could only be an imaginary one who beholds the potentialities—and Kirzner says that is not what he means.

Entrepreneurial Discovery Often Upsets Other People's Plans (or, III Does Not Imply a Fulfillment Version of II)

By all intuitive accounts, entrepreneurial discovery often upsets people's plans. Entrepreneurs often surprise established businesses, upset customs, and frustrate some customers. Had the entrepreneurial discovery not occurred, those customs and businesses would have gone forward as planned—actual expectations would have been fulfilled.

Kirzner notes (2000: 142, 250) that he has received this objection many times. Kirzner deals with the objection by saying that the plans and expectations held by the other businesses and their customers were erroneous all along, that they did not correctly take into account the realities of the situation. It will be useful to scrutinize Kirzner's discourse on this matter.

In a subsection called "Entrepreneurial Innovation—Coordinative or Disruptive?" (2000: 249–252), Kirzner takes up the challenge:

> To see why and how I believe it is possible and accurate to insist on my use of the term 'coordinative' to describe the entrepreneur's behavior, it will be useful to focus on an example of bold, creative, innovative Schumpeterian entrepreneurship responsible for a dramatic technological breakthrough, revolutionizing an entire industry.
>
> (250)

Notice that Kirzner promises an example of "the entrepreneur's behavior"—in the singular—but in the ensuing pages we never find such an example. The next sentence reads: "Consider the invention and innovation of the automobile in the U.S." He elaborates on the example, but henceforth, at least four times, it is now "entrepreneurs"—plural—who wrought the changes. Rather than the unique action of one individual, several entrepreneurs have come up with the same discovery and are simultaneously carrying it out or are poised to carry it out. In this story, no single entrepreneur really upsets the plans of the buggy makers, because if entrepreneur A fails to make the discovery, the buggy makers' plans will be devastated just as thoroughly and just as swiftly by B, C, D, and E. Thus, Kirzner writes, "The truth, as we now know, is that it was an industry sitting on a powder keg waiting to explode" (251). Thus, Kirzner has shifted from "the entrepreneur" to an example that does not face up to the challenge. Suppose there is one pioneering entrepreneur without like in sight. If we compare the world with and without that entrepreneur's discovery, we see that without his discovery some buggy makers will go on better, their plans will be fulfilled, at least for a longer stretch. Dealing with the buggy makers' disappointment and the incompatibility that *does* result from the entrepreneurial discovery, then, must lead Kirzner into issues of aggregation.

Another notable instance of Kirzner attempting to address the same challenge is at Kirzner (2000: 142f), where he answers Klein (1997). Again we fail to see Kirzner zeroing in on the comparison of worlds with and without a particular entrepreneurial discovery. Again, human experience—*verstehen*—is not to be credited: "The apparent earlier calm which, as a result of the aggressive new competition, has been followed by sudden disruption, was in fact utterly misleading. That calm was a façade..." (143). In sketching the example, Kirzner does not make explicit an assumption about multiple simultaneous entrepreneurs; instead, this example carries an implicit assumption that the incumbents who foolishly thought they were experiencing calm actually themselves had access to the opportunities in question, and could have taken them into account. Under that assumption, Kirzner is interpreting his claims under rubric II strictly in the "takes into account" version, and not at all in the fulfillment/compatibility version—the distinction based on how things go along a chosen plan and retrospection regarding the chosen path. Thus we find shifting from one version of II to another so as to sustain the various pieces, as though the versions of II all cohere as one. At any rate, one should insist: If we stick to the original simple example, in which the opportunity exists for only a single potential entrepreneur, then we must see that some disappointment or upset comes *only* in the entrepreneurial event. In judging it to be coordinative nonetheless, Kirzner must be engaging in some kind of aggregation—which he denies—or not really invoking rubric II in any fundamental way at all.

Fulfillment and Compatibility Need Not Imply No Further Profit Opportunities (or, a Fulfillment Version of II Does Not Imply III)

Here we deal with the fulfillment/compatibility version of the claims under rubric II. We contend that the fulfillment and compatibility of plans and expectations do not imply that there are no betterment opportunities out there. A network of people may carry on spontaneously, each making plans and forming expectations about the doings of the others, and they may find their plans and expectations to be fulfilled and mutually compatible in every reasonable and intuitive sense, and yet they may be overlooking opportunities for both individual and social betterment. There may be an opportunity for a better mousetrap out there, but the overlooking of that opportunity by everyone does not necessarily involve any upset to their plans or expectations. When the discovery occurs, people might make their future plans accordingly, but there is no necessary implication that their plans up to or at such time go unfulfilled or encounter incompatibilities.

Presumably, that is why, within this rubric, Kirzner at times couches the condition in terms of *taking things into account*, as when he characterizes coordination as entailing that one "correctly takes into account" how things would go for oneself "were one's own actions to be different" (2000: 136). If one had, instead, built that better mousetrap (and by implication, we are to suppose, in the first instance discovered the opportunity), then things would have gone better for him. So Kirzner's "takes into account" can do the work necessary to get II to imply III, but fulfillment and mutual compatibility, by themselves, do not deliver that result.

We now replay the point in the contrapositive—that is, we examine the Kirznerian notion that not-III implies not-II: Does the nonexistence of a betterment opportunity imply that people do not feel disappointment, discord, or regret? Here we must make use of our earlier distinction between how things go along a chosen path and retrospection regarding the chosen path. The nonexistence of a betterment opportunity *does* imply that people do not feel retrospective regret about the chosen path (assuming of course that they do not come to new spurious notions about what opportunities had existed). As we understand the terms, regret goes with error, and the non-existence of a betterment opportunity implies no error. The nonexistence of a betterment opportunity does not imply, however, that people do not feel disappointment or discord. That is, things might not go as hoped or expected, even though there was no particularly better way to go about things. It was the sentiments and expectations that were faulty, not the decisions or actions.

We believe that, all within rubric II, Kirzner has mixed together the two different sets of sentiments about a plan: fulfillment vs. retrospective affirmation. Hayek's words about equilibrium and order—which Kirzner treats as words about coordination—involve fulfillment and compatibility (or, in the negation, disappointment and incompatibility). As Kirzner wishes to claim Hayek as his own, Kirzner uses fulfillment and compatibility, but Kirzner seems to sense that what really does go with his discovery ideas (rubric III) is, rather, "taking into account" (or, in the negation, regret). It is only that version of II that implies III.[13]

PROBLEMS IN SEEING KIRZNER'S TWO IDEAS AS CHARACTERIZATIONS OF COORDINATION

The previous section considered the Kirznerian ideas of II and III in Fig. 16.2. That consideration was primarily immanent criticism of the purported cohesion between those pieces, not criticism of those ideas as necessary characterizations of coordination. Now we focus on the characterizations of coordination in those terms.

Problems in Fulfillment, etc., as Characterization of Coordination

Kirzner (1992a: 141–143) develops a traffic signaling system example to explicate coordination. The example proceeds from the point of view of the traffic engineer, not any of the motorists. Kirzner speaks without reservation of programming the system "to control the flow of traffic in some optimal manner" (141), to avoid collisions and delays. The purpose

---

13. To carry through on the scheme here, we note that III does not imply that (or any other version) of II. That is, as we have already argued, entrepreneurial discovery does not imply disappointment, incompatibility, or regret. The reason we have the relation (that is, the relation between the "takes into account" version of II and III) as *only one-way* is that we have narrower conceptions of what constitutes an entrepreneurial discovery and what constitutes an error, with the narrowness being a matter of how obvious the opportunity is (or was)—with obviousness understood within and depending upon the context of the discourse. Following Chapter 7, entrepreneurial discovery is only discovery of nonobvious opportunities, and error is only the nondiscovery of obvious opportunities. Thus, entrepreneurial discoveries do not imply previous errors.

to which Kirzner puts the example is to distinguish between the coordination achieved by a static signal program and that achieved by an adaptive signal program that changes based on the history of traffic patterns. This is all well and good—Kirzner at his best. We say that in both aspects the coordination of which Kirzner speaks is naturally interpreted as concatenate coordination.

Now, suppose the signal program was quite bad—by standards relevant to those likely to be talking in a concerned way about such things. Following Kirzner: "Southbound drivers find themselves waiting at red lights, let us say at three o'clock in the afternoon, for several minutes during which no traffic flows at all in the east-west directions. Clearly this waiting is unnecessary; it means that north-south drivers are compelled to act in a fashion that is not co-ordinated with the decisions of the east-west drivers" (141–142). Our point is this: Where, in this sorry concatenation, is there any necessary disappointment, incompatibility, or regret in plans or expectations? Suppose that motorists are familiar with the system. They get into their cars expecting a dreary journey with long delays; their plans and expectations are fulfilled. Moreover, they have no opportunity to improve their situation. There is no sense of regret, nor any feeling of discord or incompatibility with the plans of other motorists.

In this example—which both Kirzner and we readily identify as discoordination—if there is any sense of disappointment, incompatibility, or regret, it must be on the part of the traffic control chiefs. But there again, there is no guarantee that such persons actually feel any disappointment, incompatibility, or regret. We would hope they care enough about motorists' delays that they come to such sentiments, and we would hope that reform of the system is viable, but, even if not, we may still describe the situation as poor coordination. It is natural to us to think about the satisfaction that a benevolent mind would feel in the achieving of a better signaling system. As for our description of the concatenation as a "sorry" one, we may say that if the benevolent being in fact guided the traffic officials so as to produce the observed system, *that being would feel regret* over the guidance it issued, a regret that derives in some aggregate manner from its sympathies with the motorists.

The previous examples of Crusoe and of the verger do not necessarily imply any disappointment, incompatibility, or regret. Likewise, people might experience disappointment and discord without there being any discoordination in decisions and actions.

The Kirznerian rubric II involves sentiments and expectations. In our view, the only part to be retained in a significant way is to associate regret or self-reproach with error[14]—an association that Kirzner strongly affirms *sometimes* (1979: 128–130, 146, 147; 1985: 56; 1994: 224–225). As for the other sentimental and expectational aspects of Kirzner's discourse about coordination—the positive notions of fulfillment and compatibility, the negative notions of disappointment, incompatibility, and discord—we see them as only very loosely related to coordination. The problem is that our actions involve hopes, visions, and vague awareness of possible contingencies. Often, our doings are better described as "muddling through." There is often ambiguity about whether "our plans" go as expected. They rarely go as well as we wish, and they almost never go in a way that is utterly surprising, and how we describe the experience might depend on the discourse situation. Further, suppose that people learn to expect little. Does fulfillment or disappointment depend on the dispositions or personalities of the individuals involved? While we accept discovery as highly consonant with concatenate coordination, we do not see the same for fulfillment and compatibility.[15]

Problems in Claiming That Every Entrepreneurial Action Is Coordinative

"All Swans Are White"

One can make a system in which all swans are white by defining certain nonwhite birds as not swans. In managing the "field of force" of our scholarly discourse (Quine 1961), we jointly manage the strength of claims (the minimal percentage of swans that are white) and the semantic distinctions so as to achieve reasonable consistency. Consistency is not our only objective, however. Not all consistent systems are equally good. We have to consider the value or usefulness of *entire fields*, one against another (Quine 1961). If you make your claims 100%, you have a much

14. In the matter of associating regret/self-reproach with agent error, we would allow the element of regret to be merely potential or vicarious. In the matter of associating regret/self-reproach with social error, we project the semantics of agent error onto beings that might only be fictitious, metaphorical, or allegorical.

15. Perhaps these terms have gotten into the swirl because of the extensive Austrian discourse involving *equilibrium* and its cognates. Austrians have a practice of speaking of "equilibrium" without reference to a model. To our mind, "equilibrium" and its cognates are tropes that only have meaning within certain genres of metaphor or storytelling involving a model. The speaker chooses model metaphors to serve the purposes of the discourse. Whether some particular phenomena are to be described as equilibrium or disequilibrium depends on the model employed.

more complicated—and possibly eccentric—set of distinctions. You might have to attend to definitional "redistricting" in myriad minute instances to protect your 100%. Consider the opposite extreme. Suppose you work with 0% statements—"Swans are white zero or more percent of the time," "Swans have feathers zero or more percent of the time," and so forth. Then, for consistency, you don't have to worry about your distinctions at all; even bananas may be counted as swans. But 0% claims aren't serviceable. In managing this Quinean problem, we adjust at both ends, finding percentages for our claims in light of the practicality and meaningfulness of the semantic options. Like Mises and Rothbard, Kirzner holds an image of science that makes him enamored of 100% claims. As a concomitant, we contend, he ends up making impractical distinctions. Adam Smith was much more attuned to the Quinean problem, much less enamored of 100%—even suspicious of it—and more respectful of semantics "plain and intelligible to common understandings" (WN: 687).

Kirzner says that 100% of successful entrepreneurial actions are coordinative. We say it is less than 100% but high enough to give the claim presumptive truth. It seems to us that many kinds of counterexamples can be creditably presented. There are surely cases in which a first mover into a market space happens to be below-average, and that things would have gone better if the first mover had *not* moved into the space and gummed it up. This first-mover problem crops up with regard to product lines, conventions, standards, internal procedures, relationships, etc. Many other kinds of examples might be given in which entrepreneurial gain is discoordinative, including monopolistic situations, speculative situations, misleading advertising, exploitation of ignorance (e.g., tourist traps), shirking and laziness, opportunism, exploitation of a commons, businesses that are obnoxious or distasteful to some of the local community, and demerit markets. Ricketts (1992: 77–78) offers the example of a putative entrepreneur getting his acquaintances drunk and talking them into a deal that they'll later regret. He also speaks (82) of interloping entrepreneurs undoing beneficial long-term practices. All of these can be voluntary, profitable, and frowned on by the moral community involved in our coordination talk. While the proper presumption is that voluntary successful entrepreneurship is coordinative, there is no basis for insisting that it *always* is.[16]

---

16. George Selgin (1983: 39) distinguished between "equilibrating" and "coordinating" and challenged Kirzner on the claim that entrepreneurial action is necessarily coordinating. At one point (39) Selgin associates coordination with "increased well-being."

When Kirzner attempts to deal with some of these challenges, he leaves us unsatisfied.

Was The Communist Manifesto Coordinative?

In a moment of entrepreneurship, a man discovers an opportunity to write a certain book, get it published, and sell many copies. He enlists a collaborator and voluntarily agrees with publishers to produce the book, who voluntarily sell it to "sovereign" consumers. The book is very popular. Gains are made by the entrepreneur and his associates. Their plans and expectations are fulfilled. They have no regrets.

The author is Karl Marx, and the book is *The Communist Manifesto*. In Kirzner's view, it seems, one would have to say that the entrepreneurial act was coordinative. It would seem to satisfy all of his diverse aspects of coordination. In our view, however, it is reasonable for those who regard *The Communist Manifesto* as pernicious to judge this entrepreneurial act as discoordinative. To a liberal, humane mind imagined to behold the vast concatenation and its potentialities, the creation of *The Communist Manifesto* is a sad and lamentable day. Even if we set aside the pernicious effects the book would have on coercive policymaking, the cultural effects were unfortunate.

Kirzner would, no doubt, say that Marx's writings are filled with errors. In Kirzner's view, however, one would have a hard time interpreting the acts involved as error in his economic sense. Marx gained, his associates gained, the activity was voluntary, and nothing was regretted. To our way of thinking, Marx's errors were not agent errors; they were errors only in the allegorical sense exposited earlier when discussing the traffic-signal system: If the imaginary benevolent being in fact guided Marx and Engels so as to have them produce *The Communist Manifesto*, that being would feel regret over the guidance it issued. Even though there is no agent error, there can be error in terms of the "sense" of the social "organism" of which Hayek (1933a/1991) spoke. Voluntary, successful entrepreneurial developments are sometimes discoordinative.

The Communist Manifesto is merely an extreme example of something that frequently occurs in cultural markets—the prosperity of unfortunate, discoordinative ideas, forms, beliefs, and sentiments. Even if we presuppose that coercion plays no role—that is, we assume that the cultural markets are perfectly free, and that there is no hazard of the cultural wares inciting coercive actions—it still makes sense to suppose that sometimes discoordinative activities will prosper. We may have good reason to believe that the very discoordinativeness of activities in such a setting gives rise to forces that tend to make the activities in question unprofitable, but there is no reason to suppose that such an invisible hand works instantaneously, which means that along the way it is likely that many agents will reap entrepreneurial gains from discoordinative actions.

"Markets" vs. "Institutions"

How would Kirzner deal with such contentions about cultural products? A clue might be found in his discussion of path-dependence. Kirzner (1992a: 166–179) confronts the possibility of inferior patterns, standards, and practices getting locked in. Kirzner even uses "inferior" and "superior" to describe them. He gives the example of using feet and inches, and notes that "a superior system of measurement might have emerged" (172). He gives the example of "some hardy soul" (175) starting a path in a deep snow and others following in his footsteps. He suggests that the path might persist through time as the route people follow even though it is very inferior to other routes that might have emerged. Kirzner seems to be acknowledging that, under the circumstances, successful entrepreneurial action by certain pathfinders can produce inferior results. He safeguards his categorical claims by saying that such cases concern "institutions," whereas his theories are about "markets." In the paragraph that concludes the essay, Kirzner writes:

> [T]hese earlier economic insights into the spontaneously co-ordinative properties of markets do not, in themselves, provide any reassurance concerning the benign quality of the long-run tendencies of institutional development ... [T]he spontaneous co-ordination which occurs in markets provides us with no basis for any extension of the welfare theorems relating to markets to the broader field of the theory of institutional evolution.
>
> (179)

Kirzner draws a line between "markets" and voluntary "institutions." How does one, though, draw the line? Will one say that any time there is any element of path-dependence—in products, in standards, in practices, in customs—the activity becomes "institutional" and hence cannot be taken as a challenge to his theory? Don't practices and customs suffuse all market activity, however? A barber shop, a grocery store, Craigslist.org, and Amazon.com are, in every sense of the term, *institutions*. The expressions and workings of demand and supply typically proceed within the context of institutions. One might wonder whether Kirzner's "market" represents merely some blackboard example devoid of institutional context. Yet, Kirzner goes about his categorical coordination claims as though they have common relevance to real-world economic affairs. Where he separates "markets" and "institutions," Kirzner (1992a: 166–179) offers no clarification of the difficulties in making that separation—he does not even acknowledge the difficulties.

Moreover, Kirzner's "inferior" and "superior" in speaking of "institutions" is quite mysterious. In speaking of "institutions," Kirzner avoids the term *coordination*, apparently because he wishes to reserve the coordination criterion for talk of markets. So what is the criterion for institutions? The only clarification is reference to Pareto rankings (170, 172). That, however, is so narrow as to be useless—indeed, shouldn't we assume that the first hardy soul who trudged through the snow did so in a way that was individually optimal? Kirzner speaks of "inferior" and "superior" without any indication of the criterion involved or of how it relates to coordination.

Brian Loasby (1982), Martin Ricketts (1992), and others have brought similar criticisms. Kirzner relates Loasby's challenge: "Loasby stresses not only the possibility of entrepreneurial mistakes in the face of an uncertain future, but also the possibility that entrepreneurs discover profit opportunities through deliberately misleading the consumer (Loasby 1982: 121) or through speculatively purchasing assets…" (Kirzner 1992a: 13–14). Kirzner sets up the challenge quite dramatically, but in the remaining thirteen pages of the essay he never seems to answer it. He essentially addresses a different challenge, namely, that sometimes entrepreneurs err and drive the market in a wrong direction (a matter that Loasby also raised). Kirzner writes: "The postulation of a tendency for profit opportunities to generate equilibration has not been put forward as an inexorable, determinate sequence. The emphasis upon the incentive to win profits has not been intended to deny the possibility of entrepreneurial losses" (21). His lengthy examples of the erroneous bicycle factory inducing a demand for steel (29–30) and of the shoe producer acting through time (32f) are examples of entrepreneurial error, not entrepreneurial success. He says at the end of the shoe-producer example: "But it is always the case, nonetheless, that appropriate entrepreneurial incentives do, at any given moment, offer themselves in regard to the path relevant to the realities" (31). The issue, however, is whether entrepreneurial incentives *not thusly appropriate,* too, might *ever* offer themselves, and Kirzner never seems to address this matter. He concludes the essay with many gestures at concession and relaxation of his claims (see esp. 34–36) but without confronting the real challenge. Similarly, in responding to Ricketts' point that sometimes profit can be had in ways that are indubitably voluntary but manipulative, Kirzner (1992b) dodges it with the pronouncement that his work is not intended to apply in contexts "[w]here property rights are not well defined, not fully protected, or otherwise not complete enough to satisfy the conditions for a fully private enterprise economy" (93).

Does Kirzner Stretch "Entrepreneurship" to Include All Action?

We suggest examples of discoordinative successful voluntary entrepreneurship, including:

- Misleading marketing practices, manipulation
- A low-quality first mover leading to lock-in
- Speculative bubble
- *The Communist Manifesto*
- Establishing an opium den in a community
- Local cultural effects (e.g., a brothel, obnoxious billboards)
- Opportunism, shirking, etc.

One way Kirzner might try to deal with some of these examples is to regard all action as entrepreneurial and to thereby disqualify some of the examples as cases of *omnilateral* successful entrepreneurship. Suppose a tourist trap sells tourist items at terms that, say, we know the consumer is very likely to quickly discover were bad terms. Suppose most such buyers will presently feel "ripped off."[17] Kirzner might say that this is not an example of successful entrepreneurship because the success is not omnilateral—the consumers, too, he might say, are entrepreneurs, and they do not feel the transaction was a success. Mises (1966) writes: "In any real and living economy every actor is always an entrepreneur" (252)—and Kirzner (1979: 28) quotes the statement approvingly.[18] Thus,

---

17. To clarify further, assume that the consumer affirms the level of trust he had put in the merchant's decency. He feels, not that he erred, but that he was "ripped off," though not quite defrauded in a sense that would make what the merchant had done coercive.
18. See also Kirzner (1973: 33f) and (2001: 87).

every consumer who walks into a 7-Eleven and buys a carton of milk instantiates the entrepreneur. We think that this indiscriminate use of "entrepreneur" or "entrepreneurship" is wrongheaded. Interpretive perception plays some role in all human action, but we think that the entrepreneurial aspect corresponds with the nonobviousness of the opportunity discovered. Following the accustomed grooves of going to 7-Eleven to buy milk usually will not qualify. Rather than seeing a continuum of interpretive perceptiveness and demarcating an exceptional category as entrepreneurial—like Schumpeter (1934: 81–82), not only for entrepreneurship but for "being able to sing"—Kirzner sometimes insists that the "zero" point of interpretive perceptiveness is mechanical and that *anything greater than zero* is entrepreneurship. It is like treating the idea of "fatness" as having more than zero fat on one's body, or saying that thin people are "a little fat." We believe that this is misguided. We believe that Kirzner conflates entrepreneurship and interpretive perceptiveness, just as the suggested analogy would conflate fatness and body weight. Properly speaking, thin people are not in the "fat" category at all, and people who show little or only ordinary interpretive perceptiveness are not in the "entrepreneur" category at all.[19]

Indeed, Kirzner seems to be inconsistent in this regard. In keeping with ordinary language, Kirzner writes of entrepreneurial discovery as an "unanticipated enjoyment" that "lifts one out of the routine sequence of everyday experience" (1992b: 86). In general, one naturally reads Kirzner's entrepreneur talk through the lens of ordinary semantics. Kirzner seems to revert to the overly expansive conception only when he needs to invoke an idea of omnilateral entrepreneurial success to get out of certain binds.

If Kirzner wants to hold that "every actor is always an entrepreneur," where does that leave him? First, his statement about the coordinativeness of activities that satisfy omnilateral successful entrepreneurship has coverage that is significantly truncated. Perhaps Kirzner would say that it simply does not apply to the tourist trap, which he might agree is discoordinative, since the consumers, too, are now counted as entrepreneurs. Could he likewise exclude the several other examples we offer? Perhaps, with enough work, but it seems to us that he will need to get

---

19. Kirzner's overly expansive conception of entrepreneurship relates to the problem with his claiming that coordinative enhancements (save those by sheerest chance) come *only* by entrepreneurial actions. One reason we rejected this claim is that we take a narrower view of entrepreneurship. To follow through on our analogy, to say that coordinative enhancements come only by entrepreneurial actions is like saying that coordinative enhancements come only by actions by fat people.

into counterfactuals about collective action (e.g., in the path-dependent cases) as well as whether we may say that people *act* in the forming of certain attitudes, sentiments, expectations, and habits, and even in adopting certain beliefs: Are we to say that one commits entrepreneurial error in investing intellectual, moral, or spiritual capital in an inferior technological system, *The Communist Manifesto*, a drug habit, or identification with a "clean" neighborhood? Now that everyone is an entrepreneur, whatever basis we have for saying that an event is discoordinative might be turned by Kirzner into an instance of some entrepreneur not having acted successfully. Thus, once we minutely, idiosyncratically snip away all the discoordinative cases, we are left with only coordinative cases.

It appears that Kirzner goes to impractical lengths to preserve certain Misesian "pure, universal truths of economic theory" (2001: 56). If this is how Kirzner would handle the challenging cases, he must admit the truncated coverage of the application of those truths. The "pure truths" do not apply universally, except in the sense that they apply universally within the hodgepodge of cases in which they apply. This is unfortunate. The vital truths that Kirzner teaches would, if rendered in by-and-large versions, be more serviceable and more widely applicable. Instead, because of problems that come with 100% conceptualizations, people jettison what is vital and good in Kirzner.

IS KIRZNER BUILDING OUT AROUND AN AXIOM ABOUT VOLUNTARY INTERACTION?

What would it mean for Kirzner for entrepreneurship to be discoordinative? Studying Kirzner's works carefully, one gets the feeling that "coordinative" is necessarily built into successful voluntary entrepreneurship—or, more generally, simply successful voluntary action—by Mises' dictum of human action.

Murray Rothbard was much more blatant in building out around an axiom about voluntary interaction. He propounds a principle of "demonstrated preference," minimizes talk of entrepreneurship and coordination, and states bluntly: "Voluntary exchanges, in any given period, will increase the utility of everyone and will therefore maximize social utility" (1962/1993: 770); *"no government interference with exchanges can ever increase social utility"* (1956/1994: 252). Rothbard makes his claim to 100% deduction quite clear: "[S]ince all government actions rest on its taxing power, we can deduce that: *no act of government whatever can increase social utility*" (252). Similarly, Joseph Salerno (1993) writes: "We may thus conclude that every act of intervention unambiguously lowers social welfare" (131). Kirzner often seems to be making the same kind of 100% claim, but much less explicitly. If so, why not make it explicit? If Kirzner is intent on having a system in which voluntary implies coordinative, why not make that clear from the outset, and then proceed to show how he proposes to alter the entire field of concepts, semantics, and statements so as to achieve that goal? Doing so would have the virtue of directness.

In an essay "The Limits of the Market" (contained in Kirzner 2000), Kirzner denies the possibility of faulty market operation; he denies the very idea of market failure. But in Kirzner's scheme, what would it mean for the market to be faulty, for there to be market failure? Has he done nothing more than twist coordination talk and its domains as needed so as to maintain that successful voluntary action in the market is always coordinative?

ECONOMIC GOODNESS AND SOME LARGER GOODNESS

Even if one accepts Kirzner's distinction between "markets" and "institutions" and supposes that there remain substantive cases and issues in the "market" category, do we find Kirzner *in that domain* taking a firm Rothbardian libertarian line? No, we do not. We find out, essentially, that while coordination is the last word in *economic* goodness, it does not necessarily agree with some larger goodness. In Kirzner's eschewal of the Rothbardian line, we encounter another distinction:

> To say that the market process works successfully in the context of externalities is certainly not to pronounce the market outcome socially optimal... Nor is it, in and of itself, to declare governmental attempts compulsorily to internalize externalities, to be a definite error (since, after all, governmental policy may seek to reflect citizens' preferences as these are understood in moral or political terms, rather than in the narrow, austerely 'scientific' terms within which economic science is confined).
>
> (2000: 82)

Kirzner seems to be saying that his coordination claims pertain only to "economic" aspects of preferences, plans, expectations, opportunities, etc., as opposed to "moral or political" aspects. In the essay, Kirzner is not dealing with issues like culture or political identity but with conventional discussion of economic externalities such as pollution. Kirzner seems to be saying that it may be socially bad if gas stations sell leaded gasoline and make profits, but the external ill effects do not count in considerations of whether selling leaded gasoline is coordinative. Somehow those ill effects are cast out as "moral or political."

Now, in a discourse situation, we do, indeed, often find it worthwhile to distinguish economic goodness from other kinds of goodness—perhaps some larger goodness that subsumes economic goodness. But even then, would the economic realm sustain Kirzner's 100% claims? To address such a question, we need to get specific about what constitutes the distinction (does "economic" merely mean voluntary?), and what, broadly, is the nature of larger goodness. Kirzner enters into nothing of the kind. He seems to make the distinction simply to maintain his 100% claims while eschewing the Rothbardian line when it comes to larger goodness.

CAN THE COORDINATION STANDARD BE USED TO CRITICIZE INTERVENTIONS?

Kirzner's works, efforts, and intellectual community are imbued with liberal purpose. The great message is that liberty is far more valuable and worthy than accorded by the public culture and public policy. The teachings on coordination are directly and deeply related to this great message. Kirzner indicates this deep connection when he writes:

> We can now understand how Mises came to believe that economic science leads us ineluctably to the conclusion that a policy favoring unfettered free markets, a policy of laissez-faire, of capitalism without any government intervention, is scientifically demonstrated to be the best policy. A free market works in a systematic way to encourage coordination among the decisions of market participants, with the motivating force being the needs and preferences of consumers.
>
> (2001: 170)

While the liberal character of Austrian discourse is plain, when we get down to specifics in Kirzner's works about the connection between coordination talk and policy argumentation, we encounter problems—and we believe that the problems arise from Kirzner's two basic errors: insisting on 100% and not embracing concatenate coordination.

Kirzner Seems to Say That We Cannot Use Coordination to Compare Policy Regimes

Despite the liberal flavor of Kirzner's coordination talk, his discourse grows abstruse and inconsistent in attempting to show how the coordination talk works in comparing coordination of policy regimes. He writes: "The criterion is itself admittedly unable to discriminate between the economic goodness of different moral/legal frameworks, unless one of them is taken as the relevant starting point" (2000: 139). This phrasing (similarly found on 138) would seem to suggest that you *can* discriminate between frameworks but that the judgment will depend on which one you start at. A full examination of the texts, however, leaves such a reading in doubt. Another possible reading is that Kirzner is saying you simply cannot make judgments of coordination across legal frameworks.

In attempting to elucidate, Kirzner offers:

> To see this at the most elementary level, imagine that agent alpha prefers a marginal unit of beef over a marginal unit of chicken, while agent beta prefers the chicken over the beef. It will make all the difference in the world, in our judgment of coordination or miscoordination in regard to the distribution of beef and chicken ownership, whether we (i) begin with a situation in which alpha and beta 'own' the chicken and beef respectively, or (ii) begin with a situation in which alpha, say, 'owns' *both* the beef and the chicken. From the perspective of situation (i), coordination would require that alpha finish up having the beef, and beta having the chicken. But from the perspective of situation (ii), it is that initial situation (in which alpha owns both the beef and the chicken) which is the coordinated situation. From a strictly economic perspective (i.e., from a perspective which is neutral in regard to the relative morality or legality of alternative initial property rights patterns of distribution) one cannot pronounce situation (ii) as economically 'bad'—even though that situation would be perceived as uncoordinated, were our initial vantage point to have been a situation in which the beef and chicken were, initially, differently distributed.

> (2000: 139)

Thus, Kirzner says that if we started with a situation in which alpha and beta each had a piece of meat, but ended with beta having both pieces, the outcome is uncoordinated. Kirzner implies, in parallel fashion, that if we started with beta owning both and ended with each having a piece of meat, it would be uncoordinated. Kirzner does not say how, from each starting point, such outcomes emerge. Kirzner's thrust seems to be that whenever there is an alteration in the "moral/legal framework," then coordination cannot be used. The meat example leaves us uncertain, however, since, in the first example, where Kirzner pronounces the outcome "uncoordinated" it would seem that beta stole alpha's chicken. If that is what Kirzner means to imply, perhaps he would say that individual coercion does not count as an alteration in the moral/legal framework.

Kirzner attempts to clarify by drawing an analogy between the coordination criterion and distance. "The question 'How far is it to Chicago?' cannot be answered except by reference to some 'arbitrarily-given' starting point" (139). True enough, but the kind of distance question that would be analogous to the question of comparative coordination is: Which is further from Chicago, St. Louis or Indianapolis? Kirzner's discussions of these matters (principally in 2000: 80f, 138f) seem to suggest, however, that there is no comparative coordination across policy regimes. On this reading, we simply cannot speak of whether a policy reform would help or hurt coordination: "[C]oordination cannot be defined except within a given, adopted moral/legal framework; nonetheless, within that framework, it offers an objective criterion" (139). To follow through on the distance analogy, Kirzner, then, would be saying that we cannot speak of whether St. Louis or Indianapolis is farther from Chicago.

If Kirzner were to stick to this line, surely it would be quite astonishing. Despite the pervasive liberal character of all the coordination talk, we would be taking Kirzner to be saying that such talk is useless in comparing regimes. On this view, we cannot say that abolishing slavery was coordinative; we cannot say whether the imposition of pre-market approval for pharmaceuticals was discoordinative; we cannot say that socializing the food industry would be discoordinative. On this view, Kirzner's coordination criterion would say that voluntary entrepreneurial actions within a regime are coordinative, and little else.

But, Kirzner Uses Coordination to Compare Policy Regimes

Although Kirzner seems to say that we cannot use coordination to compare policy regimes, he then on the next page (2000: 140) uses it to compare policy regimes. The sole policy example addressed there is the issue of central planning versus free markets. Again Kirzner is abstruse and it is necessary to quote at length:

What Mises showed, of course, was that at a deeper level, the central planner cannot create a true plan, since he cannot engage in 'economic calculation,' i.e., each part of the 'plan' is necessarily made without full awareness of its true implications for other parts of the attempted plan. What this means, in terms of our notion of coordination is that the actions called for by the attempted central plan are uncoordinated in the sense that, were the various agents in the socialized economy to have the freedom to make their own decisions (with full awareness of each other's decisions and potential decisions), (i.e., were they to be assigned specific property rights), they would find it mutually beneficial not to follow the pattern of actions in fact dictated by the central plan—even if the central planner's objective was that of fulfilling the preferences of agents, to the greatest socially possible extent. The economic inadequacy of socialist planning is thus to be understood as seen from the hypothetical starting point of some (i.e., any) pattern of property rights.

(140–141)

The passage seems to be saying the following: If we assume that the central plan was intended to fulfill "the preferences of agents, to the greatest socially possible extent," and if instead of the socialist regime there was a pervasive assignment of private property rights, then the various agents would have done differently than the erstwhile plan, and, on that basis, "the actions called for by the attempted central plan are uncoordinated."

Kirzner deems the central plan "uncoordinated" on the basis that, acting under laissez-faire capitalism, "the various agents in the socialized economy…would find it mutually beneficial not to follow the pattern of actions in fact dictated by the central plan." Kirzner does not clarify the principle here, but he seems to be saying that any policy regime that results in outcomes other than those which would prevail under laissez-faire capitalism is uncoordinated. Since any significant departure from laissez-faire capitalism will result in different outcomes, the only thing that such a principle achieves is to render a binary criterion of economic goodness: Laissez-faire private enterprise regimes are coordinated, and all the others are uncoordinated. Such a criterion of economic goodness would be neither useful nor reasonable.

At other moments, Kirzner makes judgments about policy in terms of coordination very plainly. Consider these two cases:

• "Imposed price ceilings may, similarly, not merely generate discoordina-tion in the markets for existing goods and services (as is of course well recognized in the theory of price controls); they may inhibit the discovery of wholly new opportunities" (1985: 38–39).

- "Quite apart from the discoordination generated by such imposed prices in the markets for *existing* goods and services, price (and also quality) restraints also may well inhibit the discovery of wholly new opportunities" (1985: 143).

Here, Kirzner casually cites the "well recognized" problems of price controls as instantiations of discoordination. Such discoordination would surely be a demerit of such regimes, in comparison to regimes without such discoordination.

Kirzner, despite himself, clearly wants to use coordination to judge policy reform. In a footnote at the conclusion of the primary essay on the matter, he seems to acknowledge that things are unsettled: "We must readily grant that even if the arguments in this chapter are accepted, we have not yet firmly established the usefulness of the coordination concept as the criterion for economic goodness. The serviceability of the coordination criterion, as a device with which to rank a series of alternative policies, has to be concretely demonstrated" (2000: 147, n. 18).

On the Evaluation of Price Controls

Now, think about the lately bulleted statements in which Kirzner says that price controls generate discoordination. How would he square that with his own characterizations of coordination? The "well recognized" disadvantages of rent control involve the deadweight loss from curtailed quantity transacted and the mal-allocation of those units that are transacted. In what way do these problems fit Kirzner's characterizations of coordination? Under rubric II, there is no way to see those problems as either a lack of fulfillment or compatibility of plans or expectations. People expect rent-controlled rates; they expect shortages, queues, and so on. Nor is there any regret on the part of market participants. As for rubric III, the well-recognized discoordination does not involve any missing of profit opportunities. The law expunges opportunities that would exist in the absence of the law. The standard analysis does not involve any unexploited opportunities. Kirzner has no basis in his characterizations for calling the well-recognized harms of rent-control "discoordination."

Indeed, if we were serious about Kirzner's characterizations of coordination, where would that leave the libertarian economist? Quite plausibly, occupational licensing, the postal monopoly, and the government school system tend toward a regimentation of affairs and bring *greater* fulfillment of plans and expectations. Plans and expectations adapt to any environment, and, thus perhaps there are more moments of frustration and regret in a dynamic system than in a regimented one. Take regimentation to the extreme and think of life within a prison or military training camp; in Kirzner's terms of rubrics II and III, these would seem to suffer little discoordination.

The problem is Kirzner's characterization. Of course, those interventions are discoordinative, for in the back of our minds is concatenate coordination. To a liberal mind imagined to know the set of possible concatenations, each of those interventions is undesirable relative to freer arrangements. The interventions are viewed as undesirable for a variety of reasons, including matters of discovery, and including standard deadweight-loss analyses.

WHY WE SHOULD OWN UP TO—AND PROPERLY LOCATE—THE "LOOSE, VAGUE, AND INDETERMINATE"

By 1973, the year of *Competition and Entrepreneurship*, the economics profession had for many generations experienced the trend toward formalization. Increasingly, human beings were being thought of as optimization machines—a trend exquisitely protested by Buchanan (1979) on moral grounds. On knowledge grounds, Kirzner illuminated crucial ways in which human beings cannot be reduced to machines. The trends against which Kirzner was leaning were part of a broader trend. Modernist social scientists felt the need to do value-free science, to establish separate scientific disciplines, and to schematize the discipline's teachings. These developments went hand-in-hand with the deterioration of any liberal consensus within the moral community—social democracy and interventionism were ascendant and socialism threatened radical change.

While Kirzner's sensitivity to knowledge's richness drew from Hayek, his image of economic science followed Mises. In developing his ideas about entrepreneurship and coordination, Kirzner attempted to preserve the Misesian praxeological vision of *wertfreiheit* and exact deduction from foundational truths. Kirzner answered one form of modernism with another. He worked hard to have a modernist economic science that incorporated his key insights, but over time the efforts grew increasingly abstruse.

In our view, economics is part of the humanities. It is really political economy, of a piece with moral and political philosophy. Inquiry, argumentation, and judgment in the field is bound to enter into realms of the "loose, vague, and indeterminate," to use Adam Smith's phrase (TMS: 175, 327). Modernism may be seen as the effort to exile the loose, vague, and indeterminate.[20] The "utility" that agents maximized was utterly vague (Coase 1977/1994),[21] but no matter: the substance of "utility" was safely placed outside the province of economic science. All such nebulae were to be eliminated from the science. The aspiration was to make the science a sort of grammar, which Smith described as "precise, accurate, and indispensable" (TMS: 175). The only way to do this is to skirt the most important things—that is, the most important issues, positions, and arguments. Any economics that speaks to the most important things is, whether it admits it, bound to enter into the loose, vague, and indeterminate. Kirzner is devoted to addressing the most important things. He ends up with plenty that is loose, vague, and indeterminate. His discourse includes ambiguities and inconsistencies such as:

- Kirzner runs together two perspectives: plan fulfillment vs. retrospective plan affirmation. Similarly, he is inconsistent on whether error entails regret.[22]
- Kirzner says that "every actor is always an entrepreneur" (1979: 28) but also that entrepreneurial discovery "lifts one out of the routine sequence of everyday experience" (1992b: 86).
- Kirzner says coordination cannot be used to make judgments across regimes, and yet he uses it to make judgments across regimes.
- Kirzner characterizes coordination with the ideas of both rubric II and rubric III, but we have argued that those two rubrics do not go hand-in-hand.

20. Incidentally, it might be proper to see "modern" as post-Newton, and David Hume and Adam Smith really as rather exceptional within the general, centuries-long stream. But modernism becomes especially virulent (and "value free") with the decline of liberalism/rise of social democracy.

21. "To say that people maximize utility tells us nothing about the purposes for which they engage in economic activity and leaves us without any insight into why people do what they do" (Coase 1977/1994: 43); "man must recognize that even within his own private sphere of action there is no maximand" (Buchanan 1979: 110): "Smith would not have thought it sensible to treat man as a rational utility-maximiser" (Coase 1976/1994:116).

22. Kirzner strongly associates regret/self-reproach with error in 1979: 128–130, 146, 147; 1985: 56; 1994: 224–225.

Kirzner also invokes distinctions that remain insufficiently clarified, including:

- "markets" vs. "institutions" (1992a: 166–179)
- "economic" vs. "political" preferences (or aspects/dimensions of preferences) (2000: 82)

It makes sense that discourse about the most important things would inevitably involve the loose, vague, and indeterminate. If the most important things could be resolved by grammar-like sciences, then those things would be settled and would no longer be most important at the operative margins of discourse. While the aspiration is always to get *more* of a grammar into our understanding of the most important things, it is vain to think that we can elude the loose, vague, and indeterminate.

Owning up to the looseness, we then may think about how best to manage and locate it in our discourse. Our view is that we ought to be open about the looseness of our sensibilities about the desirable, about goodness, and specifically here about the aesthetic aspects of *coordination*, even when such is confined to only "economic" considerations. Being confessedly loose in that matter will enable us to accentuate the grammatical nature of other parts of our discourse, particularly the distinction between voluntary and coercive action; we want an economics that justifies a presumption of liberty. Kirzner, by contrast, claims to have "a clear-cut, objective criterion" (2000: 133), with the result that muddleness erupts throughout his teachings.

Mainstream economists have tried to relieve discomfort with the looseness that inheres in their doings by replacing concatenate coordination with "efficiency," "optimality," and "the social welfare function." These are served up as precise and accurate maximands, but in fact they become vague and indeterminate when put to important social purposes. On our view, economists should resist translating concatenate coordination as *efficiency* or *optimality* precisely because coordination does not pretend to or aspire to a maximand.

When an economist says, "Rent-control hurts coordination," the statement addresses certain narrow consequences of rent control as well as the concept of coordination itself; in making the statement, the economist aims to edify listeners with regard to the relevant moral and aesthetic sensibilities—what Charles Griswold has called the protreptic quality of discourse (see Chapter 3). The economics literature that used "coordination" in discussing the vast concatenation had a similar protreptic quality, in that it addressed the aesthetic sensibilities that ponder the vast concatenation. The protreptic quality—addressed to edification of basic attitudes, aesthetics, and outlooks—did not fit the "value-free" values of putatively scientific economics, and hence was discouraged and displaced by more formal discourse. In the modernist century, each journal article or textbook chapter arranged for itself a neat setting and story, and "efficiency," "optimality," and "the social welfare function" were represented in those analytic settings. Yet as game theorists from John Von Neumann (Dore et al. 1989: xiv) to Robert Aumann (1985: 42) have acknowledged, there is an aesthetic lurking behind such genres as well. The problem is that model-building aesthetics are typically ill suited to addressing important social purposes. If we are going to make the aesthetic element accountable to important social purpose, we ought not to keep it in the dark.

Kirzner writes: "What is needed for an objectively-based normative economics, is a criterion which, like the criteria which identify a particular disease, can be unambiguously identified by economic science and which, again as in the case of disease, seems likely to be able to serve as a norm for goodness in the light of independently established, widely shared or otherwise assumed moral principles" (2000: 134). Kirzner writes as though "disease" is hammered out by science, and then the business of human affairs puts that learning to use. Similarly, he thinks that science hammers out the coordination criterion, and then the morally relevant community may adopt the criterion as a norm in evaluating policies. The separation is false and unnatural. If the morally relevant public did not perceive beauty to inhere in coordination, what sense would it make to use that protreptic term? Suppose the morally relevant public was virulently closed and illiberal. What kind of discourse situation would have an economist talking to them of coordination (whatever it is, but assuming it is broadly liberal) and calling it "coordination"? The auditors might listen to him and say, "Ah, thank you, now we understand better what we must do to achieve discoordination."

In the case of medicine, perhaps it is much easier to separate grammar and aesthetics. "Mental illness" aside, a disease is quite distinct from the organism it afflicts. It is simple to assume that we are rooting for the organism and against the disease. In social policy, however, the "disease" is societal practices, interests, and beliefs. It is often a matter of individuals being unenlightened, of their beliefs being their affliction. The dialectics of discourse drive it toward those disagreements in which interlocutors invoke sensibilities that are not so widely shared that we may usefully fashion them "objectively-based normative economics."

Kirzner writes: "Use of the coordination criterion involves no such moral commitment at all, on anybody's part. Use of the coordination-criterion presumes that those advised by the economist are morally concerned that members of society [achieve better coordination]" (2000: 145). Wouldn't cooperating with policymakers entail a kind of commitment to their moral concerns, though? If advising the makers of public policy—or using the protreptic "coordination" in teaching nineteen-year-olds how to interpret political and economic affairs—does not often or even typically entail moral commitments, then what does?

Kirzner elaborates on how Mises presupposes a value of "consumer sovereignty" among his readers (2001: 169). Kirzner does not deal with whether it was reasonable to suppose that "consumer sovereignty" is an unrivaled value. Specifically, he does not explore what would happen to Mises' claims under the alternative assumption that people value collectivism. What would "coordination" mean to them? Suppose a social democrat favors the government school system relative to a voucher system, saying that it enhances coordination. Kirzner's formal characteristics of coordination (rubrics II and III) do not help much to dispute the claim, but, more importantly, Kirzner would be unwilling to negotiate the substance of "coordination." In contrast, a Smithian would dispute the claim but be upfront that what he deems misguided are not just narrower beliefs about specific consequences but broad beliefs as well. Most likely the social democrat will make claims that must drag us into a discussion of much wider consequences, including moral, sentimental, and cultural consequences.

Every economics can be thought of as the thought of some imaginary composite economist. As Polanyi put it: "The words I have spoken and am yet to speak mean nothing: it is only *I* who mean something *by them*" (1962: 252).

Kirzner's attitude is to relegate anything loose and vague into not-economic-science quarters. For example, when he speaks of "a possibly erroneous initial distribution of rights" (2000: 86), it is clear that the "erroneous" is, to his mind, completely separate from economic science, as though "economics" is what remains after all the loose and vague stuff has been separated out. By trying to relegate looseness to other quarters, Kirzner in fact ends up with brittle 100% claims surrounded by abstruse doctrine erupting with problems. It is a bit like managing vice: Attempts to eradicate it are vain—and discoordinative.

If, instead, we allow more of the loose and vague in our idea of coordination and confess the protreptic nature of it, then our by-and-large claims will be more robust and we can enter more concretely and plainly into argumentation about issues, positions, and points with fewer worries about whether a particular concession upsets some axiom and fewer inhibitions about getting into waters muddied with moral, sentimental, and cultural consequences.

Economists can preserve the important presumptive claim that coordination is advanced better by free markets than by intervention, a claim true to Hayek. It is sound to see both competition and entrepreneurship as being coordinative, in that they usually—not always—bring about changes in the grand concatenation that make it better coordinated in the eyes of the humane mind imagined to behold it. Lower-cost firms replace higher-cost firms, consumers find new and better goods and services, people find more satisfaction in their work, and so on. Such general sensibilities help to justify Adam Smith's presumption of natural liberty and ultimately entail a sense of beauty "not unlike that which we ascribe to any well-contrived machine" (TMS: 326). Government intervention typically brings a variety of effects that the imagined mind regards as baneful. With the indicated modifications, the coordination teachings of the Austrian economists remain basically true and important—but it is doubtful that they remain distinctively Austrian.

CHAPTER 17

༄

Some Fragments

FRAGMENTS ON THE DEEPSELF

When Kierkegaard (1989: 43) says, "The self is a relation which relates to itself," perhaps he points to what I have called the deepself.

The individual inhabits a realm of latent potentialities; his interpretations give rise to new interpretations, making a series calling for subscripts and for ellipses at both ends.

In making a decision, he formulates and selects alternatives; he formulates their advantages and disadvantages. If no alternative emerges as obviously worthy, he may hesitate and search for more information and better interpretations. But he must get on with it, and the decision takes form. As he judges he chooses; he acts, and consequences follow. He looks back and may affirm or regret his decision, or any part of it. If he feels he has erred, he may learn to overcome his erring. He learns.

He gropes his way toward—what? Particular objects, aims, and goals. All toward—what? His happiness? His utility? His joys? His contentment? Each day we enjoy our breakfast, but the items on today's to-do list have connections to larger objects, aims, and goals.

Larger objects, aims, and goals all toward—what? Joys and contentment again, the enjoyment of beauties greater than breakfast. Also, again, still larger or improved objects and aims. Man learns, but also, he must make commitments; his selfhood is a work in progress.

"But time is short and I must stop here at level t." That is sometimes what "happiness" and "utility" signify, bounding the discourse and drawing it to a close. But we should not pretend that, resources allowing, we cannot proceed to t+1. We do not gain by pretending that there is a definitive uppermost when there isn't, and likewise for a definitive lowermost.

*   *   *

In Episode I of *Star Wars*, Qui-Gonn Jinn counsels little Anakin Skywalker: "Your focus determines your reality." You decide your focus, and thus your reality.

On the other hand, there is much to be said for the reverse, that your reality, your experience, determines your focus.

Here we perhaps have a yin-yang that recommends another exalted straddle, at one turn avoiding what the impartial spectator would deem delusion and at another what she would deem fatalism, actualization of a candid and composed vitality.

*   *   *

Virtue is chiefly the matter of what it is that one makes his self-interest.

A DECLARATION OF OUTLOOK

- A common tendency is to make incentives the master principle, to reduce knowledge problems to more fundamental incentive problems, by specifying a cost to thinking and to the acquisition of information. But any understanding of a set of incentives emerges from a deeper body of knowledge. Any understanding of the actor's incentives, I_n, can be explained by his knowledge conditions, K_n, which can in turn be explained by a larger or deeper plain of incentives, I_{n+1}, which can be explained by K_{n+1}, and so on. Whenever Stigler maintains that Hayek/Kirzner stands on the turtle of incentives, Hayek/Kirzner may retort that Stigler stands on the turtle of knowledge. It's knowledge and incentives intermeshed all the way down, and they should be dual articles in discourse.
- Machines are not human beings, because machines quickly come to a final level, full stop. At the final level, a machine cannot make a joke, take a hint, or regret its behavior. Hence the adage: "Computers are stupid: They do what you say, not what you mean." Therein also lies one of the virtues of machines, for, at that highest level, a machine also cannot go *meshugge*.
- If we give primacy to incentives, we turn actors into machines and imperil our understanding of human beings and social processes.
- Articulate knowledge entails information, interpretation, and judgment.
- Much of modern political economy has miscarried by proceeding as though knowledge were merely information—that is, as though interpretation were symmetric and final.

- Economic prosperity depends greatly on new knowledge, or discovery, of profit opportunities that translate into social betterment. These discoveries are often a transcending of the working interpretation, not merely the acquisition of new information.
- Models generally assume common knowledge. Often, however, the sets of relevant knowledge of the relevant actors do not approximate the common knowledge assumption, and model metaphors mislead us.
- We need better appreciation of asymmetric interpretation. The need is not for the purpose of developing some body of scientific economics; it is for the purpose of counteracting the hubris of self-styled scientists and experts. Appreciation of asymmetric interpretation is key to appreciating the presumption of liberty.
- Though Kirzner would have Mises our greatest teacher, I prefer to regard the foregoing as Kirzner's service to Hayek and Hayek's service to Smith (who enjoyed better times than Mises). Kirzner aids Hayek in getting us back to being leading voices in our communities, engaging others in sensible conversation about how people's conditions and lives can be bettered.
- Smith taught that bad public policy is partly the result of not knowing better, of misguided cooperation, not of greed or malice. Economists may justify their efforts and their salaries chiefly by teaching citizens to know better. Such is the economist's calling.

FRAGMENTS AGAINST OPPRESSION BY SCIENCE

Moving through our worlds of languages, people acquire, and make a home from, points of view, ways of seeing and speaking. Re-examining one's positions—*re-viewing* one's point of view—is a trying business, because one must view from some ground, and once we begin to question our home ground, how do we choose another? Eventually, people must claim their ground and their sanity. They must stop inquiring into their own core beliefs, so they install smoke detectors and sprinkler systems to prevent the fire of inquiry from reaching their own precious ground. It is a necessary and fully human strategy. My only objection is that some people call their systems for extinguishing inquiry "science."

*   *   *

When we say that science is conversation, they jibe: "Ha! Maybe *your* 'science.'"
  Yes, and *our* conversation.

*   *   *

The 1984 suspense film *Blood Simple* tells a story of a killer, a husband, a wife, and a beau who meet tragic ends. The husband hires the killer to kill his wife and her beau. The killer pretends to have carried out the job and is paid by the husband but then kills him. The beau finds the body, concludes that the wife did it, and disposes of the body. The woman concludes that the beau killed her husband. The woman and her beau love each other, cooperate, and try to protect each other. Overwhelmed with shock and anguish, when they converse, each interprets their conversation as though it is common knowledge that the other did the killing, to make their love viable. They greatly misinterpret each other's words. They do not figure out that neither of them did the killing, and their misguided actions lead the real killer to kill the beau. And finally, in self-defense, the woman kills the killer.

The woman and the beau had shared goals: being together and staying out of trouble. They failed terribly. The knowledge and resources available to the team were not utilized wisely, from the team's own point of view. Their story is fraught with misinterpretation, error, and regret. Even from the *ex ante* position, the team did not achieve a point on its welfare frontier. Such is how one movie critic—a Kirznerian critic—might describe the events of the story.

Another critic—a "Neoclassical" (in a narrow sense of the term)—takes issue with the Kirznerian telling.

Neoclassical critic: As theorists, we ought to employ a framework that gives no place to "misinterpretation," "error," and "regret." The proper way to tell the story is that *each individual* did optimize. When the beau spoke, he chose words that seemed best suited to the situation, and the woman responded and reacted in ways that, given her imperfect information, best suited the situation. The selected strategies of each turned out badly, but optimization does not mean that things always turn out well. Each individual simply faced resource constraints and experienced bad luck.

Kirznerian critic: There is nothing against logic in excluding notions of error and regret. Such a telling, however, does a poor job of relating the meaning and interest of the film. The problems that the characters encountered would, in your description, be expressed within an artificial framework of optimization—a framework that would seem alien indeed to the characters themselves, and to viewers who put themselves in the character's position. Your telling obscures the root of their problems: misinterpretation, misunderstanding. The moral of the story—that sometimes we fundamentally misinterpret our situation and misunderstand each other—is lost. By your telling, the messsage of the story would simply be that sometimes our luck is *really* bad.

Neoclassical critic: No, it's not just about bad luck. We movie reviewers have a way of talking about uncertainty and communication problems: information costs. The characters in the film made their search choices optimally and experienced bad luck. People think information and thinking are costless, but they're not! The film is really about the high costs of acquiring information. You Kirznerians should read the literature sometime. It is filled with papers about asymmetric information, papers that study what you talk of, only in a rigorous way.

Kirznerian critic: The woman and the beau had similar information: Both knew that the husband was dead or missing. And they wanted to help each other. The problem was that each interpreted the facts differently. It wasn't so much asymmetric information, as *asymmetric interpretation*. How many papers are there in the literature about asymmetric interpretation?

Neoclassical critic: Now look, what you Kirznerians say has a sort of layman's appeal, but remember: We're scientists. Do you offer a rigorous way of representing "interpretation," "understanding," and "error"?

Kirznerian critic: What do you mean by "rigorous"?

Neoclassical critic: Can you study it scientifically?

Kirznerian critic: What do you mean by "scientifically"?

Neoclassical critic: Can you define it and make it work in a formal model? Can you quantify "interpretation," measure it in the real world, and test your descriptions using statistical methods that scientists use?

Kirznerian critic: Well, not in the way you mean. But ...

Neoclassical critic: You Kirznerians have to realize that once we stray from rigorous thinking, we put standards in jeopardy. We can't allow any sort of loose, nonrigorous thinking to pass as science. Just think what would become of the good journals! We'd fight constantly over what work is good and what bad, with no objective way to decide.

Kirznerian critic: There is something to what you say. However ...

Neoclassical critic: Look, it is darling the way you Kirznerians buck the mainstream and celebrate free markets—I'm for free markets, too—but we have a profession to run.

Kirznerian critic: But your way of speaking leaves out important things. And I notice that nobody reads your movie reviews.

Neoclassical critic: I beg your pardon! My movie reviews are very successful. They are on reading lists in graduate courses across the country.

Kirznerian critic: Well, I guess that is one kind of success.

* * *

In the *Journal of Political Economy*, Benjamin Klein reviewed Israel Kirzner's *Competition and Entrepreneurship* (1973):

> Because of its peculiar methodology and language, this book is unlikely to have a large impact on the profession...The book, on the other hand, is likely to have a large impact (or at least large sales) in the nonprofessional libertarian market. This is mainly due to the general appeal among this group of Austrian analysis and with Kirzner's indirect rationalization of a laissez-faire policy... But the effectiveness of particular institutional arrangements in specific imperfect-information contexts must be determined by much more thorough theoretical and empirical analysis...What Kirzner presents as analysis is merely a turgid terminological system with no clearly stated propositions that could, in principle, be refuted.
>
> (B. Klein 1975: 1304–1305)

But what of the following proposition: Restrictions on liberty, including high taxes, reduce the motivation, range and prowess of the interpretive faculties that make for the kind of discovery that Kirzner calls "entrepreneurial."

Everyone agrees that bringing statistical evidence to bear on this proposition is difficult. But is refutation possible "in principle"? If so, then, according to the indicated criterion, Kirzner's body of work becomes real science (and rather important science, at that).

Otherwise, would the utterers of positivist precepts kindly explain the "principle" that this proposition fails to satisfy, and why that principle ought to be considered the marker of real science?

*   *   *

To maintain with Hayek that opportunities and knowledge are highly particularistic is to say that cases differ and performance cannot be readily evaluated. To show that liberal arrangements perform better, Hayek must show the opportunities that governmentalized arrangements *fail* to make use of. It is precisely such knowledge that eludes mastery.

The strongest evidence for Hayek's view would be the failure of able opponents to show its unsoundness. They withhold this evidence merely by ignoring the liberal outlook. Liberal theorists are defeated by silence.

*   *   *

The academic economist is often squeamish about engaging in plain talk about policy issues, maybe because policy debate is a painful reminder that he cannot base his political opinions on his opinion of what science is.

*   *   *

Dilemmas of the Hayekian in academe:

- He needs to show himself knowledgeable in professing that society, economy, and self are unknowable.
- He must commune with colleagues in the intellectually marginal, while differing on the inframarginal.
- He dreams of vindicating certain central verities and presumptions, but taboos deter him from even stating them.
- In departmental meetings, if 51% know and oppose his cause, his open efforts contribute to its defeat.
- For twelve years, he must refrain from trying to explain that there is such a thing as water and that it runs downhill; the tenured professor then finds that again he is a mere novice.
- To the ordinary citizen, he says: "In stupendously many ways, each painfully complicated, grotesque, and insulting, government intervention keeps you from living better. Neither you, nor I, nor anyone else can do much to fix the situation. Now, join with us in attending to these matters."
- He must entreat them to think about governmental matters and to hope that we may get to a social arrangement in which they need not think about such matters.
- When he applies to an official agency for a grant, he says to himself, "The institution shouldn't exist," and he says to the institution, "I'm the man for the job."
- He continually finds reason to hope that things will get better, and reason to believe that things are worse than he had thought.

DEAR SOCIAL DEMOCRATS

Knowledge and Incentives in *Ninotchka*

In the 1939 Hollywood film *Ninotchka* (which stars Greta Garbo and Melvyn Douglas), three Soviet officials travel to France carrying a box of czarist jewels to be sold off for Mother Russia. Once in Paris, Iranoff and Kopalski favor staying at a luxurious hotel, but the scrupulous Buljanoff objects to the burden the expense would put on comrades. Iranoff explains that Lenin himself would have them take the fine hotel, to show the prestige of the Bolsheviks. "Okay then, who am I to contradict Lenin?"

They ask the hotel manager for a room with a vault large enough to hold the large box of jewels. The manager says that one suite has a vault that size, but it might give offense: The Royal Suite.

What would Moscow think?

The Russians confer:

"We just tell them that we had to do it on account of the safe. There was no other safe big enough."

"That's right, that's right!" they agree.

It dawns on Buljanoff: "But of course, we could take out the jewels and distribute them in three or four boxes in the vault and take a small room. That's an idea, isn't it?"

"Yes that's an idea," Iranoff replies, "but who said we have to have an idea?"

"That's right, that's right!"

They beam to the manager: "Give us the Royal Suite!"

* * *

Isaac Asimov once said: "If knowledge can create problems, it is not through ignorance that we can solve them."

Yes, but sometimes the knowledge needed to solve problems is not new or even expert. The solution may lie in knowledge forsaken. Pride yourself for being progressive in a sense expressed by C.S. Lewis: "We all want progress. But... [i]f you are on the wrong road, progress means doing an about-turn and walking back to the right road; and in that case, the man who turns back soonest is the most progressive" (1952/2000: 28).

CHAPTER 18

༺ঙ༻

In Defense of Dwelling in Great Minds

A Few Quotations from Michael Polanyi's The Study of Man

I am a member of the economics department at George Mason University. When the department has a job opening and is looking at candidates, I often have only a few minutes to speak with each. I want to get a sense of the candidate's mind, character, and vision. I often ask the candidate: *Who are some of the economists you most admire?* The question is always revealing and sometimes awkward. Many candidates have no certain response and, apparently, no great admiration for any economist.

Among economists, concern for the great, the epic, seems weak, and seems to be receding. Most economists seem not to have heroes. It is but a shrinking minority who feel reverence for individuals such as Smith, Mill, Marx, Marshall, Veblen, Keynes, Mises, Hayek, Rothbard, Galbraith, and Friedman. The practical men and women of the economics profession sometimes derogate such reverence as cultish idolatry. They commend *appreciation*, but not reverence. Meanwhile, those who *do* revere great figures often feel bashful and guard their reverence furtively.

In 1958, Michael Polanyi delivered a set of lectures at the University College of North Staffordshire, published as a small book, *The Study of Man* (1963). His topic led into remarks that speak to the worthiness of a sense of reverence and greatness. The following passages were chosen for that purpose. By implication, they would seem to support the cause of making the history of economic thought a staple of economic training and practice:

> To contemplate a person as an ideal is to submit to his authority. The admirer of Napoleon does not judge him by independent previously established standards, but accepts, on the contrary, the figure of Napoleon as a standard for judging himself. Such an admirer may be mistaken in the choice of his hero, but his relation to greatness is correct. We need reverence to perceive greatness, even as we need a telescope to observe spiral nebulae.
>
> (96)

> A man who has learned to respect the truth will feel entitled to uphold the truth against the very society which has taught him to respect it. He will indeed demand respect for himself on the grounds of his own respect for the truth, and this will be accepted, even against their own inclinations, by those who share his basic convictions.
>
> (61–62)

> The mind is a comprehensive feature of man. It is the focus in terms of which we are subsidiarily aware of the play of a man's features, utterances and whole behaviour. A man's mind is the meaning of these workings of his mind. It is false to say, as Ryle does, that these workings *are* his mind. To say this is to commit a category mistake (to use Professor Ryle's term) of the same kind as we should commit if we said that a symbol *was* its own meaning. A comprehensive entity is something else than its particulars known focally, in themselves.
>
> (65)

> Every pebble is unique, but profoundly unique objects are rare. Wherever these are found (whether in nature or among the members of human society) they are interesting in themselves. They offer opportunity for intimate indwelling and for a systematic study of their individuality. Since great men are more profoundly unique than any object in nature, they sustain a far more elaborate study of uniqueness than any natural object can. Hence the peculiar position of dramatic history at the end of a row of sciences of increasing intimacy and delicate complexity, yet offset against all of them by an exceptionally vigorous and subtle participation in its subject-matter.
>
> (85)

> Now take into account also that the participation of the knower in the thing he knows increases steadily as the objects of knowledge ascend to ever higher

levels of existence, and that, correspondingly, the observer also applies ever higher standards of appreciation to the things known by him. These two trends will combine to an ever more ample and also more equal sharing of existence between the knower and the known, so that when we reach the point at which one man knows another man, the knower so fully dwells in that which he knows, that we can no longer place the two on different logical levels. This is to say that when we arrive at the contemplation of a human being as a responsible person, and we apply to him the same standards as we accept for ourselves, our knowledge of him has definitely lost the character of an observation and has become an encounter instead.

(94–95)

We are now being led back to these ultimate matters by our examination of historiography in its relation to the natural sciences. A reverent submission to greatness has been found to form the ultimate member of a series of studies applied to an ascending sequence of realities. Starting from physics, we passed through the rising levels of biological sciences and arrived at the study of man as the agent of responsible choices; and then, when from this encounter of equals we went on to the study of heroes, we found ourselves paying homage to our subject and educating ourselves in its image. Clearly, when arrived here, we can no longer think of ourselves as observers occupying, as such, a logical level above that of our object. If we can still distinguish two levels we are now looking *up* to our object, not down.

I have purposely chosen as my example the figure of Napoleon to remind us that this process of education may amount to a corruption. This should show how we both submissively depend for our whole universe of thought on the masters whose deeds and works we reverently study, and yet how independent we are, and indeed how hazardously self-reliant, in accepting them as our masters. This choice must indeed ultimately fall back on us, since no authority can teach us how to choose between itself and its rivals. We must enter here on an ultimate commitment which coincides essentially with the act of deciding to what extent we should accept as given the social and mental milieu within which we shall deploy our own thoughts and feelings. By recognizing our heroes and masters we accept our particular calling.

At this point the study of man is definitively transformed into a process of self-education. Instead of observing an object, or even encountering a person, we are now apprenticing ourselves to the understanding and imitation of the great minds of the past. We are dedicating ourselves to the service of obligations for which they have legislated. We are entering on a framework of expressions and standards by the guidance of which our minds will be enlarged and disciplined.

(97–98)

Looking up to Polanyi, I add a few words that speak to the currents of liberal economics.

The passages conclude that we are now apprenticing ourselves to the understanding and imitation of the great minds of the past, entering on a framework of expressions and standards.

It is only natural that we enter more knowingly and easily into minds situated nearer to us in time and place, for we better understand their expressions and standards; we may even have encountered their living being or others who have done so.

But what if the past century represents an epoch of heightened philosophical and semantic confusion, in which even the greatest minds were ensnared, beset, and compromised? If liberal semantics and philosophy are the jewels of virtuous civilization, what if their greatest epoch is now two centuries behind us? One gravitates by proximity to minds within living memory. Polanyi authorizes reverence and even a kind of submission. But, here in 2012, there is a special hazard: Our devotion to, our expertise in great minds of the twentieth century might keep us from understanding those earlier and greater figures that become for us really approachable only later.

GLOSSARY

Asymmetric information: You and I having different sets of information, as when I do not get to see your cards.

Asymmetric interpretation: You and I having different interpretations. We might have the same information, but you alone might see a great opportunity by virtue of an interpretation not in my intellectual portfolio. Asymmetric interpretation seems to be an essential ingredient in humor; every joke, it seems, provides an illustration of asymmetric interpretation.

Coincidence of interest: You and I have a coincidence of interest if in promoting my interest, I also promote your interest, as when I avoid colliding with you or I work to complete a voluntary exchange with you. This is not to say that our interests coincide perfectly or entirely.

Common knowledge: Something is common knowledge among a set of people if everyone knows it, everyone knows that everyone knows it, everyone knows that everyone knows that everyone knows it, etc. Game theorists often assume common knowledge among players to give closure to the model and, thereby, impose symmetric interpretation among the players.

Concatenate coordination: A concatenation is said to be better coordinated if its components or elements find an order more pleasing or desirable according to some relevant standard. Concatenate coordination was what economists, including Simon Newcomb, Friedrich Hayek, and Ronald Coase, usually meant by "coordination" from the time that the term first found usage in economics in the 1880s until the 1970s.

Concatenation: A series of interconnected or interrelated things, activities, or events; a chain, order, netting, or constellation of such things.

Convention: A way of acting or behavior regularity in a recurring situation, a regularity corresponding to a coordination equilibrium in that situation. Driving on the right is the convention in the United States.

Cooperation: You and I cooperate if we have a common awareness of our working together. It can be parsed in terms of the two coordinations: The mutual coordinating of each one's actions in a context in which each cooperator perceives himself to be contributing to the same referent concatenation. There is mutual consciousness of each one's contributing to the pleasing concatenation. The spirit of cooperation is especially pronounced when there is not only mutual awareness but also mutual sentiment: "We did it together!"

Coordination: It is important to distinguish between *concatenate coordination* and *mutual coordination*. In virtually any social setting they coexist, for they are two different ways of thinking about doings. For concatenate coordination, the perspective is synoptic, beholding the whole concatenation of actions, whereas mutual coordination builds from the several perspectives of the individuals doing their activities. Concatenate and mutual are two different sets of lenses, entailing different rubrics of ideas.

Coordination equilibrium: In a game-theoretic model, an equilibrium is, in the purest sense, a coordination equilibrium if and only if no player can make *any* player better off by deviating from the coordination equilibrium. Thus, there is mutual coordination in the equilibrium. But a coordination equilibrium is not necessarily a very good outcome. It may be a coordination equilibrium for Americans to use the Imperial system of weights and measures, but those conventions are inferior to the metric system. Also, note that coordination equilibrium is far from synonymous with Nash equilibrium: Every coordination equilibrium is a Nash equilibrium, but not every Nash equilibrium is a coordination equilibrium.

Correction: For a mistake, correction can be fixing in the instance, as with a typo. For an error, correction may entail contemplation resulting in reformulation or reformation of one's habits, routines, relationships, purposes, or interpretations—leading, one hopes, to better judgment.

Decision (as opposed to *Choice*): Again I quote Kenneth Burke (1932/1966: 215): "If decisions were a choice between alternatives, decisions would come easy. Decision is the selection and formulation of alternatives."

Deepself: A "society of mind" approach to the human being, with asymmetric knowledge within the being. Most importantly, the approach sees the human being as layered but with neither an uppermost nor a lowermost layer or level. Thus it rejects flattening the human being down to a machine or mathematical function (man as "Max U"), even one that is multileveled.

Disappointment: A sentiment arising from things not going as expected or planned. Being disappointed is different from regretting the plan itself. Disappointment does not imply regret, and regret does not imply disappointment.

Discoordination: In the context of mutual coordination, this term means failure to coordinate our actions, as when each of goes to a different place when trying to meet up; it would not mean coordinating on an inferior outcome (such as meeting on a rainy street-corner). In the context of concatenate coordination, this term means an upset to the workings of the system. I wonder whether it would be useful to use "discoordination" when thinking of mutual coordination and "malcoordination" when thinking of concatenate coordination. Thus, we would describe universal defection in a prisoners' dilemma game as malcoordination but not as discoordination, since mutual coordination is not even possible. Also, in a coordination game, we could describe an inferior coordination equilibrium as malcoordination, but not as discoordination. Discoordination would be reserved for outcomes like our failing to meet up at the same place (an outcome that, in a concatenate light, could also be called malcoordination).

Discovery: Coming to new knowledge. The new knowledge may be more a matter of a new interpretation than a matter of new pieces of information.

Disjointed knowledge: Knowledge that is fragmented, which means asymmetric in either or, more likely, both information and interpretation.

Dovetailing: In woodworking joinery, a dovetail joint is a joining of two pieces, usually in a perpendicular configuration, such as two walls or two sides of a drawer. At the joint, the end of one or both of the pieces resembles a dove's tail.

This joining has served as a metaphor for meshing or interlocking activities, as when we say that our plans dovetail—a usage found extremely infrequently in the writings of Hayek but more frequently in Kirzner and others. The dovetail joint can be interpreted alternatively as a sort of mutual coordination, if we imagine the two pieces of wood as shaping themselves so as to be snug with one another, or as concatenate coordination, in that the joint makes for a sturdy building or drawer. Whereas Kirzner (2010) has invoked the dovetail joint as a primary metaphor for what he means by "coordination," my view is that, while the dovetail joint nicely highlights the co-existence and even interrelation of mutual and concatenate coordination, it does not represent a coherent, separate, third notion of coordination.

Efficiency: Increasing the ratio of output to input, as with the efficiency of an engine. Defined this way, usage of the term would seem to imply a pretty exact idea of the output and the input.

Emergence, emergent convention: Emergence implies that the emergent things come into view by their own force, as when baby sea turtles emerge from the sand. Conventions are emergent when they come into prominence by the growing practice of such convention, by "catching on," as opposed to by central direction or imposition. Note that, as with the QWERTY keyboard, it is the *adoption*, not the composition, of the rule or standard that is said to be emergent.

Entrepreneurship: I associate entrepreneurship with the discovery of nonobvious opportunity, rather like Kirzner does. That association is useful for appreciating liberty, but other associations are useful for other purposes.

Epiphany: In comic strips, when a character has this experience it is represented by a light-bulb flash over her head. It is coming to an important new and better interpretation, and hence an opportunity, that was not obvious. It is the kind of discovery most appropriately associated with entrepreneurial discovery.

Error: A course of action about which you feel you should have known to do otherwise; an action that gives rise to regret—if not actual regret, then potential or vicarious regret.

Facts: When you and I converse, we treat a statement as factual if we mutually understand that we both accept and use it; we care about the statement, and we do not care to take issue with it.

Flat-talk: Discourse that flattens knowledge down to information.

Focal point: A feature that from its salience, prominence, uniqueness, or conspicuousness is focal, and that people in the context expect to be mutually focal and hence as quite possibly effective in mutually coordinating their actions. Focal points are sometimes called Schelling points.

Hayek, Friedrich A. (1899–1992): A social philosopher born and raised in Austria but who spent most of his career in Britain, the United States, and Germany. Originally a soft socialist, he converted to liberalism during his early twenties, influenced particularly by the writings and personal influence of Ludwig von Mises. In 1974, Hayek was a co-recipient of the Riksbank Prize in Economics in Honor of Alfred Nobel.

Hume, David (1711–76): A Scottish moral philosopher and good friend of Adam Smith. The most characteristic feature of his writings, in my view, is his remarkable understanding of ideas under the rubric of mutual coordination (including focal points and convention). He tended to interpret features of the world through that lens, including causation, ownership, voluntary agreement, justice, political authority, human identity and human consciousness.

Impartial spectator: Adam Smith's term (in *The Theory of Moral Sentiments*) for the imagined beholder of the whole, whose judgment is impartial and is presupposed by all of us to be worthy of our sympathy and allegiance. In this book I have dubbed the impartial spectator "Joy." We disagree in our characterizations of Joy, but we agree to a set of conversational ground rules that presuppose a single Joy universal to all of us (though recognizing the historical and contextual particularity of the circumstances of the individual actions judged of). The impartial spectator is not one's conscience, which Smith rather calls one's "representative" of the impartial spectator, but rather more like the unreachable ideal: one's conscience's conscience's conscience's ... conscience.

Incentive: An incentive is articulable, and, hence, perhaps manipulable, as within a means-ends framework that is commonly understood—as opposed to *motivation*, which suggests more subterranean sources and vaguer aims.

Information: Facts as they are understood through the basic or working interpretation.

Interpretation: A way of understanding or reading the facts. Different interpretations give rise to different arrays of information.

Invisible hand: Without anyone guiding, superintending, or possibly even minding the overall coordination of the concatenation, its many constituent actions nonetheless advance its coordination as though directed or induced by a wise and benevolent god-like being. Like *spontaneous order*.

Judgment: Taking stock in certain interpretations by acting on them—that is, by judging them to be worth investing in. The action facet of knowledge.

Kirzner, Israel M. (b. 1930): The leader of the wing of Austrian economics that tends to homogenize Mises and Hayek. A protégé of Mises at New York University, Kirzner has focused on entrepreneurial discovery as the driving force of economic progress. In my view, and in my terminology, Kirzner's great contribution has been to defy the flattening of knowledge down to information by highlighting how liberal policy conduces to better interpretations and the realization of opportunities with wide social benefits. For more than four decades, Kirzner led a program in Austrian economics at New York University, where he is now professor emeritus.

Knowledge: We know more than we can tell, and what we can tell is not merely a matter of information, but also interpretation and judgment.

Liberalism: By "liberalism" I mean a rather libertarian political sensibility akin to the original liberal persuasion, particularly as it existed in Britain (as opposed to the Continent, where *liberalism* was more associated with notions of revolution and matters of political form and participation), emerging especially in the eighteenth century, perhaps best represented by Adam Smith, and politically by Liberal Party politicians Richard Cobden, John Bright, and William Gladstone, and pervasively understood in the Anglosphere merely as "liberalism" up to the end of the nineteenth century and in much of the world still today.

Liberty: Others not messing with one's stuff.

Minsky, Marvin (b. 1927): An American cognitive scientist and leader in artificial intelligence. Among his works is *The Society of Mind* (1986).

Mistake: A slip-up, as by a subordinate who executes badly. Like a typo.

Mises, Ludwig von (1881–1973): An epic figure in the drama of human liberty. During the 1930s he was driven from Austria and settled in New York in 1940. He propounded liberalism and his system of economics or "praxeology," which was fashioned as a deductive, categorical science based on axioms such as "Man acts." In Vienna, he greatly influenced the young Friedrich Hayek, and in New York he was mentor to many students, notably Murray Rothbard and Israel Kirzner.

Motivation: Motivation is not necessarily articulable or manipulable—as opposed to *incentive*.

Mutual coordination: We mutually coordinate our actions when we drive on the same side of the road; or use the same word, such as "apple," to refer to an object; or use the same medium of exchange. Our actions mesh according to a situational coincidence of interest. Mutual coordination is generally manifest from the interactor's point of view. The ideas of mutual coordination came forward especially with Thomas Schelling's book *The Strategy of Conflict* (1960) and the rise of game theory. Nowadays, it is what economists usually mean by *coordination*.

Path-dependence: The dependence of the current set of alternatives on past circumstances or decisions that are otherwise no longer relevant. Technological standards are often said to be path-dependent, in that once a standard catches on, the practice of it becomes the cause of its own perpetuation. From path-dependence, inferior conventions can become locked in. There is mutual coordination, but concatenate coordination is lacking relative to what would be the case with a superior standard or convention. Path-dependence and lock-in are more important in matters of culture, politics, and morals than of technology.

Plan affirmation: Looking back on the plan and affirming the plan or the decision to pursue it; not regretting it, not feeling as though it was an error. Plan affirmation does not imply plan fulfillment.

Plan fulfillment: Things going pretty much as planned. The plan is fulfilled. Plan fulfillment will not necessarily be accompanied by plan affirmation. Even a fulfilled plan might be regretted.

Polanyi, Michael (1891–1976): A Hungarian-British polymath who wrote about spontaneous order in *The Logic of Liberty* (1951) and the richness of knowledge in *Personal Knowledge* (1962), *The Study of Man* (1963), and *The Tacit Dimension* (1966).

Regret: Wishing you had done things differently, a sentiment most relevant when you feel that you *could* have done things differently. Feeling that you erred.

Respondence: Perceiving and responding to incoming bits of information that one was not searching for, as when one notes useful information shown in a billboard while driving along on a highway. Respondence does not involve major interpretive shifts. It is like *search*, except that search is the active pursuit of information, such as looking up a phone number, while respondence is passive, as useful information just comes your way.

Rothbard, Murray N. (1926–95): A student of Mises in New York, Rothbard was from an early age an ambitious and prodigious polymath, working to erect axiomatic and paradigmatic systems in political ethics and economics—both based explicitly on the distinction between voluntary and coercive action—all woven together, along with bold interpretive scholarship in political, economic, and intellectual history, to offer a libertarian (even anarchist) political worldview.

His economics follow and develop Mises' praxeological approach. Like Kirzner, he fashioned and nurtured an Austrian economics; his brand is centered on Mises and, if only implicitly, on Rothbard himself, whereas Kirzner has worked to integrate Hayek more centrally into a set of tenets deemed Austrian. Many of Rothbard's followers today tend to dehomogenize Mises and Hayek, and prefer Mises. Rothbard saw Hayek and himself as the leading representatives of rival visions for liberalism in his times. Rothbard has been a much more important figure than is generally recognized; a great many Austrians and libertarians are influenced more by Rothbard than by Mises, Hayek, or anyone else, but trade externally on labels and figures that soften and obscure Rothbard's radical politics and rationalistic approach to policy and ethical discourse.

Schelling, Thomas C. (b. 1921): An American economist who has developed and explored most of the important elements of strategic and situational analysis, many of which were later distilled in game theory. His book *The Strategy of Conflict* (1960) contains (among much else) the seminal exposition of many of the ideas of the mutual coordination rubric, including focal points. The book also grapples with issues of asymmetric interpretation, as it explores how people interpret a situation differently, based in part on things that a formal analysis might regard as incidental or unimportant features of the setting. Focalness is a matter of interpretation and, as such, is not amenable to formalization. Thus his book stands as something of a critique of attempting to flatten matters down to symmetric interpretation or common knowledge. Like Adam Smith, Schelling infuses his terms with meaning by rich illustration and application. His book *Micromotives and Macrobehavior* (1978) develops ideas later discussed as path-dependence and lock-in of conventions and technological standards. *Choice and Consequence* (1984) contains two essays that discuss self-command problems by thinking of the human being as a multiple-self; these essays were significant in getting economists to think beyond the consistent, integrated agent. In 2005, Schelling was a co-recipient of the Riksbank Prize in Economics in Honor of Alfred Nobel.

Search: Actively hunting down bits of information within a working interpretation (whereas *respondence* is passively receiving and responding to incoming bits).

Self-reproach: A sentiment arising from error and impelling correction.

Serendipity: The discovery of an opportunity involving a major interpretive shift that, in the context of discovery, is obvious to the discoverer—as opposed to *epiphany*, which is nonobvious.

Smith, Adam (1723–90): The Scottish moral philosopher whose two principal works were *The Theory of Moral Sentiments* (1st ed. 1759, 6th ed. 1790) and *The Wealth of Nations* (1776).

Spontaneous order: An order (or concatenation) whose overall coordination is without central direction or superintending; usually said of an order that impresses in its coordination—whether that of the molecules in a crystal or snowflake, or of the activities in the free-enterprise economy. In public policy argumentation, the relevant frame for "spontaneous" is typically that of more or less free; governmental restrictions are thus said to make the order less spontaneous, and liberalizations more spontaneous.

Symmetric information: Information whose exposure and possession is symmetric. In chess, information is symmetric. In bridge and poker, information is asymmetric.

Symmetric interpretation: Two people who interpret an affair or set of statements the same way have symmetric interpretation. The common-knowledge assumption in model building is the imposing of a sort of symmetric interpretation among the agents of the model.

Sympathy: The mutual coordination of sentiment.

Synoptic: A description or account is said to be synoptic if it covers the whole, front to back, beginning to end. The description is not necessarily detailed, but it gives a complete account of things it accounts for. A table of contents is a synoptic account of the book's contents. We evoke a synoptic view of a concatenation when we speak of its coordination.

Transcendence: Moving up to a higher or superior interpretation.

REFERENCES

Adamson, Robert E. 1952. "Functional Fixedness as Related to Problem Solving: A Repetition of Three Experiments." *Journal of Experimental Psychology* 44(4): 288–291.

Akerlof, George A. 1970. "The Market for 'Lemons': Quality Uncertainty and the Market Mechanism." *Quarterly Journal of Economics* 84 (August): 488–500.

Alchian, Armen A. 1950. "Uncertainty, Evolution and Economic Theory." *Journal of Political Economy* 58: 211–221.

———. 1977 [1969]. "Corporate Management and Property Rights." In Alchian, *Economic Forces at Work*. Indianapolis: Liberty Press.

Alchian, Armen A., and Harold Demsetz. 1977 [1972]. "Production, Information Costs and Economic Organization." In Alchian, *Economic Forces at Work*. Indianapolis: Liberty Press.

Alvarez, Sharon A., and Jay B. Barney. 2007. "Discovery and Creation: Alternative Theories of Entrepreneurial Action." *Strategic Entrepreneurship Journal* 1: 11–26.

Alwin, Duane F., Ronald L. Cohen, and Theodore M. Newcomb. 1991. *Political Attitudes over the Life Span: The Bennington Women after Fifty Years*. Madison: University of Wisconsin Press.

Arrow, Kenneth J. 1971 [1962]. "Economic Welfare and the Allocation of Resources for Invention." In Arrow, *Essays in the Theory of Risk-Bearing*: 144–163. Chicago: Markham Publishing Co.

———. 1963. "Uncertainty and the Welfare Economics of Medical Care." *American Economic Review* 53 (December): 941–973.

———. 1974a. *The Limits of Organization*. New York: W.W. Norton.

———. 1974b. "Limited Knowledge and Economic Analysis." *American Economic Review* 64: 1–10.

———. 1984. *The Economics of Information*, Vol. 4 of the *Collected Papers of Kenneth J. Arrow*. Cambridge, Mass.: Harvard Belknap.

———. 1992. "I Know a Hawk from a Handsaw." In *Eminent Economists: Their Life Philosophies*, edited by M. Szenberg: 42–50. New York: Cambridge University Press.

———. 2003. Letter to Daniel Klein (October 21), *Econ Journal Watch* 2(1). http://econjwatch.org/articles/symposium-on-information-and-knowledge-arrow-correspondence (Accessed 30 August 2011).

Arthur, Brian, W. 1994. *Increasing Returns and Path Dependence in the Economy*. Ann Arbor: University of Michigan Press.

Aumann, Robert. 1985. "What Is Game Theory Trying to Accomplish?" In *Frontiers of Economics*, edited by Kenneth Arrow and Seppo Honkapohja: 28–76. Oxford: Basil Blackwell.

Bain, Alexander. 1868. *Mental and Moral Science*. London: Longmans, Green, and Co.

Bagehot, Walter. 1915 [1876]. "Adam Smith as a Person." In Bagehot, *The Works and Life of Walter Bagehot*, Vol. 7, edited by Mrs. Russell Barrington: 1–32. London: Longmans, Green, and Co.

Ball, Laurence, and David Romer. 1991. "Sticky Prices as Coordination Failure." *American Economic Review* 81(3): 539–552.

Barry, Norman. 1982. "The Tradition of Spontaneous Order." *Literature of Liberty* 2(2): 7–58.

Bastiat, Frédéric. 1996 [1850]. *Economic Harmonies*. Translated by W. Hayden Boyers, edited by George B. de Huszar. Irvington-on-Hudson, N.Y.: The Foundation for Economic Education, Inc.

Bauer, Peter T. 1981. *Equality, the Third World, and Economic Delusion*. Cambridge, Mass.: Harvard University Press.

Beales, Howard, and Steven Salop. 1980. "Selling Consumer Information." *Advances in Consumer Research* 7: 238–241.

Beales, Howard, Richard Craswell, and Steven C. Salop. 1981. "The Efficient Regulation of Consumer Information." *Journal of Law and Economics* 24 (December): 491–539.

Beito, David T. (with Bruce Smith). 1990. "The Formation of Urban Infrastructure Through Nongovernmental Planning: The Private Places of St. Louis, 1869–1920." *Journal of Urban History* 16: 263–303.

Beltramini, Richard F., and Edwin R. Stafford. 1993. "Comprehension and Perceived Believability of Seals of Approval Information in Advertising." *Journal of Advertising* 12(3) (September): 3–13.

Bentham, Jeremy. 2008 [1787]. "Gulphs in Mankind's Career of Prosperity: A Critique of Adam Smith on Interest Rate Restrictions." *Econ Journal Watch* 5(1): 66–77.

Bierce, Ambrose. 1993 [1911]. *The Devil's Dictionary*. New York: Dover.

Biglaiser, Gary. 1993. "Middlemen as Experts." *Rand Journal of Economics* 24: 212–223.

Binmore, Ken. 1992. *Fun and Games: A Text on Game Theory*. Lexington, Mass.: D.C. Heath and Co.

Bitterman, Henry J. 1940. "Adam Smith's Empiricism and the Law of Nature: I." *Journal of Political Economy* 48(4): 487–520.

Block, Walter. 1979. "Free Market Transportation: Denationalizing the Roads." *Journal of Libertarian Studies* 3(2): 209–238.

Boettke, Peter J. 2001. *Calculation and Coordination: Essays on Socialism and Transitional Political Economy*. New York: Routledge.

Bond, Eric W. 1982. "A Direct Test of the 'Lemons' Model: The Market for Used Pickup Trucks." *American Economic Review* 72 (September): 836–840.

Booth, Wayne C. 1974. *Modern Dogma and the Rhetoric of Assent*. Chicago: University of Chicago Press.

Briggeman, Jason, Daniel B. Klein, and Kevin D. Rollins. 2010. "44 Economists Answer Questionnaire on the Pre-Market Approval of Drugs and Devices." *Econ Journal Watch* 7(2): 162–173.

Brin, David. 1998. *The Transparent Society: Will Technology Force Us to Choose Between Privacy and Freedom?* Reading, Mass.: Addison-Wesley.

Brittan, Samuel. 1985. "Two Cheers for Self-Interest." Adapted and reprinted in *Capitalism with a Human Face* (Cambridge, Mass.: Harvard University Press, 1995).

Brown, Vivienne. 1994. *Adam Smith's Discourse: Canonicity, Commerce, and Conscience.* London: Routledge.

Brubaker, Lauren. 2006. Why Adam Smith Is Neither a Conservative nor a Libertarian. *Adam Smith Review* 2: 197–202.

Bryant, John. 1983. "A Simple Rational Expectations Keynesian-Type Model." *Quarterly Journal of Economics* 98: 525–529.

Buchanan, James M. 1965. "An Economic Theory of Clubs." *Economica* 32: 1–14.

———. 1979. "Natural and Artifactual Man." In Buchanan, *What Should Economists Do?*: 93–112. Indianapolis: Liberty Fund.

———. 1999. *The Logical Foundations of Constitutional Liberty.* Indianapolis: Liberty Fund.

Buckle, Henry T. 1904 [1861]. *Introduction to the History of Civilization in England,* edited by J.M. Robertson. London: George Routledge & Sons.

Bukharin, Nicolai I. 1971 [1920]. *Economics of the Transformation Period.* New York: Bergman.

———. 1972 [1917]. *The Economic Theory of the Leisure Class.* New York: Monthly Review Press.

Burke, Kenneth. 1966 [1932]. *Towards a Better Life.* Berkeley: University of California Press.

Bush, Vannevar. 1937. "The Engineer and His Relation to Government." *Science* 86 N.S. (2222): 87–91.

Butler, Joseph. 1736. *Analogy of Religion, Natural and Revealed to the Constitution and Course of Nature to Which Are Added, Two Brief Dissertations.* http://www.ccel.org/ccel/butler/analogy.toc.html (Accessed 30 August 2011).

Calkins, Earnest Elmo. 1928. *Business the Civilizer.* Boston: Little, Brown and Co.

Cannan, Edwin. 1896. Editor's Introduction to *Lectures on Justice, Police, Revenue and Arms* by Adam Smith. Oxford: Clarendon Press.

———. 1902. "The Practical Utility of Economic Science." *Economic Journal* 12(48) (December): 459–471.

Caplan, Bryan. 2005. "From Friedman to Wittman: The Transformation of Chicago Political Economy." *Econ Journal Watch* 2(1): 1–21.

———. 2007. *The Myth of the Rational Voter: Why Democracies Choose Bad Policies.* Princeton: Princeton University Press.

Cheung, Steven. N. S. 1983. "The Contractual Nature of the Firm." *Journal of Law and Economics* 26: 1–21.

Chisholm, Donald. 1989. *Coordination Without Hierarchy: Informal Structures in Multiorganizational Systems.* Berkeley: University of California Press.

Chwe, Michael S. 2001. *Rational Ritual: Culture, Coordination, and Common Knowledge.* Princeton: Princeton University Press.

Clark, John Bates. 1899. *The Distribution of Wealth.* New York: Macmillan Company.

Clark, John Maurice. 1923. *The Economics of Overhead Costs.* Chicago: University of Chicago Press.

Clark, Michael J. 2011. *The Virtuous Discourse of Adam Smith: The Political Economist's Measured Words on Public Policy.* PhD dissertation. George Mason University, Fairfax, Va.

Coase, R.H. 1972. "Industrial Organization: A Proposal for Research." In *Policy Issues and Research Opportunities in Industrial Organization,* edited by Victor R. Fuchs: 59–73. New York: National Bureau of Economic Research.

———. 1981 [1938]. "Business Organization and the Accountant." In *L.S.E. Essays on Cost*, edited by James M. Buchanan and G.F. Thirlby: 97–132. New York: New York University Press.

———. 1988 [1937]. "The Nature of the Firm." In Coase, *The Firm, the Market, and the Law*: 33–55. Chicago: University of Chicago Press.

———. 1988 [1960]. "The Problem of Social Cost." In Coase, *The Firm, the Market, and the Law*: 95–156. Chicago: University of Chicago Press.

———. 1992. "The Institutional Structure of Production" (Nobel lecture). *American Economic Review* 82: 713–719.

———. 1994 [1975]. "Economists and Public Policy." In Coase, *Essays on Economics and Economists*: 47–63. Chicago: University of Chicago Press.

———. 1994 [1976]. "Adam Smith's View of Man." In Coase, *Essays on Economics and Economists*: 95–116. Chicago: University of Chicago Press.

———. 1994 [1977]. "Economics and Contiguous Disciplines." In Coase, *Essays on Economics and Economists*: 34–46. Chicago: University of Chicago Press.

Comanor, William S., and Thomas A. Wilson. 1974. *Advertising and Market Power*. Cambridge, Mass.: Harvard University Press.

Comte, Auguste. 1896. *The Positive Philosophy of Auguste Comte*. 3 vols. Translated and condensed by Harriet Marineau. London: George Bell & Sons.

Cooper, Russell, and Andrew John. 1988. "Coordinating Coordination Failures in Keynesian Models." *Quarterly Journal of Economics* 103: 441–463.

Cowen, Tyler. 1985. "Public Goods Definitions and Their Institutional Context: A Critique of Public Goods Theory." *Review of Social Economy* 43: 53–63.

DeLong, Bradford J. 1991. "Did J.P. Morgan's Men Add Value? An Economist's Perspective on Financial Capitalism." In *Inside the Business Enterprise: Historical Perspectives on the Use of Information*, edited by Peter Temin: 205–236. Chicago: University of Chicago Press.

Demsetz, Harold. 1983. "The Neglect of the Entrepreneur." In *Entrepreneurship*, edited by Joshua Ronen: 271–280. Lexington, Mass.: D. C. Heath and Co.

DeSalvo, Joseph S. 1973. "The Economic Rationale for Transportation Planning." In *Perspectives on Regional Transportation Planning*, edited by Joseph D. DeSalvo: 21–89. Lexington, Mass.: Lexington Books.

DeVany, Arthur, and Ross D. Eckert. 1991. "Motion Picture Antitrust: The Paramount Case Revisited." *Research in Law and Economics* 14: 51–112.

Diamond, Peter. 1982. "Aggregate Demand Management in Search Equilibrium." *Journal of Political Economy* 90: 881–894.

Diandas, John and Gabriel Roth. 1995. "Alternative Approaches to Improving Route Bus Service in Sri Lanka." Unpub.

Dodgson, John S., and Y. Katsoulacos. 1991. "Competition, Contestability and Predation: The Economics of Competition in Deregulated Bus Markets." *Transportation Planning and Technology* 15: 263–275.

Dore, Mohammed, Sukhamoy Chakravarty, and Richard Goodwin. 1989. *John von Neumann and Modern Economics*. Oxford: Clarendon Press.

Dunker, Karl. 1945. "On Problem-Solving." *Psychological Monographs* 58(5), whole no. 270.

Durkheim, E. 1964. *The Division of Labor in Society*. Translated by George Simpson. New York: The Free Press.

Eckert, Ross and George Hilton. 1972. "The Jitneys." *Journal of Law and Economics* 15: 293–325.

Ellickson, Robert C. 1991. *Order Without Law: How Neighbors Settle Disputes.* Cambridge, Mass.: Harvard University Press.

Elster, Jon. 1979. *Ulysses and the Sirens: Studies in Rationality and Irrationality.* New York: Cambridge University Press.

Ely, Jeff. 2009. "Don't Link to This Post" (August 10), *Cheap Talk.* http://cheaptalk.org/2009/08/10/dont-link-to-this-post/ (Accessed 10 August 2011).

Ely, Richard T. 1903. *Studies in the Evolution of Industrial Society.* New York: Macmillan.

Epstein, Richard. 1997. *Simple Rules for a Complex World.* Cambridge, Mass.: Harvard University Press.

Foldvary, Fred. 1994. *Public Goods and Private Communities: The Market Provision of Social Services.* Aldershot: Edward Elgar.

Foldvary, Fred E., and Daniel B. Klein, eds. 2003. *The Half-Life of Public Policy Rationales: How New Technology Affects Old Policy Issues.* New York: New York University Press.

Forman-Barzilai, Fonna. 2005. "Sympathy in Space(s): Adam Smith on Proximity." *Political Theory* 33(2): 189–217.

Foxwell, Herbert Somerton. 1887. "The Economic Movement in England." *Quarterly Journal of Economics* 2(1): 84–103.

Frankena, Mark, and Paul Pautler. 1986. "Economic Analysis of Taxicab Regulation." *Transportation Research Record* 1103: 2–5.

Friday, David. 1922. "An Extension of Value Theory." *Quarterly Journal of Economics* 36(2): 197–219.

Friedman, David. 1994. "A Positive Account of Property Rights." *Social Philosophy and Policy* 11(2): 1–16.

Friedman, James W. 1986. *Game Theory with Applications to Economics.* New York: Oxford University Press.

Friedman, Jeffrey. 2009. "A Crisis of Politics, Not Economics: Complexity, Ignorance, and Policy Failure." *Critical Review* 21(2–3): 127–183.

Friedman, Milton, and Rose D. Friedman. 1980. *Free to Choose: A Personal Statement.* New York: Harcourt Brace Jovanovich.

Friedman, Thomas L. 1999. *The Lexus and the Olive Tree.* New York: Farrar, Straus and Giroux.

Fuller, Lon. 1969. *The Morality of Law.* New Haven: Yale University Press.

Garrison, Roger W. 1993. "On the Relevance of Policy to Kirznerian Entrepreneurship: Comment." In *Effects of Taxes and Regulation on Entrepreneurship*: 71–79. Hayward, Calif.: Smith Center for Private Enterprise Studies.

George, Henry. 1886. *Protection or Free Trade.* New York: Robert Schalkenbach Foundation, undated reprint.

Gilder, George. 1984. *The Spirit of Enterprise.* New York: Simon and Schuster.

Gombrich, E.H. 1960. *Art and Illusion: A Study in the Psychology of Pictorial Representation.* New York: Pantheon Books.

Grava, Sigurd. 1980. "Paratransit in Developing Countries." In *Transportation and Development Around the Pacific*: 278–289. New York: American Society of Civil Engineers.

Griswold, Charles L. Jr. 1999. *Adam Smith and the Virtues of Enlightenment.* Cambridge: Cambridge University Press.

Grossman, Sanford J. 1981. "The Informational Role of Warranties and Private Disclosure about Product Quality." *Journal of Law and Economics* 24 (December): 461–483.

Gwartney, James, Joshua Hall, and Robert Lawson. 2010. *Economic Freedom of the World, 2010 Annual Report*. Vancouver: Fraser Institute.

Gwilliam, K.M., C.A. Nash, and P.J. Mackie. 1985. "Deregulating the Bus Industry in Britain—The Case Against." *Transport Reviews* 5: 105–132.

Haakonssen, Knud. 1981. *The Science of a Legislator: The Natural Jurisprudence of David Hume and Adam Smith*. Cambridge: Cambridge University Press.

Harrison, Glenn W., and Peter Morgan. 1990. "Search Intensity in Experiments." *Economic Journal* 100 (June): 478–486.

Hayek, Friedrich A. 1936. "The Mythology of Capital." *Quarterly Journal of Economics* 50(2): 199–228.

———. 1939 [1933b]. "Price Expectations, Monetary Disturbances and Malinvestment." In Hayek, *Profits, Interest and Investment*. London: George Routledge and Sons.

———. 1944. *The Road to Serfdom*. Chicago: University of Chicago Press.

———. 1948 [1937]. "Economics and Knowledge." In Hayek, *Individualism and Economic Order*: 33–56. Chicago: University of Chicago Press.

———. 1948 [1940]. "Socialist Calculation III: The Competitive 'Solution'." In Hayek, *Individualism and Economic Order*: 181–208. Chicago: University of Chicago Press.

———. 1948 [1945]. "The Use of Knowledge in Society." In Hayek, *Individualism and Economic Order*: 77–91. Chicago: University of Chicago Press.

———. 1948 [1946]. "Individualism: True and False." In Hayek, *Individualism and Economic Order*: 1–32. Chicago: University of Chicago Press.

———. 1948. *Individualism and Economic Order*. Chicago: University of Chicago Press.

———. 1952. *The Sensory Order: An Inquiry into the Foundations of Theoretical Psychology*. Chicago: University of Chicago Press.

———. 1955. *The Counter-Revolution of Science: Studies on the Abuse of Reason*. New York: Free Press.

———. 1960. *The Constitution of Liberty*. Chicago: University of Chicago Press.

———. 1964. "Kinds of Order in Society." *New Individualist Review* 3: 3–12.

———. 1967 [1961]. "The Non Sequitur of the 'Dependence Effect.'" In Hayek, *Studies in Philosophy, Politics and Economics*: 313–317. Chicago: University of Chicago Press.

———. 1967 [1963]. "Rules, Perceptions, and Intelligibility." In Hayek, *Studies in Philosophy, Politics and Economics*: 43–65. Chicago: University of Chicago Press.

———. 1973. *Law, Legislation and Liberty: Vol. 1, Rules and Order*. Chicago: University of Chicago Press.

———. 1976. *Law, Legislation and Liberty, Vol. 2, The Mirage of Social Justice*. Chicago: University of Chicago Press.

———. 1978 [1974]. "The Pretence of Knowledge" (Nobel lecture). In Hayek, *New Studies in Philosophy, Politics, Economics and the History of Ideas*. Chicago: University of Chicago Press.

———. 1978a. "Coping with Ignorance." *Imprimis* 7(7) (July): 1–6.

———. 1978c. "The Atavism of Social Justice." In Hayek, *New Studies in Philosophy, Politics, Economics and the History of Ideas*: 57–68. Chicago: University of Chicago Press.

———. 1978d. "Competition as a Discovery Procedure." In Hayek, *New Studies in Philosophy, Politics, Economics and the History of Ideas*: 179–190. Chicago: University of Chicago Press.

———. 1979. *Law, Legislation and Liberty: Vol. 3, The Political Order of a Free People.* Chicago: University of Chicago Press.

———. 1981 [1978b]. Foreword to Ludwig von Mises's *Socialism*. Indianapolis: Liberty Fund.

———. 1983. An Interview with F.A. Hayek. *Cato Policy Report* 5(2).

———. 1988. *The Fatal Conceit: The Errors of Socialism*. Chicago: University of Chicago Press.

———. 1991 [1933a]. "The Trend of Economic Thinking." In Hayek, *The Trend of Economic Thinking: Essays on Political Economists and Economic History*, edited by W.W. Bartley III and S. Kresge: 17–34. Chicago: University of Chicago Press.

———. 1994. *Hayek on Hayek: An Autobiographical Dialogue*. Edited by S. Kresge and L. Wenar. Chicago: University of Chicago Press.

———. 1997 [1939]. "Freedom and the Economic System." In Hayek, *Socialism and War: Essays, Documents, Reviews*, edited by Bruce Caldwell: 189–211. Chicago: University of Chicago Press.

———. 1997 [1941]. "The Economics of Planning." In Hayek, *Socialism and War: Essays, Documents, Reviews*, edited by Bruce Caldwell: 141–147. Chicago: University of Chicago Press.

———. 2007 [1941]. *The Pure Theory of Capital*. Edited by L.H. White. Chicago: University of Chicago Press.

Hazlitt, Henry. 1998 [1964]. *The Foundations of Morality*. Irvington-on-Hudson, N.Y.: Foundation for Economic Education.

Hedengren, David, Daniel B. Klein, and Carrie Milton. 2010. "Economist Petitions: Ideology Revealed." *Econ Journal Watch* 7(3): 288–319.

Hensher, David A. 1988. "Productivity in Privately Owned and Operated Bus Firms in Australia." In *Bus Deregulation and Privatization*, edited by J.S. Dodgson and N. Topham: 141–170. Aldershot: Avebury.

High, Jack C. 1982. "Alertness and Judgment: Comment on Kirzner." In *Method, Process, and Austrian Economics*, edited by Israel M. Kirzner: 161–168. Lexington, Mass.: D.C. Heath.

———. 1986. "Equilibration and Disequilibration in Market Processes." In *Subjectivism, Intelligibility and Economic Understanding: Essays in Honor of Ludwig M. Lachmann on His Eightieth Birthday*, edited by Israel Kirzner: 111–121. New York: New York University Press.

Hirsch, Max. 1901. *Democracy versus Socialism*: London: Macmillan.

Hodgskin, Thomas. 1966 [1827]. *Popular Politcal Economy*. New York: Augustus M. Kelley.

Horwitz, Steven. 2004. "Monetary Calculation and the Unintended Extended Order: The Misesian Microfoundations of the Hayekian Great Society." *Review of Austrian Economics* 17(4): 307–321.

Hume, David. 1902 [1748]. *An Enquiry Concerning Human Understanding*. Edited by L.A. Selby-Bigge in a volume containing both Enquiries. Oxford: Clarendon Press.

————. 1902 [1751]. *An Enquiry Concerning the Principles of Morals*. Edited by L.A. Selby-Bigge in a volume containing both Enquiries. Oxford: Clarendon Press.

————. 1978 [1740]. *A Treatise of Human Nature*. Edited by L.A. Selby-Bigge and revised by P.H. Nidditch, 2nd edition. Oxford: Clarendon Press.

————. 1987. *Essays: Moral, Political, and Literary*. Edited by E.F. Miller. Indianapolis: Liberty Fund.

Hutcheson, Francis. 2008 [1726]. *An Inquiry into the Original of Our Ideas of Beauty and Virtue*. Edited by W. Leidhold. Indianapolis: Liberty Fund.

Hutt, W.H. 1934. "Co-ordination and the Size of the Firm." *South African Journal of Economics* 2(4) (December): 383–402.

Ikeda, Sanford. 1990. "Market-Process Theory and 'Dynamic' Theories of the Market." *Southern Economic Journal* 57(1) (July): 75–92.

Ippolito, Pauline M. 1986. "Consumer Protection Economics: A Selected Survey." In *Empirical Approaches to Consumer Protection Economics*, edited by Pauline M. Ippolito and David T. Scheffman: 1–33. Washington, D.C.: Federal Trade Commission.

Ippolito, Pauline M., and Alan D. Mathios. 1990. "Information, Advertising and Health Choices: A Study of the Cereal Market." *Rand Journal of Economics* 21 (Autumn): 459–480.

Jakee, Keith, and Heath Spong. 2003. "Praxeology, Entrepreneurship and the Market Process: A Review of Kirzner's Contribution." *Journal of the History of Economic Thought* 25(4): 461–486.

Jennings, M. Kent. 1990. "The Crystallization of Orientations." In *Continuities in Political Action*, edited by M. Kent Jennings and Jan W. van Deth et al.: 313–348. New York: Walter de Gruyter.

Keeler, Theodore E. 1983. *Railroads, Freight, and Public Policy*. Washington, D.C.: Brookings Institution.

Keynes, John M. 1930. *Treatise on Money I*. London: Macmillan.

————. 1951. *Essays in Biography*. New edition. London: Rupert Hart-Davis.

Kierkegaard, Søren. 1978. *Parables of Kierkegaard*. Edited and translated by T.C. Oden. Princeton: Princeton University Press.

————. 1989. *The Sickness unto Death*. Translated by A. Hannay. New York: Penguin.

Kirzner, Israel M. 1963. *Market Theory and the Price System*. Princeton: Van Nostrand.

————. 1973. *Competition and Entrepreneurship*. Chicago: University of Chicago Press.

————. 1979. *Perception, Opportunity, and Profit: Studies in the Theory of Entrepreneurship*. Chicago: University of Chicago Press.

————. 1985. *Discovery and the Capitalist Process*. Chicago: University of Chicago Press.

————. 1992a. *The Meaning of Market Process: Essays in the Development of Modern Austrian Economics*. New York: Routledge.

————. 1992b. "Entrepreneurship, Uncertainty and Austrian Economics: Commentary on Ricketts." In *Austrian Economics: Tensions and New Directions*, edited by Bruce J. Caldwell and Stephan Boehm: 85–102. Boston: Kluwer Academic Publishers.

————. 1994. "A Tale of Two Worlds: Comment on Shmanske." In *Advances in Austrian Economics* 1, edited by Peter Boettke and Mario Rizzo: 223–226. Greenwich, Connecticut: JAI Press.

————. 1999 [1983]. "Does Anyone Listen to Economists?" In *What Do Economists Contribute?*, edited by Daniel B. Klein. London: Macmillan.

————. 2000. *The Driving Force of the Market*. New York: Routledge.

————. 2001. *Ludwig von Mises: The Man and His Economics*. Wilmington: ISI Books.

————. 2010. "The Meaning of 'Economic Goodness': Critical Comments on Klein and Briggeman." *Journal of Private Enterprise* 25(2): 55–85.

Kitzmann, Jana and Dirk Schiereck. 2005. "Entrepreneurial Discovery and the Demmert/Klein Experiment: Another Attempt at Creating the Proper Context." *Review of Austrian Economics* 18(2): 169–178.

Klamer, Arjo, Deirdre McCloskey, and Stephen Ziliak. 2007. "Is There Life after Samuelson's *Economics*? Changing the Textbooks." *Post-Autistic Economics Review* 42(18) (May): 2–7.

Klein, Benjamin. 1975. "Review of Kirzner's *Competition and Entrepreneurship*." *Journal of Political Economy* 83 (December): 1305–1309.

Klein, Benjamin, and Keith B. Leffler. 1981. "The Role of Market Forces in Assuring Contractual Performance." *Journal of Political Economy* 89(4): 615–641.

Klein, Daniel B. 1997. "Convention, Social Order, and the Two Coordinations." *Constitutional Political Economy* 8: 319–335.

————. 1998. "Planning and the Two Coordinations, With Illustration in Urban Transit." *Planning and Markets* 1(1).

————. 2005. "The People's Romance: Why People Love Government (As Much as They Do)." *The Independent Review* 10(1): 5–37.

————. 2006. "Free Parking versus Free Markets." *The Independent Review* 11(2): 289–297.

————. 2007. "The Myth of the Rational Voter: Towards a Future Edition—Remarks on Bryan Caplan." Unpub. http://econfaculty.gmu.edu/klein/Assets/Caplan_critique.doc (Accessed 30 August 2011).

————. 2008. "Colleagues, Where Is the Market Failure? Economists on the FDA." *Econ Journal Watch* 5(3): 316–348.

Klein, Daniel B., and Jason Briggeman. 2010a. "305 Economists Called to Answer Questionnaire on the Pre-Market Approval of Drugs and Devices." *Econ Journal Watch* 7(1): 99–106.

Klein, Daniel B., and Michael J. Clark. 2010. "Direct and Overall Liberty: Areas and Extent of Disagreement." *Reason Papers* 32 (Fall): 41–66.

Klein, Daniel B., and John Majewski. 2006. "America's Toll Road Heritage: The Achievements of Private Initiative in the Nineteenth Century." In *Street Smart: Competition, Entrepreneurship and the Future of Roads*, edited by Gabriel Roth: 277–303. New Brunswick, N.J.: Transaction Publishers.

Klein, Daniel B., Adrian Moore, and Binyam Reja. 1997. *Curb Rights: A Foundation for Free Enterprise in Urban Transit*. Washington, DC: Brookings Institution.

Klein, Daniel B., and Aaron Orsborn. 2009. "Concatenate Coordination and Mutual Coordination." *Journal of Economic Behavior and Organization* 72: 176–187.

Klein, Peter G. 2008. "Opportunity Discovery, Entrepreneurial Action, and Economic Organization." *Strategic Entrepreneurship Journal* 2: 175–190.

Knight, Frank H. 1921. *Risk, Uncertainty, and Profit*. Boston: Houghton Mifflin.

————. 1965 [1951]. *The Economic Organization*. New York: Harper and Row.

Koppl, Roger. 2000. "Policy Implications of Complexity: An Austrian Perspective." In *The Complexity Vision and the Teaching of Economics*, edited by D. Colander: 97–117. Northampton, Mass.: Edward Elgar.

Kreft, Steven F., and Russell S. Sobel. 2005. "Public Policy, Entrepreneurship, and Economic Freedom." *Cato Journal* 25(3): 595–616.

Lachmann, Ludwig M. 1971. *The Legacy of Max Weber*. Berkeley: Glendessary Press.

———. 1978 [1956]. *Capital and Its Structure*. Kansas City: Sheed Andrews and McMeel.

———. 1986. *The Market as an Economic Process*. New York: Basil Blackwell.

Landa, Janet T. 1994. *Trust, Ethnicity, and Identity: Beyond the New Institutional Economics of Ethnic Trading Networks, Contract Law, and Gift-Exchange*. Ann Arbor: University of Michigan Press.

Lange, Oskar, and Fred M. Taylor. 1964 [Lange's contribution first published in 1938]. *On the Economic Theory of Socialism*. Edited by B. E. Lippincott. New York: McGraw-Hill.

Lauderdale, James Maitland. 1966 [1819]. *The Nature and Origins of Public Wealth*. 2nd ed. New York: Augustus M. Kelly.

Lavoie, Donald. 1985a. *National Economic Planning: What Is Left?* Cambridge, Mass.: Ballinger Publishing Co.

———. 1985b. *Rivalry and Central Planning: The Socialist Calculation Debate Reconsidered*. New York: Cambridge University Press.

Leibenstein, Harvey. 1966. "Allocative Efficiency vs. 'X-Efficiency.'" *American Economic Review* 56 (June): 392–415.

Leijonhufvud, Axel. 1981. *Information and Coordination: Essays in Macroeconomic Theory*. Oxford: Oxford University Press.

Leland, Hayne E. 1980. "Minimum-Quality Standards and Licensing in Markets with Asymmetric Information." In *Occupational Licensure and Regulation*, edited by Simon Rottenberg: 265–284. Washington, D.C.: American Enterprise Institute.

Leslie, T.E. Cliffe. 1888 [1879]. "The Known and the Unknown in the Economic World." In Leslie, *Essays in Political Economy*: 221–242. London: Longmans, Green, & Co.

Lewis, C. S. 2000 [1952]. *Mere Christianity*. San Francisco: Harper Collins.

Lewis, David K. 1969. *Convention: A Philosophical Study*. Cambridge, Mass.: Harvard University Press.

Lindgren, J. Ralph. 1969. "Adam Smith's Theory of Inquiry." *Journal of Political Economy* 77(6): 897–915.

Little, I.M.D. 1957. *A Critique of Welfare Economics*. 2nd edition. Oxford: Oxford University Press.

Loasby, Brian J. 1982. "Economics of Dispersed and Incomplete Information." In *Method, Process and Austrian Economics: Essays in Honor of Ludwig von Mises*, edited by I.M. Kirzner. Lexington, Mass.: D.C. Heath.

———. 1983. "Knowledge, Learning and Enterprise." In *Beyond Positive Economics*, edited by Jack Wiseman. London: Macmillan.

Luce, R. Duncan, and Howard Raiffa. 1957. *Games and Decisions: Introduction and Critical Survey*. New York: John Wiley & Sons.

Lynd, Robert S. 1948. *Knowledge for What? The Place of Social Science in American Culture*. Princeton: Princeton University Press.

MacCallum, Spencer Heath. 1970. *The Art of Community*. Menlo Park, Calif.: Institute for Humane Studies.

Macfie, A. L. 1967a. *The Individual in Society: Papers on Adam Smith*. London: Allen and Unwin.

———. 1967b. "The Moral Justification of Free Enterprise: A Lay Sermon on an Adam Smith Text." *Scottish Journal of Political Economy* 14(1): 1–11.

———. 1971. "The Invisible Hand of Jupiter." *Journal of the History of Ideas* 32(4): 595–599.

Macpherson, Hector C. 1899. *Adam Smith*. Edinburgh: Oliphant, Anderson & Ferrier.

Maitland, Frederic William. 2000 [1875]. *A Historical Sketch of Liberty and Equality*. Indianapolis: Liberty Fund.

Marshall, Alfred. 1927. *Industry and Trade*. 3rd edition. London: Macmillan and Co.

Marx, Karl. 1936. *Capital: A Critique of Political Economy*. Vol. 1. Translated by S. Moore and E. Aveling. New York: Modern Library.

———. 1967 [1867]. *Capital: A Critique of Political Economy*. Vol. 1, *The Process of Capitalist Production*. New York: International Publishers.

———. 1967 [1885]. *Capital: A Critique of Political Economy*. Vol. 2, *The Process of Circulation of Capital*. New York: International Publishers.

———. 1974 [1871]. "The Civil War in France: Address of the General Council." In Marx, *The First International and After: Political Writings, Vol. 3*: 187–268. Edited by D. Fernbach. New York: Random House.

———. 1998. *Capital*. Vol. III. Vol. 37 of *Karl Marx-Frederick Engels Collected Works*. London: Lawrence B. Wishart.

Maugham, W. Somerset. 1952. "The Verger." In *The Complete Short Stories of W. Somerset Maugham*, Vol. III: 572–578. Garden City, N.Y.: Doubleday.

McCloskey, D.N. 1985. *The Rhetoric of Economics*. Madison: University of Wisconsin Press.

———. 1994. *Knowledge and Persuasion in Economics*. New York: Cambridge University Press.

———. 2006. *Bourgeois Virtues: Ethics for an Age of Commerce*. Chicago: University of Chicago Press.

———. 2010. *Bourgeois Dignity and Liberty: Why Economics Can't Explain the Modern World*. Chicago: University of Chicago Press.

McCloskey, D.N., and Arjo Klamer. 1995. "One Quarter of GDP Is Persuasion." *American Economic Review*, Papers and Proceedings 85(2): 191–195.

Menger, C. 1985 [1883]. *Investigations into the Method of the Social Sciences With Special Reference to Economics*. Edited by Louis Schneider, with a new introduction by Lawrence H. White. New York: New York University Press.

———. 1994 [1871]. *Principles of Economics*. Trans. J. Dingwall and B.F. Hoselitz. Grove City, Pa.: Libertarian Press.

Merriam-Webster's Collegiate Dictionary. 1994. 10th ed. Springfield, Mass.: Merriam-Webster.

Merry, Sally Engle. 1984. "Rethinking Gossip and Scandal." In *Towards a General Theory of Social Control, Vol. 1, Fundamentals*, edited by Donald Black: 271–302. New York: Academic Press.

Mill, James. 2005 [1818]. Letter to David Ricardo (September 23). In *The Works and Correspondence of David Ricardo*, edited by Piero Sraffa with M.H. Dobb. Vol. 7 Letters 1816–1818. Indianapolis: Liberty Fund.

Mill, John Stuart. 1909 [1871]. *Principles of Political Economy*. Edited by William James Ashley. London: Longmans, Green and Co.

Miller, Terry, and Kim R. Holmes. 2010. *2010 Index of Economic Freedom*. Washington, D.C.: Heritage Foundation and The Wall Street Journal.

Minsky, Marvin. 1986. *The Society of Mind*. New York: Simon & Schuster.

Mises, Ludwig von. 1935. [First published in German in 1920]. "Economic Calculation in the Socialist Commonwealth." In *Collectivist Economic Planning*, edited by F.A. Hayek. London: George Routledge & Sons.

———. 1966. *Human Action: A Treatise on Economics*. 3rd edition. Chicago: Henry Regnery.

———. 1981 [First German edition 1922]. *Socialism: An Economic and Sociological Analysis*. Translated by J. Kahane. Indianapolis: Liberty Fund.

Mohring, Herbert. 1972. "Optimization and Scale Economies in Urban Bus Transportation." *American Economic Review* 62: 591–604.

Moore, Adrian T., and Ted Balaker. 2006. "Do Economists Reach a Conclusion on Taxi Deregulation?" *Econ Journal Watch* 3(1): 109–132.

Morrow, Glenn R. 1923. *The Ethical and Economic Theories of Adam Smith*. New York: Longmans Green & Co.

———. 1927. "Adam Smith: Moralist and Philosopher." *Journal of Political Economy* 35(3): 321–342.

Morison, Samuel Eliot. 1965. *The Oxford History of the American People*. New York: Oxford University Press.

Myrdal, Gunnar. 1969. *Objectivity in Social Research*. New York: Pantheon Books.

Nash, Christopher A. 1988. "Integration of Public Transport: An Economic Assessment." In *Bus Deregulation and Privatisation: An International Perspective*, edited by J.S. Dodgson and N. Topham: 97–223. Brookfield, Mass.: Avebury.

Newcomb, Simon. 1880. "The Organization of Labor I: The Organizer as a Producer." *Princeton Review* 1 (May): 393–410.

———. 1886. *Principles of Political Economy*. New York: Harper & Brothers.

Nichols, Mark W. 1998. "Advertising and Quality in the U.S. Market for Automobiles." *Southern Economic Journal* 64(4): 922–939.

O'Driscoll, Gerald P. 1976. "The American Express Case: Public Good or Monopoly?" *Journal of Law and Economics* 19(1) (April): 163–175.

O'Driscoll, Gerald P. Jr., and Mario J. Rizzo. 1996. *The Economics of Time and Ignorance*. New York: Routledge.

Otteson, James. 2002. *Adam Smith's Marketplace of Life*. Cambridge: Cambridge University Press.

———. 2008. Review of Craig Smith's *Adam Smith's Political Philosophy*. *Adam Smith Review* 4: 303–306.

Parkinson, Thomas L. 1975. "The Role of Seals and Certifications of Approval in Consumer Decision-Making." *Journal of Consumer Affairs* 9 (Summer): 1–14.

Pashigian, Peter B., and Brian Bowen. 1994. "The Rising Cost of Time of Females, the Growth of National Brands and the Supply of Retail Services." *Economic Inquiry* 32 (January): 33–65.

Philbrook, Clarence. 1953. "'Realism' in Policy Espousal." *American Economic Review* 43(5):846–859.

Phillipson, Nicholas. 2010. *Adam Smith: An Enlightened Life*. New Haven: Yale University Press.

Plant, Arnold. 1974 [1937]. "Centralise or Decentralise?" In Plant, *Selected Economic Essays and Addresses*: 174–198. London: Routledge & Kegan Paul.

Polanyi, Michael. 1951. *The Logic of Liberty: Reflections and Rejoinders*. Chicago: University of Chicago Press.

————. 1962. *Personal Knowledge: Towards a Post-Critical Philosophy*. Chicago: University of Chicago Press.

————. 1963. *The Study of Man*. Chicago: University of Chicago Press.

————. 1966. *The Tacit Dimension*. New York: Doubleday & Co.

Pool, Ithiel de Sola, and Manfred Kochen. 1978. "Contacts and Influence." In *The Small World*, edited by Manfred Kochen: 3–51. Norwood, N.J.: Ablex Publishing.

Quine, Willard van Orman. 1961. "Two Dogmas of Empiricism." In Quine, *From a Logical Point of View*, 2nd edition: 20–46. Cambridge, Mass.: Harvard University Press.

Rabelais. 1946 [1533]. *The Portable Rabelais*. Edited by Samuel Putnam. New York: Viking Press.

Rasmusen, Eric. 1989. *Games and Information: An Introduction to Game Theory*. New York: Basil Blackwell.

Reeder, John, ed. 1997. *On Moral Sentiments: Contemporary Responses to Adam Smith*. Bristol: Thoemmes Press.

Rees, Albert. 1966. "Information Networks in Labor Markets." *American Economic Review* 56 (May): 559–566.

Ricketts, Martin. 1992. "Kirzner's Theory of Entrepreneurship—A Critique." In *Austrian Economics: Tensions and New Directions*, edited by Bruce J. Caldwell and S. Boehm: 67–102. Boston: Kluwer.

————. 1994. *The Economics of Business Enterprise: An Introduction to Economic Organization and the Theory of the Firm*. 2nd edition. New York: Harvester Wheatsheaf.

Robertson, John. 2005. *The Case for the Enlightenment: Scotland and Naples 1680–1760*. Cambridge, UK: Cambridge University Press.

Romer, Paul. 1994. "New Goods, Old Theory, and the Welfare Costs of Trade Restrictions." *Journal of Development Economics* 43: 5–38.

Romilly, Samuel. 1840. *Memoirs of the Life of Sir Samuel Romilly, with a Selection from His Correspondence*. 3 vols. London: John Murray.

Rosen, Harvey S. 1992. *Public Finance*. 3rd edition. Homewood, Ill.: Irwin.

Roth, Gabriel, and George C. Wynne. 1982. *Free Enterprise Urban Transportation*. New Brunswick, N.J.: Transaction Books.

Roth, Gabriel, ed. 2006. *Street Smart: Competition, Entrepreneurship, and the Future of Roads*. New Brunswick, N.J.: Transaction Publishers.

Rothbard, Murray N. 1993 [1962]. *Man, Economy and State: A Treatise on Economic Principles*. Auburn, Ala.: Ludwig von Mises Institute.

————. 1994 [1956]. "Toward a Reconstruction of Utility and Welfare Economics." In *On Freedom and Free Enterprise*, edited by Mary Sennholz: 224–262. Irvington-on-Hudson, N.Y.: Foundation for Economic Education.

Rothenberg, Jerome. 1993. "Social Strategy and the Tactics in the Search for Safety." *Critical Review* 7: 159–180.

Rubin, Paul H. 1978. "The Theory of the Firm and the Structure of the Franchise Contract." *Journal of Law and Economics* 21: 223–233.

Russo, J. Edward, Richard Staelin, Catherine A. Nolan, Gary J. Russell, and Barbara L. Metcalf. 1986. "Nutrition Information in the Supermarket." *Journal of Consumer Research* 13 (June): 48–70.

Salerno, Joseph T. 1993. "Mises and Hayek Dehomogenized." *Review of Austrian Economics* 6(2): 113–146.

———. 2008. "The Entrepreneur: Real and Imagined." *Quarterly Journal of Austrian Economics* 11: 188–207.

Sautet, Frédéric E. 2000. *An Entrepreneurial Theory of the Firm*. London: Routledge.

Savage, Ian. 1986. "Evaluation of Competition in the British Local Bus Industry." *Transportation Research Record* 1064: 1–10.

Scheerer, Martin. 1963. "Problem-solving." *Scientific American* 208 (April): 118–128.

Schelling, Thomas C. 1960. *The Strategy of Conflict*. Cambridge, Mass.: Harvard University Press.

———. 1966. *Arms and Influence*. New Haven: Yale University Press.

———. 1978. *Micromotives and Macrobehavior*. New York: Norton.

———. 1984. *Choice and Consequence*. Cambridge, Mass.: Harvard University Press.

Schneider, Louis. 1985 [1963]. Introduction to Carl Menger's *Investigations into the Method of the Social Sciences*: 1–21. New York: New York University Press.

Schneider, Lynne, Benjamin Klein, and Kevin M. Murphy. 1981. "Government Regulation of Cigarette Health Information." *Journal of Law and Economics* 24 (December): 575–612.

Schopenhauer, Arthur. 1970 [1851]. *Essays and Aphorisms*. New York: Penguin Books.

Schotter, Andrew, and Yale M. Braunstein. 1981. "Economic Search: An Experimental Study." *Economic Inquiry* 19 (January): 1–25.

Schultz, Theodore W. 1975. "The Value of the Ability to Deal With Disequilibria." *Journal of Economic Literature* 13 (September): 827–846.

———. 1990. *Restoring Economic Equilibrium: Human Capital in the Modern Economy*. Cambridge, Mass.: Basil Blackwell.

Schumpeter, Joseph A. 1934. *The Theory of Economic Development*. Translated by R. Opie. Cambridge, Mass.: Harvard University Press.

Scott, William R. 1900. *Francis Hutcheson: His Life, Teaching and Position in the History of Philosophy*. Cambridge: Cambridge University Press.

Sears, David O., and Carolyn L. Funk. 1999. "Evidence of the Long-Term Persistence of Adults' Political Predispositions." *Journal of Politics* 61(1) (February): 1–28.

Selgin, George A. 1983. "Praxeology and Understanding: An Analysis of the Controversy in Austrian Economics." *Review of Austrian Economics* 2(1): 19–58.

Shaftesbury (Anthony Ashley Cooper). 2001 [1709]. *Characteristicks of Men, Manners, Opinions, Times*. Indianapolis: Liberty Fund.

Shearmur, Jeremy. 1996. *Hayek and After: Hayekian Liberalism as a Research Programme*. London: Routledge.

Shipe, Richard Thomas. 1992. *Cost and Productivity in the U. S. Urban Bus Transit Sector, 1978–1989*. PhD dissertation. University of California, Berkeley.

Shmanske, Stephen. 1994. "On the Relevance of Policy to Kirznerian Entrepreneurship." In *Advances in Austrian Economics* 1, edited by Peter Boettke and Mario Rizzo: 199–222. Greenwich, Conn.: JAI Press.

Shoup, Donald. 2005. *The High Cost of Free Parking*. Chicago: Planners Press of the American Planning Association.

Silber, Norman Isaac. 1983. *Test and Protest: The Influence of Consumers Union*. New York: Holmes and Meier.

Smith, Adam. 1976 [1776]. *An Inquiry into the Nature and Causes of the Wealth of Nations*. Oxford: Oxford University Press.

———. 1977. *The Correspondence of Adam Smith*. Edited by E.C. Mossner and I.S. Ross. Oxford: Oxford University Press.

———. 1978. *Lectures on Jurisprudence*. Edited by R. L. Meek, D. D. Raphael and P.G. Stein. New York: Oxford University Press.

———. 1980. *Essays on Philosophical Subjects*. Edited by W.P.D. Wightman, J.C. Bryce and I.S. Ross. Oxford: Oxford University Press.

———. 1982 [1790]. *The Theory of Moral Sentiments*. Edited by D.D. Raphael and A.L. Macfie. New York: Oxford University Press.

———. 1985 [1761]. "Considerations Concerning the First Formation of Languages." Reprinted in *Glasgow Edition of the Works and Correspondence Vol. 4 Lectures on Rhetoric and Belles Lettres*, edited by J.C. Bryce: 203–226. New York: Oxford University Press.

Smith, Vernon L., and James M. Walker. 1993. "Monetary Rewards and Decision Costs in Experimental Economics." *Economic Inquiry* 31 (April): 245–261.

Spencer, Herbert. 1862. *First Principles*. New York: D. Appleton.

———. 1901 [1871]. "Morals and Moral Sentiments." In Spencer, *Essays: Scientific, Political, & Speculative*, Vol. 1: 331–350. London: Williams and Norgate.

———. 1969 [1884/1892]. *The Man Versus the State*. Edited by Donald Macrae. Baltimore: Penguin Books.

———. 1970 [1851]. *Social Statics*. New York: Robert Schalkenbach Foundation.

Stephen, James Fitzjames. 1993 [1873]. *Liberty, Equality, Fraternity*. Edited by S.D. Warner. Indianapolis: Liberty Fund.

Stephen, Leslie. 1876. *History of English Thought in the Eighteenth Century*, Vol. II. London: Smith, Elder & Co.

Stewart, Dugald. 1982 [1794]. *Account of the Life and Writings of Adam Smith*. In Adam Smith, *Essays on Philosophical Subjects*. Indianapolis: Liberty Fund.

———. 1997 [1828]. "Of Sympathy." In *On Moral Sentiments: Contemporary Responses to Adam Smith*, edited by John Reeder: 121–126. Bristol: Thoemmes Press.

Stigler, George J. 1961. "The Economics of Information." *Journal of Political Economy* 69: 213–225.

———. 1966. "The Formation of Economic Policy." In *Current Problems in Political Economy*: 57–76. Greencastle, Ind.: Depauw University.

———. 1967. "Imperfections in the Capital Market." *Journal of Political Economy* 75(3): 287–292.

———. 1971. "Smith's Travels on the Ship of State." In Stigler, *The Economist as Preacher and Other Essays*: 136–145. Chicago: University of Chicago Press.

———. 1976. "The Xistence of X-Efficiency." *American Economic Review* 66(1): 213–216.

———. 1978. "Wealth, and Possibly Liberty." *Journal of Legal Studies* 7(2): 213–217.

———. 1982. "The Economist as Preacher." In Stigler, *The Economist as Preacher and Other Essays*: 3–13. Chicago: University of Chicago Press.

Stiglitz, Joseph A. 1994. *Whither Socialism?* Cambridge, Mass.: MIT Press.

Sugden, Robert. 1986. *The Economics of Rights, Cooperation and Welfare*. Oxford: Basil Blackwell.

Thaler, Richard H., and Hersh M. Shefrin. 1981. "An Economic Theory of Self-Control." *Journal of Political Economy* 89: 392–406.

Thomsen, Estaban. 1992. *Prices and Knowledge: A Market-Process Perspective*. London: Routledge.

Tucker, Robert. 1961. *Philosophy and Myth in Karl Marx*. Cambridge: Cambridge University Press.

Tullock, Gordon. 1971. "Public Decisions as Public Goods." *Journal of Political Economy* 79(4): 913–918.

———. 1993. "Thoughts on Private Roads." University of Arizona Discussion Paper 93-6. http://econ.arizona.edu/docs/Working_Papers/Archives/1993/WP_93-6.pdf (Accessed 29 October 2011).

Ullmann-Margalit, Edna. 1977. *The Emergence of Norms*. Oxford: Oxford University Press.

Viscusi, W. Kip. 1978. "A Note on 'Lemons' Markets with Quality Certification." *Bell Journal of Economics* 9: 277–279.

Viton, P. A. 1981. "A Translog Cost Function for Urban Bus Transit." *Journal of Industrial Economics* 29: 287–304.

Von Neumann, John and Oskar Morgenstern. 1953. *Theory of Games and Economic Behavior*. 3rd edition. Princeton: Princeton University Press.

Wagner, Eric R. 1989. "Types of Managed Health Care Organizations." In *Managed Health Care Handbook*, edited by Peter R. Kongstvedt: 11–18. Rockville, Md.: Aspen Publishers.

Weisberg, Robert W. 1993. *Creativity: Beyond the Myth of Genius*. New York: W.H. Freeman and Co.

Whately, Richard. 1966 [1832]. *Introductory Lectures on Political Economy*. New York: Augustus M. Kelley.

White, Lawrence H. 1985. Introduction to Carl Menger's *Investigations into the Method of the Social Sciences*: vii–xviii. New York: New York University Press.

White, Peter. 1995. "Deregulation of Local Bus Service in Great Britain: An Introductory Review." *Transport Reviews* 15: 185–209.

Wicksteed, Philip H. 1967 [1910]. *The Common Sense of Political Economy*. New York: Augustus M. Kelley.

Winston, Clifford. 1993. "Economic Deregulation: Days of Reckoning for Microeconomists." *Journal of Economic Literature* 31(3): 1263–1289.

Wittgenstein, Ludwig. 2001 [1953]. *Philosophical Investigations*. Translated by G.E.M. Anscombe. New York: Blackwell.

Wittman, Donald. 1989. "Why Democracies Produce Efficient Results." *Journal of Political Economy* 97(6): 1395–1424.

———. 1995. *The Myth of Democratic Failure: Why Political Institutions Are Efficient*. Chicago: University of Chicago Press.

Young, H. Peyton. 1996. "The Economics of Convention." *Journal of Economic Perspectives* 10(2) (Spring): 105–122.

Young, Jeffrey T. 1997. *Economics as a Moral Science: The Political Economy of Adam Smith*. Cheltenham: Edward Elgar.

INDEX

CPSIA information can be obtained at www.ICGtesting.com
Printed in the USA
LVOW07s1921060913

351387LV00007B/16/P